An Introductory English Grammar

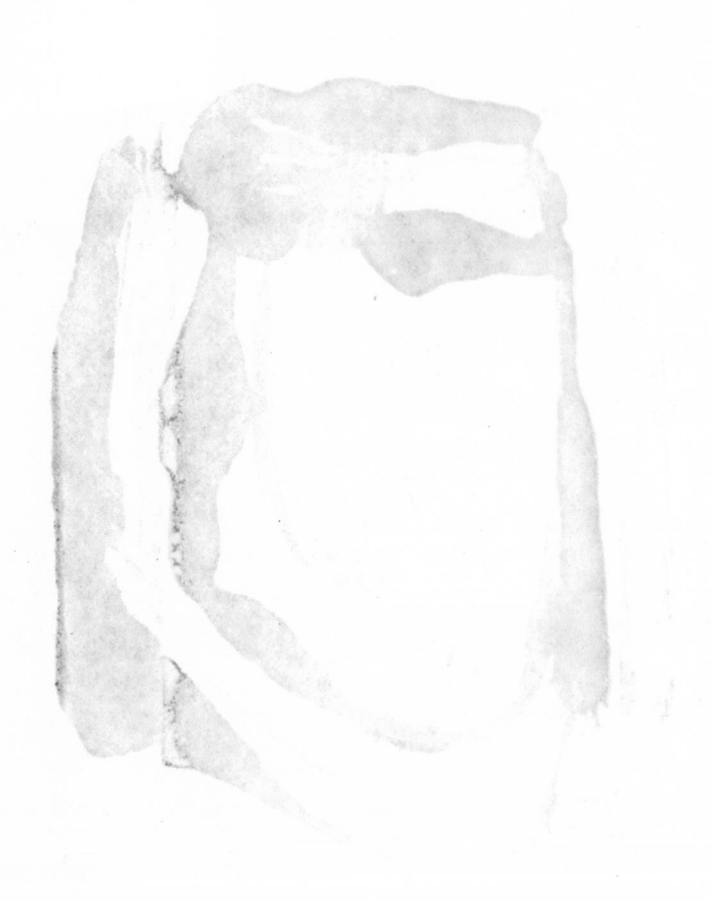

An Introductory English Grammar

Norman C. Stageberg
STATE COLLEGE OF IOWA

With a chapter
on TRANSFORMATIONAL GRAMMAR
by
Ralph Goodman
STATE COLLEGE OF IOWA

Holt, Rinehart and Winston, Inc.
New York • Chicago • San Francisco • Toronto • London

Library of Congress Catalog Card Number 65–14864
SBN 03-051300-6
Printed in the United States of America
0123 40 987

To the Instructor

THIS is a college textbook of English grammar. The first and longer part is a structural grammar, supplemented by occasional borrowings from transformationism. Then follows an introduction to transformational grammar which is closely meshed with the preceding structural description. This order is desirable, for students will comprehend transformational grammar more readily if they have first had a grounding in structural grammar. The book is designed for a three-hour, one-semester course for undergraduates.

The limitations of a one-volume grammar must be acknowledged. No one has ever written a grammar describing completely the English language. The fullest grammars are those of Poutsma and Jespersen, running respectively to five and seven bound volumes; and these — admirable as they are and packed with fine material — do not cover the ground. We must therefore expect that a single volume can at best present only the central features of English grammar and offer methods of description which the student can use in analyzing any further data he may collect. And we must expect to find rigorously curtailed or omitted altogether those refinements, exceptions, moot points, and extended developments that might be included in a comprehensive grammar. Thus this book does not pretend to completeness of coverage or to a set of inviolable grammatical statements. The fact is that for most if not all of the generalizations that you will meet here, or in any compact grammar, one can readily bring up counterexamples.

Let us illustrate counterexamples in the area of adjectives. If you point out to your class that one-syllable adjectives are compared with *-er* and *-est*, a dormant figure in the back row is likely to emerge from his cocoon long enough to inquire, "What about *mere* and *due?*" If you show that adjectives not compared with *-er* and *-est* will take *more* and *most* as substitutes, someone will call your attention to words like *dental* and *lunar*. If you use the common frame sentence

The _______ (NOUN) is very _______
adj *adj*

as a key to adjectives, you may have to face up to *content* and *unable*, which do not occupy the first slot, and to *principal* and *olden*, which do not occur in the second one. If, following the usual rule, you say that the position for a single attributive adjective is before, not after, its noun head, the expressions *money necessary* and *something bad* may be brought on the floor. If you mention the well-known fact that adjectives are modified by qualifiers like *very*, an enterprising student may remind you of *daily* and *weekly*.

This kind of situation can and should be handled openly and honestly. Students must be made to realize early in the course that a grammatical generalization or rule is a descriptive statement of customary, not universal, usage. If the counterexamples are few, they can be listed as exceptions. If they are numerous and follow a pattern, the rule can be refined. If they are limited to a particular region, to a certain social group, to some trade or profession, or to an age or sex group, they can be assigned to the group which habitually uses them. Thus a class can, by its own observations, elaborate the basic grammar presented here. As a result those who will go on to teach English grammar in the schools may be less dogmatic and more respectful of language data, however recalcitrant, than if counterexamples had been ignored or forced into a Procrustean bed.

Definitions also present a problem. A grammar is a closed system, a circle. Wherever one begins in this circle, say at X, he finds himself having to use undefined terms. But if he goes back to W to cover these terms, there will be still other terms that need defining. And so one can go backward around the circle until he finds himself at X again. Thus undefined terms are inevitable. In this book I have tried to devise an effective order of presentation with as few undefined terms as possible.

A word of explanation about the phonology may be pertinent. The phonemic system used is a simple one following the Kenyon-Pike tradition. Into this system I have imported the barred i /ɨ/. That this is a genuine phoneme is no longer questioned, but it has a low functional load. That is to say, there are relatively few cases in English where /ɨ/ is in contrast with another phoneme. The result of this infrequency of contrasts is that your students will have difficulty in distinguishing /ɨ/ from /ə/ and /ɪ/ and will not be able to utter it in isolation without a good deal of guided practice. It is tempting, for pedagogical expedience, to treat it as an allophone of /ə/, and if you yield to this temptation, little harm will be done. After all, generations of phoneticians did pretty well without /ɨ/ before 1951, when Trager and Smith first revealed its existence to a skeptical world.

The vowel sound in *fur*, *sir*, and *her* is for the vast majority of Americans a single *r*-colored vowel and therefore might be shown by a single symbol such as /ɝ/. But this would mean adding another symbol to the system, and I have elected to use the two symbols /ər/ instead to represent this sound, thus avoiding the extra symbol. This procedure is theoretically justifiable, for in a few parts of the East the /ər/ is pronounced as two sounds, and the single r-colored vowel is therefore in free variation with

with the vowel-plus-/r/ combination.* Furthermore I use /ən/ to represent phonemically both [ən] and the syllabic [n̩], as in /bətən/. So there is consistency here.

In method the exposition in this book advances by short-step progression, with an exercise after nearly every step. I have chosen this method because I believe that the student must work actively with the language if he is to achieve a firm understanding of it. The exercises are self-corrective, providing the student with an immediate feedback.

A question may arise here. If the explanations are clear — and I have done my best to make them so — and if the exercises are provided with answers, what is there left for the instructor to do in the classroom? At the risk of expounding the obvious, permit me to mention a few classroom procedures that I have found useful.

1. Ask for questions on the text and on the exercises. The answers to the exercises on the phonology in particular will evoke questions, for the student, when asked to write a given word in phonemic script, will sometimes record a pronunciation different from that shown in the answer. This is entirely normal because of the dialectal and idiolectal variations among speakers of English. For example, if you have your students pronounce in turn the word *wash*, they are very likely to produce at least these three pronunciations: /waš/, /wɔš/, and /wɔrš/. Students should be shown at the beginning that all persons do not speak English in exactly the same way.
2. During the first unit, on phonology, have daily transcription practice. This will sharpen auditory perception and develop a ready command of the phonemic symbols.
3. Have your class furnish original illustrations of the grammatical concepts presented in the text. The search for and discussion of such illustrations may help to strengthen understanding more than the performance of preshaped exercises.
4. Have your students justify their answers in those exercises which ask for the what but not the why. In this way you can find out which students really understand what they are doing.

* See Hans Kurath and Raven I. McDavid, Jr., *The pronunciation of English in the Atlantic States* (Ann Arbor, University of Michigan Press, 1961), pp. 31–100.

Acknowledgments

ACKNOWLEDGMENTS can never be made to all who have nourished one's intellectual life.

Among the classroom teachers who have given me sustenance, I cannot fail to mention Miles Hanley, R.-M. S. Heffner, Robert C. Pooley, and William E. Leonard of the University of Wisconsin; Albert Marckwardt, then at the University of Michigan; and B. J. Whiting of Harvard University.

For particular works, I owe an especially heavy debt of gratitude to three linguists. Ilse Lehiste's *An Acoustic-Phonetic Study of Internal Open Juncture* furnished the information for my pages on internal open juncture. Archibald A. Hill's chapter on phonotactics in his *Introduction to Linguistic Structures* is the source of my treatment of the distribution of phonemes. James Sledd's *A Short Introduction to English Grammar* provided the pattern for the double-track system of parts of speech that I have adopted.

Of the other writers with whose work on grammar I have become familiar, there are many to whom I owe thanks. From across the Atlantic I have found valuable the books of R. H. Close, A. S. Hornby, Otto Jespersen, E. Kruisinga, E. Maetzner, and H. Poutsma. On our own continent I am indebted to a much larger group, among whom are Noam Chomsky, R. B. Lees, Hans Kurath, Raven McDavid, Jr., C. C. Fries, Kenneth Pike, Harold King, Eugene Nida, W. F. Twaddell, C. F. Hockett, H. A. Gleason, Jr., H. L. Smith, George Trager, Hans Marchand, W. N. Francis, Paul Roberts, Harold Whitehall, John S. Kenyon, Edward Sapir, and Leonard Bloomfield.

In addition there are the professional articles and monographs, conference discussions, correspondence and chats with colleagues — all these have furnished grist to the mill: a felicitous example, an apposite phrase, a new insight, a challenging position. These enter into one's intellectual bloodstream and become part of one's being; eventually their origin is lost. For all such, my thanks to the unknown benefactors.

Professor Andrew MacLeish of Northern Illinois University taught parts of the material in prepublication form and offered useful suggestions for improvement. Professor Ralph Goodman, my colleague at the State College of Iowa, brought the keen eye of a transformationist to bear on the text and offered valuable criticisms. Professor Frederic G. Cassidy of the University of Wisconsin read the final draft with meticulous care and called attention to matters that needed correction or revision. Professors

Harold B. Allen of the University of Minnesota and W. Nelson Francis of Brown University read the first draft of the phonology and made thoughtful suggestions that resulted in an improved treatment. The Committee on Research at the State College of Iowa, under the chairmanship of Professor Gordon Rhum, kindly gave financial assistance for the construction of teaching materials which, after classroom use, were incorporated into this book. To these scholars I am deeply indebted for their friendly assistance.

Diagrams six and seven have been reprinted with permission of the Regents of the University of Wisconsin from Professor R.-M. S. Heffner's *General Phonetics*, 1950, published by the University of Wisconsin Press. To them and to Professor Heffner I am deeply obliged. And last but most, I am grateful to my wife Amy, who faced the ordeal of a scrivening husband with patience and good nature.

To the Student

At this very moment you have an excellent command of English grammar. This is an operational command that functions below the threshold of awareness. As you speak, you select — with little conscious thought or effort — the precise forms and arrangements of words that signal the meanings you wish to express. The process is almost automatic.

Now you are about to undertake a systematic study of the structure of this language that you handle so easily. Your situation is not unlike that of a skillful automobile driver who is about to begin a course in auto mechanics. But there is this difference: the English language is a machine vastly more complex than the finest car you could buy. And when you have completed this study of your language, you should have a good idea of what makes it go.

As you progress through this book you will be given exercises at each step along the way. These are necessary and should be done with care, for they will enable you to get a firm grasp of matters that you might otherwise only half learn and quickly forget. The answers to these exercises are in the back of the book. As soon as you have finished each exercise, you should correct it at once. Then, if you have made any mistakes, restudy the text to master the points that you did not learn on your first attempt.

There are two dangers for you in this procedure. An exercise may seem so easy that you will be tempted to do it orally instead of writing it out. This seems harmless enough, but it will exact its penalty later on. Research in programed learning reveals that students who work orally know as much at the time as those who do the writing; but several months later, those who have faithfully written out their work show a higher retention rate.

The second danger is that you may merely use the answers instead of thinking through the exercises. But just as you cannot learn to swim on a piano stool, so you cannot master the complexities of language by only reading about them. You must work actively with the language itself, and this is what the exercises give you a chance to do. If you work honestly and seriously, there is no reason why you should not succeed in this course.

Contents

part two

THE MORPHOLOGY OF ENGLISH

part three
SYNTAX

part four

TRANSFORMATIONAL GRAMMAR

part one

THE PHONOLOGY OF ENGLISH

I.

The Production and Inventory of English Phonemes

A descriptive grammar of English progresses upward through three levels of structure. The first or lowest level deals with the system of speech sounds employed by native speakers of English. The study of this level is called phonology. The next higher level is concerned with the meaningful forms made from the individual speech sounds. Generally speaking, we may say that it deals with words and their meaningful parts. This is the realm of morphology. The top level treats of the ways in which words are arranged to form sentences, and here we are in the area of syntax. Hence we begin our study of English grammar, logically and properly, at the first level with a consideration of the speech sounds of English.

At the outset, as we approach our study of English phonology, we must bear in mind two important facts.

First, language itself is ORAL — it lives on the lips and in the ears of its users — and writing is a visual symbolization of language itself. To realize that language is independent of writing, we have only to recall the many tribes, nations, and ethnic groups whose members possess no form of writing but whose LANGUAGES are being avidly studied today by linguistic scientists and anthropologists. When we study the grammar of a language through the medium of writing, as we shall do in this book, we must often supplement the writing with special marks to indicate the stresses, pitches, and breaks of oral speech; and sometimes we must replace writing with a different set of symbols to represent the sounds of the living voice.

Second, the English language as spoken in the United States is not uniform. It is made up of numerous dialects and subdialects, about which our knowledge is yet far from complete. We have chosen to present here the phonology of what may be loosely called Mid-Western English.

A. The Speech-producing Mechanism

Speech sounds are sound waves created in a moving stream of air. They are disturbances of the medium such as you would observe if you were to drop a stone on the quiet surface of a pool. The air is expelled from the lungs, passes between the two vocal cords in the larynx (Adam's apple),

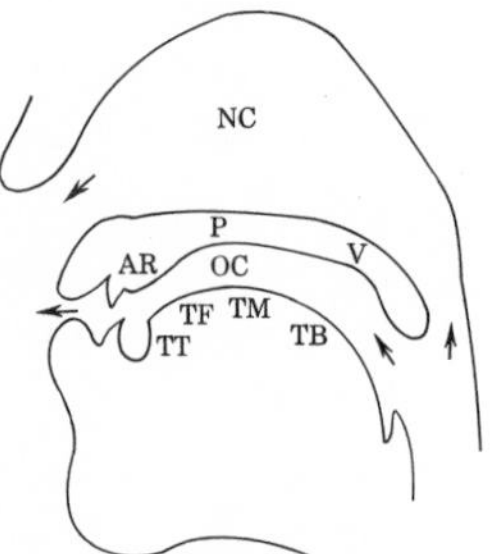

AR	Alveolar ridge
NC	Nasal cavity
OC	Oral cavity
P	Hard palate
V	Velum, or soft palate
TT	Tongue tip
TF	Tongue front
TM	Tongue middle
TB	Tongue back

Diagram 1 **Speech-producing mechanism.**

and proceeds upward. As you will note on Diagram 1, this moving stream of air has two possible outlets. It can pass through the nasal cavity and emerge through the nose, or it can pass through the oral cavity and come out through the mouth. But why doesn't it go through both passages, which are shown to be open on the diagram? Because in speech one of them is ordinarily closed. And how does this happen? Let us consider the oral sounds first. On diagram 1 you will notice the velum, marked *V*. This is a movable curtain of flesh. If you will run your finger back along the roof of your mouth, you will feel at first the bony structure of the hard palate, marked *P*. Just behind this hard palate you will feel the soft flesh of the velum. It ends in a pear-shaped pendant, called the uvula, which you can see hanging in your throat if you look in the mirror. Now, when you produce any oral sound, one that goes out through the mouth, for example a-a-a-a-a-a-a, you at the same time raise the velum until it touches the back of the throat, closing the nasal cavity. You can actually see this raising of the velum if you will open your mouth wide, flash a light into your mouth, look in the mirror, and say a-a-a-a-a-a several times in succession. The process is illustrated in diagram 2.

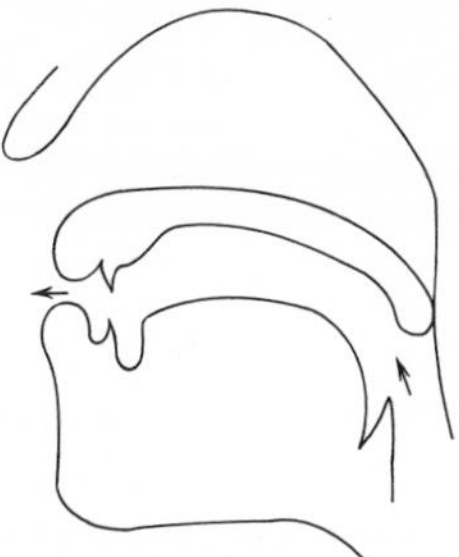

Diagram 2
Air passing through oral cavity. Tongue position for /a/.

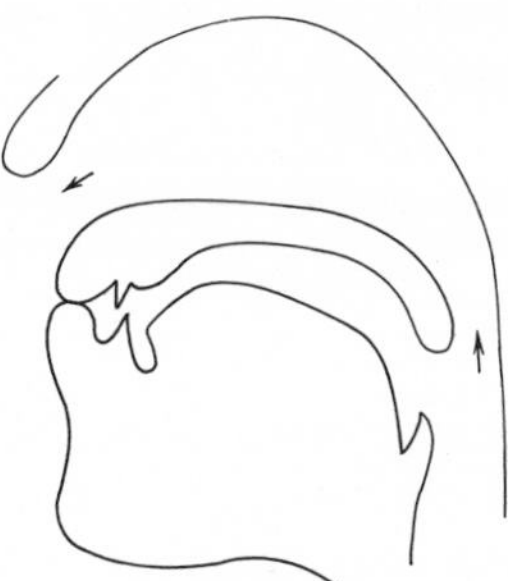

Diagram 3
Air passing through nasal cavity. Lip position for /m/.

Now let us turn from the oral sounds to the nasals, those that pass through the nasal cavity. To make the three nasal sounds of English, you leave the velum in the position shown on diagram 1 and block off the oral cavity in one of three ways: with the lips (diagram 3), with the tongue tip (diagram 4), or with the tongue back (diagram 5). Thus, with the oral

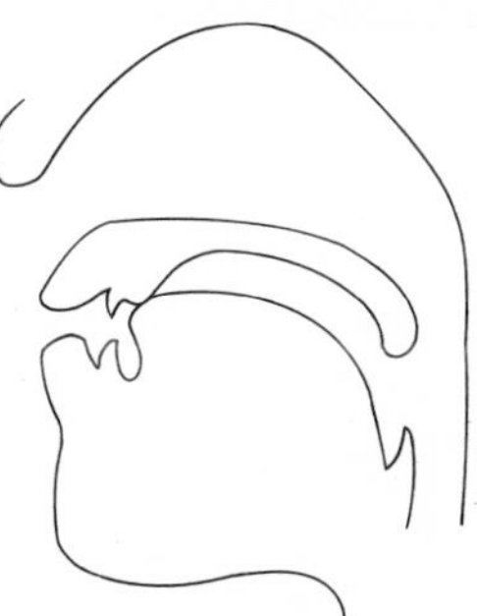

Diagram 4
Air passing through nasal cavity. Tongue position for /n/.

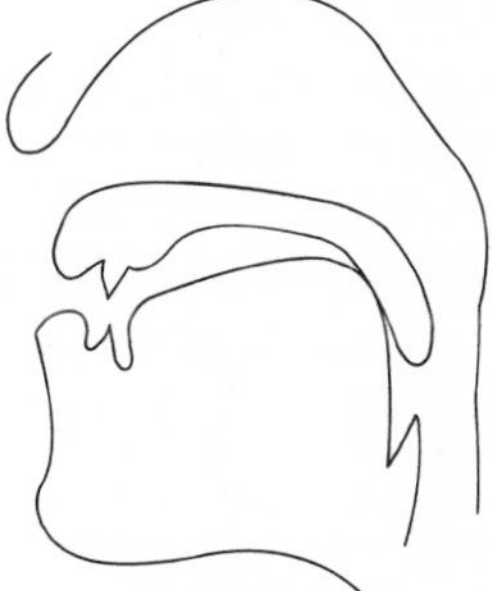

Diagram 5
Air passing through nasal cavity. Tongue position for /ŋ/.

cavity blocked off, the sound can emerge only through the nasal cavity. It is evident now that every speech sound we utter is either an oral or a nasal sound. For illustration, try exercise 1.

EXERCISE 1

★ As you pronounce the following words, hold the final sound for some time. As you hold the final sound, stop your nose with your fingers. If this action stops the sound, the sound is obviously a nasal. But if the sound continues, then close your lips. The sound will thereupon be cut off, demonstrating that it is an oral sound. After each word write "nasal" or "oral" to label the final sound.

1. rim ________	4. see ________	7. trim ________
2. saw ________	5. sing ________	8. pain ________
3. bin ________	6. tall ________	9. wrong ________

You may wonder about the "nasal twang" that you occasionally hear. This is caused by the habit of slightly lowering the velum for sounds that are normally oral, thus permitting some of the air to go out through the nasal cavity.

You have now learned the three nasals of English, which we symbolize in a special notation as /m/, /n/, and /ŋ/. The /m/ is a bilabial nasal, made by closing the two lips. The /n/ is an alveolar nasal, made by stopping the flow of air with the tongue tip against the alveolar ridge. The /ŋ/ is a velar nasal, made by stopping the flow of air with the back of the tongue against the velum. In all three the air moves through the nasal cavity. They are illustrated on diagrams 3, 4, and 5.

But one element is missing from our description of the three nasals. Where does the sound come from? To answer this question we must examine the vocal cords.

Inside the larynx (Adam's apple) are two short bands of flesh and muscle stretching from front to rear. In breathing and during the production of some speech sounds, like /f/ and /s/, these are held open, allowing free ingress and egress of air, as shown in diagram 6. But with many sounds they are pressed tightly together, and the air passing between them causes them to vibrate, as shown in diagram 7. These vibrations are given reso-

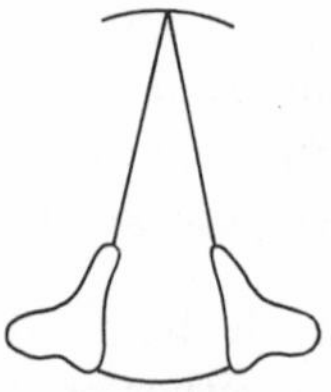

Diagram 6
Position of vocal cords during exhalation.*

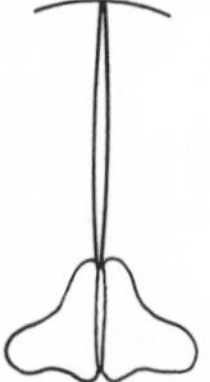

Diagram 7
Position of vocal cords when vibrating.*

---

* Reprinted with permission of the copyright owners, the Regents of the University of Wisconsin, from R.-M. S. Heffner, *General Phonetics*, 1950, the University of Wisconsin Press.

nance by the cavities of the mouth and nose, and the result is the phenomenon called voicing. In the making of every speech sound, then, these vocal cords are either vibrating or not vibrating. If they are vibrating, the sound is called voiced. If they are not vibrating, the sound is called voiceless. An exercise will illustrate.

EXERCISE 2

★ Hold your hands tightly over your ears and pronounce the last sound in each of the following words. Write "voiced" after those during the pronunciation of which you hear the vibration of your vocal cords, which will sound like a strong hum. Write "voiceless" after those during the pronunciation of which such vibration is absent.

1. less ________	4. pin ________	7. mush ________
2. hum ________	5. sheath ________	8. fin ________
3. if ________	6. among ________	9. song ________

We see now that to our description of the three nasals we must add the fact that each one is voiced, that their sound comes from the vibration of the vocal cords.

Let us now turn for a moment to examine the voicing or voicelessness of speech sounds other than the nasals. It was pointed out above that every speech sound is either voiceless or voiced. The next two exercises will give you practice in distinguishing these two kinds.

EXERCISE 3

★ Pronounce the first sound in the following words with your hands over your ears. Write "voiced" after each word in which you hear the hum of your vocal cords during the pronunciation of this first sound. Write "voiceless" after those which are pronounced without the hum.

1. fine ________	4. then ________	7. shock ________
2. vine ________	5. seal ________	8. late ________
3. thin ________	6. zeal ________	9. rate ________

EXERCISE 4

★ This is a little harder. Do the same as you did in exercise 3, but be very careful to keep the first sound in each word separate from the one that follows in the same word.

1. pin ____________	3. time ____________	5. coon ____________
2. bin ____________	4. dime ____________	6. goon ____________

At this point from the foregoing discussion of nasals, orals, and voicing, you should have acquired a working knowledge of these parts of the speech-producing mechanism: nasal cavity, oral cavity, lips, alveolar ridge, hard palate, velum, tongue tip, tongue back, and the vocal cords. Test yourself by writing these terms in the appropriate places on diagram 8 below. Then verify your answers by consulting diagram 1 and correct any errors.

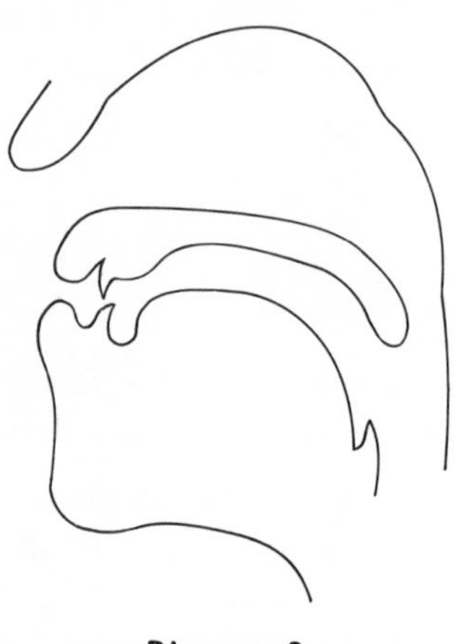

Diagram 8

B. The Phoneme

Before continuing with an inventory of English speech sounds and the ways of producing them, we must clearly understand one basic concept — the phoneme.

The phoneme is easily understood: it is a speech sound that signals a difference in meaning. Consider, for example, the words *dime* and *dine*. They sound exactly alike except for the /m/ and the /n/, yet their meanings are different. Therefore it must be the /m/ and /n/ which make the difference in meaning, and these two nasals are thereby established as English phonemes. Likewise, if we compare the sounds of *sin* and *sing*, we find only one difference between them: *sin* ends in the alveolar nasal /n/ and *sing* in the velar nasal /ŋ/. (Don't be deceived by the spelling of *sing;* the letters *ng* represent a single sound /ŋ/, one which you can prolong as long as your breath holds out.) This contrast is evidence that /n/ and /ŋ/ are both phonemes. Pairs of words like those above which demonstrate a phonemic contrast are called minimal pairs.

EXERCISE 5

★ After each minimal pair write the phonemes that are established by the sound contrast between them. Be sure to contrast pronunciations, not letters. Since you have not yet learned most of the phonemic symbols, use letters to represent the phonemes.

1. pin ______	6. rattle ______	11. sad ______
bin ______	tattle ______	sat ______
2. big ______	7. fine ______	12. made ______
dig ______	vine ______	make ______
3. late ______	8. zoo ______	13. tool ______
rate ______	too ______	tomb ______
4. pill ______	9. hot ______	14. fate ______
kill ______	got ______	feign ______
5. go ______	10. sick ______	15. thin ______
so ______	wick ______	thing ______

A phoneme may be pronounced in different ways, depending on its position in the utterance, and still remain the same phoneme. As an example, let us take /l/. If you pronounce *lit* and *well* slowly and distinctly, you will hear two different [l]s. The second one seems to be preceded by an "uh" sound. With a little practice you can place your tongue tip on the alveolar ridge and change from the first to the second [l] without moving the tongue tip. Now, if you pronounce *well* with the [l] of *lit*, the word will sound different, a little un-English, but the meaning will not be changed. The use of one or the other of these two [l]s never makes a difference in meaning; hence they are not two phonemes but merely variants of the /l/ phoneme. You will sometimes hear still another [l] in words like *play* and *sled*. Here there may be a voiceless [l̥], whereas the [l]s of both *well* and *lit* were voiced. But whether you pronounce *play* and certain other words with a voiced or a voiceless [l], the meaning remains unchanged; so this third [l̥] is another variant of the /l/ phoneme.

Such variants of a phoneme are called allophones. Allophones are enclosed in brackets with the occasional addition of diacritical marks to indicate the exact pronunciation. Phonemes are enclosed in slants. Thus we may say that the /l/ phoneme has three allophones: [l] as in *lit*, [ɫ] as in *well*, and [l̥] as in *play*. A phoneme then is not an individual sound but a small family or class of similar sounds.

With this introduction to the concept of the phoneme, we are now ready to examine the inventory of English phonemes.

C. The English Phonemic System: Vowels

The classification of English vowels is a complex and controversial matter; it is even difficult to define a vowel with precision. But we can make four statements about vowels that will help to show their nature:

1. Vowels are oral sounds. In some dialects and in certain contexts, vowels may become partially nasal, but normally they are orals, not nasals.
2. Vowels are voiced.
3. Vowels are characterized by a free flow of air through the oral cavity.
4. The distinguishing features of the different vowels are determined largely by tongue position.

English may be said to have thirteen vowels — five front, four back, and four central vowels — which we shall now take up systematically.

Front Vowels. If you pronounce the final sound of *be*, symbolized by /i/, and hold the /i/, you will find that the tongue front and middle are humped high in the mouth, leaving a narrow passage for the flow of air between the hard palate and the surface of the tongue. The tongue position of /i/ is the top one on diagram 9.

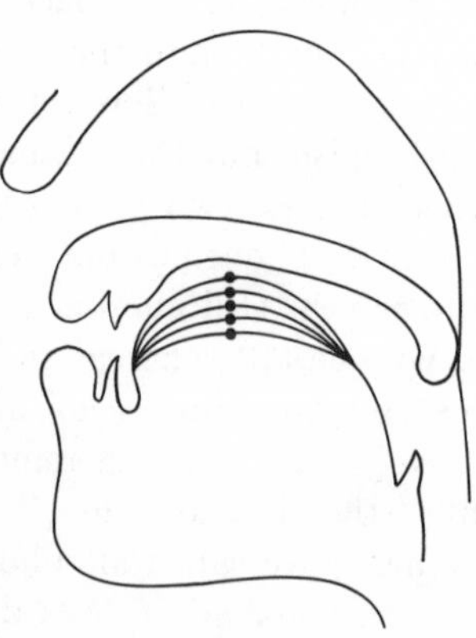

Diagram 9 **Front vowels.**

Next, say the same vowel /i/, holding your jaw in your hand, and then say the first sound of *add*, symbolized by /æ/. You will observe a considerable drop of the jaw and some flattening of the tongue. The tongue position of the vowel /æ/ is the bottom one on diagram 9. To fix these differences of position in your mind, hold your jaw and say /i/, /æ/ rapidly a number of times in succession.

Between these two extremes, /i/ and /æ/, are three other vowels. To hear them in order from the top tongue position to the bottom one, pronounce the following words, noting the middle sound: *beat, bit, bait, bet, bat.* Now say just the vowels in the same order, holding your jaw, and observe how the jaw drops a little as each one is uttered. These five vowels are called the FRONT VOWELS, because they are formed in the front of the mouth by the position of the tongue front. For each front vowel the lips are spread, or unrounded. The tongue positions and the symbols for them are indicated on diagram 9, although this diagram and diagrams 10 and 11 do not show the dropping of the jaw for successively lower vowels.

English spelling cannot be used to represent accurately the speech sounds of English because of its inconsistencies. How, for example, would you symbolize the vowel of *bait* in English spelling? By *ai* as in *wait, eig* as in *reign, ey* as in *they, ay* as in *say, a* as in *late, ei* as in *vein, au* as in *gauge, ea* as in *steak?* So, to represent the sounds of words, we shall use a special alphabet in which one symbol always represents one and the same speech sound, and each sound is always represented by only one symbol. In this alphabet the five illustrative words in the preceding paragraph are written as follows:

beat = /bit/ bat = /bæt/
bait = /bet/ bit = /bɪt/
bet = /bɛt/

The symbols and words written in these symbols are enclosed in slants, like /bæt/.

In exercise 6, which follows directly, you are given transcription practice employing the five front vowels and six consonants. The phonemic symbols for these eleven sounds are written by hand as follows:

/i/ m*ee*t	/p/ *p*ie
/ɪ/ m*i*t	/b/ *b*y
/e/ m*a*te	/t/ *t*en
/ɛ/ m*e*t	/d/ *d*en
/æ/ m*a*t	/k/ *c*ob
	/g/ *g*ob

EXERCISE 6

★ In the second column transcribe the words in the first column as you normally pronounce them. The first two are done to show you how.

1. pack pæk
2. cape kep
3. Pete ______
4. pit ______
5. pate ______
6. pet ______
7. pat ______
8. keep ______
9. kid ______
10. cat ______
11. beak ______
12. big ______
13. date ______
14. debt ______
15. kick ______
16. cap ______
17. peck ______
18. pick ______
19. peek ______
20. gad ______
21. get ______
22. gate ______
23. gat ______
24. back ______
25. bake ______
26. tap ______
27. tape ______
28. tip ______

Back Vowels. Pronounce the final sound of *too,* symbolized by /u/. For this vowel, /u/, the lips are rounded and the back of the tongue is raised to a position near the velum, leaving a little space for the air to flow. The tongue position is the top one on diagram 10.

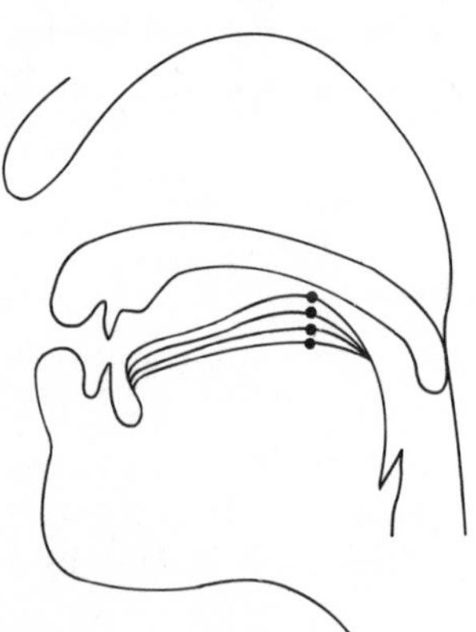

Diagram 10 **Back vowels.**

Now pronounce the sound you make when you say "aw," as in "Aw, come on." For most Americans this is the vowel of *saw, raw,* and *jaw.* It is symbolized by /ɔ/. The tongue position is the bottom one on diagram 10. Next, utter the vowels /u/ and /ɔ/ in rapid succession, with your hand on your jaw. This will show you the upper and lower extremes of the range of the four vowels that are called back vowels. If you will also look in the mirror while uttering the successive /u/s and /ɔ/s, you will see the close rounding of the lips for /u/ and the open rounding for /ɔ/.

As the back of the tongue is lowered from the /u/ position, it reaches in turn the positions for the three other back vowels: /ʊ/ as in *pull,* /o/ as in *note,* and /ɔ/ as in *ought, law,* and *ball.* And at each of these three positions the rounding of the lips is successively opened, as you can observe in the mirror. The four back vowels, from top to bottom, are illustrated by this series:

fool = /ful/ full = /fʊl/ foal = /fol/ fall = /fɔl/

In exercise 7 below, you are given transcription practice in the back vowels and are introduced to these nine new consonants:

/f/ as in *f*ine
/v/ as in *v*ine
/θ/ as in *th*in
/ð/ as in *th*en
/s/ as in *s*eal
/z/ as in *z*eal
/š/ as in *sh*un
/ž/ as in a*z*ure
/h/ as in *h*ow

EXERCISE 7

★ Transcribe in the second column the words in the first column.

Spelling	*Transcription*	*Spelling*	*Transcription*
1. food	__________	11. voodoo	__________
2. foot	__________	12. shook	__________
3. foe	__________	13. who	__________
4. fought	__________	14. hoe	__________
5. shoe	__________	15. zone	__________
6. show	__________	16. zoo	__________
7. though	__________	17. thought	__________
8. thaw	__________	18. those	__________
9. soup	__________	19. oath	__________
10. ought	__________	20. vision (Use /ə/ for the second vowel.)	__________

Central Vowels. English has four central vowels. The first one is a high central vowel symbolized by /ɨ/. It is often heard in unstressed positions, as in the unstressed *just* of "Just a minute." In uttering this phrase you probably have an /ɨ/ in *just* unless you stress it or unless you have schooled yourself to use the vowel of *us* in the word. This unstressed *just* contrasts in pronunciation with *gist*, which is usually pronounced with the lower high front vowel /ɪ/. You can easily hear this contrast if you are able to pronounce *just* the same way in isolation that you pronounce it in the key phrase above. This high central vowel /ɨ/ is also heard in the unstressed *can* of "I can do more." This *can* /kɨn/ contrasts with *kin* /kɪn/ and with stressed *can* /kæn/. The /ɨ/ is made by raising the tongue rather high in the central part of the mouth and spreading the lips, though not as widely as for /ɪ/. One way to find the /ɨ/ position is to pronounce the vowel of *up* and then to raise the tongue toward the roof of the mouth. Its position is shown in diagram 11, and it is often called *barred i*.

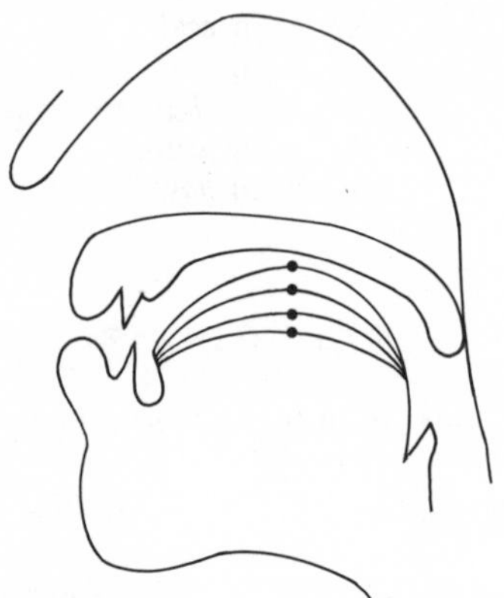

Diagram 11 **Central vowels.**

The second central vowel may be illustrated by the first sound of *up* and *upon*. It is written /ə/, like an upside-down *e*, and its position is shown in diagram 11. It is heard as the pronunciation of the italicized vowels in the following words:

Stressed: s*u*n, d*o*ne, fl*oo*d
Unstressed: sof*a*, *a*lone, sci*e*nce, kingd*o*m, c*o*nnect, diffic*u*lt, s*u*ppose

The /ə/ is a vowel of high frequency in English, especially in unstressed syllables, and is technically called schwa. You will find it a good practice exercise to pronounce repeatedly the word *hunted*, using for the *-ed* the three vowels /ɪ/, /ɨ/, and /ə/. Which do you find is your normal pronunciation?

The third central vowel requires special consideration. If you pronounce *fur*, *sir*, *her*, you are uttering, as the final sound, a mid-central r-colored vowel, that is, if you belong to the majority of Americans who do not "drop their r's." But there are other Americans who pronounce words like these with an /ə/ plus an r sound, as in hurry /həri/, instead of with the single r-colored vowel. Thus we shall use the pair of symbols /ər/ to represent both pronunciations — the single, central, r-colored vowel and also the schwa-plus-an-r sound.

The fourth central vowel is the sound you make when the doctor says, "Open your mouth wide and say a-a-a-a." For most Americans this is the vowel of *not* and the first vowel of *father*. It is symbolized by /a/. In sounding this vowel you will note that the mouth is widely opened and that the tongue is nearly flat. The tongue position is the bottom one in diagram 11.

In the exercise below on the central vowels, three new consonant symbols are added to your repertoire:

/č/	churn	/čərn/
/ǰ/	judge	/ǰəǰ/
/r/	rap	/ræp/
	fur	/fər/
	earn	/ərn/
	part	/part/

EXERCISE 8

★ Transcribe in phonemic symbols the following words as you normally pronounce them. The italicized letters will require careful listening to reveal whether you pronounce them as /ɪ/, /ɨ/, /ə/, or /i/.

1. d*i*nner ________	7. start*e*d ________
2. s*i*ster ________	8. fold*e*d ________
3. ch*i*ldren ________	9. r*e*gard ________
4. Ros*a*'s ________	10. d*e*gree ________
5. ros*e*s ________	11. hab*i*t ________
6. thes*i*s ________	12. judg*e*s ________

EXERCISE 9

★ Transcribe in phonemic symbols the following words as you normally pronounce them.

1. urge ________	3. cut ________	5. rug ________
2. stop ________	4. sofa ________	6. above ________

7. bird ________ 12. urban ________ 17. today ________

8. rust ________ 13. odd ________ 18. cupboard ________

9. run ________ 14. affḗct ________ 19. journey ________

10. church ________ 15. effḗct ________ 20. hot ________

11. leisure ________ 16. pocket ________

CHART OF ENGLISH VOWEL PHONEMES

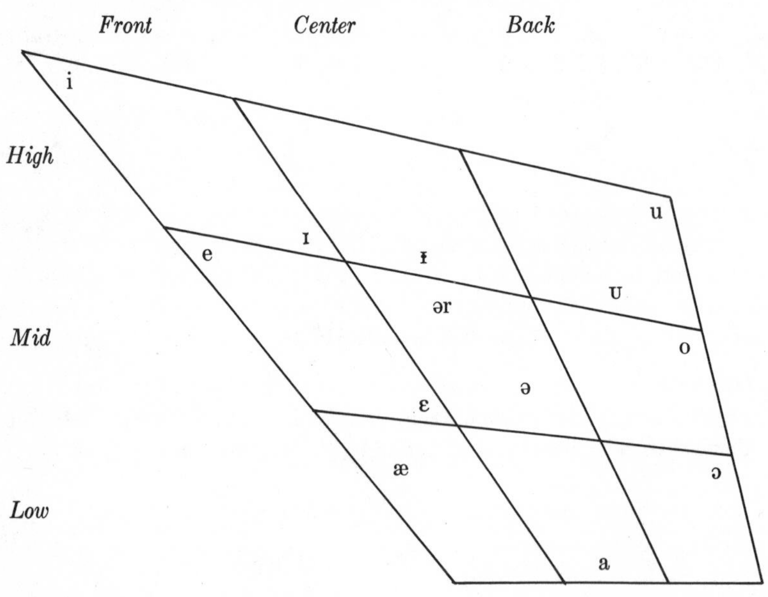

The thirteen vowel phonemes of English can be seen in relation to one another on the vowel chart just above, a two-dimensional grid of tongue positions, the mouth being at the left and the throat at the right. Using this chart we can easily give to the thirteen vowels descriptive names which will be useful in discussing them. The names are these:

/i/ High-front	/ɨ/ High-central	/u/ High-back rounded
/ɪ/ Lower high-front	/ər/ Higher mid-central	/ʊ/ Lower high-back rounded
/e/ Higher mid-front	/ə/ Mid-central	/o/ Mid-back rounded
/ɛ/ Lower mid-front	/a/ Low-central	/ɔ/ Low-back rounded
/æ/ Low-front		

It must be realized that the foregoing classification of vowels by tongue position is imprecise and generalized. Their relative positions, however, are correct. Also, there are further classifications — tense, lax; close, open; narrow, wide; long, short — that we are bypassing in the interest of a stringent simplicity. But by and large the above description and classification of vowel phonemes will serve for the fleeting glance to which we are limited.

The Syllable. Before moving ahead to the next group of phonemes, the diphthongs, it is necessary for us to examine the nature of the syllable.

When we speak we can observe that certain sounds have a greater sonority or carrying power than others. For example, in *soap* /sop/, the /o/ has greater sonority than the /s/ or the /p/, even though all are spoken with equal force. If /sop/ is spoken at some distance from the listener, he may hear distinctly only the /o/. In *potato* /pəteto/, the /ə/, /e/, and /o/ are more sonorous, more audible, than the /p/ and the /t/s. The sounds which have this greater inherent sonority or carrying power are mostly the vowels. Thus, as we utter connected discourse, we become aware of a peak-and-valley effect of sonority or audibility. The peaks of sonority are the vowels; and the valleys of less distinctness are the consonants, as in *echo* /ɛko/, or the slight diminution of loudness, as in *create* /kri-et/. This brings us to the syllable. A syllable is a sound or a short sequence of sounds which contains one peak of sonority. This peak is usually a vowel, and the vowel is said to be the center of the syllable. A segment of speech, then, contains as many syllables as there are peaks. Here are some examples of words with the peaks, or syllabic centers, underlined.

One syllable:	be	/bi/
	string	/strɪŋ/
Two syllables:	believe	/bɨliv/
	being	/biɪŋ/
	stirring	/stərɪŋ/
Three syllables:	believing	/bɨlivɪŋ/
Four syllables:	unbelieving	/ənbɨlivɪŋ/
Five syllables:	unbelievingly	/ənbɨlivɪŋli/

EXERCISE 10

★ Transcribe the following words in phonemic symbols, underline the peaks, and indicate how many syllables each word has.

Word	*Transcription*	*No. of Syllables*
spoonful	/spunfʊl/	2
1. seat	____________	____________
2. infect	____________	____________
3. paper	____________	____________
4. disenchant	____________	____________
5. unostentatious	____________	____________

We have seen that vowels are peaks of sonority and are therefore syllabic centers. But there are four consonants — /m/, /n/, /ŋ/, and /l/ — which also have considerable sonority and which can constitute syllables.

As our first example, let us take the two-syllable expression *stop 'em.* This can be uttered in two ways. The first is /stap əm/. After the lips are closed to make the /p/, they are opened for the /ə/, and closed again for the /m/. But there is a second way. Here the lips are closed for the /p/ and remain closed for the /m/. Try it and see for yourself. While you are making the /p/, no air can escape from the mouth. The closed lips shut off the mouth exit and the raised velum shuts off the nasal exit. Now, holding the lips closed, you open the velum by lowering it, and what happens? The air escapes with a slight explosion through the nasal cavity. Here the /m/ is a peak of sonority and by itself constitutes a syllable. This /m/ is called a syllabic /m/.

ORAL EXERCISE A

★ Practice saying these expressions, using for the last syllable both (1) a schwa plus /m/ or /n/, and (2) a syllabic /m/.

1. leap 'em
2. rob 'em
3. open

The syllabic /n/ is formed similarly. Consider, for example, *button.* You may pronounce it /bətən/ by dropping the tongue from the /t/ position on the alveolar ridge, uttering the /ə/, and then replacing the tongue for the /n/. But you can also pronounce *button* without removing the tongue. At the /t/ position the air is prevented from escaping by the tongue against the alveolar ridge and by the closed velum, which shuts off the nasal cavity. If you hold the tongue in the /t/ position, and open the velum, you will get an /n/ as the air escapes through the nasal cavity.

ORAL EXERCISE B

★ Practice saying these expressions, using for the last syllable both (1) a schwa plus an /n/, and (2) a syllabic /n/.

1. beaten
2. cotton
3. sudden

The syllabic /ŋ/, which is less frequent, is heard in expressions like *Jack and Jill,* /ǰækŋǰɪl/. At the /k/ position the air is held in by the back of the tongue against the velum and by the velum, which has been raised to cut off the nasal cavity. With a lowering of the velum, the nasal cavity is opened and the syllabic /ŋ/ is heard.

ORAL EXERCISE C

★ Practice saying these expressions in two ways. At the /k/ or /g/ position, use first the schwa plus an /n/ and then the syllabic /ŋ/.

1. back and forth
2. bag and baggage
3. rack and ruin

The syllabic /l/ is somewhat differently articulated. To make the common /l/, you place the tongue on the alveolar ridge, vibrate the vocal cords, and let the air flow over and off the tongue on one or both sides and escape through the mouth. Now, to make the syllabic /l/, as in *rattle*, you first have the air completely closed off by the tongue in the /t/ position on the alveolar ridge and by a raised velum cutting off the nasal cavity. Then you open one or both sides of the tongue, without removing the tip from the alveolar ridge, letting the air go around the tongue and out the mouth.

ORAL EXERCISE D

★ Pronounce the following words in two ways, using for the last syllable both (1) a schwa plus /l/, and (2) a syllabic /l/.

1. cattle
2. saddle
3. beetle

Although it is easy to locate the peaks of sonority that indicate syllable centers, the vowels and syllabic consonants, it is sometimes impossible to find the boundary between syllables, that is, the point of minimum sonority. In the two-syllable *hushing* /həšɪŋ/, for example, where is the syllable boundary? After the /ə/? Before the /ɪ/? Or in the middle of /š/? It is like trying to establish in a valley the exact line separating the two hills on either side. For our purpose here, we need not be much concerned with syllable division, and where the boundary is not audible, we can resort to an arbitrarily selected break.

Diphthongs. A diphthong consists of two vowels which occur in the same syllable, the tongue moving smoothly from one position to the other without hiatus, as in *sigh*, /sai/, *sow* (female pig), /sau/, and *soy*, /sɔi/. The two vowels together represent the peak of sonority, though one always has greater prominence than the other. Many of our vowels are diphthongized in various subareas of English, and four of them are normally diphthongized in Standard English: /i/, /e/, /u/, and /o/. For these, however, we shall use the symbols just given, since there is no phonemic difference between the pure vowels and the diphthongized vowels.* According to the system we are using, the diphthongs are only three: /ai/ as in *by*, /au/ as in *bough*, and /ɔi/ as in *boy*.

EXERCISE 11

★ Transcribe the following words into phonemic symbols, using your own natural pronunciation.

1. my ____	6. joy ____	11. high ____	16. try ____
2. toy ____	7. chives ____	12. ouch ____	17. stripe ____
3. how ____	8. thou ____	13. mighty ____	18. rowdy ____
4. tie ____	9. shy ____	14. roil ____	19. Kilroy ____
5. cow ____	10. rye ____	15. coy ____	20. destroy ____

Under the heading of "diphthongs" we shall give attention to the knotty problem of the r sounds. You have already met the /r/ consonant as in *race* /res/ and the higher mid-central r-colored vowel as in *cur* /kər/. This leaves us to consider the r sound that occurs after vowels in the same syllable. Our practice here will be to consider these r's as consonantal and to transcribe them with the /r/ symbol, thus: *farm* /farm/; *pore* /por/; *poor* /pur/; *fair* /fɛr/; *fear* /fɪr/. The symbols /ər/ will be reserved for occasions when this sound is the center of a syllable, as in the two-syllable *stirring* /stərɪŋ/ contrasted with the one-syllable *string* /strɪŋ/.

EXERCISE 12

★ Transcribe the following words into phonemic symbols, following your own natural pronunciation.

1. we're ____	3. they're ____	5. care ____
2. beer ____	4. there ____	6. merry ____

* You may think that you are uttering single vowels in words like *cease* /sis/, *maim* /mem/, *noon* /nun/, and *moan* /mon/. But the vowel sounds you are actually making are diphthongized vowels something like these: 1. [ɪi], 2. [ei], 3. [ʊu], and 4. [ou]. If you can find a tape recorder which plays backward, you can easily hear them for yourself: simply record these four words and then play them backward.

7. Mary ________
8. marry ________
9. barge ________
10. morning ________
11. mourning ________
12. north ________
13. northern ________
14. floor ________
15. here ________
16. tour ________
17. horse ________
18. hoarse ________
19. pair ________
20. payer ________
21. stair ________
22. stayer ________
23. mare ________
24. mayor ________
25. spurring ________
26. spring ________
27. cur ________
28. crowd ________
29. purr ________
30. proud ________
31. burr ________
32. bread ________
33. sure ________
34. shoer ________
35. dire ________
36. dyer ________

D. The English Phonemic System: Consonants

Vowels, you have learned, are characterized by a free flow of air. Consonants, on the other hand, are produced by stopping or obstructing this flow of air, except for the three nasals. The first six consonants presented here are those produced by a stoppage of air: /p b t d k g/.

***Stops:* /p/, /b/.** If you hold your velum and lips closed and exert outward air pressure, nothing will happen except that your cheeks may puff out. Now if you suddenly open your lips the air explodes outward and you have made a /p/. This consonant is called a voiceless bilabial stop because (1) the vocal cords do not vibrate, (2) two lips are used, and (3) a complete stop of the air flow is made. If during the same process you vibrate your vocal cords, you will produce a /b/, a voiced bilabial stop.

***Stops:* /t/, /d/.** Instead of using the lips, you can stop the air flow by holding the tongue against the alveolar ridge, with the velum closed, and exerting outward air pressure. A sudden removal of the tongue will then produce a /t/, a voiceless alveolar stop. But if the vocal cords vibrate during the process, you will produce a /d/, a voiced alveolar stop.

***Stops:* /k/, /g/.** The third pair of stops is produced by raising the tongue back against the velum, which is also raised to cut off the nasal cavity. When the tongue back is released, the outrushing air results in a /k/, a voiceless velar stop, or a /g/, a voiced velar stop, depending on whether or not the vocal cords are vibrating.

EXERCISE 13

★ To increase your awareness of the three stop positions, pronounce slowly and in succession /p/, /t/, and /k/, and try to feel, tactually and kinesthetically, what is going on inside your mouth. Do this six times and then repeat the process in reverse.

EXERCISE 14

★ Transcribe the following words into phonemic symbols.

1. pip ________	8. stopgap ________	15. hands ________
2. bib ________	9. hiccough ________	16. liquor ________
3. tot ________	10. subpoint ________	17. six ________
4. deed ________	11. fast ________	18. guest ________
5. coke ________	12. fasten ________	19. keep ________
6. gag ________	13. oozed ________	20. coop ________
7. stopped ________	14. hand ________	

EXERCISE 15

★ In *keep* and *coop* there are two different [k]s, which are allophones of /k/. In what way are they different? To answer this, try whispering the [k] of *keep* and that of *coop* alternately and note your tongue position and lip rounding. Furthermore, if you bear in mind the positions of the two vowels, you may be able to explain why the [k]s differ.

Fricatives. English contains nine consonants which are produced by an obstruction of the air stream causing audible friction. These nine fricatives are:

/f v θ ð s z š ž h/

We shall discuss these in pairs, beginning with those in the front of the mouth and moving to the back.

The first pair, /f/ and /v/, are heard in *fail* and *vale.* They are produced when the outgoing air is obstructed by the lower lip touching the upper teeth. The /f/ is called a voiceless labiodental fricative, and /v/ a voiced labiodental fricative. They differ only in the fact that /v/ is voiced. You can feel the vibration of the vocal cords for /v/ if you press your fingers around the top of the larynx, sound a continuous /f/, and then change without stopping to a /v/. The next three pairs of fricatives can be tested in the same way for voicelessness and voicing.

The second pair, /θ/ and /ð/, are heard in *ether* and *either*. They are made with the tongue between the upper and lower teeth, obstructing the air stream between its tip and the upper teeth. The /θ/ is a voiceless interdental fricative, and /ð/ a voiced interdental fricative.

The third pair is /s/ and /z/, as in *face* and *faze*. These are pronounced by the tongue permitting a small stream of air to hiss over its surface at the alveolar ridge. The /s/ is a voiceless alveolar fricative, and /z/ a voiced alveolar fricative.

The fourth pair of fricatives are /š/, the third consonant in *dilution*, and /ž/, the third consonant in *delusion*. These are made by the friction of moving air between the tongue front and the palatal region just behind the alveolar ridge. The /š/ is a voiceless alveopalatal fricative, and /ž/ a voiced alveopalatal fricative. To get the feel of the voiceless alveolar and alveopalatal fricatives, take a deep breath and on a continuous stream of air repeat /s/ and /š/ in alternation, noting the movements of the tongue and the lips.

The last fricative is /h/, as in *hat* contrasted with *at*. This is produced by the breath rushing through the vocal cords closing to a position for vibrating. Its tongue and lip position is that of the following sound. You can see this easily by preparing your mouth to say *ha, he, who*. It is called the voiceless glottal fricative, the glottis being the space between the vocal cords.

EXERCISE 16

★ Transcribe the following words in phonemic symbols:

1. enough _______	8. scent _______	15. luxury _______
2. wife _______	9. close (adjective) _______	16. luxurious _______
3. wives _______	10. clothes (noun) _______	17. measure _______
4. fifth _______	11. news _______	18. humble _______
5. south _______	12. newspaper _______	19. honest _______
6. southern _______	13. house _______	20. homage _______
7. with _______	14. husband _______	

EXERCISE 17

★ For each word below, find a word that, with it, forms a minimal pair demonstrating the phonemic status of the fricative. Write this word in phonemic notation.

1. *f*ind ____________ 4. *th*us ____________ 7. *sh*irk ____________

2. *v*ase ____________ 5. *s*eem ____________ 8. a*z*ure ____________

3. bo*th* ____________ 6. ja*zz* ____________ 9. *h*ang ____________

Affricates. English has two affricates — the voiceless /č/ as in *chill*, and the voiced /ǰ/ as in *Jill.* The /č/ begins with the voiceless stop /t/, which is exploded as a voiceless fricative /š/. Thus it is sometimes written /tš/. It is known as the voiceless alveopalatal affricate. The /ǰ/ consists of a voiced stop /d/, which is exploded as a voiced fricative /ž/, and is sometimes written /dž/. It is called the voiced alveopalatal affricate.

Nasals. The three nasals — /m/, /n/, and /ŋ/ — have already been described on pages 5–6.

Lateral. The lateral /l/, as in *louse*, is made by placing the tongue tip on the alveolar ridge and vibrating the vocal cords as the air passes out on one or both sides of the tongue. To feel the tongue position, hold the tongue firmly at the alveolar ridge and make a series of /l/s and /n/s, noting how the sides of the tongue open and close as you alternate sounds.

Glides. The three glides — /y/, /r/, and /w/ — are signalized by a moving, not a stationary, tongue position. They are all voiced.

With /y/, as in *yoke* contrasted with *oak*, the tongue begins in the /i/ region and moves toward the position for the following vowel. It is called the high front glide. In the case of /r/, as in *rate* contrasted with *ate*, the tongue begins in the position of the r-colored vowel of *purr*, /ər/, and moves toward the following vowel. It is known as the retroflex alveolar glide, though this name is not descriptive of some /r/s. The third glide is /w/, as in *will* versus *ill.* Here the tongue takes an /u/ position and then moves into the following vowel. It is called the high back glide.

EXERCISE 18

★ Transcribe the following words into phonemic notation:

1. literature ____________ 3. champagne ____________

2. champion ____________ 4. soldier ____________

5. judge ________________
6. solemn ________________
7. pneumonia ________________
8. singer ________________
9. linger ________________
10. strong ________________
11. stronger ________________
12. illusion ________________
13. folk ________________
14. milk ________________
15. use (verb) ________________
16. opinion ________________
17. try ________________
18. wear ________________
19. where ________________
20. berate ________________

We have now covered briefly the thirteen vowels and twenty-four consonant phonemes of English. These are charted on the diagrams on page 16 and below. You will find that memorizing these charts is an excellent way to keep in mind the basic facts about each sound.

Note in the consonant chart that, like the vowel chart, the arrangement is from the front of the mouth at the left to the throat at the right.

CHART OF ENGLISH CONSONANT PHONEMES

	Bilabial	Labio-dental	Inter-dental	Alveolar	Alveo-palatal	Velar	Glottal
Stops vl	p			t		k	
Stops vd	b			d		g	
Fricatives vl		f	θ	s	š		h
Fricatives vd		v	ð	z	ž		
Affricates vl					č		
Affricates vd					ǰ		
Nasals	m			n		ŋ	
Lateral				l			
Glides				r	y	w	

EXERCISE 19

★ As a review of the vowel and consonant symbols, write in phonemic notation one illustrative word for each phoneme given below.

Vowels

1. /i/ ______________
2. /ɪ/ ______________
3. /e/ ______________
4. /ɛ/ ______________
5. /æ/ ______________
6. /ɨ/ ______________
7. /ər/ ______________
8. /ə/ ______________
9. /a/ ______________
10. /u/ ______________
11. /ʊ/ ______________
12. /o/ ______________
13. /ɔ/ ______________

Consonants

1. /p/ ______________
2. /b/ ______________
3. /t/ ______________
4. /d/ ______________
5. /k/ ______________
6. /g/ ______________
7. /f/ ______________
8. /v/ ______________
9. /θ/ ______________
10. /ð/ ______________
11. /s/ ______________
12. /z/ ______________
13. /š/ ______________
14. /ž/ ______________
15. /h/ ______________
16. /č/ ______________
17. /ǰ/ ______________
18. /m/ ______________
19. /n/ ______________
20. /ŋ/ ______________
21. /l/ ______________
22. /r/ ______________
23. /y/ ______________
24. /w/ ______________

EXERCISE 20

★ Read aloud the following words and word groups. Watch out for this danger: You may recognize a word and pronounce it as you ordinarily do instead of following the notation. A stress mark /ˊ/ has been added to show the syllable of greatest emphasis. In the blanks write out in ordinary spelling the word or word group. These are all real pronunciations made by native American speakers.

Single Words

1. frag ______
2. sári ______
3. hwai ______
4. rum ______
5. rʊm ______
6. príti ______
7. wʊ́mən ______
8. wímɨn ______
9. čifs ______
10. laivz ______
11. sɛns ______
12. sɛnts ______
13. paunz ______
14. əkrɔ́st ______
15. əfɛ́kt ______
16. waš ______
17. wɔš ______
18. wɔrš ______
19. hɔrs ______
20. hors ______
21. sʌ́mpθɪŋ ______
22. lǽŋgwɨǰ ______
23. kántækt ______
24. kəntǽkt ______
25. tyúzdi ______

Word Groups

1. lɛmi gó ______
2. am gənə krái ______
3. hu æst yú ______
4. ai tóld ɪm ______
5. wi tól ðəm ______
6. aišt θɪŋk i wʊ́d ______
7. šiz pərdi číki ______
8. ðe kʊdəv bɔ́t ðəm ______
9. ail míšu ______
10. al tríču ______

II.

Assimilation and Other Phonetic Processes

A. Assimilation

Up to this point we have been dealing mainly with words in isolation. The pronunciation of such words is called the citation form. But the citation form of words is often not the pronunciation heard in everyday living speech. For words are compounded with other words to make new ones; they take on prefixes and suffixes; and usually they are met as part of a continuous stream of speech. Thus the sounds with which a word begins and ends are frequently in contact with adjoining sounds. When two sounds occur cheek by jowl, a change is likely to occur in one (or both) of them: it becomes more like its neighbor in some respect. A few examples will make this tendency clear.

The citation form of *news* is /nuz/ or /nɪuz/. Let us take *news*, with its final /z/, and add *paper* to it. Now the voiced /z/ of *news* is juxtaposed to the voiceless /p/ of *paper*. Do the two sounds remain the same? In the speech of many persons the voiced /z/ changes to a voiceless /s/ — /nuspepər/. The change can also work the other way, from voicelessness to voicing. The citation form of *north*, /nɔrθ/, ends in a voiceless /θ/, but when the voiced suffix *-ern* /ərn/ is added, the /θ/ becomes /ð/, thus *northern* /nɔrðərn/.

The process we have just illustrated is called assimilation. Assimilation may be defined as the phonetic process by which one speech sound comes to resemble or become identical with a neighboring sound. In the cases above, we were concerned with voice assimilation, a very common kind. In many two-syllable words like *matter*, *butter*, *dirty*, where the voiceless /t/ is surrounded by voiced sounds, there is a tendency to voice the /t/, making it a kind of /d/. In cases like *sit down* /sɪdaun/, the /t/ becomes identical with the /d/; that is to say, it disappears.

EXERCISE 21

★ Transcribe the following. Use double underlining to show voice assimilation to neighboring sounds. Be able to explain each assimilation.

1. letter ________	7. goose ________
bottle ________	gooseberry ________
dirty ________	8. shut ________
2. south ________	shut up ________
southern ________	9. have ________
3. it ________	I have to fish ________________
it is ________	I have two fish ________________
4. worth ________	10. How many guests will you have to feed?
worthy ________	a. ________________________
5. got ________	b. ________________________
I've got it ________	11. used ________
6. cup ________	He used to dance ________________
cupboard ________	He used two eggs ________________

Voice assimilation plays a role in the formation of English s plurals. In spelling, the s plural consists of the addition of an *s* or *es* to the singular form of the noun. But in the spoken language, there are three s plurals. You can readily discover these by means of the next exercise.

EXERCISE 22

★ Transcribe the following words in both their singular and plural forms. When you have finished, compare the plural suffix you added with the final sound of the singular to see what the two have in common. Then answer these two questions:

1. What are the three forms of the s plural?
2. What principle governs the choice of the plural suffix?

Spelling	*Singular*	*Plural*	*Spelling*	*Singular*	*Plural*
1. stop	______	______	11. son	______	______
2. right	______	______	12. song	______	______
3. cake	______	______	13. doll	______	______
4. muff	______	______	14. fear	______	______
5. breath	______	______	15. glass	______	______
6. mob	______	______	16. rose	______	______
7. ride	______	______	17. dish	______	______
8. frog	______	______	18. garage	______	______
9. wave	______	______	19. ditch	______	______
10. sum	______	______	20. edge	______	______

There are apparent exceptions to the principle governing the choice of the s plural suffix, for example, pairs like *life, lives* and *wreath, wreaths,* which can be explained historically. The principle is also operative with two other grammatical suffixes — the noun possessive, as in *Jack's, John's,* and the *s* ending of the verb in the third person singular, as in *bakes, begs.* All this we shall take up later in the study of English morphology.

A case of assimilation similar to that of the s plural exists with the past-tense suffix *-ed.* Here again we shall proceed inductively with an exercise.

EXERCISE 23

★ Transcribe each word both in the present-tense form given, and in the past-tense form. Then study your results and answer two questions:

1. How many phonemic forms does the *-ed* suffix have?
2. What principle governs the choice of suffix?

Spelling	*Present*	*Past Tense*	*Spelling*	*Present*	*Past Tense*
1. pass	________	________	11. hug	________	________
2. laugh	________	________	12. rave	________	________
3. mop	________	________	13. mill	________	________
4. back	________	________	14. stir	________	________
5. rush	________	________	15. rot	________	________
6. wrench	________	________	16. load	________	________
7. rob	________	________	17. seat	________	________
8. seem	________	________	18. sod	________	________
9. loan	________	________	19. need	________	________
10. wrong	________	________	20. repeat	________	________

Assimilation may stem not only from the action or inaction of the vocal cords but also from the action of other parts of the speech-producing apparatus. As two adjoining speech sounds are uttered, the set of movements producing one of these sounds may accommodate itself to the movements that produce the other sound. In brief, the production of the two sounds is short-cut, resulting in economy of effort and a change in the sounds themselves. An example will clarify this point. Consider the last two sounds of *length* /lɛŋθ/. This is sometimes heard in the assimilated form of /lɛnθ/, in which the velar nasal /ŋ/ has become the alveolar nasal /n/. In the first form, /lɛŋθ/, the tongue back is raised to the velum for /ŋ/; then the tongue tip is placed at the bottom of the upper teeth for /θ/. Two tongue movements are needed. But in /lɛnθ/ the two tongue movements are reduced to one. The tongue tip goes immediately to the bottom of the upper teeth to produce a dental instead of an alveolar /n/, and then remains in exactly the same position for /θ/. Thus production is short-cut with a consequent alteration of sound. The phonetician describes this by saying that the /ŋ/ has been assimilated to (= made like) the /θ/, becoming /n/. This kind of assimilation is called place assimilation.

In the preceding example of *length,* one sound was made to resemble another: the /n/ became partially like the dental /θ/ in that it changed from an alveolar to a dental. In the next example of place assimilation, one sound becomes identical with the second. If we utter *horse* and *shoe* individually, we find that *horse* ends in /s/ and *shoe* begins with /š/. But if we utter them as one word *horseshoe,* the final /s/ of *horse* is assimilated to the initial /š/ of *shoe*, becoming identical with it in /hɔršu/. In short, the /s/ disappears. The assimilative disappearance of sounds in spoken discourse is not uncommon. When /t/, for instance, becomes part of a consonant cluster, usually enclosed by consonants, as in *softness*, it tends to disappear.

EXERCISE 24

★ Transcribe the following expressions and be able to explain in class, in terms of the vocal apparatus, just what assimilation is likely to occur at the italicized places.

1. stren*gth* ____________
2. thi*s* *s*ugar ____________
3. gra*ndp*a ____________
4. gra*ndm*a ____________
5. ha*ndk*erchief ____________
6. wi*dth* ____________
7. brea*dth* ____________
8. co*nq*uer (Cf. contact) ____________
9. wa*s* *y*our ____________
10. He le*ft* *th*e town ____________
11. Ju*st* *th*ink ____________
12. Di*d* *y*ou? ____________
13. the mos*t* *f*un ____________

EXERCISE 25

★ Answer the following questions:

1. In the sixteenth century the two forms *unpossible* and *impossible* existed side by side. Why do you think *impossible* survived as the standard form?
2. In *Webster's Third New International Dictionary* we find the variant verb forms *enplane* and *emplane*. Which do you believe will survive? Why?
3. The Latin *cum*, meaning "with," became *con-* in many words. The *n* of *con-* represents either /n/ or /ŋ/. Which is it in these words: *condemn, congress*. Why?
4. A sentence like "She was writing this morning" is sometimes misunderstood as "She was riding this morning." Explain.
5. Chinese *san pan*, meaning "three planks," appears in English as *sampan*. Explain the *m*.
6. The Vulgar Latin *patrem*, meaning "father," developed into Italian *padre*. Explain the *d*.

B. Metathesis

Metathesis is the transposition of speech sounds. The person who says *tradegy* for *tragedy* or *revelant* for *relevant* is metathesizing. The dialect form *axe* /æks/ for *ask* /æsk/ is another case, going back a thousand years to Old English. The most commonly heard metatheses occur in the phonetic situation of /r/ plus a vowel. Take *pretty* for example. In the sentence "She's a pretty girl," we are likely to say /prɪti/. But when *pretty* is given minimal stress, as in "That's pretty good," the word tends to become /pərti/. If you listen carefully to the pronunciation of *hundred, apron, pronounce,* and similar words with /r/ plus vowel in an unstressed position, you will notice many metathesized /ər/s in the speech of educated people.

EXERCISE 26

★ In word history, metathesis has been occasionally responsible for changing pronunciations and spellings. As examples, look up the etymology of these words and write the early unmetathesized forms in the blanks.

Present Word	*Form before Metathesis*
1. bird	________________
2. third	________________
3. grass	________________
4. clasp	________________
5. dirt	________________

C. Epenthesis

Epenthesis is the insertion of an extra sound within a word, such as the /p/ you may hear in *something,* or the /t/ in *sense.* The extra sound is termed excrescent. Of the various epenthetic situations, we shall discuss one that is rather common.

After an /m/ an excrescent /p/ may occur before these voiceless consonants: /t/, /k/, /f/, /θ/, /s/, and /š/. The /p/ occurs because of a slight lack of coordination in the speech-making mechanism, which can be illustrated with *something.* To pronounce *something* as /səmθɪŋ/ requires a precise functioning of the speech apparatus at the critical point of /-mθ-/. For /m/ the lips are closed, and velum is lowered, and the vocal cords vibrate as the /m/ hums through the nose. Now, in shifting to the /θ/, four actions must take place at exactly the same time: the vocal cords must cease vibrating, the tongue tip take an interdental position, the velum rise to close off the nasal passage, and the lips open. However, if the velum closes off the nasal passage a fraction of a second before the lips open, then air pressure builds up behind the lips, and when they are opened the air bursts out in a /p/.

In other words in which /m/ is followed by a voiceless consonant, the reason for the excrescent /p/ is fundamentally the same: the velum closes the nasal passage before the lips open.

EXERCISE 27

★ Answer the following questions:

1. Is the *p* in *glimpse* and *empty* the result of epenthesis? To find out, look up etymologies of these words.
2. What variant spellings do *Samson* and *Thomson* have? Explain.
3. Which of these words may be heard with an excrescent /p/: *comfort, combat, warmth, warmly, Tomkins, Tomlin, dreamt.*

D. Epithesis

Epithesis is the addition of an extra consonant to the end of a word. It occurs after a final /n/ or /s/. Suppose we consider the word *sound.* In Middle English this was *soun* /sun/. First, we must note that /n/ and /d/ are homorganic; this means that both are made at the same position of the speech organs — the tongue tip at the alveolar ridge. If, when /n/ is being sounded, the vocal cords stop vibrating as the tongue is released from the alveolar ridge, the /n/ merely ceases. But if the velum should be raised, closing off the nasal passage, before the tongue is lowered, air pressure builds up behind the tongue, and upon release of the tongue, a /d/ is produced. It was doubtless the latter set of articulatory movements, made by many people in early England, that gave *sound* its /d/, which later appeared in the spelling. The same /d/ can be heard today in /draund/, a substandard pronunciation of *drown.*

After final /s/ an epithetic /t/ occasionally appears. It is caused by the fact that the tongue, instead of being lowered to end the /s/ sound, is pressed against the alveolar ridge while the breath is moving outward; then when the tongue is lowered, the release of air pressure produces a /t/. You will now and then hear this /t/ at the end of *once* and *across.*

EXERCISE 28

★ Look up the etymology of the following words to determine the source of the final sound: *lend, bound* (adjective), *against, midst, amongst.*

III.

Spelling and Pronunciation

A. Relations Between Spelling and Pronunciation

Languages are reduced to writing by means of three kinds of writing systems. Some systems, like Cherokee, use one symbol for each syllable. Others, like Chinese, use one symbol for each morpheme, the smallest segment of an utterance that carries meaning. But most languages, including English, use an alphabetic, that is to say, a phonemic system. This means that the letters stand for phonemes. An ideal alphabetic writing system would be one in which each letter always stood for the same phoneme, and each phoneme was always represented by the same letter. Such a two-way one-for-one correspondence between letters and phonemes does not exist in any standard alphabet now in general use. Of course you have been using such a phonemic system in this book but systems like this are used only by the relatively few who are students of language.

English is far from the ideal writing system, as anyone with spelling difficulties is well aware. In fact, English does not contain a single instance of a two-way one-to-one correspondence — letter to sound and sound to letter. Small wonder. Our language has thirteen vowel phonemes and twenty-four consonant phonemes — thirty-seven in all. And to represent these thirty-seven, it has only twenty-six letters, of which three are superfluous. A few illustrations will reveal this inadequacy of letter-sound and sound-letter correspondences. The first letter of the alphabet, *a*, represents at least eight phonemes, as shown by this series: *dame, fare, pan, father, ball, pillage, lunar, opera.* If we go the other way, from sound to letter, we find that nearly all phonemes have from two to over a dozen spellings. In this respect, the vowel phonemes are worse offenders than the consonants. Here are some ways in which the phoneme /i/ is spelled: *ee*, feet; *e*, me; *ae*, Caesar; *eo*, people; *ea*, beat; *ei*, deceive; *oe*, amoeba; *ie*, relieve; *i*, ravine; *ey*, key; *ay*, quay.

EXERCISE 29 (From letter to sound)

★ Write in each blank the phonemic symbol for the italicized letter:

a. 1. *s*uch ______

2. devi*s*e ______

3. *s*ure ______

4. trea*s*ure ______

5. ai*s*le ______

b. 6. *c*ite ______

7. *c*opper ______

8. deli*c*ious ______

c. 9. b*e* ______

10. m*e*t ______

11. *E*nglish ______

12. sil*e*nt ______

13. s*e*rgeant ______

EXERCISE 30 (From sound to letter)

★ a. Write one word illustrating each of the spellings of the phoneme /š/ listed below:

Spelling	*Example*	*Spelling*	*Example*
1. sh	______________	7. s	______________
2. ch	______________	8. se	______________
3. ce	______________	9. si	______________
4. ci	______________	10. ti	______________
5. sch	______________	11. ss	______________
6. sci	______________	12. ssi	______________

★ b. Write one word illustrating each of the spellings of the phoneme /o/ listed below:

Spelling	*Example*	*Spelling*	*Example*
1. o	________________	6. ow	________________
2. oh	________________	7. eo	________________
3. oa	________________	8. au	________________
4. oe	________________	9. ew	________________
5. ou	________________	10. eau	________________

11. ough ________________

Illustrations like the foregoing, which could be multiplied, suggest that English spelling is unpredictably capricious. But we must remember that they are selective, having been chosen to demonstrate this one aspect of spelling, its irregularity. If all English spelling were like this, it would be virtually useless as a writing system. Yet we do succeed in representing the spoken language with our spelling; witness the fact that most persons can read aloud with little trouble. Furthermore, when we meet new words in our reading, we seldom have trouble in pronouncing them. An exercise in nonsense words will illustrate this point:

EXERCISE 31

★ a. *Spelling to sound.* Write the following nonsense words in phonemic notation to show your pronunciation of them:

1. lete ____________	6. theet ____________
2. vake ____________	7. noot ____________
3. zite ____________	8. deat ____________
4. noke ____________	9. poat ____________
5. fube ____________	10. boe ____________

★ b. *Sound to spelling.* The following words are given in phonemic notation. Write them out in conventional spelling.

1. /dɪt/ ____________	3. /ǰæt/ ____________
2. /tɛt/ ____________	4. /zat/ ____________

5. /čət/ __________	8. /bæməəm/ __________
6. /zel/ __________	9. /sail/ __________
7. /omɛkt/ __________	10. /əut/ __________

Up to this point we have seen that English spelling contains both regularities and irregularities. Professor Robert A. Hall, Jr., in his excellent *Sound and Spelling in English,* divides English spellings into three groups — the regular, the semiregular, and the downright irregular. He offers a list of forty-seven phonemes and combinations of phonemes which have regular letter equivalents and concludes, "English orthography does afford to each phoneme of the language at least one regular, clear and consistent alphabetic representation." The semiregular spellings, he points out, are irregular only in the way they symbolize one or two phonemes of a word; furthermore, these spellings fall into subsets which are consistent within themselves. The downright irregular are relatively few. As examples of the last, Hall lists such words as *quay, busy, schism, who, debt, choir.*

Here is an exercise which will give you instances of some of the simpler regularities in English spelling.

EXERCISE 32

★ Begin with the syllable /ɪn/. Go through the chart of English consonant phonemes, diagram 13, and list all the words you can make by placing single consonants at the beginning of /ɪn/. Write each word in both phonemic notation and in conventional spelling. Then do the same for /æt/ and /at/. What correspondence do you find between the consonant phonemes and the letters representing them?

	/ɪn/		/æt/		/at/	
	Phon. Not.	*Spelling*	*Phon. Not.*	*Spelling*	*Phon. Not.*	*Spelling*
1.						
2.						
3.						
4.						
5.						
6.						
7.						

8. ________ ________ ________ ________ ________ ________

9. ________ ________ ________ ________ ________ ________

10. ________ ________ ________ ________ ________ ________

11. ________ ________ ________ ________ ________ ________

12. ________ ________ ________ ________ ________ ________

13. ________ ________ ________ ________ ________ ________

14. ________ ________ ________ ________ ________ ________

15. ________ ________ ________ ________ ________ ________

16. ________ ________ ________ ________ ________ ________

17. ________ ________ ________ ________ ________ ________

18. ________ ________ ________ ________ ________ ________

Exercise 32 suggests, within its limited data, that English consonant phonemes have one spelling that may be considered regular and stable. In addition to one regular spelling, nearly all consonant phonemes have others. The number of spellings varies considerably. At one end of the scale is /θ/, which is always spelled *th*. At the other end are /k/, which has eleven spellings, and /š/, which has fourteen. Within all this irregularity, however, are subsets of words which tend to be regular and consistent within each set. The phoneme /f/ will serve to illustrate these subsets. In initial position its regular spelling is *f*, as thousands of words will attest. But a large subset spell this initial /f/ as *ph*, words like *physics, phenomenon, philosophy, pheasant, pharmacy*. In final position the /f/ phoneme has its regular spelling in words like *if, loaf, serf, spoof, beef*. But the subsets give us more possibilities.

ff as in *biff, miff, off, scoff, buff*
gh as in *laugh, cough, tough, rough, enough*

And there are the less frequent final spellings of *fe* as in *knife*, *ph* as in *epitaph*, and *ffe* as in *giraffe*.

Subsets like these are manifold. They are the basis of the spelling "rules" that you learned in school, e.g., "*i* before *e* except after *c*," which were often accompanied by lists of exceptions. The presence of such subsets, which lead a random existence in our minds, both aids and misleads us in our spelling. They aid us in that they limit spelling choices. If a word begins with the phoneme /f/ we know automatically that it begins with *f* or *ph* and that it does not begin with *ff* or *gh*. Or if we wish to spell a word containing the sounds /ait/ we are reasonably sure that the spelling will be either *-ight,* following the subset *might, night, light, right, sight, fight, delight* — or *-ite,* following *mite, kite, site, recite, bite.* But such dual sets mislead us, too, for the sounds do not tell exactly which spelling to choose; and also there are exceptions to harass us, like *height.*

EXERCISE 33

★ English has numerous subsets involving the addition of a suffix. In subsets *a* and *b* below, state the principle that governs the spelling of a word when a suffix beginning with a vowel-letter — *-ed, -ing,* or *-er* — is added.

a.		b.	
1. hope	hoped hoping	1. hop	hopped hopping
2. dine	diner dining dined	2. din	dinned dinning
3. ride	rider riding	3. rid	ridder ridding
4. cite	cited citing	4. sit	sitter sitting
5. dote	doting doted	5. dot	dotting dotted

a. ______________________________

____

b. ______________________________

____

EXERCISE 34

★ This is a continuation of exercise 33. Study the words below ending in silent *e* and state the spelling principle governing the addition of suffixes.

1. care + ed = cared + ful = careful
2. love + ing = loving + ly = lovely
3. blame + able = blamable + less = blameless
4. fine + ed = fined + ness = fineness
5. game + est = gamest + ly = gamely
6. disgrace + er = disgracer + ful = disgraceful

____

____

____

We may conclude that English spelling is far removed from an ideal phonemic system with a two-way one-to-one correspondence between sounds and letters; but that, despite the uncertain and insecure relations between spelling and pronunciation, it does have many regularities that are available to the alert writer.

B. Spelling Pronunciation

In the act of reading we not infrequently meet words that we have never heard sounded, that are familiar to our eyes but not to our ears. In such cases we do the natural thing — we give them the most plausible pronunciation suggested by the spelling. If, for instance, a plains dweller, in reading a sea story, comes across the words *boatswain* and *gunwale,* he is likely to pronounce them /botswen/ and /gənwel/; whereas one reared in a boating environment would have learned by ear the traditional pronunciations of /bosən/ and /gənəl/. This contrast affords an illustration of spelling pronunciation, which is simply a pronunciation that departs from the traditional pronunciation and conforms closely to the spelling.

The words we acquire in childhood, before learning to read, are those that are resistant to spelling pronunciation. The word *cupboard* is a good example. This is normally spoken as /kəbərd/, and few persons notice how far this traditional pronunciation has moved away, by assimilation and weakening of stress on the last syllable, from an aural combination of *cup* and *board.* Now let us compare *cupboard* with *clapboard,* which has gone through exactly the same processes of change and has the traditional pronunciation of /klæbərd/. Many Americans have never heard this word, certainly not in childhood, and others have seen it only in print. Thus it is only to be expected that it should be given the spelling pronunciation of /klæpbɔrd/.

Place names, which may endure for centuries, tend to develop vagaries of pronunciation known only to those in intimate association with the places. It is not surprising then that strangers to these places, with only the spelling to guide them, will mispronounce the names. Countless Americans pronounce *Edinburgh* as /ɛdɪnbərg/, not realizing that in Scotland the city is known as /ɛdɪnbəro/. Personal names too tend to change through the influence of spelling. A well-known instance is *Theobald.* When Pope slandered "piddling Theobald" some two centuries ago, he created in the word combination an especially effective collocation of sounds, for *Theobald* still had at that time its traditional pronunciation of /tɪbəld/. Today it is generally known by the spelling pronunciation of /θiəbɔld/.

It is not uncommon for spelling pronunciation to be generally adopted by all speakers of English, thus becoming the standard pronunciation. A special class of such words deserves mention. English contains hundreds of words borrowed from Latin and French with a *th* spelling. In these words the *th* was pronounced /t/ in Latin and French, and it was with this voiceless stop /t/ that they came into English. Two examples are *theme* and *theater*, both first recorded in English in the fourteenth century. In that century they were spelled in English with either *th* or *t*, the latter reflecting the actual pronunciation. The spelling *th* eventually prevailed, and with it came the spelling pronunciation /θ/ that we use today. In personal first names with *th*, an interesting situation exists that can be made clear by an exercise.

EXERCISE 35

★ After each name in the first column write in phonemic notation your pronunciation of it. In the second column spell out your nickname for each personal name. In the third column write in phonemic notation your pronunciation of the nickname.

1. Anthony __________ __________ __________
2. Theodore __________ __________ __________
3. Dorothy __________ __________ __________
4. Arthur __________ __________ __________
5. Elizabeth __________ __________ __________
6. Matthew __________ __________ __________
7. Nathaniel __________ __________ __________

Explain the /θ/–/t/ disparity in these names. What two Biblical names with *th* have resisted spelling pronunciation and are still pronounced with a /t/?

__________ __________

EXERCISE 36

★ After each word write in phonemic notation your pronunciation of it. Then look it up in your desk dictionary to see whether you have used a spelling pronunciation. If your dictionary records two or more pronunciations, try to decide whether one is a spelling pronunciation which has become acceptable. Sometimes the Middle English form of the word will give you a clue to the traditional pronunciation. After your notation write SP (spelling pronunciation) or TP (traditional pronunciation) to show which pronunciation you used.

1. breeches ____________________ _____
2. blackguard ____________________ _____
3. comptroller ____________________ _____
4. almond ____________________ _____
5. nephew ____________________ _____
6. coxswain ____________________ _____
7. Greenwich ____________________ _____
8. falcon ____________________ _____
9. Pall Mall ____________________ _____
10. arctic ____________________ _____

That the spelling of words has at times wrought changes in their pronunciation does not mean at all that spelling is an infallible guide to pronunciation. Yet you will frequently hear a person justify a pronunciation by an appeal to spelling. He may insist, for example, that *often* should be pronounced /ɔftɪn/, because it is spelled with a /t/, though he does not remember to apply this argument to *soften.* Or he may wish to pronounce the *h* in *vehicle,* the *b* in *subtle,* or the *l* in *calm* or *salmon* because his eye has seen these letters in the printed word. Such a principle is rendered impossible of application by the irregularities of English spelling, as we have already seen. The answer to the person who appeals to spelling to justify pronunciation is to ask him to apply his principle to words like those in the next exercise.

EXERCISE 37

★ Write in phonemic notation your pronunciation of the following words:

1. come ______________
   home ______________
2. move ______________
   shove ______________
3. friend ______________
   fiend ______________
   sieve ______________

4. swore ________________

   sword ________________

5. hornet ________________

   hour ________________

6. house (noun) ________________

   carouse ________________

   famous ________________

7. corps ________________

   island ________________

   debt ________________

   sovereign ________________

   pneumatic ________________

8. colonel ________________

IV.

Stress

A. Stress Phonemes

In our discussion of phonemes up to now, we have been concerned with the thirty-seven phonemes of English. These are called segmental phonemes because each is a segment of the continuous flow of speech. But this is only part of the phonemic story. We utter phonemes with varying degrees of prominence or stress; we sound voiced phonemes on different pitch levels; and we employ breaks or disjunctures to break up the whole utterance into groupings. The consequence of these three oral practices is that three more language elements require scrutiny — stress, pitch, and juncture (the common term for disjuncture). All three are phonemic; and as they accompany, and are said to be superposed on, the segmental phonemes, they are called suprasegmental phonemes. In this chapter we shall investigate the first of these three suprasegmental phonemes, that of stress.

Stress refers to the degree of prominence a syllable has. In *agree*, for example, the *gree* sounds more prominent than the *a*. In any utterance there may be as many degrees of stress as there are syllables, but many of the differences will be slight and even imperceptible. We are concerned here only with those differences of stress that have the power to distinguish meanings, namely the stress phonemes. Of these there are three, when we limit our analysis to individual words. Going from the most prominent to the weakest, we distinguish them by the following diacritics and names:

´ Primary stress
` Mid stress
˘ Weak stress (usually not indicated)

They are all illustrated in the word *légĕndàry*.

To demonstrate that stress is phonemic we shall again employ a minimal pair. If we contrast /pə̀rmít/ with /pə́rmìt/, we see that the segmental phonemes are identical and that the two words differ only in the position of their primary and mid stresses. So it must be these stresses that distinguish them as signifying a verb and a noun respectively, and the stresses must therefore be phonemes.

Since some students have difficulty in differentiating various degrees of stress, a few graduated exercises may be useful.

EXERCISE 38

★ Place a primary stress mark over the syllable that has the greatest prominence.

1. defer
2. differ
3. pervert (verb)
4. pervert (noun)
5. conflict (verb)
6. conflict (noun)
7. evil
8. superb
9. romance
10. detail
11. research
12. defense

EXERCISE 39

★ Place a mid-stress mark over the syllable that has the next to the greatest prominence. The primary stress marks are supplied.

1. díctionary
2. sécretary
3. separátion
4. íntellect
5. fundaméntal
6. aviátion
7. perpendícular
8. académic
9. univérsity
10. absolútely

EXERCISE 40

★ Mark the primary and mid stresses on the following words.

1. accent (noun)
2. austere
3. ambush
4. humane
5. blackbird
6. forgive
7. irate
8. pathos
9. diphthong
10. phoneme

EXERCISE 41

★ Mark all degrees of stresses that you hear in the following words.

1. intellectual
2. designate
3. education
4. busybody
5. interruption
6. humanitarian
7. socialized
8. ceremony
9. military
10. uninspired

In the preceding exercises you have been putting stress marks of three degrees on isolated words, the citation forms. When we turn our attention to word groups and sentences, we shall need four degrees of stress. These are indicated as follows:

ˊ Primary stress
ˆ Secondary stress
ˋ Third stress (same as mid stress on words)
˘ Weak stress

The word *ìntelléctual* has all three degrees of word stress; but when it occurs in a phrase, *ìntellêctual cùriósity*, its primary stress is demoted to second, as the markings show, and four degrees of stress are needed to describe the stress patterning. An exercise will furnish more illustrations.

EXERCISE 42

★ Place a primary stress mark on the single words, and both primary and the secondary stress marks, /ˊ/ and /ˆ/, on the longer expressions. Omit the third and weak stress marks.

1. remarkable
2. remarkable invention
3. tiresome
4. tiresome job
5. contract (noun)
6. contract bridge
7. praiseworthy
8. praiseworthy remark
9. academic
10. academic procession
11. blooming
12. blooming plant

B. Shifting Stress

Many words in English have what is called shifting stress. In isolation or before weakly stressed syllables, these words have a primary stress on the last syllable, like *unknówn*. But when they are used before a stressed syllable, this primary stress is shifted toward the front of the word, as in

The *ûnknòwn* thíef is still ùnknówn.

In the first *unknown* of the sentence, front-shifting has occurred because of the primary stress on *thief*. The stress on *un-* has been demoted from primary to secondary, but this syllable still has the strongest stress in the word, in contrast with the second *unknówn*. An exercise will show you shifting stress in action.

EXERCISE 43

★ Place the primary, secondary, and third stress marks, /ˊ/ and /ˆ/, and /ˋ/, on the words in italics.

1. She's an *ideal girl.*
2. That girl is *ideal.*
3. Our *overnight guests* did not stay *overnight.*
4. The *cut-glass bowl* was not really *cut-glass.*
5. *Inlaid tiles* are always *inlaid.*
6. Wasn't he *almost killed? Almost.*
7. He went *overseas* for his *overseas job.*
8. The soldiers are *Chinese* in the *Chinese army.*
9. He waited to be *fourteen* for *fourteen years.*
10. A *left-handed pitcher* doesn't always bat *left-handed.*

C. Grammatical Stress Patterns

Grammatical patterns are accompanied by regular stress patterns. Sometimes such stress patterns are the sole means of differentiating one grammatical pattern, with its concomitant meaning, from another. At other times the stress patterns just ride along. Of the many in English we shall take up only six, for it is difficult to deal with stress apart from pitch and juncture, all three of which cooperate in conveying meanings.

Pattern 1. A compound noun is usually accompanied by the stress pattern of ˊ ˋ. It is exemplified by *blúebìrd, hígh schòol, díning ròom.* A compound may be spelled as two words, as one, or as a hyphenated word. Both *sidewalk* and *drug store* are compounds, because of their stress pattern, regardless of the fact that one is written as a single word and the other as two.

EXERCISE 44

★ Place the compound noun stresses over the following words.

1. blackboard
2. hotbed
3. paleface
4. mailman

5. shortcake
6. roundhouse
7. paperback
8. rocking chair
9. spinning wheel
10. flying officer

Pattern 2. The modifier + noun pattern is signaled by the stress pattern of ˆ ´, as in *sîck núrse, pôor hóuse, wôrking mán.*

EXERCISE 45

★ Place the modifier + noun stresses over the following words.

1. hot house
2. dark room
3. black bird
4. tender foot
5. handy man
6. red skin
7. funny bone
8. dancing teacher
9. mowing machine
10. humming bird

EXERCISE 46

★ Here are twelve pairs of words and phrases distinguished by stress. The items in column 1 have modifier + noun stress; those in column 2 have compound noun stress. Write a brief statement of the meaning of each.

1a. hîgh cháir ________________	1b. hígh chàir ________________
2a. gâme físh ________________	2b. gáme fìsh ________________
3a. blûe bóok ________________	3b. blúebòok ________________
4a. grêen hóuse ________________	4b. gréenhòuse ________________
5a. dôuble ú ________________	5b. dóuble ù ________________
6a. râcing hórse ________________	6b. rácing hòrse ________________

7a. smôking róom	7b. smóking ròom
__________	__________
8a. trâveling mán	8b. tráveling màn
__________	__________
9a. dâncing gírl	9b. dáncing gìrl
__________	__________
10a. côoling lótion	10b. cóoling lòtion
__________	__________
11a. Frênch téacher	11b. Frénch tèacher
__________	__________
12a. lông hánd	12b. lónghànd*
__________	__________

Pattern 3. A qualifier + adjective or adverb often takes the stress pattern ^ ʹ. A qualifier is a word that can occupy the position of *very*. It qualifies, or modifies, an adjective or adverb. Common qualifiers are *very, quite, more, rather, somewhat, too.*

---

* The distinction between compound noun {ʹ ˋ} and modifier-plus-noun {^ ʹ} cannot be consistently maintained in English. Here are a few of the complications:
1. Compare *his pêrsonal ínterests* with *his párty ìnterests.* By our rules the first is a modifier-plus-noun and the second a compound noun. Now let's make a sentence out of them:

He has both *pêrsonal* and *párty* interests.

Here *personal* and *party* are coordinated by *and*, so that *party* must be a modifier and not part of a compound noun. You can repeat this coordination test with pairs like *mîlitary clóthes–búsiness clòthes.*
2. Apart from the stress patterns, there seems to be no structural difference between *Fírst Strèet* and *Fîrst Ávenue, páperbàck* and *pâper dóll, bóy frìend* and *bôy scíentist, tálking màchine* and *flŷing sáucer*, and similar pairs. Thus it does not appear sensible to call the first member of each pair a compound noun and the second a modifier-plus-noun.
3. English contains expressions like *grêat grándfather, sprîng féver, grând júry* which have modifier-plus-noun stress but whose meanings are certainly not the additive total of those of their components. Furthermore, when the first member is an adjective, we cannot add a second modifier after the first without destroying the meaning, e.g., *great old grandfather.* Hence these seem to be compound nouns with a secondary-primary stress pattern.

Despite such limitations, we shall maintain the distinction because it is so widely operative.

EXERCISE 47

★ Place qualifier + adjective or adverb stress marks over the following phrases. (Other stress patterns also occur here.)

1. very tired
2. rather old
3. quite happily
4. more sophisticated
5. too beautiful
6. pretty bad
7. mighty happy
8. awfully glad
9. really sorry
10. real sorry

Pattern 4. The verb + noun-object grammatical pattern has a stress pattern of ˆ ˊ, as in *They lôve bírds* and *They are bâking ápples.* This pattern occasionally contrasts with the compound noun stresses ˊ ˋ, as you will see in the next exercise.

EXERCISE 48

★ Restate the following sentences so as to explain the meaning of the word combinations that have stress marks.

1. They are râcing hórses. ______________________________

____

2. They are rácing hòrses. ______________________________

____

3. Rûnning gréyhounds is his favorite sport. ______________________________

____

4. He raises rúnning grèyhounds. ______________________________

____

5. They are côoking ápples. ______________________________

____

6. They are cóoking àpples. ______________________________

____

7. Smóking tùrkeys are more expensive than ordinary ones. ______________________________

____

8. Smôking túrkeys gives a good income. ______________________________

We have seen that the stress pattern ^ ´ is used for both a modifier plus a noun and for a verb plus a noun-object. This situation results in ambiguity when we do not know which of the two grammatical patterns is intended by the ^ ´. For example, in "Flŷing plánes can be dangerous," the first two words can mean either "planes which are flying" or "the act of piloting planes."

EXERCISE 49

★ State briefly the two meanings of the italicized phrases.

1. She abhors *scrâtching dógs.*

 ____

 ____

2. *Môving bóoks* always disturbed him.

 ____

 ____

3. We enjoy *entertâining vísitors.*

 ____

 ____

4. They are *encôuraging repórts.*

 ____

 ____

5. *Bûrning óil* frightened him.

 ____

 ____

EXERCISE 50

★ Place stress marks over the words to indicate the verb + noun-object and the compound-noun patterns.

1. *Jump ropes* are used by boxers.
2. They *jump ropes* for exercise.
3. He has to *wash rags* after cleaning his gun.
4. *Wash rags* are hard to get.
5. She likes to *map routes* for travel.

6. We never follow *map routes.*
7. The guards *flash lights* into the dark corners.
8. They all carry *flashlights.*
9. We *watch dogs* with great interest during the hunting season.
10. There are three *watchdogs* on their farm.

Pattern 5. The verb + adverbial grammatical pattern also has a ^ ʹ stress pattern, as in *You must lôok óut* and *The tent had been pûshed óver.* The compound noun derived from such verb + adverbial combinations has the usual ʹ ˋ pattern, as in *The lóokòut had a long vigil* and *This problem is no púshòver.*

EXERCISE 51

★ Place stress marks over the italicized words to indicate the verb-adverbial and the compound noun combinations.

1. George is always *cutting up.*
2. He is an inveterate *cutup.*
3. This information is not to be *handed out.*
4. These *handouts* will give you the necessary information.
5. The movie was *held over.*
6. This movie is a *holdover* from last week.
7. She doesn't want to *come down.*
8. What a *comedown* she had.
9. She gave Jack the *comeon,* and he *came on.*

Pattern 6. In pattern 1 we observed the compound-noun stress pattern of ʹ ˋ, as in *gréenhoùse.* This is heard extensively. There is also another compound noun stress pattern which reverses that of pattern 1. It is ˋ ʹ, as in *Rhòde Ísland.* This pattern is used in a smaller number of words, many of which are proper names. Some compound nouns take either of the two, as *shórt stòry* or *shòrt stóry.*

EXERCISE 52

★ Place the compound-noun stress you use, presumably ʹ ˋ or ˋ ʹ, on the following words.

1. St. Paul
2. Great Britain
3. roast beef
4. loudspeaker

5. old-timer
6. ice cream
7. parched corn
8. headmaster
9. fourth-grader
10. left wing

EXERCISE 53

★ Paraphrase these sentences to bring out clearly the meanings of the words in italics.

1. A *shòrt stóry* is not necessarily a *shôrt stóry.*

____

____

2. An *òld máid* is not necessarily an *ôld máid.*

____

____

3. *Clèar Láke* is not a *clêar láke.*

____

____

4. A *Nèw Yórker* is not a *nêw Yórker.*

____

____

5. *Lòng Práirie* [a town in Minnesota] is not a *lông práirie.*

____

____

D. Gradation

Let us approach gradation through examples. The vowel of the word *and* is pronounced /æ/ when it is uttered with any of the three upper degrees of stress, as in

Not Tom ór I but Tom ánd /ænd/ I.

But when *and* is spoken with weak stress, as is customary, its vowel is likely to change to schwa /ə/, as in

Tom ănd /ən/ I have been appointed.

Or consider *to.* With primary stress the vowel is /u/, as in

He came tó. /tu/

But under weak stress the vowel will probably become a barred *i*, that is, the high central vowel /ɨ/, as in

He came tŏnight. /tɨnait/

As a third example, let us take *way*. Here the vowel is /e/ when it has one of the stronger stresses, as in

She went awáy. /əwe/

Now if the stress is reduced to the weakest, the vowel tends to change to the high central vowel /ɨ/, as in

She is alwăys /ɔlwɨz/ late.

A final example will complete our case. Some words with a vowel plus /r/, like *for* and *are*, also have a change of vowel quality under weak stress. The vowel of *for* is /ɔ/ under strong stress, as in

What is it fór? /fɔr/

Under weak stress, however, the combination /ɔr/ may become the higher mid central r-colored vowel /ər/, sometimes spelled "fer" in dialect stories and comic strips. You will hear this frequently in expressions like

This is fŏr /fər/ you.

Now, with these examples in mind, we are ready to define gradation. Gradation is a change in vowel quality, when stress is reduced to weak stress, to one of the central vowels /ə/, /ɨ/, or /ər/. As spoken discourse contains many weakly stressed syllables, it is obvious that occurrences of these vowels are very frequent in daily speech. This frequency is disguised by the fact that there are many spellings for these vowels.

EXERCISE 54

★ Write the following items in phonemic notation as you say them in natural speech.

1. He's a jûst man. ____________
2. Jŭst a minute. ____________
3. áre ____________
4. They ăre gone. ____________
5. depóse ____________
6. depŏsition ____________

7. háve ______________________

8. He must hăve left. ______________________

9. ór ______________________

10. Will it be wind ŏr rain? ______________________

11. He cán but he won't. ______________________

12. He căn do it. ______________________

13. thé ______________________

14. Thĕ best one ______________________

15. Ăs you see ______________________

16. Just ăs good ______________________

17. lént ______________________

18. silĕnt ______________________

19. bé ______________________

20. bĕcause ______________________

V.

Pitch Levels and Terminals

A. Intonation Contours

Because vowels and many consonants are voiced, they possess the tonal quality of pitch, for pitch is a necessary concomitant of the vibration of the vocal cords. In English we made use of this pitch as a part of our signaling system. Although we employ many degrees of pitch in speaking, we use only four levels of relative pitch as phonemes, that is, to make distinctions in meaning. These four are as follows:

4. extra-high
3. high
2. normal
1. low

This is to say, the normal pitch of your speaking voice, whatever its actual height, is called level 2; and from this you make departures upward and downward. Take a simple sentence:

2 I'm going **3** hóme. **1**

You begin on level 2, your natural and normal level, and remain there until you reach the last primary stress. Here your voice rises one level and then drops to level 1. This 2 3 1 pattern is the pitch signal for statements.

The extra-high level, 4, is reserved as a substitute for level 3 when you wish to express special emphasis or excitement. It is rather sparingly used.

Pitches combine into patterns to make meaningful melodies — like the 2 3 1, meaning that a statement or proposition is being uttered. These melodies have three methods of closure, which are called terminal junctures, or merely terminals.

The first terminal, which occurs at the end of a sentence, is the fading terminal. It is characterized by a rapid fadeaway of the voice into silence and by a considerable prolongation of the preceding word with pitch level 3. It is symbolized by /↓/. This symbol should be used to indicate the closure of our last example sentence:

2 **3** **1**
I'm going hóme↓

To sense the prolongation of *home*, the pitch 3 word, compare it with the length of *home* in the next sentence:

2 **3** **1**
I'm going home Thúrsday↓

The second terminal is the rising terminal. It is a short, slight rise in pitch from the last level heard, but does not go all the way up to the next level. The preceding pitch 3 word is somewhat prolonged, but less so than for the fading terminal. It is symbolized by /↑/ and commonly occurs at the end of yes-or-no questions:

2 **3** **3**
Are you thére↑

Patterns of pitch, with their accompanying terminals, like the two above — 2 3 1 ↓ and 2 3 3 ↑ — are called intonation contours.

The third terminal is the sustained terminal. One recognizes this terminal by a slight lengthening of the preceding pitch 3 word, less than before the second terminal, and by a sustaining of the last-heard pitch. The following word, however, may be at a different pitch level. Its symbol is /→/, and it may be heard at the end of a long sentence-subject:

2 **3** **2** **2** **3** **1**
All the occupants of the cár → seemed dazed by the shóck.

To hear this terminal more sharply, compare what happens at *car* with what you hear in this sentence:

2 **3** **1**
The car is réady↓

Note that of the two preceding examples, the first has two intonation contours and the second only one.

Every sentence, as well as some grammatical word-group units within a sentence, has its own intonation contour. In symbolizing contours you should indicate the pitch levels at three places: the beginning of the grammatical unit, the beginning of the syllable bearing the primary stress, and the end of unit before the terminal. You also use a pitch number for any other changes of level. There will be a primary stress in each grammatical unit; in other words, there must be a primary stress somewhere between every two terminals. Primary stress usually accompanies pitch level 3.

We are now ready to examine some of the more commonly used intonation contours in American English, and the kinds of grammatical units they accompany. But first a word of caution. The contours described below are widely employed, but not to the total exclusion of variant ones. For instance, instead of the 2 3 1 pattern for "I'm going home," some speakers will use a 2 2 1 pattern. So, when you do the exercises, don't try to slavishly follow the contours described in the text; just put down exactly what you hear yourself say.

1. 2 3 1 ↓. This contour occurs in three kinds of sentences.

a. Statement or declarative sentence:

2 **3** **1**
We drove to the lake ↓

b. Command:

2 **3** **1**
Go to your room ↓

c. QW question:

This means a question that begins with a question word, like *who, what, which, when, where, why, how.*

2 **3** **1**
Who is your friend ↓

It is interesting to note that the ordinary statement contour can be used for this kind of question because the sentence already contains a sure signal that a question is coming: the question word at the beginning. Compare this kind of question with the next one.

2. 2 3 3 ↑. This contour is used in three common situations.

a. Yes-or-no question in statement form:

2 **3** **3**
He's gone ↑

Here a special contour is needed to signal a question, for without it the sentence would be a statement.

b. Yes-or-no question in question form:

2 **3** **3**
Are you there ↑

c. Initial grammatical unit (phrase or clause):

2 3 3
In short ↑

2 3 3
If you'll wait ↑

EXERCISE 55

★ For each sentence or grammatical unit, supply the marks of the intonation contour — the pitch levels and terminal junctures. If you wish, put in the primary stress first to help you.

1. He walked to the lab.
2. Get out of my sight!
3. Where is my necktie?
4. She won't be home till twelve?
5. Are you going to the game early?
6. To tell the truth, I haven't learned to dance.
7. Unless you take the car, I won't go.

3. 2 3 2 → or ↑. This contour signals incompleteness. In the first situation below, it is an alternate for 2 3 3 ↑.

a. Initial phrase or clause:

2 3 2
Under the circumstances → or ↑

2 3 2
When you leave → or ↑

b. Statement, to indicate that the speaker has more to say:
Often the word following this contour is *but*.

2 3 2
She's a nice girl → or ↑

4. 3 2 →. This is a call, such as you hear from neighborhood mothers:

3 2
Harry →

5. 3 3 ↑. On an individual question word, this contour signals a request for repetition of some part of the preceding message.

2 3 1 3 3
Jane has a new piano teacher ↓ Who ↑

6. 3 1 ↓. On an individual question word, this contour constitutes a request for further information.

2 3 1 3 1
Jane has a new piano teacher ↓ Who ↓

EXERCISE 56

★ For each sentence or grammatical unit, supply the marks of the intonation contour — the pitch levels and terminal junctures.

1. When do we eat?
2. If you'll wait,
3. For the most part,
4. He's very handsome, (but)
5. George, (come home at once).
6. We're going to eat in Chicago. Where? (= In what city did you say?)
7. We're going to eat in Chicago. Where? (= In which restaurant?)

7. 2 3 ↑. This contour is used on a stressed word, phrase, or clause in a series, with the exception of the last item. Note that in each example there are three contours because there are three primary stresses.

2 2 3 2 3 2 3 1
She prefers óranges ↑ ápples ↑ and chérries ↓

2 2 3 2 2 3 2 3 1
She looked under the béd ↑ in the dráwers ↑ and in the clóset ↓

8. REPETITION OF PREVIOUS PITCH. This is used for a quoter clause of the "he said" kind in medial or final position.

2 3 3 3 3 3
Are you going ↑ he asked ↑

2 3 1 1 1 1
I'm through ↓ he said ↓

9. 1 2 ↑ OR 3 3 ↑. The name of the person whom you are addressing is accompanied by various contours, of which these are quite common.

2 3 1 1 2
Why are you washing → Jane ↑

2 3 1 1 2
What did you put on the table → Mellon ↑

2 3 3 3 3
Are you coming ↑ George ↑

10. 2 3 3 ↑ 2 3 1 ↓. In this and the following section, two contours combine to make a distinction in meaning. This one signals a choice of two possibilities:

2 3 3 2 3 1
Do you want tea ↑ or coffee ↓

This means, "Which of the two do you want, tea or coffee?"

11. 2 3 3 ↑ 2 3 3 ↑. This contour proposes a yes-or-no question.

2 3 3 2 3 3
Do you want tea ↑ or coffee ↑

The meaning is "Do you want tea or coffee in preference to something else?"

EXERCISE 57

★ For each sentence or grammatical unit, supply pitches and terminals.

1. Will you have hot chocolate or milk? (one or the other)
2. Will you have hot chocolate or milk? (or something different)
3. I'm taking physics, chemistry, German, and American history.
4. "When are you driving home?" she asked.
5. Give me a lift, Bill.

B. Variations for Emphasis

The contours described above are modified when we single out certain words for emphasis. One way to get special emphasis is to give primary stress and a higher pitch level to the word we wish to emphasize.

2 3 1
Normal: He wants to eat all the tíme ↓

2 3 2 2 3 1
Emphatic: He wants to éat → all the tíme ↓

Sometimes such a primary stress on the emphasized word abrogates the primary stress that would normally come later in the sentence.

2 3 1
Normal: He fell into the pónd ↓

2 3 1
Emphatic: He féll into the pond ↓

In sentences like the foregoing the pitch slopes gradually down from level 3 to level 1. If the emphasized word has more than one syllable, it is the syllable with the highest word-stress that is given the primary stress and the higher pitch level.

2 3 1
Normal: Fifi does not enjoy intellectual gámes ↓

2 3 1
Emphatic: Fifi does not enjoy intelléctual games ↓

Another mode of emphasis is found in yes-or-no questions. The word to be emphasized takes a primary stress and higher pitch level, just as in the previous examples, but the pitch remains at this higher level for the duration of the question. The next illustrative sentences show the contours used when the emphasis is placed on different words.

	2 3 3
Normal:	Are you walking to the párty this evening ↑
	2 3 3
Emphatic:	Are yóu walking to the party this evening ↑
	2 3 3
Emphatic:	Are you wálking to the party this evening ↑
	2 4 4
Emphatic:	Are you walking to the párty this evening ↑
	2 3 3
Emphatic:	Are you walking to the party this évening ↑

EXERCISE 58

★ You are given below four groups of sentences. For the first sentence in each group indicate the normal intonation contour and primary stress. For the others indicate the contours and primary stresses that take into account the emphasized (italicized) word.

1a. My sister wallowed in the mud.
 b. My sister *wallowed* in the mud.
2a. Is the library in your college quite large?
 b. Is the *library* in your college quite large?
 c. Is the library in *your* college quite large?
 d. Is the library in your college *quite* large?

C. Review Exercises on Stress, Pitch Levels, and Terminals

EXERCISE 59

★ In these pairs of sentences the segmental phonemes are identical, but the intonation contours and the positions of the primary stresses are different. Explain briefly the difference of meaning in each pair.

2 3 1
1a. He met Sarah Smith going to the líbrary ↓

____

2 3 1 2 3 1
1b. He met Sarah Smíth ↓ going to the líbrary ↓

____

2 3 1
2a. I called Bill an ámateur↓

____

2 3 1 2 3 1
b. I called Bíll↓ an ámateur↓

____

2 3 1
3a. Why are you scratching Béss↓

____

2 3 1 1 2
b. Why are you scrátching↓ Béss↑

____

2 3 1
4a. You'd better dó it↓

____

2 3 1
b. You'd bétter do it↓

____

2 3 1 1 2
5a. What are we having for súpper → Hám↑

____

2 3 1 2 3
b. What are we having for súpper↓ Hám↑

____

EXERCISE 60

★ On each expression place the stress marks that will result in the meaning stated.

1a. fair crowd	a. a medium-sized crowd
b. fair crowd	b. a crowd at the fair
2a. girl hunter	a. a girl who is a hunter
b. girl hunter	b. a hunter of girls
3a. a record sale	a. a sale of records
b. a record sale	b. a sale that breaks the record
4a. a secondary road program	a. a program for secondary roads
b. a secondary road program	b. a road program that is secondary
5a. They're wading pools	a. They are pools for wading
b. They're wading pools	b. They are wading through pools

EXERCISE 61

★ Supply sustained junctures /→/ where needed to make, or help make, the differentiation in meaning. Some of the stresses are supplied. Remember that sustained juncture is a matter of the lengthening of the preceding pitch-3 word.

1a. Every dáy passengers enjoy a meal like thís.
= Passengers enjoy the meal every day.

b. Everyday pássengers enjoy a meal like thís.
= Ordinary passengers enjoy a meal like this.

2a. The blue dréss particularly ínterested her.
= interested her particularly

b. The blue dress partícularly ínterested her.
= particularly the blue dress

3a. French pláne with twenty-four cráshes
= The plane has had twenty-four crashes.

b. French plane with twenty-fóur cráshes
= Plane crashes with twenty-four aboard.

4a. I consider thése érrors.
= I consider these things to be errors.

b. I consider these érrors.
= I think about these errors.

5a. The sóns raise méat.

b. The sun's ráys méet.

EXERCISE 62

★ Indicate the primary stress, pitch, and juncture in the area of the italicized words. Use your own natural pronunciation as your guide.

1. He was looking for a *lake that* always offered good fishing.
2. Every Saturday Sam drove to Clear *Lake, which* was about thirty miles away.
3. The *freshmen who* make a B average will be given a picnic by the national honorary society.
4. The incoming *freshmen, who* will arrive during the weekend, will take their examinations on Monday and Tuesday.
5. He chose the *canoe that* seemed the most durable.
6. May I present Michael *Smith, who* is from Seattle?
7. There will be a meeting of *students who* are from California.
8. The neighbors did not approve of the *shrubs which* we had planted.
9. The hedge was composed of French *lilacs, which* flowered in May.
10. Dr. *Bloom,* who specializes in bone surgery, built a new clinic.

EXERCISE 63

★ Indicate the primary stress, pitch, and juncture in the area of the italicized words. Use your own natural pronunciation as a guide.

1. That young man is Harry *Boulder, a promising junior.*
2. *Hoskins, a first-string quarterback,* was on the bench with an injured ankle.
3. *Typhoon, a well-known novel,* is famous for its descriptive writing.
4. She was reading the *novel Typhoon.*
5. For Christmas she gave him a silk *necktie, a hand-painted beauty.*
6. My *sister Karen* is trying out for a national merit scholarship.
7. We all hoped that *Karen, my younger sister,* would win a scholarship.
8. He lives in Elk *Valley, a county seat.*
9. Her favorite opera was *Carmen, a work by Bizet.*
10. The *opera Carmen* was her favorite.

EXERCISE 64

★ State the meaning of each expression.

2 **3** **1**
1a. Còmic strîp àrtist díes ↓

____

2 **3** **1**
b. Cômic strìp àrtist díes ↓

____

2 **3** **1**
2a. He àccidêntally drôwns a wânted mán ↓

____

2 **3** **1** **2** **3**
b. He àccidêntally drówns ↓ a wânted mán ↓

____

3a. Automâtic brídge tòll collèctors

____

b. Automâtic brîdge tóll collèctors

____

4a. A shôrt stóry èditor

____

b. A shórt stòry èditor

____

2 3 1
5a. Ôh bóy ↓

---

2 3 3
b. Ôh bóy ↑

6a. Gêorge's bódy wòrks

---

2 3 1
b. Gêorge's bôdy wórks ↓

---

2 3 1
7a. I am an oútdòor lòver ↓

---

2 3 1
b. I am an ôutdôor lóver ↓

8a. a gôod réading còurse

---

b. a gòod réading coùrse

---

2 3 1
9a. Hè gâve the líbrary bòoks ↓

---

2 3 1
b. Hè gâve the lîbrary bóoks ↓

10a. (About a women's organization in the Essex village of Ugley)
the Ûgley Wómen's Ìnstitute

---

b. the Ûgley wômen's ínstitute

VI.

Internal Open Juncture

In the preceding chapter we studied the three terminal junctures and noted that they occur at the end of grammatical units or sentences. The fourth juncture of English differs from the others in that it occurs within grammatical units or sentences. It is found between words and between parts of words, and is called internal open juncture. Like the other three it is phonemic, as this minimal pair will show:

keep sticking
keeps ticking

Internal open juncture is indicated by a plus sign /+/ and is sometimes called plus juncture. Here it is with a complete phonemic notation of the pair above:

```
2      3    1
kîp + stíkɪŋ ↓
2       3   1
kîps + tíkɪŋ ↓
```

By means of internal open juncture we are able to make distinctions between homophonous pairs like these: *an ice man, a nice man; its praise, it sprays; Grade A, gray day; see Mabel, seem able.* But although most native speakers have little difficulty in perceiving internal juncture, they have trouble in explaining just what gives them a sense of break or separation at the junctural point. It is only through the combined efforts of sharp-eared linguists and spectographic analysts that we have been able to learn the conditions under which internal juncture occurs. In general, it is the nature of the sounds surrounding the juncture that serves to locate it. The details are numerous and complex and vary with the kinds and positions of the sounds involved. All we can do here is to examine a few examples of the sound characteristics that define junctures. You will find it good ear training to try to detect for yourself the differences in sounds between the members of each pair before you read the explanation that follows each.

1a. kêep stícking

b. kêeps tícking

There are three differences here between *a* and *b* in the sounds around the junctures. First, the /p/ of *keep* is longer than the /p/ of *keeps;* that is to say, the lips remain closed for a longer time. Second, the /s/ of *sticking* is longer than the /s/ of *keeps.* Initial (postjunctural) consonants are usually longer than those in other positions. Third, the /t/ of *ticking* has more aspiration than that of *sticking.* This means merely that there is more air following the explosion. See for yourself. Hold the back of your hand an inch from your mouth, say *stick* and *tick*, and notice which /t/ is followed by the stronger blast of air. The same difference is true of all three voiceless stops /p t k/. In initial position they have heavy aspiration, but after an /s/ (with no juncture intervening), only slight aspiration. Such are the differences in sound that cue the listener to differentiate between *keep sticking* and *keeps ticking.*

2a. a + níce màn (with emphatic stress)

b. an + íce màn

In 2*a* the /n/ of *nice* is about twice as long as the /n/ of *an.* This is the clue that it belongs in initial position with *nice.*

3a. it + swings

b. its + wings

Here we find two sound differences that determine internal juncture. The first you already know — the initial /s/ of *swings* is longer than the final /s/ of *its.* The second is a kind of assimilation. In *wings* the /w/ is voiced, as it normally is in initial position, but in *swings* the /w/ is wholly or partly devoiced because of the preceding voiceless /s/. This kind of devoicing is common; a voiceless consonant tends to make voiceless a following /w/, /l/, /r/, /m/, /n/. A few examples of this devoicing are *twist, flee, cream, smoke, snow.*

4a. why + choose

b. white + shoes

In this pair the /ai/ is longer in *why* than it is in *white.* In general, final (prejunctural) vowels and diphthongs are longer than those in other positions. The /š/ of *shoes*, being initial, is longer than the /š/ that is the second component of /č/ in *choose*. (Remember that /č/ consists of /t/ plus /š/ uttered as a single speech sound.)

The foregoing examples illustrate a few of our speech habits that enable us to distinguish internal open junctures between words. Now let us recapitulate those that you will find helpful in doing exercise 65.

1. Initial (postjunctural) consonants are longer than those in other positions. For example, the /m/ in *may* is longer than the /m/ in *seam*.

2. Initial voiceless stops /p t k/ are strongly aspirated. Examples are *pot, tot, cot*. If, however, these are preceded by /s/, the aspiration is greatly reduced. Compare the aspiration of these pairs: *pan, span; top, stop; kill, skill*. But when there is a juncture between the /s/ and the /p/, /t/, or /k/, there is no reduction of aspiration. For example, you can feel on your hand the aspiration after the /p/ in *this + pot* but not in *this + spot*.

3. In initial position these consonants are voiced: /w l r m n/, as in *way, led, ray, might*, and *nag*. But after a voiceless consonant they tend to become devoiced, as in *sway, fled, pray, smite*, and *snag*.

4. Final (prejunctural) vowels and diphthongs are longer than those in other positions. For example, the /u/ is longer in *new* /nu/ than in *nude* /nud/, and the /ɔ/ is longer in *I saw + Ted* than in *I sought + Ed*.

5. Final (prejunctural) consonants are longer than internal consonants. The /p/ in *keep* is longer than that in *keeps*.

EXERCISE 65

★ Write the following expressions in phonemic notation with segmental phonemes and internal junctures. After each pair, explain what characteristics of the surrounding sounds identify the position of the internal junctures. All the information you need for these cases has been included in the foregoing discussion.

1a. I scream ____________________

b. ice cream ____________________

____

____

2a. night-rate ____________________

b. nitrate ____________________

____

____

3a. that stuff ____________________

b. that's tough ____________________

4a. seem able ____________________

b. see Mabel ____________________

5a. its lid ____________________

b. it slid ____________________

6a. new deal ____________________

b. nude eel ____________________

7a. it sprays ____________________

b. its praise ____________________

EXERCISE 66

★ Can you distinguish by ear between *a name* and *an aim?* Many persons find this difficult because there may be no internal juncture between a weakly stressed and a strongly stressed syllable. In the history of English such a difficulty has led to some changes in spelling, as this exercise will reveal.

Look up the etymology of each of the following words in your desk dictionary, write down its ME (Middle English) original, and show how each received a new spelling through incorrect division.

Present Form	*ME Form*	*Process*
newt	an ewte	became "a newt"
1. adder	________	____________
2. apron	________	____________

3. auger ________ _____________

4. nickname ________ _____________

5. umpire ________ _____________

An accurate and exceptionless statement about the distribution of internal junctures cannot be made, because the habits of speakers vary too much. It can be said that in running discourse many words are separated from one another by /+/. But also, there are cases where words run together in close transition without the /+/, like the unstressed *tŏ thĕ* in *tŏ thĕ ăbóve*. Contrariwise, internal juncture may occur within words, as in *sly* + *ness* compared with *minus*. We can at best just offer a few principles that will help guide your ear to the presence of internal junctures, with the warning that they are not inviolable.

1. If two vowels in successive syllables carry primary or secondary stresses, there will be a /+/ somewhere between them.

lîkes + méat   blûe + dréss

But if two such vowels carry primary and third stresses, there may or may not be a /+/ between them.

bóathoùse   bóot + blàck

2. Two adjoining vowels are usually separated by /+/.

ăn ópĕră + ŏf   thĕ + ĭdéă + ămúses

3. A vowel with weak stress followed by a consonant is often in close transition with the consonant, and there is no /+/.

ăbóve   ă bág   thĕ bést

4. A consonant followed by a vowel with weak stress is in close transition, with no intervening /+/.

móst ŏf   fóund ĭn

5. Between successive syllables with weak stress there is no /+/.

ŏf thĕ wátĕr
awfŭl ĭn ĭts ìmplĭcátĭons

EXERCISE 67

★ Put in internal junctures where they belong, following the five principles given above. Then read these expressions aloud, following the markings, and try to hear the difference between internal juncture and close transition.

1. fîne jób
2. môst of the tíme

3. a sôlo of Jím's
4. the párty
5. thât párty
6. tâlk wísely
7. sòme of the inspîred ártists
8. Jâne lôves cándy
9. stône fénce
10. bîrd in the búsh
11. óutlòok
12. Lòng Îsland

Internal open juncture is the last phoneme in our enumeration of the suprasegmentals. Now we shall revert to the segmental phonemes and see how they pattern in English words.

VII.

The Distribution of Phonemes

The English language, we have seen, has thirty-seven segmental phonemes. These phonemes are peculiar to English in that no other language has exactly the same inventory. The *th* phonemes that seem so natural to us, /θ/ and /ð/, are not found in most European languages; and the high front rounded vowel /y/ of French, German, and Chinese does not exist in English. (This symbol /y/ does not represent the initial sound of *yes*, as it does in this book.)

When phonemes are joined together in syllables and words, it becomes apparent that there are limitations to the positions they may occupy and to the ways in which they may be arranged in sequences. For example, an English word never begins with /ŋ/ or ends with /h/. An English word may begin with /st/ but not with /ts/. Spanish words, on the other hand, do not begin with /st/ and German words do begin with /ts/. Thus languages vary not only in their stock of phonemes, but also in the ways they permit these phonemes to associate together. The totality of the positions in which any language element may occur is called its distribution, and it will now be our task to examine in part the distribution of English phonemes. We shall begin with the consonants.

First, however, we must be clear about the meaning of two terms that will be used frequently in this chapter — "initial position" and "final position." "Initial position" means a position that follows a juncture and precedes a vowel; it is also called "postjunctural position." Thus a group of consonants in initial position, like /str/, will occur not only at the beginning of words but also within a word following an internal juncture, as in *restress* /ri + strɛs/. Compare this with *restrain*, in which /str/ is not "initial" or "postjunctural" because it does not follow an internal juncture. The second term, "final position," means a position that follows a vowel and precedes a juncture, and is also known as "prejunctural position." It ordinarily means the position at the end of words.

English consonant phonemes occur singly or in groups, and in the word they occupy three positions — initial, medial, and final. This descriptive statement is not as trite as it appears, for it is not necessarily true of other languages. In Japanese, for instance, consonants occur only singly, not in groups, and in Mandarin Chinese, consonants do not appear in final position, except for nasals. Our immediate concern now will be with consonants in groups in the initial positions. A group of two or more consonants which adjoin each other is called a consonant cluster; and a cluster after a juncture, an initial consonant cluster.

A preliminary exercise with nonsense words will perhaps reveal that you, as a native speaker, are already aware of which initial consonant clusters are permitted and which are not permitted in English, even though you have given the matter no thought.

EXERCISE 68

★ Write E after each nonsense word that sounds English to you, and NE after each one that sounds non-English.

1. /ŋwa/ _____	6. /frun/ _____
2. /spro/ _____	7. /kpadi/ _____
3. /pfunt/ _____	8. /twab/ _____
4. /glɪŋ/ _____	9. /psalmist/ _____
5. /šči/ _____	10. /plon/ _____

It is the odd-numbered words above that contain the non-English initial consonant clusters. They are real words taken from these languages: 1. ancient Chinese, 3. German, 5. Russian, 7. Loma (Liberian), and 9. French.

In English initial consonant clusters, the maximum number of phonemes is three. These clusters of three have the following positional characteristics:

1. Only /s/ can occupy first position.
2. Only the voiceless stops /p t k/ appear in second position.
3. Only /l r y w/ appear in third position.

But all possible combinations do not occur, and we actually have only the nine of the following exercise.

EXERCISE 69

★ Give in conventional writing one word beginning with each of the following three-consonant clusters. Note carefully here and in the following exercises that /y/ at the end of a cluster is always followed by /u/. In words like *student, duty, tune, suite, chew, juice, lute* the pronunciation may vary between /u/ and /yu/.

1. /spl-/ ______________
2. /spr-/ ______________
3. /spy-/ ______________
4. /str-/ ______________
5. /sty-/ ______________
6. /skl-/ ______________ (In learned words only)
7. /skr-/ ______________
8. /sky-/ ______________
9. /skw-/ ______________

From the three-consonant initial clusters, we derive four classes of two-consonant clusters. Each class has one consonant position vacant, and the two remaining consonants retain the same order as that of the three-consonant cluster. All clusters in these derived classes are listed in the next exercise.

EXERCISE 70

★ Give in conventional writing one word beginning with each of the following two-consonant clusters. (Numbers refer to the three positions listed above exercise 69.)

a. Derived 1–2 class

1. /sp-/ ______________
2. /st-/ ______________
3. /sk-/ ______________

b. Derived 2–3 class

1. /pl-/ ______________
2. /pr-/ ______________

3. /py-/ ______________
4. /tr-/ ______________
5. /kl-/ ______________
6. /kr-/ ______________
7. /ky-/ ______________
8. /kw-/ ______________
9. /tw-/ ______________

c. Derived 1–3 class

1. /sl-/ ______________
2. /sw-/ ______________
3. /sy-/ ______________

d. Derived 3–3 class

1. /ly-/ ______________

In addition to the three-consonant and the two-consonant derived clusters in initial position, there is also a sizable group of nonderived two-consonant clusters. Each of these contains only one consonant found in the three-consonant clusters. Therefore it is not a derived but a nonderived cluster.

EXERCISE 71

★ Give in conventional writing one word to exemplify each of the following nonderived two-consonant initial clusters.

1. /sn-/ ______________
2. /sm-/ ______________
3. /bl-/ ______________
4. /br-/ ______________
5. /by-/ ______________
6. /dr-/ ______________
7. /dy-/ ______________
8. /dw-/ ______________
9. /gl-/ ______________
10. /gr-/ ______________
11. /gy-/ ______________
12. /sf-/ ______________
13. /my-/ ______________
14. /ny-/ ______________

15. /fl-/ ______________ 21. /šr-/ ______________

16. /fr-/ ______________ 22. /vy-/ ______________

17. /fy-/ ______________ 23. /hw-/ ______________

18. /θr-/ ______________ 24. /hy-/ ______________

19. /θy-/ ______________ 25. /čy-/ ______________

20. /θw-/ ______________ 26. /ǰy-/ ______________

The two-consonant clusters you have just seen in exercises 70 and 71 are the ones that are thoroughly English. Besides these there are some which exist in a sort of twilight zone. They belong to foreign words which have come into English retaining something of their foreign pronunciation, like *moire* and *pueblo*, and especially to foreign personal and place names, like *Buena Vista*, *Schmidt*, and *Vladivostok*. It is difficult to say whether or not such consonant clusters belong in the inventory of initial English consonant clusters. If you'd like to try your hand at them, do the next exercise.

EXERCISE 72

★ Give in conventional writing one word exemplifying each of the following two-consonant clusters. For some you may have to resort to names of persons or places. An unabridged dictionary will help you with the more resistant ones.

1. /pw-/ ______________ 11. /šm-/ ______________

2. /bw-/ ______________ 12. /šn-/ ______________

3. /gw-/ ______________ 13. /šw-/ ______________

4. /mw-/ ______________ 14. /ts-/ ______________

5. /nw-/ ______________ 15. /vl-/ ______________

6. /sv-/ ______________ 16. /vr-/ ______________

7. /šp-/ ______________ 17. /vw-/ ______________

8. /št-/ ______________ 18. /zl-/ ______________

9. /šk-/ ______________ 19. /zw-/ ______________

10. /šl-/ ______________ 20. /žw-/ ______________

EXERCISE 73

★ When we turn to the single-consonant phonemes that may occupy initial position, we find that all but two may begin a word. Go through the chart of English consonant phonemes, diagram 13 (page 25), find these two, and list them:

1. ______ 2. ______

So much for initial consonants and consonant clusters. The clusters that remain, those in medial and final positions, are numerous. We shall deal with them scantly, however, since our look at initial clusters will be sufficient to illustrate this area of language patterning known as phonotactics.

In final position, that is, after a vowel and before a juncture, the maximum number of consonants that can cluster together is five, though it is doubtful whether clusters of five are ever sounded in normal speech.

EXERCISE 74

★ In the first column write in phonemic notation your pronunciation of the final consonant or consonant clusters in each of the following words. In the second column write down the number of consonants in the final clusters.

1. pass	______	______	9. strength	______	______
2. ask	______	______	10. text	______	______
3. asked	______	______	11. first	______	______
4. health	______	______	12. sixth	______	______
5. eighth	______	______	13. twelfth	______	______
6. attempt	______	______	14. texts	______	______
7. chintz	______	______	15. sixths	______	______
8. mince	______	______	16. twelfths	______	______

The answer-key to this exercise will give the greatest number of consonants that might possibly be heard in deliberate speech. But you will probably, like many speakers, assimilate and take shortcuts through the prickly maze of consonant sounds. For instance, in number 3 one can easily say /æskt/, but more often the /k/ is assimilated to the /t/, giving /æst/. And in *sixths*, instead of the full /sɪkstθs/, one is likely to produce a shortened form, like /sɪks:/. The [:] here is a diacritic standing for greater length.

Vowels do not cluster. When two or more of them occur successively, one of two things happens: (1) one glides effortlessly into the other, as in /trai/ and /kɔi/; or (2) they are separated by juncture, as in *naïve* /na+iv/. So, in the distribution of English vowels, one has only position to consider. Here we shall just look quickly at the initial and final positions by means of a few exercises.

EXERCISE 75

★ To see if every English vowel can be used at the beginning of a word, write in phonemic notation one word beginning with each of the thirteen vowels.

1. /i/ __________
2. /ɪ/ __________
3. /e/ __________
4. /ɛ/ __________
5. /æ/ __________
6. /ɨ/ __________
7. /ər/ __________
8. /ə/ __________
9. /a/ __________
10. /u/ __________
11. /ʊ/ __________
12. /o/ __________
13. /ɔ/ __________

EXERCISE 76

★ The vowels /u/ and /ʊ/ have a low frequency in initial position. List in phonemic notation all the words you can think of in ten minutes that begin with /u/ and /ʊ/.

/u/	/ʊ/
__________	__________
__________	__________
__________	__________
__________	__________
__________	__________

Now we shall see which vowels occur in word-final position.

EXERCISE 77

★ Write in phonemic notation one word ending with each of these vowels.

1. /i/ ____________________ 5. /a/ ____________________

2. /e/ ____________________ 6. /u/ ____________________

3. /ər/ ____________________ 7. /o/ ____________________

4. /ə/ ____________________ 8. /ɔ/ ____________________

The five remaining vowel phonemes — /ɪ/, /ɛ/, /æ/, /ɨ/, and /ʊ/ — never or seldom occur in final position.

The phonotactic patterns of a language have a compulsive effect upon its speakers in that these speakers find it hard to break the patterns of their native tongue and habituate themselves to the use of new ones. If, for example, you try to teach a Spaniard to pronounce *student,* he is likely to persist in saying /ɛstudɛnt/ for some time because /st-/ is not an initial consonant cluster in Spanish, whereas /ɛst-/ is common. Likewise an American in India has great difficulty in pronouncing the native term for washerman, *dhobi* /dʰobi/, because /dʰ-/ does not occur initially in English. Instead, he will say /dobi/. Yet this same American can say *Toby* /tʰobi/ with perfect ease because initial /tʰ-/ is a normal word beginning in English.

The general tendency is for a speaker to pronounce words borrowed from another tongue with the phonotactic patterns of his own language, even when he can utter the foreign clusters. For instance, it is easy for us to say /šn-/ at the beginning of a word, as in the German *Schnorchel,* but we normally change the word to /snɔrkəl/ to conform to our own English initial cluster /sn-/.

OPTIONAL EXERCISE

★ Here are a few words beginning with consonant clusters that are not native to English. Assume that you hear each one and wish to pronounce it. Write in phonemic symbols your probable pronunciation.

1. German *Pfund* /pfʊnt/, pound ____________________

2. German *Zeit* /tsait/, time ____________________

3. French *Psyché* /psiše/, Psyche ____________________

4. Mazahua (Mexican) /ndišu/, woman ____________________

5. African *Mboya* /mbɔya/, = a proper name ____________________

part two

THE MORPHOLOGY OF ENGLISH

VIII.

Morphemes

We now turn our attention to the study of the internal structure of words, known as morphology. The term *word* we shall use loosely in its familiar sense, since a strict definition will not be necessary till later.

A. Definition of Morpheme

Before we can examine the structure of words, we must become acquainted with an entity known as the morpheme. A morpheme is a short segment of language that meets three criteria:

1. It is a word, or a part of a word that has meaning.
2. It cannot be divided into smaller meaningful parts without violation of its meaning or without meaningless remainders.
3. It recurs in differing verbal environments with a relatively stable meaning.

Let us examine the word *straight* /stret/ in the light of these criteria. First of all, we recognize it as a word and can find it listed as such in any dictionary. Second, it cannot be divided without violation of meaning. For example, we can, by dividing straight /stret/, get the smaller meaningful forms of *trait* /tret/, *rate* /ret/, and *ate* /et/, but the meanings of these violate the meaning of *straight.* Furthermore, when we divide it in these ways we get the meaningless remainders of /s-/, /st-/, and /str-/. Third, *straight* recurs with a relatively stable meaning in such environments as *straightedge, straighten,* and *a straight line.* Thus *straight* meets all the criteria of a morpheme.

As a second example, let us compare the morpheme *bright* (= light) with the word *brighten* (= make light). In sound the only difference between the two words is the added /ɪn/ of *brighten;* and in meaning the difference is the added sense of "make" in *brighten.* This leads us to conclude that /ɪn/ means "make." Thus we see that /ɪn/ is a part of a word that has meaning. We also know that it cannot be divided into smaller meaningful units and that it recurs with a stable meaning in words like *cheapen, darken, deepen, soften,* and *stiffen.* It is therefore obvious that /ɪn/ must be considered a morpheme.

EXERCISE 78

★ After each word write a number showing how many morphemes it contains.

1. play ___	11. keeper ___
2. replay ___	12. able ___
3. date ___	13. unable ___
4. antedate ___	14. mahogany ___
5. hygiene ___	15. rain ___
6. weak ___	16. rainy ___
7. weaken ___	17. cheap ___
8. man ___	18. cheaply ___
9. manly ___	19. cheaper ___
10. keep ___	20. capsize ___

EXERCISE 79

★ Write the meaning of the italicized morphemes.

1. *ante*date ____________________
2. *re*play ____________________

3. man*ly* ______________________________
4. keep*er* ______________________________
5. *un*able ______________________________
6. rain*y* ______________________________
7. cheap*est* ______________________________
8. *in*active ______________________________
9. *im*possible ______________________________
10. *mal*function (noun) ______________________________

B. Free and Bound Morphemes

Morphemes are of two kinds, free and bound. A free morpheme is one that can be uttered alone with meaning. For instance, in reply to "What are you going to do now?" you might answer "Eat." This is a free morpheme. A bound morpheme, unlike the free, cannot be uttered alone with meaning. It is always annexed to one or more morphemes to form a word. The italicized morphemes in exercise 79 above are all bound, for one would not utter in isolation forms like *ante-*, *re-*, *-ly*, *-er*, and *un-*. Here are a few more examples: *pre*view, play*ed*, activ*ity*, super*vise*, *con-*, *-vene*.

EXERCISE 80

★ Underline the bound morphemes. It is possible for a word to consist entirely of bound morphemes.

1. speaker
2. kingdom
3. phonemic
4. idolize
5. selective
6. delivery
7. intervene
8. revise
9. dreamed
10. undone

C. Bases

Another classification of morphemes puts them into two classes: bases and affixes. A base is that morpheme in a word that has the principal meaning.* The italicized morphemes in these words are bases: *deni*al, *lov*able, *annoy*ance, re-*enter*. Bases are very numerous, and most of them in English are free morphemes; but some are bound, like *-sent* in *consent, dissent,* and *assent.* A word may contain one base and several affixes. *Readability,* for example, contains the free base *read* and the two affixes *-abil-* and *-ity;* and *unmistakable* has the free base *take* and the affixes *un-*, *mis-*, and *-able.*

EXERCISE 81

★ Underline the bases in these words.

1. womanly
2. endear
3. failure
4. famous
5. infamous
6. lighten
7. enlighten
8. friendship
9. befriend
10. Bostonian
11. unlikely
12. prewar
13. subway
14. falsify
15. unenlivened

D. Bound Bases

All the bases in the preceding exercise are free bases. Now we shall look at bound bases, to which it is sometimes hard to attach a precise meaning. A good number of bound bases in English come from the Latin and Greek, like the *-sent-* in *sentiment, sentient, consent, assent, dissent, resent.* The standard way to pin down the meaning is to search for the meaning common to all the words which contain the base. A base may have more than one form. In the above list it has these forms: /sɛntɪ-/, /sɛnš-/, /-sɛnt/, and /-zɛnt/. Here is an exercise in this method.

EXERCISE 82

★ Write in the blanks the meaning of the italicized bound bases. To be exact, we should write these words below in phonemic script to show the

* This *ad hoc* definition will do for our present purpose. A more exact definition, which requires terms that you will not meet until later, would go something like this: A base is a linguistic form which meets one or more of these requirements:

1. It can occur as an immediate constituent of a word whose only other immediate constituent is a prefix or suffix.

   Examples: re*act*, *act*ive, re*ceive*.

2. It is an allomorph of a morpheme which has another allomorph that is a free form.

   Examples: *dep*th (*deep*), *wolv*es (*wolf*)

3. It is a borrowing from another language in which it is a free form or a base.

   Examples: *bio*metrics, *micro*cosm, phraseo*logy*

The third point is open to the theoretical objection that it imports diachronic lore to clarify a synchronic description.

various forms of the base, but this would involve a complication that will be explained later. So here we must be content to indicate the base in a loose way with spelling.

1. *audi*ence, *aud*ible, *audit*ion, *audit*ory ____________
2. sui*cide,* patri*cide,* matri*cide,* infanti*cide* ____________
3. *or*al, *or*ation, *or*acle, *orat*ory ____________
4. *aqua*plane, *aqua*tic, *aqua*rium, *aqua*duct ____________
5. *mort*uary, *mort*al, *mori*bund, im*mort*al ____________
6. *corps, corpse, corpor*ation, *corpor*eal ____________
7. *ten*able, *ten*ant, *ten*ure, *tenac*ious ____________
8. *pend*ulum, *pend*ant, sus*pend*ers, im*pend*ing ____________
9. *manu*al, *mani*cure, *manu*script, *man*acle ____________
10. e*ject*, in*ject*, pro*ject*ile, re*ject* ____________

This method can be difficult and baffling. An easier way that often works is to look up in your dictionary the word in question, like *consent,* and in the etymology find out the Latin meaning of the base. Under *consent* you will find that *sent* means "feel" in Latin, and this area of meaning seems to have been retained for the base of all the words in the *-sent* list.

EXERCISE 83

★ Look up in your desk dictionary the meaning of the bound bases italiziced in the words below. Write these meanings in the first column. In the second column write another English word that contains the same bound base.

1. re*vise* ____________ ____________
2. contra*dict* ____________ ____________
3. re*gress* ____________ ____________
4. inter*vene* ____________ ____________
5. com*prehend* ____________ ____________
6. re*cur* ____________ ____________
7. in*spect* ____________ ____________

8. op*pose* ____________ ____________

9. in*spire* ____________ ____________

10. *rod*ent ____________ ____________

11. *port*able ____________ ____________

12. *rupt*ure ____________ ____________

13. *annu*al ____________ ____________

14. *carn*al ____________ ____________

15. bi*gamy* ____________ ____________

EXERCISE 84

★ Below, you are given a list of prefixes and another of bound bases, all from Latin. For each the area of meaning is roughly indicated. Combine each base with as many prefixes as possible to form words. In some cases you will have to add a suffix, as in *receptive,* because there is no simple form like *recept.* In each instance note the contribution of each morpheme to the meaning of the word. Prefixes that end in a consonant tend to assimilate to the first phoneme of the base. For example, the Latin *in-*, meaning "not," retains its form in *inconsistent* but assimilates in *illegal, impossible,* and *irregular*. The assimilated forms of prefixes are given in parentheses. Use other paper for this exercise.

Prefixes

ad-	(ac-, at-) to, toward
com-	(con-) with, together, jointly, in
de-	from, down, away
dis-	(dif-) apart
ex-	from, out from, out of
in-	(im-) in, into, within, toward, on
inter-	between
per-	through, thoroughly
pre-	before, in advance
pro-	forward, before, forth, for
re-	back, again
sub-	(sup-) under
trans-	across, beyond, through

Bound Bases

1.	-tain	hold
2.	-ceive -cept -ceit	take
3.	-fer	carry, bear
4.	-clude	shut, close
5.	-port	carry

E. Affixes

An affix is a bound morpheme that occurs before or behind a base. There are two kinds, prefixes and suffixes, both of which you have already met in passing. Now we shall deal with them in greater detail.

F. Prefixes

Prefixes are those bound morphemes that occur before a base, as in *im*port, *pre*fix, *re*consider. Prefixes in English are a small class of morphemes, numbering about seventy-five. Their meanings are often those of English prepositions and adverbials.

EXERCISE 85

★ Look up in your desk dictionary each italicized prefix. (Be careful here. If you are looking up the prefix *in-* in the *American College Dictionary*, you will find eight entries for *in*. The first is the word *in* itself, which you don't want. The next three are prefixes, indicated as such by a hyphen after the morpheme, thus: *in-*. One of these is what you are looking for. Sometimes, when you have located the exact entry you want, you will find several meanings for it, as is the case with *de-*. Now back to the assignment.) From the meanings given for the prefix, choose the one that fits the word and write it in the first column. In the second column write another word containing the same prefix with the same meaning. Numbers 3, 10, 11, and 14 contain variants of a prefixal morpheme.

1. *anti*dote __________ __________
2. *circum*vent __________ __________
3. *co*pilot __________ __________
   *col*lapse __________ __________
   *com*pact __________ __________
   *con*vene __________ __________
   *cor*rode __________ __________
4. *contra*dict __________ __________
5. *de*vitalize __________ __________
6. *de*louse __________ __________

7. *de*value ____________ ____________

8. *dis*union ____________ ____________

9. *dis*agreeable ____________ ____________

10. *in*secure ____________ ____________

*im*perfect ____________ ____________

*il*legible ____________ ____________

*ir*reverent ____________ ____________

11. *in*spire ____________ ____________

*im*bibe ____________ ____________

12. *inter*vene ____________ ____________

13. *intra*mural ____________ ____________

14. *ob*struct ____________ ____________

*op*pose ____________ ____________

15. *pre*war ____________ ____________

16. *post*war ____________ ____________

17. *pro*ceed ____________ ____________

18. *retro*active ____________ ____________

19. *semi*professional ____________ ____________

20. *sub*way ____________ ____________

21. *super*abundant ____________ ____________

22. *un*likely ____________ ____________

23. *un*dress ____________ ____________

G. Suffixes

Suffixes are bound morphemes that occur after a base, like shrink*age*, fail*ure*, nois*y*, real*ize*, nail*s*, dream*ed*. Suffixes may pile up to the number of three or four, whereas prefixes are commonly single, except for the negative *un-* before another prefix. In *normalizers* we perhaps reach the limit with four: the base *norm* plus the four suffixes *-al*, *-ize*, *-er*, *-s*. When suffixes multiply like this, their order is fixed: there is one and only one order in which they occur.

EXERCISE 86

★ In these words the base is italicized. After each word write the number of suffixes it contains.

1. *organ*ists ______
2. *person*alities ______
3. *flirt*atiously ______
4. *atom*izers ______
5. *friend*liest ______
6. contra*dict*orily ______
7. *trust*eeship ______
8. *greas*ier ______
9. *countr*ified ______
10. *respons*ibilities ______

EXERCISE 87

★ Each group contains a base and suffixes. Make each into a word. In each case, see if more than one order of suffixes is possible.

1. -ed, live, -en ______________________
2. -ing, -ate, termin ______________________
3. -er, -s, mor, -al, -ize ______________________
4. provinc, -s, -ism, -al ______________________
5. -ly, -some, grue ______________________
6. -ity, work, -able ______________________
7. in, -most, -er ______________________
8. marry, -age, -ity, -abil ______________________
9. -dom, -ster, gang ______________________
10. -ly, -ion, -ate, affect ______________________

H. Derivational Suffixes

A distinction that we must now understand is that between inflectional and derivational suffixes. For the time being, let us dispose of the inflectional suffixes by simply listing them. Later we shall study them. The inflectional suffixes are these:

1. Noun possessive *-'s* (*dog's*)
2. Noun plural *-s* (*dogs*)
3. Verb present third-person singular *-s* (*vacates*)
4. Verb present participle *-ing* (*barking*)
5. Verb past tense *-ed* (*dreamed*)
6. Verb past participle *-en* (*chosen*)
7. Comparative *-er* (*sweeter*)
8. Superlative *-est* (*sweetest*)
9. Adverbial *-ly* (*sweetly*)

All other suffixes are derivational. Among the characteristics of derivational suffixes, there are three that will be our immediate concern.

1. The words with which derivational suffixes combine is an arbitrary matter. To make a noun from the verb *adorn*, we must add *-ment*, and no other suffix will do, whereas the verb *fail* combines only with *-ure* to make a noun, *failure*.

EXERCISE 88

★ The left-hand column contains ten words. The right-hand column contains thirteen derivational suffixes used to make nouns and having the general meanings of "state, condition, quality, or act of." By combining these suffixes with the words listed, make as many nouns as you can.

Words	*Noun-Forming Derivational Suffixes*	
1. happy	1. -hood	11. -ance
2. friend	2. -acy	12. -th
3. girl	3. -ism	13. -ure
4. compose	4. -ness	
5. shrink	5. -ment	
6. active	6. -age	
7. supreme	7. -y	
8. true	8. -ation	
9. pagan	9. -ship	
10. discover	10. -ity	

Nouns: ________________ ________________ ________________

________________ ________________ ________________

________________ ________________ ________________

________________ ________________ ________________

________________ ________________ ________________

2. In many cases a derivational suffix changes the part of speech of the word to which it is added. The noun *act* becomes an adjective by the addition of *-ive,* and to the adjective *active* we can add *-ate,* making it a verb, *activate.* Although we have not yet taken up the parts of speech, you probably know enough about them to distinguish between nouns, verbs, and adjectives, as you are asked to do in the next exercise.

EXERCISE 89

★ The words in the second column are formed by the addition of a derivational suffix to those in the first column. After every word in both columns indicate its part-of-speech classification by N (noun), V (verb), or A (adjective).

1. break	___	breakage	___
2. desire	___	desirable	___
3. conspire	___	conspiracy	___
4. rehearse	___	rehearsal	___
5. ideal	___	idealize	___
6. false	___	falsify	___
7. plenty	___	plenteous	___
8. doubt	___	doubtful	___
9. mouth	___	mouthful	___
10. sing	___	singer	___
11. familiarize	___	familiarization	___
12. passion	___	passionate	___
13. host	___	hostess	___
14. gloom	___	gloomy	___
15. martyr	___	martyrdom	___
16. novel	___	novelist	___
17. day	___	daily	___
18. prohibit	___	prohibitory	___

19. excel	___	excellent	___
20. create	___	creative	___
21. vision	___	visionary	___
22. cube	___	cubic	___
23. ripe	___	ripen	___
24. real	___	realism	___
25. accept	___	acceptance	___

3. Derivational suffixes need not close off a word; that is, after a derivational suffix one can sometimes add another derivational suffix and can frequently add an inflectional suffix. For example, to the word *agreeable,* which ends in a derivational suffix, one can add another one, *-ness,* and to *agreeableness* one can add the inflectional suffix *-es,* closing off the word.

EXERCISE 90

★ Add a derivational suffix to each of these words, which already end in a derivational suffix.

1. reasonable ______________________
2. formal ______________________
3. organize ______________________
4. purify ______________________
5. purist ______________________

EXERCISE 91

★ Add an inflectional suffix, one of those listed on page 94, to each of these words, which end in derivational suffixes. In the third column put any words you can think of that are formed by a suffix following the inflectional suffix you added in the second column.

1. kindness ______________ ______________
2. beautify ______________ ______________
3. quarterly ______________ ______________

4. popularize ______________ ______________

5. depth ______________ ______________

6. pressure ______________ ______________

7. extemporaneous ______________ ______________

8. orientate ______________ ______________

9. friendly ______________ ______________

10. loud ______________ ______________

A glance in the dictionary will reveal that many words have relatives, close and distant, and in grammatical study it is often necessary to examine families of related words. To label such families we employ the word *paradigm*. There are two kinds of paradigms, inflectional and derivational. The inflectional will be explained later. The derivational paradigm is a set of related words composed of the same base morpheme and all the derivational affixes that can go with this base. Here is an example: *man, manly, mannish, manful, manhood, manikin, unman, manliness, manward.*

EXERCISE 92

★ You are given here five bases, or words with their bases italicized. Give all the words in the derivational paradigm of each. Do not include words with two bases, like *manhunt* or *manpower*.

1. sin
2. kind
3. live /laiv/
4. trans*port* (-port = carry)
5. *aud*ible (aud- = hear)

I. Immediate Constituents

Up to this point we have scrutinized the three sorts of morphemes — bases, prefixes, and suffixes — of which words are composed. Now we shall see how these are put together to build the structure that we call a word.

A word of one morpheme, like *blaze,* has, of course, just one unitary part. A word of two morphemes, like *cheerful,* is obviously composed of two parts, with the division between them:

cheer | ful

But a word of three or more morphemes is not made up of a string of individual parts. It is built with a hierarchy of twosomes. As an illustration, let us examine the formation of *gentlemanly*, a word of three morphemes. We might say that *man* and *-ly* were combined to form *manly* and that *gentle* and *manly* were then put together to produce the form *gentlemanly*. But the total meaning of *gentlemanly* does not seem to be composed of the meanings of its two parts *gentle* and *manly*, so we reject this possibility. Let's try again. This time we'll say that *gentle* and *man* were put together to give *gentleman*. And if we remember that *gentle* has the meanings of "distinguished," "belonging to a high social station," we see that the meaning of *gentleman* is a composite of those of its two constituents. Now we add *-ly*, meaning "like," and get *gentlemanly*, like a gentleman. This manner of forming *gentlemanly* seems to make sense.

Now when we analyze a word we show this process but in reverse. We usually divide a word into the two parts of which it seems to have been composed. Thus

gentleman | ly

We continue in this way, cutting every part into two more until we have reduced the word to its ultimate constituents, that is, to the unit morphemes of which it is composed. Our analysis of *gentlemanly* would look like this:

gentle | man | ly

Next, let us suppose that the word to be analyzed is *ungentlemanly*. If we make the same first cut as before, cutting off the *-ly*, we get *ungentleman* plus *-ly*. But as English contains no such word as *ungentleman*, our word could not be composed of the two parts *ungentleman* and *-ly*. Instead, let's cut after the *un-*. This gives *un-* plus *gentlemanly*, a common English negative prefix plus a recognizable English word. This seems to be the right way to begin, and as we continue we get this analysis.

un | gentle | man | ly

We have now shown the layers of structure by which the word has been composed, down to the ultimate constituents — *un-*, *gentle*, *man*, and *-ly*.

In doing word diagrams, like those above, to show layers of structure, we make successive divisions into two parts, each of which is called an immediate constituent, abbreviated IC. The process is continued until all component morphemes of a word, the ultimate constituents, have been isolated.

Here are three recommendations on IC division that will assist you in the exercise to follow:

1. If a word ends in an inflectional suffix, the first cut is between this suffix and the rest of the word. So:

pre conceiv | ed mal formation | s

2. One of the IC's should be, if possible, a free form. A free form is one that can be uttered alone with meaning, e.g., *egg, enlarge, supportable.* Here are examples of wrong and right first cuts:

Wrong:	en	large ment	**Right:**	en large	ment
	in depend	ent		in	depend ent
	in support	able		in	support able

3. The meanings of the IC's should be related to the meaning of the word. It would be wrong to cut *restrain* like this:

rest | rain

because neither *rest* nor *rain* has a semantic connection with *restrain.* Nor would a division of *starchy* as

star | chy

be right because this would give an unrelated morpheme and a meaningless fragment. The two examples are properly cut in this way:

re | strain starch | y

Thus the ultimate constituents are the morphemes of which the word is composed.

EXERCISE 93

★ One of the following IC diagrams showing the layers of structure is wrong. Which one is it and why?

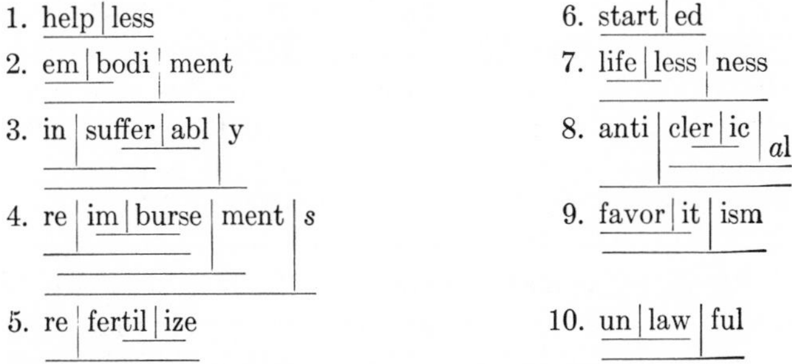

1. help | less
2. em | bodi | ment
3. in | suffer | abl | y
4. re | im | burse | ment | s
5. re | fertil | ize
6. start | ed
7. life | less | ness
8. anti | cler | ic | al
9. favor | it | ism
10. un | law | ful

EXERCISE 94

★ Diagram these words to show the layers of structure.

1. item ize d
2. pre pro fess ion al
3. news paper dom
4. counter de clar ation

5. mal con struc tion
6. contra dict ory
7. dis en throne
8. mid after noon
9. Ice land ic
10. super natur al
11. un com fort able
12. fest iv al
13. en gag ing
14. ex press ion ism
15. mis judg ment

J. Allomorphs

It is now time to sharpen and extend our understanding of the morpheme. So far we have been treating the morpheme as if it were invariable in phonemic form, that is, in the way it is pronounced. But in the preceding exercises you may have noticed occasional variations in phonemic form. In exercise 91 (page 96), for instance, the morpheme {press} of *pressure* ends in an /š/, whereas the same morpheme standing alone as the word *press* ends in /s/. Likewise, the first morpheme in *depth* is pronounced /dɛp/, but the same morpheme occurring as the word *deep* has the phonemic form of /dip/. So we see that a morpheme may have more than one phonemic form.

Next, we'll go back to the past-tense ending, the morpheme {-d_1}. We learned in exercise 23 of the phonology that this morpheme has three phonemic forms, the choice depending on the preceding sound. After an alveolar stop, /t/ or /d/, the sound is /ɨd/, as in *parted* /partɨd/ and *faded* /fedɨd/. After a voiceless consonant other than /t/, it is /t/, as in *passed* /pæst/ and *laughed* /læft/. After a voiced sound other than /d/, it is /d/, as in *seemed* /simd/ and *begged* /bɛgd/. Furthermore, these three phonemic forms of {-d_1} are not interchangeable. The occurrence of one or another of them depends on its phonological environment, in this case, the preceding sound. This pattern of occurrence of related forms, according to which each form occupies its own territory and does not trespass on the domain of another, is called complementary distribution, abbreviated CD. When the related forms of a set, like the three forms of {-d_1}, have the same meaning and are in complementary distribution, they are called allomorphs and belong to the same morpheme. So we say that the morpheme {-d_1} has three allomorphs: /-ɨd/, /-t/, and /-d/. This is expressed in the formula:

{-d_1} = /-ɨd/ ~ /-t/ ~ /-d/

Braces are used for morphemes and slants for allomorphs; a tilde (~) means "in alternation with." It must be emphasized that many morphemes in English have only one allomorph, for example, the morphemes {boy} and {-hood} each has one allomorph — /boi/ and /-hud/ — as in *boyhood.*

EXERCISE 95

★ Explain why *a/an* are allomorphs of one morpheme.

EXERCISE 96

★ Write the base morpheme and its allomorphs for each group.

Examples: steal, stealth {steal} = /stil ~ stɛl-/

1. wide, width
2. broad, breadth
3. wolf, wolves
4. able, ability
5. supreme, supremacy
6. divine, divinity
7. fame, famous, infamy, infamous
8. vision, televise, revise
9. sun, sunny, sunward
10. atom, atomic (Supply stresses in answer.)

EXERCISE 97

★ This exercise concerns the plural morpheme $\{\text{-s}_2\}$, which (we'll say for the moment) has three allomorphs. Write out each plural word in phonemic script. Then, using these as evidence, list the allomorphs of $\{\text{-s}_2\}$ and describe their complementary distribution.

1. sons ______	6. fizzes ______	11. churches ______
2. naps ______	7. dishes ______	12. gorges ______
3. passes ______	8. garages ______	13. sums ______
4. hogs ______	9. hoes ______	14. heaths ______
5. sacks ______	10. staffs ______	15. gongs ______

Allomorphs and CD:

____

____

____

____

K. Conditioning: Phonological and Morphological

In examining the past-tense morpheme {-d_1}, we saw that the three allomorphs /-ɨd ~ -d ~ -t/ were in CD and that this distribution was determined by the phonological environment, in this case by the nature of the preceding sound. The same was true of the plural morpheme {-s_2} in exercise 97, where the addition of /-ɨz/, /-z/, or /-s/ was also determined by the kind of sound immediately preceding the suffix. In these and similar cases, when the phonological environment determines which allomorph is used, we say that the selection of allomorphs is phonologically conditioned.

But the plural morpheme {-s_2} has further allomorphs, as shown by the /-ɨn/ of *ox-oxen* and by the /ø/ (zero) suffix of *sheep-sheep*. These two, /-ɨn/ and /ø/, are in CD with all the others in that they stay in their own territory, associate only with specific words, and do not overlap in positions where /-ɨz/, /-z/, and /-s/ are found. But the positions in which they occur, that is, the words they attach themselves to, have nothing to do with their phonological environment. Instead the use of /-ɨn/ as the plural of *ox* is determined by the specific morpheme *ox;* in other words, *ox* simply takes /-ɨn/ and that's that. Likewise, the occurrence of the plural ø allomorph in a few words — *swine, deer, sheep, trout, pike, quail, grouse,* and others — is determined by the fact that these special morphemes require a ø plural. In such cases, when we can describe the environment that requires a certain allomorph only by identifying specific morphemes, we say that the selection of allomorphs is morphologically conditioned.

To describe by formula these five allomorphs of {-s_2}, we write

{-s_2} = /-ɪz/~/-z/~/-s/ ∞ /-ɨn/ ∞ /ø/

The ~ refers to a phonologically conditioned alternation and the ∞ to a morphologically conditioned alternation.

EXERCISE 98

★ Write the formula to express the fact that the past-tense morpheme {-d_1} has, in the verb *be*, the two morphologically conditioned allomorphs, *was* and *were*.

____

____

L. Replacive Allomorphs

Most of the allomorphs we have been dealing with have been additive; that is, we have been forming words by adding prefixes and suffixes to bases. Now we must look at an allomorph of a different kind, the replacive, which can be illustrated by going back again to the past-tense {-d_1}. We noted that this morpheme has three allomorphs, /-ɨd ~ -t ~ -d/. But if this is all, how do we account for forms like *sang?* It would appear to contain an allomorph of {-d_1} since it is a parallel formation with regular past-tense forms:

Yesterday we *parted* /partɨd/
Yesterday we *laughed* /læft/
Yesterday we *played* /pled/
Yesterday we *sang* /sæŋ/

What happens is that there is a replacement here instead of an additive. The /ɪ/ of *sing* is replaced by the /æ/ of *sang* to signal the past tense. This is symbolized as follows:

/sæŋ/ = /sɪŋ/ + /ɪ > æ/

Here the /ɪ > æ/ is another allomorph of {-d_1}, and you can readily see how it is in CD with the others.

EXERCISE 99

★ Write the allomorphic formula for each of the following past-tense forms.

Examples: spin, *spun* /spən/ = /spɪn/ + /ɪ > ə/

1. see, *saw*
2. begin, *began*
3. bite, *bit*
4. give, *gave*
5. grow, *grew*
6. ride, *rode*
7. grind, *ground*
8. take, *took*
9. tear, *tore*
10. speak, *spoke*

M. Homophones

You are acquainted with many pairs and trios of words in English which sound alike but differ in meaning: *heir, air; pare, pair, pear*. Such words are called homophones. In morphology, it must be remembered that words like these are allomorphs of different morphemes. This becomes apparent as soon as we recall our definition of allomorphs. Let's take an example:

Did you like the *meet?* /mit/ (track meet)
Did you like the *meat?* /mit/ (roast beef)

Now, to be allomorphs of one morpheme, each allomorph must have the same meaning. These do not, and must therefore be allomorphs of different morphemes. The same is true of bound forms. Compare

Verbal inflectional suffix:	It feels /-z/ good
Noun plural inflectional suffix:	Those frogs /-z/
Noun possessive inflectional suffix:	John's /-z/ book

These three homophonous /-z/s, having different meanings, are allomorphs of three different morphemes.

EXERCISE 100

★ Write the morphemes to which each of these homophonous allomorphs belongs.

Examples: /et/ = {ate}
/et/ = {eight}

1. /mit/
   /mit/
   /mit/
2. /mait/
   /mait/
   /mait/
3. /yu/
   /yu/
   /yu/
4. /pɛr/
   /pɛr/
   /pɛr/
5. /ɪts/
   /ɪts/
6. /tu/
   /tu/
   /tu/
   /tu/

N. Stress Morphemes and Intonation Contours

The next stage in this brief morphology of English is the examination of the kinds of words that result from combinations of morphemes or from single morphemes. But first we must take into account the suprasegmental morphemes.

You recall that in your study of phonology, English was seen to have four stress phonemes: /ˊ/, /ˆ/, /ˋ/, and /˘/. And these phonemes, you remember, combine in meaningful ways. For example, in *transfer*, the pronunciation /trǽnsfə̀r/ signaled a noun, whereas /træ̀nsfə́r/ indicated a verb. Since the segmental phonemes are the same, it is the combination of stresses that conveys the meaning of "noun" or "verb." Such a meaningful combination of stresses, with or without plus juncture, is called a superfix, which is a suprasegmental morpheme. Superfixes accompany words and phrases. You met numerous superfixes in the phonology, which seemed the strategic if not logical place to present them. It was superfixes, for instance, that distinguished between *pálefàce* and *pâle fáce*. Since a word cannot be spoken without stress, stress may be considered to participate somehow in the conveyance of its meaning. Thus it is conventional to label all word stress-patterns as superfixes, whether or not they are demonstrably conveyors of meaning. As we define words in this section we shall adopt the practice of ignoring the superfixes, since they go with all words.

The second kind of suprasegmental morpheme is the intonation contour, which consists of pitches and a terminal juncture. Again you will recall a number of these morphemes from the phonology, e.g., the 2 3 1 ↓ for a statement, the 2 3 3 ↑ for a yes-or-no question, and the 2 3 ↑ on a word as a request for repetition. This morpheme accompanies phrases, clauses, and sentences.

IX.

Words

A. Definition of "Word"

That the word is a genuine linguistic unit is scarcely questioned, and everyone seems to know what it is. Teachers have no difficulty in making up spelling lists, which consist of words. Lexicographers produce dictionaries, whose entries are mainly words. When we read, we recognize words by the white spaces between them. Occasionally, however, we are puzzled by printed forms of words which are inconsistent one with another. Here are several examples from one page of a new scholarly desk dictionary, *Webster's Seventh New Collegiate Dictionary*. This book lists *woodcut* as one word and *wood block* (with the same meaning) as two. In the same column it lists the one-word *woodcock* but does not mention *wood duck*, which can be found in almost any bird book. All four words have the same superfix, ´ \`, and no formal criteria are evident for differences in the printed form. Such moot cases apart, however, we commonly have no doubt about the identity of words.

But all these instances are concerned with written words, whereas in linguistic analysis our main interest is in the spoken word. Here again, the isolation of the unit called a word appears easy. If one asks "What does ____ mean?" or "How do you pronounce ____?" the blank usually represents a word. And there is a high correlation between the written and the spoken forms of words. Yet the task of devising an exact definition of *word* is a prickly one that has engendered much controversy. We shall begin here by repeating the definition of *free form* mentioned earlier: "A free form is any segment of speech that can be spoken alone with meaning in normal speech." From this we can go on to a widely adopted definition of *word*: A word is a free form that cannot be divided wholly into smaller free forms.*

EXERCISE 101

★ Indicate which of the items below may be classified as words *according to the definition given above*. Use W for word and NW for nonword.

1. single _____
2. outlook _____
3. dance _____
4. misapprehension _____
5. milkman _____
6. happiness _____
7. breakfast _____
8. driver _____
9. undergo _____
10. redhead _____

B. Simple and Complex Words

English words may be classified on the basis of the kinds and combinations of morphemes of which they are composed. We shall adopt a classification of two main classes: simple and complex.

1. Simple words consist of a single free base.

Examples: slay, flea, long, spirit, eucalyptus

2. Complex words contain at least one bound morpheme as an immediate constituent. They fall into two subclasses:

a. Complex words – BB (bound base) have a bound form for each IC.

Examples:

tele | vise	pre | clude
ex | tract	termin | ate
rupt | ure	somnifer | ous
matri | cide	

* By way of experiment, you might like to see where this definition of *word* would lead: "A word is . . . any segment of a sentence bounded by successive points *at which pausing is possible*." Charles F. Hockett, *A Course in Modern Linguistics* (New York: Macmillan, 1958), p. 167.

b. Complex words – FB (free base) have one free form as an IC.

Examples:

lion | ess — eras | er
un | certain — re | birth
dipso | mania — tele | phone

EXERCISE 102

★ Make the first IC cut in the words below which permit such cutting. Then classify each word as:

S Simple
C–BB Complex with two bound forms as IC's
C–FB Complex with one free form as an IC

1. knave	_____	11. philosophical	_____
2. knavish	_____	12. sophistic	_____
3. graph	_____	13. sophomore	_____
4. telegraph	_____	14. misogynist	_____
5. merge	_____	15. refusal	_____
6. emerge	_____	16. carnal	_____
7. moron	_____	17. enable	_____
8. democracy	_____	18. mete	_____
9. purist	_____	19. meter	_____
10. comical	_____	20. chronometer	_____

C. Word Compounds

While doing the last two exercises, you may have wondered how to classify the nonwords like *undergo* in exercise 101 and the compound nouns like *high school* and *old maid* that you met in the phonology. None of these is a word, according to the definition on page 107, because each of them can be divided wholly into smaller free forms; e.g., *under* + *go*, *high* + *school*, *old* + *maid*.

Such terms occupy a position intermediate between the word and the grammatical structure. They are wordlike in two respects:

1. They are distributed like words.

Examples: a. Mary was picking *flowers* (*bluebells*).
b. He sat *near* (*outside*) the door.

2. They take some of the inflectional suffixes.

Examples: a The highway*s* were crowded.
b. You are upsett*ing* the boat.

Also, they have a resemblance to grammatical structures in that they imply, though they do not state, a grammatical relationship. Here are a few examples:

Term	*Implied Grammatical Structures*
kíllj̀oy	. . . kills joy (verb-object)
dównpòur	. . . pours down (verb adverbial)
hígh chàir	. . . high chair (modifier noun)
wórkmàn	. . . man works (subject verb)
íngròup	. . . group is in (*be* adverbial)
wáshing machìne	. . . machine for washing (noun plus modifier)

Terms like these, which are composed of free forms as their IC's, we shall call word compounds.

Examples: head | strong   over | come
how | ever   pay | day

Of the various ways of identifying word compounds, here are three that will prove useful:

1. Word compounds cannot be divided by the insertion of intervening material between the two parts, but grammatical structures can be so divided. As illustration, let us compare two sentences:

a. She is a sweetheart.
b. She has a sweet heart.

In the first, the word compound *sweetheart* is indivisible: you cannot insert anything between *sweet* and *heart*. But in the second sentence you could say

She has a sweet*er* heart than her sister,
She has a sweet, *kind* heart,
She has a sweet, *sweet* heart,

thereby dividing the components *sweet* and *heart*. Thus sentence *b* contains a grammatical structure, not a word compound. Following this principle of divisibility, we find that the next sentence is ambiguous:

She loves sweet potatoes.

When *sweet potatoes* means the yellow kind, the expression cannot be divided and is therefore a word compound. But when the words refer to white potatoes which are sweet, then division is possible, as in

She loves sweet, fresh potatoes,

and we have a grammatical structure.

2. A member of a word compound cannot participate in a grammatical structure. Compare *hârd báll* and *básebàll. Hârd báll* is a grammatical structure of modifier plus noun, and its first member, *hard*, can participate in the structure *very hard*:

It was a very hard ball.

But one cannot say

It was a very baseball,

as *baseball* is a word compound. Ambiguous cases can occur in sentences like

He is fond of sparkling water.

When *sparkling water* refers to ordinary water that sparkles, the first member, *sparkling*, can participate in a grammatical structure, e.g., *brightly sparkling water*. So *sparkling water* with this meaning is a grammatical structure. But when the expression refers to carbonated water, such participation cannot occur and we have a word compound.

3. Some word compounds are differentiated from grammatical structures by superfixes, as you have already learned. The superfixes /ˊ ˋ/ and /ˋ ˊ/ enable us to contrast compound nouns like *blúebìrd* and *òld-tímer* with the grammatical structure of modifier plus noun, as in *blûe bírd* and *ôld tímer*.

EXERCISE 103

★ Indicate whether each italicized expression is a word compound (C) or a grammatical structure (GS). Pay no attention to hyphens or spaces, for these are deceptive.

1. Jim's new car is a *hardtop*. ___
2. This jar has a rather *hard top*. ___
3. It was a *jack-in-the-box*. ___
4. There was a *plant in the box*. ___
5. A *hót dòg* is not a *hôt dóg*. ___ ___
6. He has a *dog in the manger* attitude. ___
7. She has a *strong hold* on him. ___
8. She has a *stronghold* in the Women's Club. ___
9. George found his *father-in-law*. ___

10. George found his *father in trouble.* ___

11. They bought it on the *black market.* ___

12. The electricity went off, and we were caught in a *black,* completely lightless, *market.* ___

13. His *spending money* was a source of annoyance to his father. ___

EXERCISE 104

★ For review, classify the following items with these symbols:

S Simple
C–BB Complex with two bound forms as IC's
C–FB Complex with one free form as an IC
WCp Word compound
GS Grammatical structure

With three classes — C–BB, C–FB, and WCp — make the first IC cut.

1. sharpshooter ________
2. a shârp shóoter ________
3. act ________
4. react ________
5. storekeeper ________
6. passbook ________
7. apparatus ________
8. detain ________
9. recur ________
10. current ________
11. unearth ________
12. referee ________
13. solve ________
14. dissolve ________
15. solvent ________
16. búll's-èye (of target) ________
17. bûll's éye (of bull) ________
18. highlander ________
19. biochemical ________
20. inaccessible ________

D. Inflectional Suffixes

The inflectional suffixes, which we have already met in passing, can be schematized as follows:

Inflectional Suffix	*Examples*	*Name*
1. $\{\text{-s}_1\}$	boy'*s*	noun possessive
2. $\{\text{-s}_2\}$	dog*s*, ox*en*	noun plural
3. $\{\text{-s}_3\}$	vacate*s*	present third-person singular

Inflectional Suffix	*Examples*	*Name*
4. {-ing$_1$}	discuss*ing*	present participle
5. {-d$_1$}	chew*ed*, r*o*de	past tense
6. {-d$_2$}	chew*ed*, chos*en*, sw*u*m	past participle
7. {-er$_1$}	bold*er*	comparative
8. {-est$_1$}	bold*est*	superlative
9. {-ly$_1$}	bold*ly*	adverb

The words to which these suffixes are attached are called stems. The stem includes the base or bases and all the derivational affixes. Thus the stem of *agreeablenesses* is *agreeableness* and that of *beautified* is *beautify*.

The inflectional suffixes differ from derivational suffixes in several ways, to which there are a few exceptions.

1. They do not change the part of speech.

Examples: *Sled* and *sleds* are both nouns.
Cough and *coughed* are both verbs.

2. They come last in the word.

Examples: shorten*ed*, villaini*es*

3. They go with all stems of a given part of speech.

Examples: bright*est*, broad*est*, loud*est*, tall*est*,

4. They do not pile up; only one ends a word.

Examples: eat*ing*, flake*s*, suppli*ed*

5. They are not replaceable by uninflected forms, except for *-er* and *-est*, which can be replaced by *more* and *most*.

Example: *Sings* in "He sings" cannot be replaced by any word except another word ending in the present third-person singular {-s$_3$}, without changing the structural sense.

6. They go with words but not with grammatical structures; that is, word groups like phrases and clauses do not take inflectional endings. It would be non-English, for example, to say "Joe is in the dark*er* than his roommate about the math problem."

EXERCISE 105

★ Write the morphemic symbol and the name for each italicized inflectional suffix. The term *suffix* here includes infixes, like those in sw*u*m, st*oo*d, r*a*ng.

1. The flagpole st*oo*d in front of Main Hall.

______ ______________________

2. Four pledge*s* were initiated.

______ ______________________

3. Shirley pledge*s* to do her best.

_____ _____________________

4. The pledge'*s* shirt was torn.

_____ _____________________

5. The pledge*s*' shirts were torn.

_____ _____________________

_____ _____________________

6. We were discuss*ing* the editorial.

_____ _____________________

7. The novel was short*er* than I had expected.

_____ _____________________

8. They wait*ed* at the dock.

_____ _____________________

9. Which is the long*est* route?

_____ _____________________

10. Have you tak*en* calculus yet?

_____ _____________________

11. Jim played skillful*ly* in the second set.

_____ _____________________

12. The dealer weigh*ed* the poultry.

_____ _____________________

13. Would you mind repeat*ing* the question?

_____ _____________________

14. The sheet*s* were soon ironed.

_____ _____________________

15. She never lock*s* the door.

_____ _____________________

E. Homophones of Inflectional Suffixes

Five of the inflectional suffixes have homophonous forms among the derivational suffixes.

The inflectional morpheme {-er_1} has two homophones. The first is the derivational suffix {-er_2}, which is attached to verbs to form nouns. This is a highly productive suffix, that is, it is used to produce hundreds of English nouns like *hunter*, *fisher*, *camper*, *golfer*, *lover*. It is often called the agent *-er* and conveys a meaning of "that which performs the action of the verb stem," as in *thriller* and *teacher*. It may also be attached to nonverbal stems, e.g., *probationer*, *New Yorker*, *teen-ager*, *freighter*. The *-er* on such words could be said to convey a more general meaning of "that which is related to"; and since this meaning is inclusive of the previous one, both these *-er* suffixes can be considered to belong to {$-er_2$}.

The second derivational *-er* morpheme appears at the end of words like *chatter, mutter, flicker, glitter, patter.* This {$-er_3$} conveys the meaning of repetition. The acceptance of this {$-er_3$}, however, is problematic and raises questions about the analysis of the remainders in words of this class.

EXERCISE 106

★ Identify the italicized *-er* as

1. [$-er_1$] inflectional suffix, as in *bigger*
2. [$-er_2$] derivational suffix, as in *singer*
3. [$-er_3$] derivational suffix, as in *flutter*

1. This is a heavi*er* tennis racket than I want. ___
2. We watched the shimm*er* of the evening light on the waves. ___
3. The fight*er* weighed in at 180 pounds. ___
4. He was tough*er* than he looked. ___
5. The jabb*er* of voices came through the open door. ___

The verbal inflectional suffix {$-ing_1$} has two homophones in *-ing.* The first one is the derivational suffix {$-ing_2$}, which is found in words like *meetings, weddings, readings.* This {$-ing_2$} is obviously derivational since it permits the addition of an inflectional suffix to close it off, the noun plural {$-s_2$}. When such a word occurs alone without the inflectional suffix, e.g., *meeting,* the *-ing* is ambiguous, for it could be either {$-ing_1$}, as in "he was meet*ing* the train" or {$-ing_2$}, as in "He attended the meet*ing.*"

The second homophone of {$-ing_1$} is the adjectival morpheme {$-ing_3$}, as in *a charming woman.* There are several tests by which the verbal {$-ing_1$} can be distinguished from the adjectival {$-ing_3$}.

The verbal {$-ing_1$} can usually occur after as well as before the noun it modifies, e.g.,

I saw a burning house.
I saw a house burning.

The adjectival {$-ing_3$} can be preceded by a qualifier like *very, rather, quite* or by the comparative and superlative words *more* and *most,* as in

It is a very comforting thought.
This is a more exciting movie.*

EXERCISE 107

★ In the blanks place a V to identify the italicized verbal {-ing$_1$} morpheme and an A to identify the italicized adjectival {-ing$_3$} morpheme.

1. It was a *charming* spot. ___
2. It was located by a sweetly *babbling* brook. ___
3. It was *exciting* to watch the flight. ___
4. From the bridge we watched the *running* water. ___
5. That *barking* dog keeps everyone awake. ___
6. He told a *convincing* tale. ___
7. The *shining* sun gilded the forest floor. ___
8. A *refreshing* shower poured down. ___
9. The attorney made a *moving* appeal. ___
10. What an *obliging* fellow he is! ___

The verbal {-d$_2$} has a homophone in the adjectival {-d$_3$}, as in

Helen was *excited* about her new job.
She was a *neglected* child.

The adjectival {-d$_3$} is characterized by its capacity for modification by qualifiers like *very*, *rather*, *quite* and by *more* and *most*. The verbal {-d$_2$} does not accept such modifiers. We would not, for example, say

*The *rather departed* guests had forgotten their dog.

---

* The adjectival {-ing$_3$} may sometimes be distinguished from the verbal {-ing$_1$} by a transformational test. Here is how it goes. Suppose you want to know whether *pleasing* is an {-ing$_3$} or an {-ing$_1$} in

a pleasing girl.

You take the stem *please* and put it in this frame:

It ______________ Mary (or any other animate noun).

This produces

It pleases Mary.

If the stem fits into this slot, its *-ing* form before a noun contains the adjectival {-ing$_3$}. Now try

a laughing girl.

The stem *laugh* put into the same frame would give

* It laughs Mary,

which doesn't make sense. Thus the prenominal *laughing* does not contain the adjectival {-ing$_3$} but the verbal {-ing$_1$}.

EXERCISE 108

★ In the blanks place a V to identify the italicized verbal {-d_2} and an A to identify the italicized adjectival {-d_3}.

1. You should read the *printed* statement. ___
2. Merle became a *devoted* mother. ___
3. This is a *complicated* question. ___
4. His *chosen* bride had lived in India. ___
5. He bought a *stolen* picture ___
6. The *invited* guests all came. ___
7. We had a *reserved* seat. ___
8. The skipper was a *reserved* (= quiet) man. ___
9. A *celebrated* painter visited the campus. ___
10. A *worried* look crossed his face. ___

EXERCISE 109

★ Ambiguity occurs when the *-ed* suffix can be interpreted as either {-d_2} or {-d_3}. This exercise will illustrate. For each sentence below write two meanings.

1. It was a finished job.

   a. ______________________________

   b. ______________________________

2. My fiancée is reserved.

   a. ______________________________

   b. ______________________________

The inflectional morpheme {-est_1} has as a homophone the derivational suffix {-est_2}, which occurs in words like *realist, typist, organist* with a meaning of "person connected with or related to." Although these two morphemes have different spellings, they are homophonous because the pronunciations /-ɪst/ or /-ɨst/ are common to both.

The inflectional suffix {-ly_1} partakes of the characteristics of both derivational and inflectional suffixes, and our assignment of it to the inflectional group is arbitrary. This {-ly_1} is added to most adjectives to form adverbs, as in *rich, richly; kind, kindly; live, lively; formal, formally; happy, happily*. A small group of adjectives does not take this {-ly_1}, among them *big, small, little, tall, long, fast.*

The adverbial {-ly_1} has as a homophone the derivational suffix {-ly_2}, an adjectival morpheme that is distributed as follows:

1. It is added to monosyllabic nouns to form adjectives that are inflected with *-er, -est.*

Examples: shape, shapely; man, manly; cost, costly

2. It is added to plurisyllabic nouns to form adjectives that are not inflected with *-er, -est.*

Examples: scholar, scholarly; coward, cowardly; mother, motherly

3. It is added to a few adjectives, giving alternate adjectival forms that are also inflected with *-er, -est.*

Examples: low, lowly; kind, kindly; live, lively

Here the adjectives *kindly* and *lively* are homophonous with the adverbs *kindly* and *lively*, which end in {-ly_1}.

4. It is added to a short list of "time" nouns to form adjectives.

Examples: day, daily; hour, hourly; month, monthly

These are not inflected with *-er, -est*, and some of them undergo functional shift to become nouns, e.g., "He subscribes to two *dailies* and three *quarterlies.*"

You might be tempted to consider these two *-ly* forms as allomorphs, since they seem to be in complementary distribution and to share the same area of meaning (= likeness), but the presence of contrasting minimal pairs like *kindly* (adverb) and *kindly* (adjective) justifies a separate morphemic status for each.

EXERCISE 110

★ Identify the italicized *-ly* as

1. -ly_1 inflectional suffix, as in *glumly*
2. -ly_2 derivational suffix, as in *fatherly*

1. The witness testified false*ly*. ___

2. Gilbert has a dead*ly* wit. ___

3. Prudence always behaved with a maiden*ly* demeanor. ___

4. He tiptoes soft*ly* into the room. ___

5. Jimmy receives a week*ly* allowance. ___

6. The dear old lady has a heaven*ly* disposition. ___

7. She spoke quiet*ly* to her grandson. ___

8. What a time*ly* suggestion! ___

9. What an unmanner*ly* helot! ___

10. It was a coward*ly* act. ___

EXERCISE 111

★ This is an exercise reviewing the inflectional and derivational suffixes. Label the italicized suffixes as DS (derivational suffix), IS (inflectional suffix), or Amb (ambiguous).

1. prince*s* ______
2. prince*ss* ______
3. find*ing*s ______
4. friendli*er* ______
5. show*s* ______
6. weav*er* ______
7. lean*er* ______
8. satir*ize* ______
9. sputt*er* ______
10. bright*en* ______
11. quick*ly* ______
12. recti*fy* ______
13. brother*ly* ______
14. respect*able* ______
15. young*er* ______
16. clean*ly* ______
17. glimm*er* ______
18. griev*ance* ______
19. dropp*ing*s ______
20. sunn*y* ______

X.

Inflectional Paradigms

A paradigm, as was explained earlier, is a set of related forms having the same stem but different affixes. As a reminder, here is a derivational paradigm with the stem *head: ahead, behead, header, headlong, headship, heady, subhead.*

Paradigms are also formed by the words to which the inflectional suffixes are attached. These are called inflectional paradigms. There are only five of them. Four are sketched below. The fifth one, that of the personal pronouns, is irregular and will be treated later.

NOUN PARADIGM

Forms:	*Stem*	*Possessive*	*Plural*	*Plural + Possessive*
Inflectional suffixes:		{-s_1}	{-s_2}	{-s_2} + {-s_1}
Models:	woman	woman's	women	women's
	doctor	doctor's	doctors	doctors'

VERB PARADIGM

Forms:	*Stem*	*Present Third-Person Singular*	*Present Participle*	*Past Tense*	*Past Participle*
Inflectional suffixes:		{-s_3}	{-ing_1}	{-d_1}	{-d_2}
Models:	show	shows	showing	showed	showed
	ring	rings	ringing	rang	rung
	cut	cuts	cutting	cut	cut

COMPARABLE PARADIGM

Forms:	*Stem*	*Comparative*	*Superlative*
Inflectional suffixes:		$\{$-er$_1\}$	$\{$-est$_1\}$
Models:	sweet	sweeter	sweetest
	lively	livelier	liveliest
	friendly	friendlier	friendliest
	soon	sooner	soonest
	near	nearer	nearest

ADVERB PARADIGM

Form:	*Adjective Stem*	*Adverb*
Inflectional suffix:		$\{$-ly$_1\}$
Model:	rough	roughly

In paradigms, the meaning of the stem remains constant, and it is the suffixes that produce the differences in meaning among the forms of each paradigm. Membership in one of these inflectional paradigms is one of the signals which enables us to group words into the four major parts of speech — nouns, verbs, adjectives, and adverbs. We shall take up this matter when we study English syntax. Now we shall examine the five paradigms one by one.

A. The Noun Paradigm

The noun paradigm is as follows:

Forms:	*Stem*	*Possessive*	*Plural*	*Plural + Possessive*
Inflectional suffixes:		$\{$-s$_1\}$	$\{$-s$_2\}$	$\{$-s$_2\}$ + $\{$-s$_1\}$
Models:	man	man's	men	men's
	doctor	doctor's	doctors	doctors'

This four-form paradigm is maximal, and not all nouns have all the four forms. Many nouns do not take the possessive forms, since an *of* structure often takes the place of the $\{$-s$_1\}$ morpheme. For example, one is more likely to say "the ceiling of the room" than "the room's ceiling." In the spoken language we cannot always be sure which s morpheme we are hearing, because the possessive and the plural have identical forms — /-s/, /-z/, and /-ɪz/ — except in the case of irregular plurals. If, for instance, you were to hear /ðə daktərz sɛmɪnar/, it could mean "the doctor's seminar," "the doctors' seminar," or "the doctors seminar."

A few so-called nouns have only a single form, that of the stem, like *tennis, courage, haste.* Another group does not have a singular form but only that of the -s plural: *clothes, environs, thanks, trousers,* and others.

These take *they/them* as a pronoun substitute and go with the plural form of the verb, e.g., "My clothes are clean." Still another group ends in the -s plural, words like *economics, linguistics, mathematics, physics,* but these take *it* as a pronoun substitute and go with a singular form of the verb, e.g., "*Linguistics* is an exacting discipline." Words in a certain, ill-defined group end in -s, like *ethics, oats, news, pliers, suds, measles,* but may be either singular or plural, depending on the context in which they occur or on the nuance of meaning expressed.

Examples:

Singular: *Measles* (= a malady) is a contagious disease.
Plural: Have you ever had them, the *measles?* (= a malady)
Singular: *Ethics* (= a philosophic discipline) is a challenging subject.
Plural: I don't approve of his personal *ethics* (= beliefs and actions).

EXERCISE 112

★ Write the paradigmatic forms of these nouns. For some slots you may have two forms or none.

Stem	*Possessive*	*Plural*	*Possessive + Plural*
1. carpenter	______	______	______
2. woman	______	______	______
3. brother	______	______	______
4. cloud	______	______	______
5. cattle	______	______	______
6. duck	______	______	______
7. Japanese	______	______	______
8. means	______	______	______
9. athletics	______	______	______
10. chaos	______	______	______

B. Noun Plurals

At this point it is convenient to set forth the ways of distinguishing singular from plural nouns. For many nouns the long-used meaning test will do: a noun is singular if it means one, and plural if it means more than one.

But meaning does not always work as a test of number. Take for instance this sentence: "I like your *hair*." Is hair singular or plural, assuming it means not a single strand but the coiffure or thatch on someone's head? Nor will form always do, since some nouns ending in an -s plural seem to be singular, e.g., *physics*, and others without an -s plural seem to be plural, e.g., *several salmon*.

There remain three useful tests for number in the noun.

1. A noun is singular if it can take one of these substitutes: *he/him*, *she/her*, *it*, *this*, or *that*. It is plural if it can take as a substitute *they/them*, *these*, or *those*.

Examples: The beach was covered with *white sand*. (= it)
Have you studied *phonetics?* (= it)
Where did you hang *my trousers?* (= them)

2. The number of a noun may be signaled by a modifier like *several*, *many*, *this*, *that*, *these*, *those*, *fifteen* or by a pronoun reference like *his/her/its*, *their*.

Examples: We saw *many fish* swimming under the bridge.
In returning to the fold, the *sheep* changed *its* direction.
In returning to the fold the *sheep* changed *their* direction.

3. When a noun functions as subject of a verb, its number is sometimes shown by the form of the verb. It is the singular noun that goes with the {-s_3} form of the verb, as in

Measles *is* a contagious disease.

Contrast this with

The goods *are* on the way

in which the verb form *are* shows that *goods* is plural. If the verb has a form that does not change for singular and plural, e.g., *came*, one can usually substitute a form that does change, e.g.,

The goods came (substitute *arrive* or *are*) late.

EXERCISE 113

★ In the blanks of the first column, write a word that you would substitute for the italicized word — *he/him*, *she/her*, *it*, *this*, *that*, *they/them*, *these*, *those*. In the blanks of the second column, write S (singular) or P (plural) to show the number of the italicized noun.

1. Miss Shen is wearing *hose* today. ______________ ______
2. What did they do with the *molasses?* ______________ ______

3. The *summons* came in the mail. ______________ ____
4. Why doesn't she call the *police?* ______________ ____
5. Jack likes to fish for *pike.* ______________ ____
6. The firm transported the *goods* to Australia. ______________ ____
7. The jar is filled with *sugar.* ______________ ____
8. Have you ever had the *mumps?* ______________ ____
9. She became fond of *mathematics.* ______________ ____
10. Does your brother eat *soap?* ______________ ____

EXERCISE 114

★ Encircle the noun modifier or pronoun reference that reveals the number of the italicized noun.

1. The hunting party saw few *deer* this season.
2. That *news* delighted her.
3. She studied *poetics* in all its complications.
4. My *scissors* lost their sharpness.
5. He shot both *quail* on the wing.

EXERCISE 115

★ Encircle the verb that reveals the number of the italicized noun.

1. The *Chinese* was preparing the dinner.
2. The *Chinese* were preparing the dinner.
3. *Oats* is his best crop.
4. The *bass* are biting today.
5. The *species* has become extinct.

One group of nouns known as collective nouns may be either singular or plural in meaning when they are singular in form. These are nouns which represent a collection or unit of individuals, like *tribe, family, team, committee, faculty, choir.* A speaker is likely to use singular forms (verbs, pronouns, determiners) in connection with such nouns when he is thinking of the unit as a single whole, but he will use plural forms when he has uppermost in mind the separate individuals within the unit.

Examples:

Singular: The family (= it, the unit) *is* sitting at the dinner table.

Plural: The family (= they, the individuals) *have* gathered from many parts of the country.

EXERCISE 116

★ Indicate in the blanks by S or P whether the italicized collective nouns are singular or plural. Decide by using the tests for number that you have learned.

1. The *band* is playing well today. ___
2. The *band* are playing well today. ___
3. The *choir* became dissatisfied with their robes. ___
4. The *choir* became dissatisfied with its singing. ___
5. The *staff* of the college paper was a high-quality group. ___
6. The *staff* of the college paper were assembled to discuss their last edition. ___
7. The *tribe* were on the warpath. ___
8. The *tribe* was the owner of the river bottom. ___
9. The *congregation* rose to its feet. ___
10. The *congregation* have all helped with the fund-raising drive. ___

The plural form of the noun usually signals the meaning of more than one. The most frequently employed plural forms are the three allomorphs of {-s_2}, such as we hear in *hats* /-s/, *fads* /-z/, and *kisses* /-ɪz/. These -s plurals are customarily considered the regular forms, not only because of their numerical preponderance but also because new nouns, either borrowed from other languages (*pizzeria*) or composed from existing morphemes (*astronaut*), tend to follow the -s plural.

In addition to the regular -s plural there are several small groups of irregular plurals.

1. Three nouns still retain an -en plural — *oxen*, *children*, and *brethren* — the last two having in addition a replacive stem vowel and a suffixal -*r*.

2. This group has a ø (zero) suffixal plural. This is a convenient way of saying that the plural is the same as the singular. It is shown in this way:

deer /dir/ = /dir/ + /ø/

The ø plural allomorph refers to a significant absence of suffix. The words in this group are the names of edible animals, game animals, fish, and birds. Among them are: *deer, sheep, swine, bear, antelope, bass, pike, carp, perch, pickerel, quail, grouse.* Beside these we may set similar words with a regular plural: *pigs, goats, suckers, muskies, bullheads, pheasants, ducks.* Some have both forms; a farmer, for example, who has *ducks* on his pond may go out hunting *duck.*

3. Seven common nouns form their plural by a replacive allomorph, like

/gis/ = /gus/ + /u > i/

These are *man, woman, goose, tooth, foot, louse,* and *mouse.* In *women* note that the replacive is not in the *-man, -men* syllable but in the first one, and goes like this:

/wɪmɨn/ = /wʊmən/ + / ʊ > ɪ / + / ə > ɨ/

4. One set of nouns has as the stem of the plural an allomorph that is different from the stem of the singular. The morpheme {calf}, for example, has /kæf/ as the singular allomorph but /kæv-/ as the plural allomorph, and the plural suffix /-z/ conforms to the voiced sound /v/. Changes in the phonemic form of allomorphs as they are grouped into words, or as they appear in different forms of a word, are called morphophonemic changes. Among the morphophonemic changes we have already noted for the plural are these:

calf	>	(= becomes) calves	/kæf/ > /kæv-/
child	>	children	/čaild/ > /čɨld-/

Each of these changes in an allomorph is an example of a morphophonemic change. Nouns in this group end in /-s/, /-f/, or /-θ/. Here are three examples:

house > houses	/hauzɨz/ = /haus/ + /s > z/ + /-ɨz/
knife > knives	/naivz/ = /naif/ + /f > v/ + /-z/
mouth > mouths	/mauðz/ = /maʊθ/ + /θ > ð/ + /-z/

Of the words in this group only *house* ends in /s/. Examples of the others are *half, loaf, self, wife, bath, path, oath.* Some nouns ending in /-f/ or /-θ/ do not make a morphophonemic change, like *chiefs;* others have two forms of the plural, like /yuθs/ or /yuðz/.

EXERCISE 117

★ Write in phonemic script the allomorphic formula for the formation of the plural of these words.

Example: brother brethren
/brɛðrɨn/ = /brəðər/ + /ə > ɛ/ + /ər > rɨn/

1. child
2. herring
3. foot
4. leaf
5. wolf

EXERCISE 118

★ Divide these words into two groups: (1) those which undergo no change of the base allomorph in the plural, e.g., "those two toughs"; (2) those which have two forms of the plural, e.g., *hoofs, hooves.* The words are *grief, scarf, chief, truth, wharf, sheath, belief, wreath, waif, staff.*

One Allomorph		*Two Allomorphs*	
______________	______________	______________	______________
______________	______________	______________	______________
______________	______________	______________	______________

Every language has its own ways of signaling plurality in nouns. In the Germanic tongues the suffixal consonants /-s/, /-n/, and /-r/ are common for this purpose. In Italian, on the other hand, the suffixal vowels /-i/ and /-e/ are employed. Chinese, an exception, does not signal plurality at all, save in the personal pronouns.

When foreign words are borrowed into English, their pronunciation becomes assimilated more or less to the phonemic system of English. This means that we follow our own native pronunciation habits as we utter these foreign words. Take, for example, the Italian noun *soprano* /soprano/. This is pronounced /səpræno/ by most Americans. We replace the first Italian /o/ by /ə/ because this accords with our way of pronouncing countless three-syllable words that have a primary stress on the medial syllable: /pəteto/, /bətænɪk/, /səfɪstɪk/, /məlɪgnənt/. And the Italian /a/ becomes /æ/ because it is our habit to pronounce *an* as /æn/ in many words like *abandon, mechanic, outlandish, pedantic, titanic.*

Now, what happens to the pluralizing morpheme of foreign nouns which are imported into English? Frequently this pluralizer is completely abandoned, and the adopted noun is made to conform to the allomorphic pattern of the English plural $\{-s_2\}$. An instance is the Italian *soprano,* which has lost its native plural of /soprani/ and is pluralized like any English word ending in a vowel /səprænoz/. And this has been the fate of many such Italian imports in *-o*: *piano, cello, solo, rondo, casino, studio, canto.* Spanish plurals — /-s/ after a vowel and /-ɛs/ after a consonant —

are so similar to the English that they seem to assimilate to English plural pattern without exception. Witness such borrowings from Spanish as *patio, mosquito, barbecue, cafeteria, guitar, cigar, lariat, canyon, alligator, tornado.*

On other occasions, the foreign spelling is retained but the pronunciation, with occasional exceptions, is modified. Thus the Latin singular and plural forms, *datum-data,* keep in English the original spelling, but the Latin plural /-a/ becomes /-ə/, whereas the Greek-Latin plural *phenomena,* with its classical /-a/ plural, may remain unchanged in English, though some speakers change it to /-ə/.

Many borrowed nouns have both plurals — their foreign ones, often modified, and the English plural, like *concerti* and *concertos, curricula* and *curriculums, syllabi* and *syllabuses.* The tendency is for such words to adopt the English $\{\text{-s}_2\}$, but some have proved resistant to change, like *agenda* and *alumni.*

EXERCISE 119

★ Look up the plurals of these words in your desk dictionary. Then write in phonemic script the pluralizing allomorph of each. If there are two pluralizers, write both.

Examples: criterion 1. /-z/ 2. /ən > ə/
thesis /ɨs/ > /iz/

1. alumna
2. formula
3. opus
4. appendix
5. stratum
6. hypothesis
7. cherub
8. apparatus
9. medium
10. stimulus
11. memorandum
12. virtuoso
13. nucleus
14. analysis
15. stadium

C. Noun Possessive

The noun possessive morpheme {-s_1} has the same phonologically conditioned allomorphs as the plural: /-s/, /-z/, and /-ɪz/. The term *possessive* is not a satisfactory label for this morpheme because a variety of different semantic relationships can exist between the possessive noun and the one that follows. The following cases will illustrate.

Relationship	*Example*
1. Possession or belongingness	John's hat Johnny's home
2. Characterization or description	a cowboy's walk men's coats
3. Origin	Raphael's paintings Cary's novels
4. Measure (time, value, space)	an hour's wait a dollar's worth a stone's throw
5. Subject of act	John's flight (John flew) the judge's decision (The judge decided)
6. Object of act	Jim's punishment was deserved (Someone punished Jim.) Eliot's critics were many. (They criticized Eliot.)

EXERCISE 120

★ Using the numbers above, indicate the relation shown between the italicized possessive and its following noun.

1. We missed the other car by a *hair's breadth.* ___
2. A *wren's song* floated through the window. ___
3. They were playing *children's games.* ___
4. The police provided for *Richard's protection.* ___
5. The *boy's jump* saved his life. ___
6. The *moon's beams* were brilliant that night. ___
7. *Willard's arrival* was a surprise. ___
8. He has never done a *day's work.* ___
9. She met *Dickie's father.* ___
10. She was irritated by *Bob's bragging.* ___

In making a choice between the possessive (*student's*) and the *of* structure (*of the student*), there is no hard-and-fast guideline, and often the form chosen depends on personal taste. The tendency, however, is to use the possessive with animate nouns, and the *of* structure with inanimate nouns; thus, *the dog's leg* but *the leg of the table.*

EXERCISE 121

★ This is an exercise to investigate the usage of the class in regard to the possessive {-s₁} in contrast to the *of* structure. You will be given pairs of sentences like this:

a. The *garage's* cement floor is cracking. ________

b. The cement floor *of the garage* is cracking. ________

If you would use only one of these forms, write *only* after the sentence containing that one. If you would use either without any particular preference, write *both* in both blanks. If you would give preference to one but might also use the other, write *pref* in the proper blank.

1a. The *building's roof* was blown off by the wind. ________

b. The roof *of the building* was blown off by the wind. ________

2a. The *soldier's* rifle had been thoroughly cleaned. ________

b. The rifle *of the soldier* had been thoroughly cleaned. ________

3a. The *lawn's* color had become brown. ________

b. The color *of the lawn* had become brown. ________

4a. We admired the *dog's* silky coat. ________

b. We admired the silky coat *of the dog.* ________

5a. The *hat's* brim was torn. ________

b. The brim *of the hat* was torn. ________

A quick tabulation on the board will show the extent to which the members of the class make a distinction between animate nouns (*soldier* and *dog*) and inanimate nouns (*building*, *lawn*, and *hat*) in their use of {-s₁} and the *of* structure.

D. Noun Feminine Forms

English has a small clutch of nouns with feminine derivational suffixes. All but one of these feminizing suffixes (*-ster*) are of foreign origin. They have been added to a masculine form or to a base morpheme. Here is a list of most of them, with examples of the feminine nouns to which they have been attached and the corresponding masculine forms.

	Suffix	*Masculine*	*Feminine*
1.	-e	fiancé	fiancée
2.	-enne	comedian	comedienne
3.	-ess	patron	patroness
4.	-etta	Henry	Henrietta
5.	-ette	farmer	farmerette
6.	-euse	masseur	masseuse
7.	-ina	George	Georgina
8.	-ine	hero	heroine
9.	-ster	spinner	spinster
10.	-stress	seamster	seamstress (= -ster + -ess)

These suffixes vary in vitality from *-ess*, the most productive, to *-stress*, which is completely dead. Two of them, *-enne* and *-euse*, occur only in words borrowed from French. The *-e*, also from French, is merely orthographic, and is not heard in the spoken word. The *-ster* is no longer a feminizing suffix but now indicates any person, usually male: *gangster*, *oldster*, *prankster*.

English also has about fifty pairs of words with separate forms for the masculine and the feminine, e.g., *bull*, *cow; uncle*, *aunt; gander*, *goose*. But these are a matter of lexicology rather than morphology, and we shall pass them by.

EXERCISE 122

★ Write the feminine form (or erstwhile feminine form) of these words.

1. Paul __________	8. equestrian __________
2. chanteur __________	9. angel __________
3. protégé __________	10. emperor __________
4. czar __________	11. launderer __________
5. songster __________	12. proprietor __________
6. major __________	13. waiter __________
7. heir __________	14. tricker __________

This concludes our look at the forms of the noun paradigm. We shall return to them again in our study of syntax. There our knowledge of the noun paradigm will help us to single out nouns in this simple way: If a word has two or more forms of the paradigm, we shall label it a noun, e.g.,

daughter daughter's daughters daughters'

But if it has only one form, like *golf*, it is not a noun by this paradigmatic test, although it may be shown to be a noun by other tests.

EXERCISE 123

★ Write N after every word that is a noun *according to the paradigmatic test* described above.

1. player ___	6. nation ___	11. chess ___
2. pray ___	7. uncle ___	12. field ___
3. sidewalk ___	8. discovery ___	13. pocket ___
4. chaos ___	9. together ___	14. game ___ (in playground context)
5. relax ___	10. shears ___	15. game ___ (in hunting context)

E. The Verb Paradigm

The next set of forms to come under our scrutiny is the verb paradigm. Verbs have three, four, or five forms. Those with four, like *learn* below, are the most common. The verb paradigm goes as follows:

Forms:	*Stem*	*Present Third-Person Singular*	*Present Participle*	*Past Tense*	*Past Participle*
Inflectional suffixes:		{-s_3}	{-ing_1}	{-d_1}	{-d_2}
Models:	learn	learns	learning	learned	learned
	choose	chooses	choosing	chose	chosen
	set	sets	setting	set	set

Each of these five forms has its own uses, which we shall now run through.

1. The first form is the stem. This occurs after *to* and after auxiliaries, such as *can* and *will*.

Examples: to *cut*, shall *look*

2. The present third-person singular is the form used with singular nouns, with *he*, *she*, *it*, and words for which these pronouns will substitute, and with word groups.

Examples: That *freshman* cuts his class every Wednesday.
He cuts his class every Wednesday.
Each is expected to do his duty.
Somebody has left a note for you.
Winning the championship cuts no ice with me.

The morpheme {-s_3} has the same allomorphs in the same distribution as the plural and possessive forms of the noun: /-s/, /-z/, and /ɪz/, as in *cuts*, *begs*, and *buzzes*.

3. The present participle is the {-ing_1} form. It combines with seven of the eight forms of *be* — *am, is, are, was, were, be, been* — to make verb phrases.

Examples: They *were writing* letters.
She must have *been sleeping*.

It is also used as a subjectless verbal in word groups like

His passion used to be *playing* golf.

4. The past tense takes on numerous forms, e.g., *shrunk, kept, led, began, rode, built, found, knew, swore, shook*. The most usual ones end in the allomorphs /-t/, /-d/, and /-ɪd/, as in *passed, pleased,* and *parted*.

5. The past participle also has numerous forms. Those most frequently occurring end in the same three sounds mentioned above, but here they are allomorphs of {-d_2}. The past participle is used with *have, has, had, having* to form verbal phrases.

Examples: She *has chosen* a stunning gown.
He *had* never *flown* in a helicopter.

It is also used with the forms of *be* to form the passive.

Examples: The orchestra *was chosen* by the committee.
By night the missing lad *had been* found.

EXERCISE 124

★ Fill out the following verb paradigms. Then indicate by a 3, 4, or 5 whether the verbs are three-form, four-form, or five-form.

Stem	*Pres. 3rd Sg.*	*Pres. P.*	*Past T.*	*Past P.*	*Number*
1. bid					
2. bite					
3. keep					
4. freeze					
5. set					
6. sell					
7. put					
8. rise					
9. tease					
10. sleep					

Most verbs follow faithfully the first three forms — the stem, the present third-person singular, and the present participle — with occasional exceptions like *does* and *says*, which have replacive allomorphs in the stem:

/dəz/ = /du/ + /u > ə/ + /-z/
/sɛz/ = /se/ + /e > ɛ/ + /-z/

And in the past tense and past participle, most verbs have identical forms, as in *learned, have learned; batted, have batted; cried, have cried.* Such are commonly known as regular verbs. It is because of the influence of this large number of verbs having this same pattern in the past tense and past participle that children utter such forms as *knowed, runned, drinked.* The child is simply following the pattern he knows best, and in so doing he creates what we call an analogical form.

There still remain, however, numerous verbs, many of them of high frequency, which form their past tense and past participle in various ways. If we should classify all English verbs according to the phonemic changes and patterns of change in the past tense and past participle, the total would amount to about fifty classes. This is hardly worth our time; an exercise in such classification will do to provide a sample of it.

EXERCISE 125

★ Write in phonemic symbols the past tense and past participle of each verb. Then classify the verbs into four classes according to the phonemic forms they have in common.

		Past Tense	*Past Participle*
Examples:	1. blow	*blu*	*blon*
	2. freeze	*froz*	*frozɨn*
	3. grow	*gru*	*gron*
	4. speak	*spok*	*spokɨn*

Class 1: *blow* and *grow*. $\{-d_1\}$ = /o > u/
$\{-d_2\}$ = /-n/

Class 2: *freeze* and *speak*. $\{-d_1\}$ = /i > o/
$\{-d_2\}$ = /i > o/ + /ɨn/

1. sting ________ ________
2. creep ________ ________
3. drive ________ ________
4. sing ________ ________
5. ride ________ ________
6. write ________ ________
7. cling ________ ________
8. ring ________ ________
9. keep ________ ________
10. deal ________ ________
11. swim ________ ________
12. spin ________ ________
13. win ________ ________
14. spring ________ ________

Class 1: ________________________________

Class 2: ________________________________

Class 3: ________________________________

Class 4: ________________________________

F. Suppletion

The next kind of verb form change we are going to examine, suppletion, had best be introduced by example. Let's look at the five-part verb *go*.

go goes going went gone

In this paradigm one form, *went*, seems out of place. It ought to be **goed*, or at least a word that begins with /g/. But the entire stem /go-/ has been replaced by a wholly different stem /wɛn-/. Such a total change within a paradigm is called suppletion, and the new form is a suppletive form. The suppletion here can be simply expressed by this diagram:

/wɛnt/ = /go > wɛn/ + /t/

One other English verb, *be*, has suppletive forms. The eight paradigmatic forms are

be am/is/are being was/were been

The stem is obviously *be*, and the alien forms that have intruded themselves into the paradigm — *am, is, are, was, were* — are the suppletive forms.

Suppletion is found in affixes as well as in stems. The plural allomorphs /-ɨn/ in *oxen* and /-rɨn/ in *children* and *brethren*, replacing the normal allomorphs of {-s_2}, are suppletive forms.

Knowledge of the verb paradigm is helpful in determining whether or not a given word should be classified as a verb. If a word can fit into three or more slots of the paradigm, we classify it as a verb. The word *begin* fits into all five positions

begin begins beginning began begun

and therefore is given the classification of verb.

With *cut*, however, the case is different. It does have three of the five possible forms:

cut cuts cutting cut cut

But it also fits partially into the noun paradigm

cut (singular) cuts (plural)

So we are faced with two homophonous *cut*'s, one a verb and the other a noun, and we cannot classify the isolated word. When it occurs in context, however, the matter is simple: "She is *cutting* the bread." *Cutting* is one verb form, and we can make substitutions showing the other verb forms:

She *cuts* the bread
She *cut* the bread yesterday

Obviously *cut* in this context is a verb. Likewise, in "He has a cut on his finger," we can substitute a plural form

He has several cuts on his finger

showing that *cut* here is a noun.

G. Auxiliaries

While we are on verbs, it will be convenient to look at a small group of structure words, ten in all, that associate with verbs and are called modal auxiliaries:

can	could
may	might
shall	should
will	would

must
ought (to)*

These modal auxiliaries precede verb stems and give them special shades of meaning like futurity, volition, possibility, probability, permission, and necessity. They are sometimes called verb markers because they signal that a verb is about to follow. The majority of the modals are said to have tense. In the first four pairs — *can, could; may, might; shall, should; will, would* — the second member may on occasion serve as the past tense of the first member. This is apparent in indirect discourse:

I think I *can* help you.
I thought I *could* help you.

Must and *ought* (*to*) do not have parallel forms, like the others. To express the past tense of *must,* in the sense of necessity, one says *had to,* e.g.,

This morning I *must* trim the hedge.
Yesterday I *had to* trim the hedge.

And for the past tense of *ought* (to), one uses *ought* (*to*)/*should* plus *have* plus a past participle, e.g.,

You *ought to* see those strawberries.
You *ought to*/*should have* seen those strawberries.

But often the ideas they express do not include an element of time. Here are all ten expressing delicate nuances of meaning exclusive of time, save that a notion of futurity is implicit in all of them.

May I help you?	You ought to be careful.
Might I help you?	Will you come again?
Can I help you?	Would you come again?
Could I help you?	Shall I return it?
You must be careful.	Should I return it?

* This account omits the uses of *dare* and *need* as auxiliaries. You might like to investigate their uses in questions and negative sentences.

On the whole, the meanings expressed are many and subtly shaded, and you are lucky that, as a native speaker, you already have a command of them.

In addition to these ten auxiliaries, there are three verbs which often function as auxiliaries and might be tagged as quasi auxiliaries. They are *be, do,* and *have.* Their forms which are used as auxiliaries are these:

have	be	do
has	am/is/are	does
having	being	—
had	was/were	did
	been	—

This group of quasi auxiliaries may precede the verb stem, the present participle, and the past participle: "I do *insist,*" "They are *studying,*" and "He has *finished.*"

When auxiliaries are employed in groups of two or three, an obligatory sequence is followed: modal + *have* + *be.*

Examples:	*modal*	*have*	*be*	
I	might	have	been	fishing/shot
George	may		be	reading/startled
They		had	been	sleeping/seen
She	must	have		quit

The quasi auxiliary *do* is a rather special case. It is reserved for questions, negative sentences, and emphatic affirmations.

Examples: *Do* you think so?
She *does* not believe it.
I *do* mean it.

EXERCISE 126

★ Give the number of auxiliaries, from 0 through 3, in each sentence.

1. I shall be waiting for you. ___
2. You ought to have done better. ___
3. Helen should have been working. ___
4. Mr. Owens has your car. ___
5. The elephant has been injured. ___

EXERCISE 127

★ Label the italicized auxiliaries as MA (modal auxiliaries) or QA (quasi auxiliaries).

1. Joyce was *being* attacked by the critics. _____

2. *Could* you hold this turkey for me? _____

3. *Did* he find the right address? _____

4. The maid *may* have committed the crime. _____

5. The net *was* lying in a heap. _____

EXERCISE 128

★ Underline the auxiliaries and make a check after those sentences which contain auxiliary sequences that do not follow the pattern of modal + *have* + *be*. The sequence may contain either two or three auxiliaries.

1. Those words must be justified. ___

2. She ought to have written her mother. ___

3. They could have come by plane. ___

4. The car could have been wrecked by that. ___

5. You might have mowed it shorter. ___

The behavior and patterning of auxiliaries differ from those of verbs in three respects.

1. A sentence with a verb can begin a conversation and be satisfactorily understood by the listener. Upon meeting a friend you might say, "I worked like a dog yesterday," and receive a nod of comprehension and sympathy. But if you used only an auxiliary in such an introductory sentence, "I could yesterday," your friend might look at you with concern and reply, "Could what?"

The point here is that an auxiliary is not used as a full verb. It may be used, however, as a substitute verb for a verb already mentioned, as in

He ate an orange and so *did* I.

Or it may be used in reference to a previously stated verb. For example, in reply to the question, "Are you going to the play?" you might say, "Yes, I may."

2. The negative of an auxiliary is made by putting *not* after it, or after the first auxiliary in a sequence:

They will *not* tell.
They have *not* been reporting the right figures.

This {nat} may take the form of *n't* /-ɪnt/, /-ənt/, or /-nt/. A negatived verb, on the contrary, requires a form of *do* plus *not* preceding the verb stem, thus:

I told him.
I *did not* tell him.

If the verb were negatived as the auxiliary is, we would get the non-English forms of

*I told not him.
*I toldn't him.

3. To make a question with an auxiliary, the subject and the auxiliary, or first auxiliary in a sequence, are reversed:

She can do a good job.
Can she do a good job?
The chairman has been told.
Has the chairman been told?

But with a verb we formulate a question by following the pattern *do* {du} + subject + stem verb:

They studied the constitution carefully.
Did they study the constitution carefully?

EXERCISE 129

★ Rewrite each sentence in two ways — as a negative and as a question. Then decide whether the italicized word is an auxiliary or a verb, using the criteria in paragraphs 2 and 3 immediately preceding this exercise. Indicate your decision by writing *Aux* or *V* in the blank at the right.

Example: She *began* working Neg. *She did not begin working.*
Q. *Did she begin working?* *V*

1. He *was* eating. Neg. ________________
Q. ________________ ______

2. He *quit* eating. Neg. ________________
Q. ________________ ______

3. The worker *was* killed. Neg. ________________
Q. ________________ ______

4. The worker *got* killed. Neg. ________________
Q. ________________ ______

5. We *must* hurry. Neg. ____________________

Q. ____________________ ______

6. We *had* to hurry. Neg. ____________________

Q. ____________________ ______

7. They *are* going. Neg. ____________________

Q. ____________________ ______

8. They *kept* going. Neg. ____________________

Q. ____________________ ______

9. He *might* have been sleeping. Neg. ____________________

Q. ____________________ ______

10. He *used* to play. Neg. ____________________

Q. ____________________ ______

One of the clues to the classification of a word as a verb is its participation in the verb paradigm. If a word fits into three or more of the five slots in this paradigm, we label it a verb.

EXERCISE 130

★ Take a quick look again at the noun and verb paradigms. Then, using membership in a paradigm as a criterion, classify these words as N (noun), V (verb), or NV (both noun and verb)

1. driver ______
2. compliment ______
3. appear ______
4. world ______
5. agency ______
6. agonize ______
7. truck ______
8. decide ______
9. emotion ______
10. book ______
11. bird ______
12. join ______
13. end ______
14. morning ______
15. variety ______
16. mother ______

17. grammar ______ 19. note ______

18. melt ______ 20. carve ______

H. The Comparable Paradigm

The comparable paradigm is as follows:

Forms:	*Stem*	*Comparative*	*Superlative*
Inflectional suffixes:		{-er$_1$}	{-est$_1$}
Models:	sweet	sweeter	sweetest
	deadly	deadlier	deadliest
	friendly	friendlier	friendliest
	soon	sooner	soonest

This paradigm is followed by these groups:

1. Nearly all one-syllable adjectives, e.g., *hot, small, proud.*
2. Some two-syllable adjectives, especially those ending in *-ly* and *-y*, e.g., *lovely, funny, polite.*
3. A few adverbials of one or two syllables, e.g., *fast, early.*
4. One preposition, *near*, as in "She sat nearest the door."

Other adjectives and adverbs usually take a preceding *more* or *most* in lieu of the inflectional *-er* and *-est.*

EXERCISE 131

★ Here is a list of two-syllable adjectives. Write the comparative and superlative forms, *-er* and *-est*, of those that you would inflect in this way.

1. angry ______ ______ 11. quiet ______ ______

2. healthy ______ ______ 12. remote ______ ______

3. bitter ______ ______ 13. severe ______ ______

4. common ______ ______ 14. solid ______ ______

5. cruel ______ ______ 15. stupid ______ ______

6. foolish ______ ______ 16. noble ______ ______

7. handsome ______ ______ 17. dusty ______ ______

8. honest ______ ______ 18. dirty ______ ______

9. mellow ______ ______ 19. lively ______ ______

10. pleasant ______ ______ 20. gentle ______ ______

EXERCISE 132

★ Here is a list of adverbials of one and two syllables. Write out the comparative and superlative forms of those that you would inflect with *-er* and *-est.* Write *no* after the adverbials which you would not use with any comparative or superlative at all.

1. often ______ ______
2. seldom ______ ______
3. already ______ ______
4. gently ______ ______
5. late ______ ______
6. ahead ______ ______
7. weekly ______ ______
8. perhaps ______ ______
9. sidewise ______ ______
10. slow ______ ______
11. under ______ ______
12. near ______ ______
13. upward ______ ______
14. far ______ ______
15. quick ______ ______
16. above ______ ______
17. loud ______ ______
18. quickly ______ ______
19. high ______ ______
20. low ______ ______

A few adjectives have suppletive and irregular forms in the comparative and superlative, like *good*:

good better best

Thus the morpheme {good} has three allomorphs: /gʊd/, /bɛt-/, and /bɛ-/. The allomorphic diagrams of *better* and *best* go like this:

/bɛtər/ = /gʊd > bɛt-/ + /-ər/
/bɛst/ = /gʊd > bɛ-/ + /-st/

In the last one, the /-st/ is an allomorph of {-est$_1$}, spelled *-est.*

EXERCISE 133

★ Write the forms of the comparative and superlative of these words.

1. well ______ ______
2. bad, ill, badly ______ ______
3. little ______ ______
4. much, many ______ ______
5. old ______ ______

The capacity to take the inflectional suffixes *-er* and *-est* is one of the signals that enables us to distinguish adjectives from nouns in the position of modifier preceding a noun. In the cluster *a stone fence,* the *stone* is not an adjective because we would never say *a stoner fence* or *a stonest fence.*

EXERCISE 134

★ In the blanks write A (adjective) or NA (nonadjective) to label the italicized words.

1. the *light* plane ______
2. the *night* plane ______
3. a *strange* idea ______
4. a *glass* vase ______
5. his *steel* file ______
6. that *clay* pot ______
7. her *red* davenport ______
8. a *dull* volume ______
9. a *bound* volume ______
10. my *close* friend ______

I. The Adverb *-ly* Paradigm

This paradigm, which is very simple, has been presented on page 120.

EXERCISE 135

★ Review the adverbial $\{\text{-ly}_1\}$ and its homophones on pages 116–117. Then place a check after each word that qualifies as an adverb.

1. swiftly ___
2. homely ___
3. softly ___
4. costly ___
5. deftly ___
6. richly ___
7. neatly ___
8. yearly ___
9. beastly ___
10. sourly ___

J. Paradigm of Personal Pronouns

The paradigm of personal pronouns is as follows:

SINGULAR

	Subject	*Object*	*Prenominal Possessive*	*Substitutional Possessive*
1st	I	me	my	mine
2nd	you	you	your	yours
3rd M	he	him	his	his
F	she	her	her	hers
N	it	it	its	its
		PLURAL		
1st	we	us	our	ours
2nd	you	you	your	yours
3rd	they	them	their	theirs
	who	whom	whose	whose

The personal pronouns might be presented like the other four paradigms, showing the stems and inflectional suffixes; but since the group is a small, closed one (not admitting new members), it will suffice to deal with its members as a set of related forms.

Let us look at them through the framework terms.

1. NUMBER. You are already acquainted with the terms *singular* and *plural*, with their meanings of "one" and "more than one." One difference from noun number here is that *we* does not mean more than one *I* but *I* and somebody else. The singular and plural have the same *you* forms. Earlier in our history the singular forms were *thou, thee, thy, thine*. These were in everyday use by the English who settled our country in the early 1600s, and you meet them in Shakespeare's plays and the King James Bible, both of the same period. They survive today in liturgical language and, partially, in the speech of the Friends.

2. FUNCTION TERMS

a. The pronouns in the *subject* column are those used in the functions of subject of the verb and subjective complement.

Examples: The Smiths and *we* are going to the ballet.
It was *she* who missed the test.

b. The pronouns in the *object* column are those which function mainly as objects of the verb and of the preposition.

Examples: I gave *her* the letter yesterday.
We saw *her* in the car.
A package came from George and *him*.

c. The prenominal possessives occur before nouns.

Example: With *my* brains and *your* industry we could make a fortune.

d. The substitutional possessives occur as substitutes for nouns.

Examples: That lawn mower is *ours* (= our lawn mower).
Yours (= your term paper) was the best.

3. PERSON
   a. The first person in the singular denotes the speaker. In the plural it denotes the speaker plus anybody else, one or more.
   b. The second person denotes the person or persons spoken to.
   c. The third person denotes those other than the speaker or those spoken to.

4. SEX REFERENCE. Only three of the horizontal rows of pronouns have sex reference — the *he, she,* and *it* rows. The *it* can refer to certain creatures of either sex — *infant, dog, pig* — and to sexless things — *story, stone, justice.*

The *who* forms are distinctive in that they are both singular and plural, masculine and feminine, and embrace all three persons. They have human reference as opposed to the non-human reference of *which,* though there are intermediate words which are referred to by both *who* and *which.*

EXERCISE 136

★ Fill in the blanks with *who* or *which* or *both.* After the sentence indicate whether the reference is H (human) or NH (nonhuman).

1. That's the girl ______________ won all the honors. ______
2. The council listened to the citizens ______________ presented the petition. ______
3. It was the spotted kitten ______________ ran under the porch. ______
4. We feared the enemy ______________ was across the hill. ______
5. The coffee ______________ you bought is stale. ______

EXERCISE 137

★ Place in each blank within the sentence either a prenominal or a substitutional possessive. In the blank after the sentence classify the one you used by a PP or a SP.

1. This is ______________ seat. ______
2. This seat is ______________. ______
3. Have you seen ______________ canary? ______
4. I compared it to ______________. ______
5. ______________ is a poor bathing suit. ______
6. I'd prefer one like ______________. ______
7. Where is ______________ friend today? ______
8. ______________ bucket is leaking. ______
9. He found it with ______________. ______
10. She bought ______________ sister a compact. ______

K. Substitute Groups

Personal pronouns furnish the basis for classifying nouns into different "substitute groups." That is to say, nouns are put into different classes according to the personal pronouns which can be substituted for them. Knowing the membership of a noun in one class or another is useful in grammatical analysis. We have already used the *it* and *they* substitute groups to settle questions of number.

The eleven substitute groups below that we shall use are those set up by Professor W. Nelson Francis.* The slant line means "or."

Pronoun Substitutes	*Examples*
1. he	father, husband
2. she	mother, wife
3. it	water, bush
4. he/she	student, cousin
5. he/it	rooster, boar
6. she/it	hen, sow
7. he/she/it	baby, chicken
8. it/they	committee, squad
9. he/she/they	everybody, person
10. it (no plural)	furniture, physics
11. they (no singular)	cattle, trousers

* From *The Structure of American English* (New York, Ronald Press, 1958), pp. 250–251. Slight change here in form of presentation.

All these classes except the tenth have *they* as a substitute for the plural forms. It must be understood that *he*, *she*, and *they* are meant to include their inflected forms *him*, *her*, *them*. Class membership depends on meaning, and as meaning shifts in the course of events, so does membership in the substitute groups. Not many years ago, for example, *nurse* would have been in the *she* group, but today, with the advent of trained male nurses, it belongs in the *he/she* group.

EXERCISE 138

★ In the blank write the number of the substitute group to which each word belongs.

1. queen __
2. duke __
3. parent __
4. cow __
5. bull __
6. shears __
7. poetry __
8. congregation __
9. sidewalk __
10. somebody __
11. sheep __
12. daughter __
13. grandson __
14. lawyer __
15. gander __
16. mare __
17. board (of people) __
18. painter __
19. book __
20. pants __

XI.

Four Processes of Word Formation

We shall now look at four common processes by which words have been formed in the past and are still being formed — clipping, acronymy, blending, and back-formation.

A. Clipping

Clipping means cutting off the beginning or the end of a word, or both, leaving a part to stand for the whole. The resultant form is called a clipped word. The jargon of the campus is filled with clipped words: *lab, dorm, prof, exam, gym, prom, math, psych, mike,* and countless others. As these examples suggest, the clipping of the end of a word is the most common, and it is mostly nouns that undergo this process. Clipping results in new free forms in the language, and sometimes in the creation of new morphemes, like *prof* and *mike.*

EXERCISE 139

★ Give the original words from which these clipped words were formed.

1. ad ________________ 3. taxi ________________

2. gas ________________ 4. cab ________________

5. frat ______ 10. memo ______

6. photo ______ 11. Fred ______

7. gin ______ 12. Al ______

8. brandy ______ 13. Tom ______

9. curio ______ 14. Joe ______

15. Phil ______

Less common than the back-clipped words, like the foregoing, are those words which lose their forepart, like *plane* and *phone*.

EXERCISE 140

★ Give the original words from which these clipped words were formed.

1. sport (game) ______ 6. wig ______

2. pike (road) ______ 7. cute ______

3. bus ______ 8. Gene ______

4. cello ______ 9. Beth ______

5. coon ______ 10. Bert ______

Only a very few words have been formed by both fore and aft clipping. Three common ones are *flu, Liz,* and *still* (apparatus for distilling hard liquor).

Clipped words are formed not only from individual words but from grammatical units, such as modifier plus noun. *Paratrooper*, for example, is a clipped form of *parachutist trooper*. In cases like this, it is often the first part that is shortened while the second part remains intact.

EXERCISE 141

★ Give the original of these clipped words.

1. Amerindian ______

2. maître d' /metər di/ ______

3. Eurasian ______

4. newsboy ______________________

5. medicare ______________________

Clipped words usually occur first in slang and argot, and some then make their way into Standard English. Most people do not realize that the following Standard English words were once longer forms: *chap, gin, mob, extra, quack*.

B. Acronymy

Acronymy is the process whereby a word is formed from the initials or beginning segments of a succession of words. In some cases the initials are pronounced, as in MP (military police, or Member of Parliament). In others, the initials and/or beginning segments are pronounced as the spelled word would be. For example, *NATO* (North Atlantic Treaty Organization) is pronounced as /neto/ and *radar* (radio detecting and ranging) as /redar/.

EXERCISE 142

★ Pronounce these acronyms and give their originals.

1. WAC ______________________
2. MC (Look up *emcee.*) ______________________
3. UNESCO ______________________
4. DDT ______________________
5. Loran ______________________
6. AWOL ______________________
7. GI ______________________
8. VIP ______________________
9. jeep ______________________
10. NAM ______________________

In the last thirty years there has been a great increase in the use of acronyms. They tend to abound in large organizations — for instance, in the army, in government, and in big business — where they offer neat ways of expressing long and cumbersome terms. The very names of some businesses have been acronymized, like *Nabisco, Socony,* and *Alcoa.* Many acronyms are used and understood only by initiates in a given field, like the military *CQ, TDY,* and *BOQ,* whereas others gain general currency, like *GI, CO,* and *PX.* It is likely that you employ some campus acronyms that would not be understood elsewhere.

C. Blending

Blending is the fusion of two words into one, usually the first part of one word with the last part of another, as in *brunch,* from *breakfast* and *lunch.* The resultant blend partakes of both original meanings. Many blends are nonce words, here today and gone tomorrow, and relatively few become part of the standard lexicon. The two classes, blends and clipped words are not sharply separated, and some words may be put into either class.

EXERCISE 143

★ Give the originals of these blends.

1. smog ________________
2. telecast ________________
3. motel ________________
4. electrocute ________________
5. splatter ________________

EXERCISE 144

★ Give the blends that result from fusing these words.

1. happening + circumstance = ________________
2. automobile + omnibus = ________________
3. escalade + elevator = ________________
4. blare or blow + spurt = ________________
5. squall + squeak = ________________

D. Back-Formation

If someone should ask you, "What does a *feeper* do?" you would probably answer, "He feeps, of course." You would answer thus because there exist in your mind such word-pairs as *tell-teller*, *reap-reaper*, *write-writer*, *sing-singer;* and you would reason, perhaps unconsciously, that on the analogy of these forms the word *feeper* must have a parallel verb *feep*. Likewise, centuries ago, after the introduction of the nouns *peddler*, *beggar*, *swindler*, and *editor* into our language, speakers followed the same analogy and created the verbs *peddle*, *beg*, *swindle*, and *edit*. This process is just the reverse of our customary method of word formation, whereby we begin with a verb like *speak* and, by adding the agent morpheme {-er$_2$}, form the noun *speaker*. The process is called back-formation. It may be defined as the formation of a word from one that looks like its derivative. A recent example is *team-teach*, from the noun *team-teacher* or *team-teaching*.

EXERCISE 145

1. The noun *greed* is a back-formation from the adjective *greedy*. Write four pairs of words that constitute an analogy for the creation of *greed*.

   ________ ________

   ________ ________

   ________ ________

   ________ ________

2. In common use in English are the pairs *revise-revision* and *supervise-supervision*. From this analogy what verb is back-formed from *television?*______

3. English has many pairs on the pattern of *create-creation*, *separate-separation*, and *deviate-deviation*. On this analogy what back-formation would you expect from *donation* and *oration?* ________________ and ________________

EXERCISE 146

★ These verbs are back-formations. Write the words from which they are formed.

1. bootleg ________________
2. typewrite ________________
3. coronate ________________
4. resurrect ________________
5. baby-sit ________________
6. advance-register __________
7. laze __________
8. jell __________
9. escalate __________
10. reminisce __________

XII.

Determiners and Prepositions

A. Determiners

With the treatment of back-formation we conclude our brisk run through English morphology. But before beginning the next section, syntax, it is desirable that we take up two small classes of words, determiners and prepositions.

A determiner is a word that patterns with a noun. It precedes the noun and serves as a signal that a noun is soon to follow, very much as the presence of an auxiliary announces that a verb is coming.

Example: *The* gymnasium

If the noun has modifiers, the determiner precedes them, too.

Examples: *The* old gymnasium
The old, red-brick gymnasium

The absence of a determiner to signal a following noun will sometimes produce ambiguity. Here is a case from a newspaper headline:

Union demands increase.

We do not know how to interpret *increase* because a signal is absent. An auxiliary would show that it is a verb:

Union demands *will* increase.

And a determiner would indicate that it is a noun:

Union demands *an* increase.

The following is a partial list of determiners:

a/an	my	this
the	our	that
her	their	these
his	your	those
its	John's (any possessive of name)	

Six of these determiners may also be used in place of a noun, that is, as noun-substitutes.

Examples: *That* will be enough.
I prefer *Elizabeth's*.
What can one do with old cars like *these?*
I can't tell Jim's tennis shoes from *his*.

EXERCISE 147

★ In the blanks write a D (determiner) or NS (noun-substitute) to show the category of the italicized word.

1. Do you like *my* new hat? ______
2. Do you like *this?* ______
3. Have you *a* match? ______
4. *These* fellows are my new teammates. ______
5. *These* are my new teammates. ______
6. We did not disturb *George's* room. ______
7. *Its* roots grew under the pavement. ______
8. Have you seen *our* formals? ______
9. *This* cold is invigorating. ______
10. *Smith's* house is for sale. ______
11. *His* is the best plan. ______
12. Where are *the* red phlox you planted? ______
13. *That* deep pool is a good place for trout. ______

14. Jack has *an* interest in grinding rocks. ______

15. *Your* slip is showing. ______

EXERCISE 148

★ Each of these newspaper headlines is ambiguous, that is, can be read in two ways. Add a determiner to each in such a way that a noun will be identified and the meaning reduced to a single one.

1. Police raid gathering ______________________________
2. Complete faculty at State ______________________________
3. Rule book not obscene ______________________________
4. Clean model house ______________________________
5. Girl shows top baby beef* ______________________________

B. Prepositions

Prepositions are words like *of*, *in*, and *to* which are usually followed by a noun, personal pronoun, or noun-substitute called the object of the preposition.

Examples: George was tired *of* them.
George sat *between* the two deans.
He liked the filling *in* the sandwich.

English has a small group of prepositions, of which the most frequently used ones are *at*, *by*, *for*, *from*, *in*, *of*, *on*, *to*, and *with*. Those in greatest use are, in order of frequency, *of*, *in*, and *to*. These one-syllable prepositions have weak or third stress in their common uses.

Examples: He came wĭth the girl.
That is the girl wĭth whom he came.
That is the girl whom he came wĭth.
That is the girl he came wĭth.

In the passive construction, formed with *be* plus a past participle, the preposition ends the structure, has no object, and takes third stress.

Examples: The clerk was spóken tò.
The speaker was láughed àt.

---

* *Baby beef* means calves, which farm boys and girls exhibit at fairs.

Monosyllabic prepositions now and then take a primary stress instead of a weak or third stress. Compare

I came wĭth hér   I came wíth hĕr
There was no cóurage ĭn hĭm.   There was no courage ín hìm.

Such changes of stress are not predictable.

EXERCISE 149

★ Underline the preposition and show by a stress mark how you pronounce it. Underline the object twice. If there is no object, write NO in the blank after the sentence.

1. The car stopped at the station. ______
2. He came from the farm. ______
3. This is the farm he came from. ______
4. These roses are for you. ______
5. The chimpanzee in the cage was yawning. ______
6. The lad stood on a barrel. ______
7. The plumber washed in the basin. ______
8. This basin has been washed in. ______
9. He objected to the last paragraph. ______
10. The part he objected to was the last paragraph. ______

Among our prepositions are a number of two-syllable ones, such as *about, above, after, against, among, before, behind, below, beneath, between, despite, except, inside, into, beyond, outside, under, upon.* These are different from the one-syllable prepositions in their stress behavior. You will find this out for yourself in the next exercise.

EXERCISE 150

★ You are given here a series of sentences containing two-syllable prepositions. The stresses are supplied. Using these sentences as your data, make a generalization explaining the operation of stresses in dissyllabic prepositions. It would be advisable to test your generalization by composing more sentences in the pattern given, to see if your conclusion is sound.

1. The sheriff came àftĕr Clarence.
2. The sheriff came áfter him.
3. We walked ùndĕr the tree.
4. We walked únder it.
5. The party advanced ìntŏ the jungle grass.
6. The party advanced ínto it.
7. Henderson stood bĕfòre the judge.
8. Henderson stood befóre him.
9. She knew everything ăbòut Einar.
10. She knew everything abóut him.

Generalization: ____

____

____

Some of these words we have been dealing with can be either prepositions or adverbials. Compare

Preposition: She looked *up* the stairs.
Adverbial: She looked *up*.
Preposition: They went *inside* the house.
Adverbial: They went *inside*.

EXERCISE 151

★ Underline the prepositions once and the adverbials twice. Put the proper stress marks on these words.

1. The swimmers waited below.
2. The swimmers waited below the dam.
3. She liked to sit near.
4. She sat near the window.
5. The paint bucket fell off the porch.
6. The paint bucket fell off.
7. The refreshments came after.
8. The refreshments came after the program.
9. I haven't seen him since.
10. I haven't seen him since yesterday.

In addition to the prepositions already mentioned, there is in English a group of *-ing* prepositions which have a verb as a stem. Here are some of the more common: *assuming, beginning, barring, concerning, considering, during, following, including, pending, regarding, succeeding.**

Examples: *Considering* your loss, the bill will not be sent.
Assuming the accuracy of the report, action must be taken at once.
We will delay the papers, *pending* arrival of the contract.

EXERCISE 152

★ Underline the *-ing* prepositions once and the *-ing* verbs twice.

1. Barring accidents, the picnic will begin at eleven.
2. There will be a smoker following dinner.
3. She is only following her orders after all.
4. May I have a conference regarding my examination?
5. He was regarding the newcomer with curiosity.
6. Considering the time, we had better stop now.
7. The entire squad, including the water boy, will make the trip.
8. I am including damage to my window in the bill.
9. The store will be closed weekends, beginning Saturday.
10. He was vague concerning the details.

The final group is composed of compound prepositions. These are relatively numerous and of various types. Often it is difficult to say whether a word group should be considered a preposition or not. Here is a short list of two types.

Two-Part	*With Noun*
together with	on account of
contrary to	in spite of
ahead of	with regard to
due to	in advance of
apart from	in front of
up to	on behalf of
out of	in place of
away from	in lieu of
up at	in addition to
as for	by way of

* The stem of *during* is *dure*, an obsolete English verb meaning "to last." The stem of *pending* is *pend-*, which comes from a French base meaning "to hang, suspend."

Two-Part	*With Noun*
inside of	in comparison with
aside from	in reference to
as concerns	with respect to
because of	in event of
owing to	for the sake of
instead of	by dint of
	in case of
	by means of

Those in the first column it is simplest to call compound prepositions. In the second column we seem to have either a compound preposition or two successive prepositional phrases (when an object is added after the last word). One argument for calling them compound prepositions is that we normally do not place modifiers before the noun following the first preposition, as we can do with ordinary prepositional phrases. For example, in *with respect to,* the word *respect* is not modified.

EXERCISE 153

★ Underline the compound prepositions.

1. We arrived ahead of time.
2. The game was called on account of rain.
3. The oldest daughter is up at the camp.
4. Contrary to our expectations, the movie was a delightful spoof.
5. The board had a meeting with reference to the new building.
6. I want to thank you on behalf of these refugees.
7. They served rice instead of potatoes.
8. They served rice in lieu of potatoes.
9. In spite of her protestations, Harriet was persuaded to join the guild.
10. The foreman received a letter with respect to alleged violations.

part three

SYNTAX

XIII.

Noun and Verb Clusters

Up to this point we have examined systematically the phonemic and morphemic structure of English. Now we shall see how words are combined into larger structures — phrases, clauses, and sentences. This is the domain of syntax. The syntactic architecture of the English sentence is extraordinarily complex and can be blueprinted by various methods, none of them perfect. In the presentation which follows, you will be shown the main outlines only, with the admonition that there are different ways of interpreting the same syntactic facts and that English syntax contains territories as yet uncharted.

A noun cluster consists of a noun and all the words and word groups that belong with the noun and cluster around it. The noun itself is called the *headword* or *head,* and the other words and word groups are modifiers of the noun.

Examples: The yellow *tulips*
The yellow *tulips* in the garden
The yellow *tulips* in the garden which were gaily blooming

In these examples *tulips* is the head. Of the rest of the words, the modifiers, we observe that the single-word modifiers, like *the* and *yellow,* precede the head and that the word-group modifiers, like *in the garden* and *which were gaily blooming,* follow the head.

EXERCISE 154

★ Underline the head of the following noun clusters.

1. The fence
2. The old fence
3. That new aluminum fence
4. The fence between the houses
5. The old fence which was painted green
6. The old fence between the houses which was painted green
7. A worn-out putter
8. My worn-out putter lying in the attic
9. A used car, broken down by abusive driving
10. The children's swings in the park which were in use all day long

EXERCISE 155

★ Make each list of words into a noun cluster and underline the headword.

1. Table, the, small, study
2. European, any, opera, great
3. Somber, evening, that, sky
4. My, shoes, roommate's, tennis, dirty
5. Linen, white, handkerchiefs, the, other, all
6. Soft, a, on the head, pat
7. Hard, a, which staggered him, blow
8. Ski, that, lying in the basement, broken
9. With a lame leg, a, who was walking on crutches, junior
10. The, in the front row, whose books he was carrying, girl

Most sentence positions which are occupied by nouns can also be occupied by noun clusters:

Examples: *Boys* often build dams in the spring.
Small boys who are not in school often build dams in the spring.
Jim wanted a *car*.
Jim wanted a *new sports car with wire wheels which would have a fast getaway*.

EXERCISE 156

★ Expand the italicized nouns by adding modifiers before, after, or both before and after. Then underline these noun clusters.

Example: The *lock* was broken.
Expanded: The rusty lock on the front door was broken.

1. *Sailboats* are beautiful to watch.
2. They sailed under the *bridge*.
3. He makes *jewelry*.
4. The player under the basket is my *brother*.
5. I gave the *cat* a dish of milk.
6. Her mother buys *chairs* at auctions and refinishes them.
7. *Camping* is not always fun.
8. She makes *pottery* on her wheel at home.
9. It is good exercise to do long cross-countries on *skis*.
10. The doctor remains in his *office* till five.

A verb cluster consists of a verb and all the words and word groups which belong with the verb and cluster around it. The verb itself is called the *headword* or *head*, and the other words and word groups are the auxiliaries, modifiers, and complements of the verb. *The complements* is the generic term for the completers of the verb, which we shall later learn to know as direct object, indirect object, object complement, and subjective complement (with its subclasses of predicate noun, predicate pronoun, and predicate adjective).

Examples: soon *arrived*
arrived late
soon *arrived* at the station
arrived just as the plane came in
was *waiting* at the door
may have been *stolen* by the cashier

EXERCISE 157

★ Underline the head in these verb clusters.

1. Stepped lightly
2. Stepped into the room

3. Quickly stepped in
4. Stepped where he was told
5. At once shouted to the crowd to stand back
6. Without hesitation shouted for help
7. Were watching for the signal
8. Had been eaten by the cat
9. Would have driven to the fair
10. Spoke loudly

Here are some verb clusters containing complements. Never mind the details now, for you will study them later; just notice that the words in the cluster are connected with the verb.

Examples: *built* a scooter
built his son a scooter
seemed gloomy and dejected
elected George a member of the fraternity
became president of his class

EXERCISE 158

★ Underline the head of these verb clusters.

1. Sold his last semester's books
2. Sold me his last semester's books
3. Appeared happy in his new job
4. Always chose Sally chairman of the dishwashing committee
5. Still remained the best candidate
6. Cheerfully gave a handsome contribution
7. Never paid his bills on time
8. At once called his uncle a brick
9. Often was weary after his workout
10. Soon returned the book he had borrowed

Many English sentences can be divided into two parts, one consisting of a noun cluster, the other a verb cluster.

EXERCISE 159

★ Draw a vertical line separating these sentences into a noun cluster and a verb cluster. Underline the noun head and the verb head.

1. The red pony in the pasture galloped along the fence.
2. Many students attended the Christmas party.

3. The senior who sells the most tickets will be honored at the prom.
4. The pipes in the classroom pounded noisily.
5. The choir in the loft sang the last hymn softly.

In sentences like these, the headword of the noun cluster is the subject of the verb, which you will hear more about shortly. The entire cluster may be called the modified or the complete subject. The verb cluster is called the predicate.

EXERCISE 160

★ Add a verb cluster to each of these noun clusters, making complete sentences.

1. The tiny leak in the hose ______________________________
2. The canoe that he wanted ______________________________
3. The pie ______________________________
4. The steaming apple pie ______________________________
5. The passenger in the front seat who was watching the speedometer ______________________________

EXERCISE 161

★ Add a noun cluster to introduce each of the following verb clusters, making complete sentences.

1. ... later regretted his decision. ______________________________
2. ... came after his dog when school was over. ______________________________
3. ... will soon return to college. ______________________________
4. ... always seemed to have a complaint to make. ______________________________
5. ... merrily swung the heavy pack on his back to begin the long hike. ______________________________

XIV.

Basic Sentence Patterns

We do not speak English by merely stringing words together in some random fashion. Instead, we carefully arrange our words, for the most part unconsciously, into patterns. In English we use a limited number of basic sentence patterns and a multitude of subpatterns. It will now be our purpose to examine the basic sentence patterns of English. Any sentence you speak will probably be based on one of these patterns. Included in the patterns are these five basic function classes: subject of verb, subjective complement, direct object of verb, indirect object of verb, object complement, and predicator (= verb).

The first three patterns have only *be* as their verb. It is necessary to give *be* this special treatment because it behaves somewhat differently from other verbs. And it is to be remembered that *be* has eight different forms: *am, is, are, was, were, be, being, been.*

A. Pattern 1: N *be* Adj

Food is good.

At first let us notice the relationship between the noun and the verb. If we change the noun to the plural form, *those foods,* we must also change the verb form *is* to *are.* We describe this noun-verb relationship by saying that the noun is "tied to" or "agrees with" the verb. And the noun in the sentence which is tied to the verb is called the subject of the verb. Thus *food* is the subject of the verb *is*. More about this concept when we reach pattern 4.

In pattern 1 the third term must be an adjective or adjectival:*

That food is *poisonous*.

You can test for pattern 1 in a simple way. It is capable of this expansion:

That food is good > That good food is very good.
That food is poisonous > That poisonous food is very poisonous.

If a sentence will not undergo this expansion, it belongs to some pattern other than pattern 1. For example, the sentence

My mother is outside

cannot be expanded to

My outside mother is very outside.

So this sentence does not belong to the pattern 1 type. The adjective in pattern 1 is in function a subjective complement, subclass predicate adjective.

EXERCISE 162

★ Apply the expansion test to see which of these sentences belong to pattern 1. Write 1 after such sentences.

1. The box is large. ___
2. The box is here. ___
3. My mother is kind. ___
4. My mother is out. ___
5. The boys were busy. ___
6. The boys were upstairs. ___
7. The dahlias have been lovely. ___
8. The party must have been enjoyable. ___
9. The party was afterward. ___
10. The car is inside. ___

---

* The difference between these two will be explained in the next chapter. In this chapter we shall use *adjective* for both.

The foregoing test for pattern 1 does not work in all cases. Nor, for that matter, does any grammatical rule or test unless accompanied by exceptions and qualifications. There is a limited number of adjectives that can occur in either the first or the second slot, but not in both, in a pattern 1 sentence like

The ________________ food (= any noun) is very ________________.

For example, many adjectives like *afraid, ashamed, aware, aghast* are used only in the second slot, and some of these do not go with *very.*

EXERCISE 163

★ Place a 1 after those adjectives which can occur only before the noun, a 2 after those which can occur only after a form of *be*, and *both* after those which may be placed in both positions.

1. main ______	6. fresh ______
2. old ______	7. mere ______
3. ablaze ______	8. principal ______
4. chief ______	9. due ______
5. alive ______	10. weekly ______

Such exceptions apart, this test does serve to distinguish pattern 1 from pattern 2.

B. Pattern 2: N *be* UW (=uninflected word)

The girl is here.

Pattern 2 differs from pattern 1 in these respects:

1. The verb *be* often, but not always, has a meaning something like "be located" or "occurs," whereas the *be* of pattern 1 means "may be described as."

2. Pattern 2 is not capable of taking the pattern 1 expansion.

3. The third position is occupied by an uninflected word like *here, there, up, down, in, out, inside, outside, upstairs, downstairs, on, off, now, then, soon, tomorrow, yesterday, over, through, above, below, before, after.* (*Up, in,* and *out* are partially and/or irregularly inflected with the forms *upper, uppermost, inner, inmost, innermost, outer, outermost, utmost, outmost.*) For most words in the third position one can substitute *there* or *then.*

Examples: The pingpong table is downstairs.
The game was yesterday.
The balls are outdoors.

Often a prepositional phrase with a *there* or *then* meaning will occupy the third position.

Examples: The wolf is at the door.
The game will be at three o'clock.

EXERCISE 164

★ After each sentence place a number 1 or 2 to identify the pattern it conforms to.

1. The picnic was outside. ___
2. The picnickers were gay. ___
3. The batter is tall. ___
4. The batter is inside. ___
5. They are on the lawn. ___
6. Our appointment is now. ___
7. The meeting will be in an hour. ___
8. The dean is in. ___
9. The dean is benevolent. ___
10. The bunks are below. ___

C. Pattern 3: N^1 *be* N^1

My brother is a doctor.

The superscript after the second noun means that this noun has the same referent as N^1; that is, both *brother* and *doctor* refer to the same person. The meaning of *be* in pattern 3 is "be classified as." The noun in the third position is called the subjective complement, subclass predicate noun. Personal pronouns also occupy this position, e.g.,

This is *shé*.
It's *mé*.
It was *théy*.
That is *míne*.

Such pronouns in the subjective complement position take primary stress.

The following sentences are examples of pattern 3:

Those coeds must be roommates.
They are my friends.
She had never been an honor student.
Harry is my favorite uncle.

EXERCISE 165

★ Indicate the pattern of each sentence by the numbers 1, 2, or 3.

1. Sandy must have been the culprit. ___
2. The dinner was over. ___
3. The dinner was tasty. ___
4. The dinner was a feast. ___
5. The Indians were the winners. ___
6. My cousin is a fool. ___
7. My cousin is proud. ___
8. The policeman may be wise. ___
9. The policeman may be there. ___
10. Policemen are the guardians of the law. ___

D. Pattern 4: N InV

Girls giggle.

At this point it is advisable to develop the concept of the subject of the verb. We said in the discussion of pattern 1 that the subject is the noun which is tied to the verb. In the sentence above the change from *Girls giggle* to *The girl giggles* shows that *girls* is the subject. Here are two absurdly simple exercises just to fix the subject-verb relationship in your mind. It will be enough to do them orally.

EXERCISE 166

★ Change the plural subjects to singular ones and make the necessary changes in the verbs. If you write out this exercise, use a double-pointed arrow to connect the subject and the verb: e.g., Children ⟷ play.

1. Cats purr.
2. Students study
3. Houses deteriorate.
4. Vases break.
5. Visitors depart.

EXERCISE 167

★ Now reverse the process, changing the subject from singular to plural.

1. The cat prowls.
2. The musician plays.
3. The professor teaches.
4. The bus waits.
5. The comedian laughs.

When a noun cluster is in the subject position, it is the headword of the cluster which is tied to the verb and is therefore the subject.

Examples: The duties of the center depend on the kind of offensive employed.

The height of the bushes varies.

EXERCISE 168

★ Below each sentence write the headword subject and the verb to which it is tied.

1. The purposes of the training make me eager to begin.

   ________________ ________________

2. The leader of the trainees selects a deputy.

   ________________ ________________

3. One among the flock of swans maintains guard.

   ________________ ________________

4. The difference between the two men appears when they are at a game.

   ________________ ________________

5. The troublemakers on the squad were hard to locate.

   ________________ ________________

If a verb is preceded by auxiliaries, the subject is tied to the first auxiliary.

Example: The visitor has gone.

The visitors have gone.

EXERCISE 169

★ Rewrite these sentences, changing the singular subjects to plural. Underline the auxiliary that is tied to the subject.

1. The patient is being watched.

   ____

2. The janitor has waxed the floor.

   ____

3. The wrestler does not smoke.

   ____

4. The car has been stolen.

   ____

5. The ship was disappearing beyond the horizon.

   ____

Thus we see that subject and verb, and subject and auxiliary, are tied together by reciprocal changes in form. But there is a difficulty here. Of all the auxiliaries, only *be, have,* and *do* can change form. The others — *can, could, may, might, shall, should, will, would, must, ought* — have the same form in the singular and plural.

Examples: **Singular:** He *will* go.
Plural: They *will* go.
Singular: The neighbor *may* help.
Plural: The neighbors *may* help.

Likewise, the forms of the verb other than the present third-person singular (which takes {-s_3}) have no singular-plural change of form that can show a subject-verb tie.

Examples: **Singular:** I *sing.*
Plural: We *sing.*
Singular: The thief *ran.*
Plural: The thieves *ran.*

How, then, can we find the subject where no tie is perceptible in the form of the verb or auxiliary? It is done this way: Change the verb or auxiliary to another form which is capable of agreement. This form will be a present *he-she-it* or *they* form of the verb or auxiliary. For example, to find the subject of

The sopranos in the choir *sang* well.

change *sang* to *sings* and *sing:*

The sopranos in the choir *sing* well.
The soprano in the choir *sings* well.

Sopranos sing are the tied forms, or those which are in agreement; hence *sopranos* is also the subject in *sopranos sang.*

EXERCISE 170

★ Below each sentence write the singular and plural noun and verb forms that enable you to find the subject.

1. The cat slept under the table.

   ________ ________ ________ ________

2. Under the table slept the cat.

   ________ ________ ________ ________

3. One junior among the students refused to sign.

   ________ ________ ________ ________

4. The milkman delivered on Tuesdays and Fridays.

   ________ ________ ________ ________

5. There went my papers.

   ________ ________ ________ ________

With auxiliaries the process is the same. If the auxiliary is accompanied by *not*, then substitute *do* and *does*:

> The men in room 217 *can* not play handball.

The substitutions

> The *men* in room 217 *do* not play handball.
> The *man* in room 217 *does* not play handball.

show that *men* is the subject of the sentence in question. Or you can test for subject by substituting the verb itself for the auxiliary:

> One of my brothers *could* play golf.

The substitutions are

> One of my brothers *plays* golf.
> Two of my brothers *play* golf.

Thus *one* is the subject of the original sentence.

In some kinds of cases the agreement test for finding the subject is not sufficient, as in questions like these:

> Who is your friend?
> What was that explosion?

We can, of course, show putative agreement by these changes:

> Who are your friends?
> What were those explosions?

But since *who* and *what* do not have singular-plural forms, they still might be considered the subjects, especially as they occupy the normal subject position before the verb. So let's try a transformation test and see what happens. We know that in a subordinate clause the subject immediately precedes the verb, e.g.,

Sentence: *The soldiers* occupied the fort.
Subclause: We know what fort *the soldiers* occupied.
Subclause: We know *what soldiers* occupied the fort.

Now, when we put the questions "Who is your friend?" and "What was that explosion?" into subordinate clauses, we get

We know who *your friend* is

and

We know what *that explosion* was.

Therefore, since *friend* and *explosion* immediately precede the verb of the subordinate clause, we say that they are the subjects of the verb in the original sentences.

EXERCISE 171

★ Put each question into a subordinate clause as indicated below. Then write the subject of the verb in the last blank.

1. Who am I?
   They found out ______________________. ___________
2. Who is he?
   We are eager to know ______________________. ___________
3. Who are they?
   The police could not discover ______________________. ___________
4. What was the amount?
   The auditor asked ______________________. ___________
5. Which one is yours?
   Can you tell ______________________. ___________

Now, back to pattern 4, which, you remember, is

N	InV
Girls	giggle.

The verb in pattern 4 is of the kind called intransitive verbs. An intransitive verb is self-sufficient; it can stand alone with its subject.

1. The sportsman *fished.*
2. The sportsmen *were fishing.*

It can be modified by words and word groups that we shall later learn to know as adverbs and adverbials.

Examples: The sportsmen fished *early.*
The sportsmen were fishing *in the stream.*
The sportsmen were fishing *when we drove up.*

But an intransitive verb is usually not completed by a noun or pronoun. For example, in

They finished late

finished is intransitive, but in

They finished the game

and

They finished it

finished is not intransitive because it is completed by a noun or pronoun. If you are in doubt whether a word following the verb is a modifier which goes with an intransitive verb or a completer of a transitive verb, a substitution can settle the matter. If you can substitute *him, her, it,* or *them,* the word is a completer and the verb is not intransitive.

Examples: 1. He hammered fast.
2. He hammered the nail.

In the first sentence you cannot substitute *it* without spoiling the structural meaning. But in the second *He hammered it* is a suitable equivalent for *He hammered the nail.* Therefore the first *hammered* is intransitive and the second one transitive.

EXERCISE 172

★ Write InV after each sentence which contains an intransitive verb. All such InV sentences will be examples of pattern 4.

1. The audience clapped. ______
2. The audience clapped loudly. ______
3. The audience clapped loudly after the main act. ______
4. The audience clapped their hands. ______
5. They were drinking quietly at the table. ______
6. They were drinking their morning coffee. ______
7. He always paid promptly. ______
8. He paid his bills on the first of the month. ______

9. Jack left early. ________

10. Jack left his clothes in the closet. ________

E. Pattern 5: N^1 TrV N^2

The girl bought a dress.

In pattern 5 the verb is completed by a noun (or pronoun), for which one can substitute *him, her, it,* or *them.* This noun, as shown by the superscript 2, does not have the same referent as the subject. It is called the direct object of the verb.

With two kinds of pronouns, however, the direct object does have the same referent as the subject. One is the set of *-self/-selves* pronouns, generally known as the reflexive pronouns. These occur as direct object in sentences like

She saw *herself.*
The life guards splashed *themselves.*

The other set consists of the reciprocal pronouns *each other* and *one another,* which function as direct objects in such sentences as

They found *each other.*
They fought *one another.*

EXERCISE 173

★ After each sentence write the pronoun that you can substitute for the italicized direct object.

1. The salesman sold *the car.* ________
2. Both soldiers saluted *the colonel.* ________
3. Mrs. Grundy grew *roses* every year. ________
4. At the desk we met *the nurse.* ________
5. The chauffeur repaired *the tire.* ________
6. Mrs. Hooper injured *her ankle.* ________
7. The collision broke *the wheel.* ________
8. I met *your sister.* ________
9. The veterinarian carried *the dog.* ________
10. We trimmed *the bushes.* ________

A verb like those above which is completed by a direct object is called a transitive verb. A transitive verb contrasts with the intransitive verb of pattern 4, which does not take a direct object.

Examples: InV She sang beautifully.
TrV She sang a beautiful folk song.

EXERCISE 174

★ In this exercise you are to distinguish between transitive verbs, intransitive verbs, and the verb *be*. After each sentence place a TrV, InV or *be* to label the verb. In the second blank write the number of the sentence pattern.

1. The center *passed* the ball to the quarterback. ________ ___
2. I'll *pass*. ________ ___
3. The sheriff *was* the leader of the posse. ________ ___
4. The sheriff was *leading* the posse. ________ ___
5. Who is *leading* now? ________ ___
6. The dean *made* an important announcement. ________ ___
7. The announcement may *be* helpful to you. ________ ___
8. The firm *sent* a form letter to all its customers. ________ ___
9. The driver *turned* sharply. ________ ___
10. The driver *turned* the car around. ________ ___

A transitive verb has two forms, which we call active and passive. The active form is the one that is followed by the direct object, which we have seen in pattern 5. From this active form we can make the passive form. Here is an illustration:

Active: The waitress poured the coffee.

Passive: The coffee was poured (by the waitress).

In this process there are three things to notice:

1. The object of the active form becomes the subject of the passive form. This is shown above in the shift of *coffee.*

2. The passive is made up of a form of the verb *be* plus a past participle, as in *was poured.*

3. The subject of the active verb may be made the object of the preposition *by*, or it may be suppressed.

EXERCISE 175

★ These sentences contain transitive verbs in the active form. Change the sentences to the passive form.

1. The maid opened the window. ______________________
2. He rolled the dice. ______________________
3. Most adolescents like dancing. ______________________
4. We chose the mountains for our vacation.

   ____
5. Jim has never read *King Lear*. ______________________
6. The tourists burned wood in the fireplace.

   ____
7. The shepherd counted his sheep. ______________________
8. We began the game at four o'clock.

   ____
9. The Smiths built a new house on the river.

   ____
10. The nature club spotted a pileated woodpecker.

    ____

EXERCISE 176

★ These sentences contain transitive verbs in the passive form. For each verb underline the *be* auxiliary once and the past participle twice. Then change the sentences to the active form. In cases where there is no *by* phrase, you will have to supply a subject.

1. The rat was killed by the terrier.

   ____
2. The pancakes were turned by the cook.

   ____
3. Much corn is raised in Iowa.

   ____

4. An early folk tune was heard.

____

5. The dishes have been washed.

____

6. A good time was had by all.

____

7. Jane was teased by her boy friend.

____

8. The flag had been lowered.

____

9. The motorcycles were stopped by the traffic officer.

____

10. A carillon concert is played at 7:45 in the morning.

____

There is in English a tiny group of transitive verbs that do not form the passive. These are illustrated in the next sentences below. Try turning each sentence into the passive and see if the result sounds English to your ears.

1. The key *fits* the lock.
2. Joe *resembles* his father.
3. I *have* a friend.
4. The settlement *suited* Mr. Jacobs.
5. This *means* war.

F. Pattern 6: N^1 TrV N^2 N^3

The mother bought the girl a dress

In pattern 6 there are five matters to be observed:

1. The superscripts 1, 2, and 3 indicate that each noun has a different referent; *mother*, *girl*, and *dress* are three separate entities.

2. We see two grammatical objects after the verb *bought.* If we omit the first one the pattern becomes number 5 and *dress* is seen to be the direct object. These two objects are called, in order, the indirect and the direct object.

3. The indirect object may often be replaced by a prepositional phrase beginning with *to* or *for*, or occasionally with a different preposition.

Examples: He sold *the student* a ticket.
He sold a ticket *to the student.*

4. The verbs that can be used in pattern 6 are in a restricted group. Some of the common ones are *give, make, find, tell, buy, write, send, ask, play, build, teach, assign, feed, offer, throw, hand, pass, sell, pay.*

5. A pattern 6 sentence may be transformed into the passive by making either the direct or the indirect object the subject of the passive verb:

A dress was bought the girl by her mother.
The girl was bought a dress by her mother.

In some cases, however, the passive transform does not sound fully natural and seems to demand a preposition, as in

The sergeant found the recruit a rifle.
A rifle was found (*for*) the recruit.

EXERCISE 177

★ The following sentences follow pattern 6. Replace the indirect object by a prepositional phrase. Put the latter where it sounds most natural.

1. The librarian found me the pamphlet.

 ____

2. He assigned Jack the toughest job.

 ____

3. The spaniel brought his master the stick.

 ____

4. Susie fed the baby robins some juicy worms.

 ____

5. Her mother sent her a new laundry box.

 ____

EXERCISE 178

★ These sentences also follow pattern 6. Transform each one into two sentences by making first the indirect and second the direct object the subject of a passive verb.

1. She gave him a dirty look.

 ____

 ____

2. The company made the manager a fine offer.

____

____

3. The dealer dealt me a bad hand.

____

____

4. He offered his roommate the car.

____

____

5. The instructor asked her a question.

____

____

EXERCISE 179

★ In the ten sentences you wrote for exercise 178, you will find an object following the passive verb. This is known as the retained object. If you wish to be more specific you can make a distinction between the retained indirect and the retained direct object. Underline the retained object in each of the rewritten sentences in exercise 178.

G. Pattern 7: N^1 TrV N^2 N^2

The players chose Harry captain

Pattern 7, like its predecessor, has two objects following the verb. But it differs from pattern 6 in three respects:

1. In the order of objects, the direct object comes first. If we eliminate the second object, we are left with pattern 5:

The players chose Harry.

The second object here is called the object complement, presumably because it completes the direct object.

2. In pattern 7 both objects have the same referent; i.e., both *Harry* and *captain* refer to the same person.

3. In pattern 7 only the first object, the direct object, can be made the subject of a passive verb. We can transform the pattern sentence into

Harry was chosen captain.

but we cannot make the object complement such a subject, for

*Captain was chosen Harry

makes no sense.

Only a very small group of verbs can be used for pattern 7. Among them are *name, choose, elect, appoint, designate, select, vote, make, consider, imagine, think, believe, suppose, find, prove, label.*

EXERCISE 180

★ In each sentence strike out the indirect object or the object complement. Then write the pattern number, 6 or 7, after the sentence.

1. She played him a trick. ___
2. We appointed George the committee chairman. ___
3. You threw us a curve. ___
4. The student body selected Arabella the beauty queen. ___
5. The faculty chose Sieverson the head counselor. ___
6. We found her a sandwich. ___
7. The dealer sold me an air mattress. ___
8. She fed him the pablum. ___
9. The city elected Mouchy mayor. ___
10. He named his new boat Belle. ___

Pattern 7 has variations in which the third position is occupied by forms other than a noun, in all cases related to the direct object.

Examples:

Adjective:	He considered her *beautiful.*
Pronoun:	I thought the caller *you.*
Uninflected word:	I thought him *upstairs.*
Past participle:	I imagined him *seated.*

EXERCISE 181

★ Underline the object complement in these sentences. In the blanks label these object complements, using the terms given for the examples above.

1. I supposed Harold outside. ______________________
2. Sally painted the kitchen yellow. ______________________
3. We believed him elected. ______________________
4. The critic thought the painting bad. ______________________
5. The test proved him fit. ______________________

H. Pattern 8: N LV Adj

The acrobat seems young

In pattern 8 the verb is called a linking verb, as it links the adjective with the subject. Any verb except *be* that may be substituted for *seems* in this frame is a linking verb.

Examples: The cyclist *appears* weary.
The physicist *grew* sleepy.

Some of the common linking verbs are *seem, appear, become, grow, remain, taste, look, feel, smell, sound, get.* If verbs like these, however, are followed by an adverb or adverbial, then the pattern is not number 8 but number 4; e.g.,

The cyclist appeared *quickly* on the scene.
The physicist grew *rapidly* in knowledge.

Here, as in pattern 1, the adjective is in function a subjective complement, subclass predicate adjective.

EXERCISE 182

★ Write the pattern number, 8 or 4, after each sentence.

1. The milk remained sweet for a week. ___
2. The newcomer remained quietly in her room. ___
3. The dog smelled hungrily at the package. ___
4. The dog smells bad. ___
5. You look sharp today. ___

6. He looked sharply to the right. ___

7. The detective felt cautiously in the box. ___

8. He feels cautious about taking the risk. ___

9. That apprentice looks careful. ___

10. The apprentice looked carefully at the new machine. ___

Linking verbs may, of course, be preceded by auxiliaries.

Examples: The party *may become* lively.
Your sister *must have seemed* friendly.

In addition to the limited number of common linking verbs, other verbs not usually thought of as linking may on occasion be followed by an adjective and therefore conform to pattern 8.

Examples: His face *went* pale.
The cow *ran* dry.
He *proved* true to the cause.

EXERCISE 183

★ Write the pattern number, 8 or 4, after each sentence.

1. The table stood near the desk. ___

2. Jameson stood loyal to his firm. ___

3. The students in the back row look sleepy. ___

4. The investigator looked outside. ___

5. Penelope turned red at the thought. ___

6. She was lying still on the hospital bed. ___

7. The tent flap blew open during the night. ___

8. The wind blew strongly through the tall pines. ___

9. The beer may stay cold until evening. ___

10. You will never keep slender that way. ___

I. Pattern 9: N^1 LV N^1

My brother remained an outstanding student.

The two superscripts show that both nouns have the same referent. The verb, which links *student* and *brother*, is a linking verb. The number of linking verbs which may occupy the verbal position in this pattern is very small. Among them are *remain, become, appear, seem, continue, stay.*

Sentences which follow pattern 9 should not be confused with those of pattern 5, in which the noun after the verb does not have the same referent as the first noun.

Examples: **9** Donald *continued* my friend, despite our differences.
5 Donald *met* my friend in the barber shop.
9 My brother *became* a doctor.
5 My brother was *seeking* a doctor.

In pattern 9, as in pattern 3, the second noun is in function a subjective complement, subclass predicate noun.

EXERCISE 184

★ Write the pattern number, 9 or 5, after each sentence.

1. The statuesque blonde became the queen of the military ball. ___
2. After two years of faithful service the corporal became a sergeant. ___
3. The military police restrained the sergeant from entering the hall. ___
4. The chief seemed a good fellow. ___
5. We saw the fellow. ___
6. We stayed boon companions for years. ___
7. The governor stayed the execution. ___
8. They appeared friends to all of us. ___
9. We shall continue the discussion tomorrow. ___
10. Johannes had remained a bachelor for reasons of his own. ___

With pattern 9 we complete the list of the nine basic sentence patterns in English.

EXERCISE 185

★ After each sentence write the number of the pattern it represents.

1. Your recital was wonderful. ___
2. Mabel was here a moment ago. ___

3. The rancher told his guests a tall tale. ___

4. The archers were not successful hunters. ___

5. The frogs were croaking in the marsh. ___

6. Jerry thought the proposal a mistake. ___

7. She had been secretary a long time. ___

8. The Romans won the first battle. ___

9. The judges believed Lightning the best horse in the show. ___

10. The director found him a new costume. ___

11. My uncle remains the worst bridge player in town. ___

12. The coach designated Joe the new manager of the team. ___

13. Migrant workers pick the strawberries in early June. ___

14. The pickles are near the wieners. ___

15. We considered his offer a fine gesture. ___

16. Your cigar smells so aromatic! ___

17. He has always seemed a serious boy. ___

18. Who is at the cottage this week? ___

19. They stayed roommates for three years. ___

20. The board elected Mr. Stoopnagel the president. ___

EXERCISE 186

★ Unless we recognize the pattern of a sentence, we do not know what the sentence means. The following sentences will illustrate this thought. Each one is ambiguous because we do not know which of two patterns it represents. After each sentence write the numbers of the patterns that it follows.

1. He found her a pig. ___ ___

2. The bouncer turned out a drunkard. ___ ___

3. The girl in the back seat looked forward. ___ ___

4. They are discouraging transfers. ___ ___

5. I'm getting her socks. — —

6. The man gave the library books. — —

7. It was a little dainty. — —

8. He accepted Wednesday. — —

9. Thorne taught himself during his young manhood. — —

10. The doctor made them well. — —

The sentence patterns you have just studied are the source of seven sentence functions, those called the subject of the verb, predicator,* object of the verb, indirect object, object complement, subjective complement, retained object, and the object of the preposition. Later you will add to these the modifier. This classification by function is only one of three major classifications that you must keep clearly in mind. The other two, classification by form and by position, are the subject of the next chapter. Since the same word or structure may sometimes be classified in three ways — by function, form, or position — there is danger of confusion here. The following preliminary table may be of help to you in understanding these three modes of classification as you go through the chapter following.

Classification by Function	*Classification by Form*	*Classification by Position*
subject of verb	noun	nominal
predicator	verb	verbal
object of verb	adjective	adjectival
indirect object	adverb	adverbial
object complement	pronoun	
subjective complement		
retained object	uninflected word	
object of preposition		
modifier		

Three examples will easily illustrate these triple classifications. Take the sentence

The *shouting boys* will play *tennis.*

1. *Shouting* is a modifier by function, a verb by form, and an adjectival by position.

---

* The predicator is that which makes a predication. This function is performed by *be* and by the InV, TrV, LV alone or in combination with auxiliaries. The term *verb* is normally used for *predicator*, since no confusion arises from this practice.

2. *Boys* is the subject of the verb by function, a noun by form, and a nominal by position.

3. *Tennis* is the object of the verb by function, an uninflected word by form, and a nominal by position.

These will become clear to you as you go ahead to study the parts of speech as classified by form and position.

XV.

Parts of Speech

An English sentence is an arrangement of words, not as words but in their capacity as parts of speech. If we do not, as listeners or readers, grasp the identity of these parts of speech, we cannot understand with certainty the message being communicated. Consider, for example,

> They are encouraging reports.

Here the word *encouraging* is the stumbling block. It may be a verb, so that the sentence means

> They encourage reports

or it may be an adjectival, giving the meaning of

> These reports are encouraging.

Not knowing the part of speech of this one word, we find the sentence ambiguous. In a carefully controlled context, of course, this sentence might not be ambiguous.

As native speakers we already have an operational command of the parts of speech. Now we shall approach them analytically and study the specific ways by which we identify them.

Let us begin with the four form-classes — noun, verb, adjective, and adverb. These are large and open classes, hospitable to strangers, and when new words enter our language they join one of these classes, usually that of nouns. Each form-class has its correlative position class, which we label as nominal, verbal, adjectival, or adverbial.

A. Nouns

Nouns are identified as nouns by two aspects of form, their inflectional morphemes and their derivational morphemes. The inflectional morphemes, you remember, are the noun possessive {-s_1} and the noun plural {-s_2}. Any word which has the possessive {-s_1} is a noun, except for phrases, like "the Queen of England's dress." Any word which has the plural {-s_2} is also a noun. And if it does not have the {-s_2} but can take it in the same position, sometimes with a readjustment of context to allow for a plural form, it is a noun. Thus in

The author seems tired

author is a noun because it can be changed to the plural in the same position, with the readjustment of *seems* to its plural form *seem:*

The *authors* seem tired.

But in the sentence

Her brother may author a new biography

author cannot be made plural in this position and hence is not a noun.

EXERCISE 187

★ Underline the words which are nouns according to the inflectional criteria just above. After each explain your choice with these numbers:

1. Has possessive morpheme.
2. Has plural morpheme.
3. Can take plural morpheme in same position, with or without a readjusted context to allow for a plural form.

The first column is for the first noun and the second column for the second noun, if there is one.

1. Our president has a new plan. _____ _____
2. The janitors had not seen the umbrella. _____ _____
3. The counselor may plan a different approach. _____ _____
4. My aunt always mothers her youngest son. _____ _____
5. Mother's cake never tasted so good. _____ _____

Nouns are identified not only by inflectional morphemes but also by noun-forming derivational suffixes added to verbs, adjectives, nouns, and bound forms. Compare these sentences:

The quality is pure.
The quality is purity.

It is the form of *purity*, with its *-ity* added to an adjective, which signifies that it is a noun. In general, the suffix itself, together with our consciousness of the part of speech to which it has been attached, provides the signal of nounness. Here is a partial list of word pairs, the second word in each containing one of the suffixes that enable us to classify a word as a noun.*

Source Verb†	*Derived Noun*
accept	acceptance
achieve	achievement
advise /z/	advice /s/
arrive	arrival
assist	assistant
block	blockade
break	breakage
complain	complaint
contemplate	contemplation
deceive	deceit
deceive	deception
decide	decision
defend	defense
deform	deformity
deform	deformation
deliver	delivery
depart	departure
draft	draftee
help	helper (-ar, -or)
paint	painting
purify	purification
save	savior

Source Adjective	*Derived Noun*
big	bigness
brave	bravery
ideal	idealist
ideal	idealism
important	importance
just	justice

* These and other derivational suffixes in this chapter are taken in part from C. C. Fries, *The Structure of English* (New York: Harcourt, Brace & World, 1952), pp. 113 ff.

† In this list and those to follow, the words labeled "source" usually provide the source in the sense that they take an affix to form the derived word. However, in a few cases — like *bath* and *bathe*, *associate* /et/ and *associate* /ət/— we have significantly contrastive forms but with no discernible source-result relationship.

Source Adjective	*Derived Noun*
pure	purity
supreme	supremacy
true	truth
violent	violence
wise	wisdom
wise	wizard

Source Noun	*Derived Noun*
Asia	Asian (-an, -ian)
book	booklet
cartoon	cartoonist
dog	doggie
friend	friendship
gang	gangster
golf	golfer
king	kingdom
labor	laborite
lemon	lemonade
mathematics	mathematician
monarch	monarchy
murder	murderess
novel	novelette
pagan	paganism
priest	priesthood
pulpit	pulpiteer
slave	slavery
Vietnam	Vietnamese

These same noun-forming suffixes are sometimes attached to bound stems, as in *dentist* and *tailor*.

OPTIONAL EXERCISE

★ You will find it rewarding to try to locate a matching set for each pair of words. This is an excellent way to become well acquainted with these noun-forming derivational suffixes.

EXERCISE 188

★ Underline each noun that can be identified by its derivational suffix. In the first blank write the source verb, adjective, or noun. In the second blank write the noun-forming suffix.

1. Jim was distressed by his failure. __________ __________
2. The payment was not large. __________ __________
3. What did the assistant say? __________ __________
4. It was a clever device. __________ __________
5. The catcher missed the ball. __________ __________
6. A collision was narrowly averted. __________ __________
7. There is a leakage under the sink. __________ __________
8. The history class was studying the Reformation. __________ __________
9. Who made the discovery? __________ __________
10. The amusement proved dull. __________ __________
11. She is often troubled by sickness. __________ __________
12. His refusal was polite. __________ __________
13. He swam the width of the river. __________ __________
14. Can you doubt his sincerity? __________ __________
15. Who does not enjoy freedom from want? __________ __________
16. Childhood is an unhappy time. __________ __________
17. Jane became a beautician. __________ __________
18. You might improve your scholarship. __________ __________
19. The fragrance was overwhelming. __________ __________
20. The intimacy of the occasion was marred. __________ __________

During the discussion just above, two questions may have occurred to you. First, since inflectional endings follow derivational suffixes and are used to identify nouns, why should we bother at all about the derivational suffixes? The reason is that in practice some words with such suffixes are seldom or never inflected. Here are a few examples: *derision, drainage, fertility, iciness, manhood,* and *nourishment.* Thus it seems best not to shortcut this mode of noun recognition. Second, why aren't the personal pronouns included among the form-classes? The personal pronouns resemble nouns in that they are inflected for the plural and the possessive and they occupy most noun positions in the basic patterns. They differ from nouns in that they have object forms and do not pattern in some ways like nouns. For instance, you can say, "Those gay girls" but not "Those gay them." Furthermore, the personal pronouns are a small closed class, whereas nouns are a large open class. Our practice here will be to consider them as a subclass of nouns with the label of "personal pronouns." In position, as you will see shortly, they are considered nominals and adjectivals.

B. Nominals

Certain sentence positions are characteristically the habitation of nouns. Of these positions we have met so far the following:

SV Subject of verb
SC Subjective complement
OV Object of verb
IO Indirect object of verb
OC Object complement
OP Object of preposition
RO Retained object

But occupancy of these positions does not positively identify nouns because words of other form-classes can occupy them as well. Here are a few illustrative cases involving the SV position.

Pattern 4: The *rich* live on the bay.

Here the SV slot is occupied by an adjective, recognizable as such because it can be inflected with *-er* and *-est*, e.g.,

The *richest* live on the bay.

Pattern 3: *Steadily* is the best way to work.

Here an adverb sits comfortably at home in the SV slot.

Pattern 5: *Swimming* develops the lungs.

We recognize *swimming* as a verb here by the *-ing* form. Though you may be tempted to call it a noun, it will not take an *-s* plural as *painting* will in "Your paintings are beautiful."

Pattern 3: *Tennis* is a superb sport for young and old.

Tennis is not a noun here because in form it takes neither the noun possessive nor the noun plural, nor any noun-forming derivational suffix. It is an uninflected word.

So we see that position cannot be used as a criterion for nouns. What we shall do, therefore, is to set up a positional class called nominal. Any word, whatever its form-class (noun, verb, comparable, pronoun, uninflected word) will be tabbed a nominal if it occupies one of the seven noun positions listed above. This gives us a double-track classification for parts of speech, one by form and the other by position. Such a procedure is perfectly sound, for any given entity may be classified in various ways by using different bases of classification. You yourself, for example, might be classified "female" by sex, "junior" by class, "brunette" by pigmentation, "Unitarian" by church affiliation, and so on. A few more examples may be pertinent.

1. We enjoyed the *game*.

Game is a noun by form, since it can be pluralized in its context, and a nominal by position, since it occupies the OV slot.

2. What can one expect from the *young?*

Young is an adjective by form because it is inflected by *-er* and *-est*. One could say "from the younger" but not "from the youngs." It is a nominal by position because it is in the OP slot.

3. *Now* is the best time.

Now is an uninflected word by form and a nominal by position, occurring in the SV position.

EXERCISE 189

★ The italicized words are nominals. In the first blank write the form-class of the word: noun, pronoun, verb, comparable, uninflected word. In the second blank indicate which noun position the word occupies: SV, SC, OV, IO, OC, OP, RO.

Example: The *poor* grew troubled. *comp.* *SV*

1. The *cheapest* are on that counter. ________ ___
2. The *seniors* held a class meeting. ________ ___
3. Can you see the game from *here?* ________ ___
4. He hated *digging*. ________ ___
5. The winners were the *men* from Homburg Hall. ________ ___
6. That car is *mine*. ________ ___
7. He had always enjoyed *physics*. ________ ___
8. We believed the letter a *hoax*. ________ ___
9. *Upstairs* is his favorite hiding place. ________ ___
10. We were given the *fattest*. ________ ___

Word groups as well as individual words can be nominals, and they occupy the usual noun positions. In this sentence

On the beach is better than in the woods

the opening word group *on the beach* is a prepositional phrase in form and a nominal by position.

EXERCISE 190

★ The italicized word groups are nominals. In each blank indicate the noun position of the group by SV, SC, OV, IO, OC, OP, RO.

1. Jerry knows *that history is never completely true.* ______
2. His greatest ambition is *to win the match.* ______
3. You made me *what I am.* ______
4. She gave *whomever she met* a warm greeting. ______
5. Do you object to *what I wrote?* ______

Whether or not a word group is a nominal can be tested by substitution. A word group is a nominal if it can be replaced by one of these: a noun or noun cluster, *this, that, these, those, he/him, she/her, it, they/them.*

EXERCISE 191

★ The italicized word groups are nominals. Write in the first blank one of the substitutes mentioned above. In the second blank indicate the noun position of the group.

1. *To win the match* was his greatest ambition.

   ______________________________ ______

2. Can you see from *where you sit?* (Try a noun.)

   ______________________________ ______

3. I always enjoy the company of *my favorite aunt from Peoria.*

   ______________________________ ______

4. He did not give *finding the cat* a second thought.

   ______________________________ ______

5. *Where we are going* has not been decided.

   ______________________________ ______

6. She became *what she had hoped.*

   ______________________________ ____

7. He hated *arriving late.*

   ______________________________ ____

8. We found *what we wanted.*

   ______________________________ ____

9. *That she is beautiful* is evident to all.

   ______________________________ ____

10. They made him *what he had always wanted to be.*

   ______________________________ ____

EXERCISE 192

★ Underline the nominal word groups. In the blank give the noun position of the word group.

1. They heard what we said. ____
2. What you do is your own business. ____
3. That was what I thought too. ____
4. You must do the best with what you have. ____
5. Jack made whoever came there the same offer. ____
6. We will name the baby whatever his grandfather wishes. ____
7. We thought of paying cash. ____
8. I'll take whichever is the most durable. ____
9. Betty forgot to bring the coffee. ____
10. George postponed mailing the letter. ____

C. Verbs

Verbs have a maximum of five different inflectional forms, as you learned in the morphology. All five are shown in the forms of *rise:*

Stem	*Present Third-Person Singular*	*Present Participle*	*Past Tense*	*Past Participle*
rise	rises	rising	rose	risen

Any word which has three or more of these inflectional forms is thereby a member of the form-class called the verb. Remember that a verb is always a single word.

EXERCISE 193

★ Underline each verb and indicate in the first column how many of the five forms it has. In the second column show which of the five forms it is. Do not include *do, be,* and *have* when they are used as auxiliaries.

1. The President met the leaders of the parade. ___ ___
2. The mines had been swept away. ___ ___
3. The bridge players would not leave the table. ___ ___
4. The water is spreading into the meadow. ___ ___
5. The canary might have been eaten by the cat. ___ ___
6. Elephantine always eats between meals. ___ ___
7. June set the table. ___ ___
8. The ruler is lying on the table. ___ ___
9. Have you bought the refreshments? ___ ___
10. The ball sank into the pond. ___ ___

The derivational affixes by which a verb is identified are rather few. This list contains verbs with such affixes and the source parts of speech from which the verbs are derived.

Source Noun	*Derived Verb*
bath	bathe
beauty	beautify
colony	colonize
friend	befriend
joy	enjoy
knowledge	acknowledge
lace	unlace
length	lengthen
strife	strive
Source Adjective	*Derived Verb*
large	enlarge
ripe	ripen
solemn	solemnize

EXERCISE 194

★ Underline each verb that can be identified by its derivational affix. In the first blank write the source noun or adjective. In the second, write the verb-forming affix.

1. The enemy city has been besieged. __________ ______
2. The judge personifies justice itself. __________ ______
3. Can you prove your contention? __________ ______
4. This paragraph will weaken your paper. __________ ______
5. Those dorm rules should be liberalized. __________ ______
6. Mann's novel may enrich your intellectual life. __________ ______
7. Why do you idolize that boob? __________ ______
8. She must have bewitched you. __________ ______
9. This agency clothes the needy. __________ ______
10. She was enraptured by the spectacle. __________ ______

D. Verbals

Verbals are those forms which occupy the verb positions. The verb positions you have seen in the nine basic sentence patterns presented in the preceding chapter. They come after the opening noun or noun phrase. These positions are the habitat of verbs and their accompanying auxiliaries and *be, have,* and *do* forms, in varying combinations. Each such word in such a position is a verbal. So we see there are four verbals in

She *must have been loafing* last week

and two in

I *should leave* the house in ten minutes.

Also, any verb form taking a subject or a complement (OV, SC, or Adj) or modified by an adverbial is a verbal, regardless of its position In these examples, the verbals are italicized:

1. *Becoming* angry, she *broke* the dish.
2. *Being* a minister, Prentice *spoke* softly.
3. After *having eaten* the turnips, Prentice *tried* to *look* satisfied.
4. The lights *having gone* out, we *lighted* candles.
5. *Giving* to the poor *is* a Christian virtue.

In brief, al! verbs and auxiliaries, including *have*, *be*, and *do*, are verbals unless they occupy a clearly established nominal, adjectival, or adverbial position. A case in point is

Giving is a Christian virtue

in which *giving* is patently a nominal in the SV position. On the other hand, in

Giving gifts is a Christmas custom,

the *giving* is a verbal because it takes the object *gifts*, and the phrase *giving gifts* is a nominal which functions as subject of the verb.

EXERCISE 195

★ Underline the verbals.

1. The sorority girls have been making floats for Homecoming.
2. A survey is being made of TV watching.
3. This society was established in 1886.
4. Our team has not been beaten this season.
5. She is waiting in the lounge.
6. Have you repaired the screens?
7. We missed seeing the parade.
8. The lawyer offered to delay action.
9. Being miserable, Charlotte put a record on the turntable.
10. George lost the match by playing badly.

A group of verbals, like most of those above, which operates as a unit is also known as a verbal, and a verbal together with its complements and modifiers is a verb cluster.

E. Adjectives

In our study of morphology you recall the comparable paradigm, with its compared words having the *-er* and *-est* inflectional suffixes. These suffixes enable us to set up a class of words called "comparables," but they do not permit us by themselves to separate into two classes the words traditionally called adjectives (e.g., *rich*, *kind*) and adverbs (e.g., *soon*, *often*). We can, however, dip into the reservoir of derivational suffixes and define adjectives by a combined test in this way: A word which is inflected with *-er* and *-est* and which is capable of forming adverbs with *-ly* and/or nouns with *-ness* is called an adjective.

EXERCISE 196

★ Fill in the blanks as follows: first column, *-er* form; second column, *-est* form; third column, *-ly* adverb form; fourth column, *-ness* noun form. Underline those words which are not adjectives by this test.

	-er	*-est*	*-ly*	*-ness*
1. close	______	______	______	______
2. icy	______	______	______	______
3. sweet	______	______	______	______
4. sad	______	______	______	______
5. high	______	______	______	______
6. sunny	______	______	______	______
7. gentle	______	______	______	______
8. small	______	______	______	______
9. little	______	______	______	______
10. fast	______	______	______	______
11. holy	______	______	______	______
12. long	______	______	______	______
13. friendly	______	______	______	______
14. ill	______	______	______	______
15. natural	______	______	______	______

In addition to the adjective test just described, we can identify adjectives by derivational suffixes alone. With most of these words the degrees of comparison are expressed by *more* and *most* rather than by *-er* and *-est*. The adjective-forming suffixes are illustrated in this list.

Source Noun	*Derived Adjective*
age	aged
athlete	athletic
child	childish
cloud	cloudy
consul	consular

Source Noun	*Derived Adjective*
crystal	crystalline
emotion	emotional
fortune	fortunate
friend	friendly
moment	momentary
penny	penniless
picture	picturesque
pomp	pompous
power	powerful
science	scientific
wood	wooden

Source Verb	*Derived Adjective*
associate /et/	associate /ət/
collect	collective
continue	continual
exist	existent
expect	expectant
prohibit	prohibitory
prosper	prosperous
read	readable
restore	restorative
shake	shaky

Source Adjective	*Derived Adjective*
dead	deadly
economic	economical

These adjective-forming suffixes and others are also added to bound forms; e.g.,

pens- + ive > pensive
cred- + ible > credible
loc- + al > local
splend- + id > splendid
frag- + ile > fragile
cert- + ain > certain
usu- + al > usual

EXERCISE 197

★ Here is a list of adjectives formed by derivational suffixes. In the first blank write the source noun, verb, adjective, or bound form. In the second, write the adjective-forming suffix.

1. golden	__________	__________
2. helpless	__________	__________
3. lovely	__________	__________
4. messy	__________	__________
5. peaceful	__________	__________
6. consular	__________	__________
7. nervous	__________	__________
8. fragmentary	__________	__________
9. repentant	__________	__________
10. affectionate	__________	__________
11. foolish	__________	__________
12. rhythmic	__________	__________
13. regional	__________	__________
14. tired	__________	__________
15. separate /ət/	__________	__________
16. recurrent	__________	__________
17. instructive	__________	__________
18. perishable	__________	__________
19. meddlesome	__________	__________
20. congratulatory	__________	__________
21. pleasant	__________	__________
22. goodly	__________	__________
23. lively	__________	__________

An especially refractory class of words is a group of about seventy-five, mostly of two syllables, which begin with the prefix *a-*. Their formation is like this:

Prefix		*Stem*	*Word*
a-	noun	-foot	afoot
		-ground	aground
		-kin	akin
a-	verb	-gape	agape
		-wake	awake
		-sunder	asunder
a-	adjective	-loud	aloud
		-fresh	afresh
		-weary	aweary
a-	bound form	-mok	amok
		-lert	alert
		-droit	adroit

These are UW's (uninflected words) because they take no inflectional endings. Although they do have the prefix *a-* in common, it seems unwise to label them formally as either adjectives or adverbs since positionally they appear in both adjectival and adverbial slots. Therefore we shall bin them as UW's. Soon however we shall meet them again in two positional classes.

F. Adjectivals

Adjectivals, like nominals, occupy certain characteristic sentence positions. The main one is that between the determiner and the noun, e.g.,

That *joyful* freshman

In this noun cluster *joyful* is an adjective by form — the source noun *joy* plus the derivational suffix *-ful* — and an adjectival by position. This position may be occupied by two other form-classes and by uninflected forms. The noun is shown in

That *college* freshman

The verb appears in

That *laughing* freshman
That *recommended* freshman

And here are uninflected words in this adjectival slot:

An *inside* job
Her *inmost* thoughts

The adjectival-plus-noun takes the modifier-plus-noun stress of secondary-primary, ^ ´. But if the stress pattern is primary-secondary, ´ `, then we have a compound noun. For illustration, compare

That âpple píe,

an adjectival-plus-noun, with

That ápple trèe,

a compound noun.

A series of adjectivals may occur between the determiner and the noun, as in

The mâny êarnest univêrsity séniors

Here there are three successive adjectivals in a fixed and unchangeable order. Because these are not interchangeable, that is, not mutually substitutable, we shall set up subclasses of adjectivals, which will be discussed in the next chapter under "Prenominal Modifiers."

EXERCISE 198

★ The italicized words are adjectivals. Indicate the form-class of each with the symbols N (noun), V (verb), A (adjective), and UW (uninflected word). Mark the stresses on the adjectival and the noun.

1. A *clean* apron ______
2. An *evening* party ______
3. A *pretty* necklace ______
4. The *class* dance ______
5. A *hopeful* sign ______
6. Their *back* yard ______
7. Those *neighborhood* cats ______
8. Sally's *new* radio ______
9. That *paper* book ______
10. A *fighting* rooster ______
11. These *broken* boxes ______
12. An *upstairs* room ______
13. Their *garage* door ______
14. The *office* typewriter ______
15. Our *school* principal ______
16. The *above* statement ______
17. That *funny* hat ______
18. A *scenic* drive ______
19. Those *chattering* girls ______
20. His *glass* eye ______

Positions other than the prenominal slot can also contain adjectivals. A common position is the third slot in pattern 8:

N	*LV*	*Adj*
The boat	remained	*wet, shiny*
The man	appeared	*aghast, aware*
The man	seemed	*in the money* (= rich)

We must be careful not to confuse such slot 3 adjectives with fillers of slot 3 in pattern 9:

N[1] LV N[1]

If a noun or noun substitute appears in this position we have, of course, a nominal and not an adjective:

They seem *friends.*
He seemed *what we expected* (= that).

Furthermore, when adverbs appear after the verb, as in

He remained *quietly*
He appeared *quickly*

We are dealing with pattern 4,

N InV,

followed by an adverb, which positionally is an adverbial. Note that these adverbials are movable:

He *quietly* remained,
He *quickly* appeared.

Compare these with

He remained *quiet,*
He appears *quick,*

where we are back again in pattern 8.

Very similar to pattern 8 is pattern 1

N *be* Adj

with its adjectival third slot, as in

Those boys are *young.*

This should not be confused with pattern 2

N *be* UW (uninflected word)

whose third slot is occupied by adverbials, e.g.,

The paper is *here.*
The meeting was *yesterday.*

EXERCISE 199

★ Underline the adjectivals which occupy position 3 in patterns 8 and 1.

1. The baby's cheeks are pink.
2. In the late afternoon the forest seemed dark.
3. The visitor became afraid.
4. The scouts seemed asleep.
5. This frog appears alive.
6. The privet hedge grew tall.
7. The privet hedge grew rapidly.
8. The grass was dewy this morning.
9. The catamaran ran aground.
10. The villagers looked hostile.

The third adjectival position is the one after the noun. It accepts adjectives, verbs, and uninflected words.

Examples:

adjectivals: The waitress, *old* and *weary*, sat heavily down.
The fellow *waving* drives a convertible.
The floor *below* is rented.
The woman *ahead* is the cashier.

EXERCISE 200

★ Underline the adjectivals and in the blanks indicate the form-class by using these symbols: A (adjective), V (verb), and UW (uninflected word).

1. One person alone heard the message. ______
2. Those coeds cheering are only sophomores. ______
3. The surface, shining and smooth, reflected the sunshine. ______ ______
4. The weather today is sultry. ______ ______
5. We started our trip homeward. ______
6. The conversation afterward was light and gay. ______ ______ ______
7. Her demeanor, excessively prim, annoyed the guests. ______
8. The two swans floating were black. ______ ______
9. His trip abroad proved expensive. ______ ______
10. The door ajar worried the housewife. ______

In this postnominal position we find word-group adjectivals of different structures:

It is time *to go.*
Andy watched his dog *swimming after a stick.*
The sweater *I prefer* is the striped one.
Mount Washington is the place *where we spent a strenuous week.*
He was a man *disturbed by many phantasies.*
The second chapter *of the book* presented the problem.

EXERCISE 201

★ Underline the word-group adjectivals and encircle the word they modify.

1. This will be a day to remember.
2. The chap sitting in that cubicle is Marge's friend.
3. This is not the size I ordered.
4. The drugstore on the corner sells the *Times.*
5. Our guests came on the week when I was housecleaning.
6. A girl spoiled by her mother is not a good roommate.
7. Just choose a time convenient to yourself.
8. Who is the head of this club?
9. Have you finished the book I lent you?
10. She was a sight to behold.

In other positions let us say that any adjective or adjective-substitute is an adjectival, unless it is in a nominal or adverbial slot. Thus in

Angry and *upset,* the applicant slammed the door

angry, being an adjective, is an adjectival; and *upset* is an adjectival because it can substitute for an adjective in normal adjectival positions, e.g.,

The child seems *upset.*
The *upset* child
The child, obviously *upset,* clamored for comforting arms.

But in a nominal position these are nominals:

The *angry* make few friends.
The *upset* sometimes need treatment.

G. Adverbs

The adverb has only three suffixes to set it apart from other form-classes. One we have already seen, the inflectional *-ly* attached to an adjective stem, e.g., *just, justly; fortunate, fortunately*. Then there are the derivational suffix *-wise* and the free form *like*.

1. *Source Noun*	*Derived Adverb*
student	student-wise

This *-wise* suffix, about five centuries old in English, has taken on renewed vitality in recent years and today may be heard attached to almost any noun to form an adverb.

2. *Source Noun*	*Derived Adverb*
student	student-like
3. *Source Adjective*	*Derived Adverb*
casual	casual-like

EXERCISE 202

★ Classify the italicized words as Adv (adverb), Adj (adjective), or UW (uninflected word). For the adverbs, write in the second column the form-class of the stem.

1. They are singing *merrily*. ______ ____________
2. They are singing *today*. ______ ____________
3. He turned the hands *clockwise*. ______ ____________
4. She studies *hard* on Sunday. ______ ____________
5. Have you seen the paper *lately?* ______ ____________
6. It's fragile. Lift it *easy-like*. ______ ____________
7. The firemen get up *daily* at seven. ______ ____________
8. *Luckily*, the brake was set. ______ ____________
9. Jack looked *downward* on the river. ______ ____________
10. Let's start *afresh*. ______ ____________
11. You *richly* deserve the prize. ______ ____________
12. Dalziel is *professor-wise* pretty knowledgeable. ______ ____________

13. Pedro sniffed *dog-like* at the garbage can. ______ ____________

14. He *carelessly* threw the match on the trail. ______ ____________

15. Our fund is faring *badly*. ______ ____________

H. Adverbials

The positional class, adverbials, cannot be pinpointed with precision and is difficult to describe without enormous complications. The difficulty is that there are numerous subclasses of one-word adverbials, and each subclass has its own positions in the various sentence patterns. To illustrate, let us look at the traditional adverbial subclasses of time, place, and manner. We'll choose two examples of each class:

Time:	a. soon	b. tomorrow
Place:	a. here	b. outside
Manner:	a. well	b. skillfully

Now we'll take a simple sentence of pattern 5 and see how these adverbials assume their positions in this pattern. We'll begin with the *a* group.

	1		2		3		4		5
		He		will		play		tennis.	
Time:	Soon		soon		soon		____		soon
Place:	Here		____		____		____		here
Manner:	____		____		____		____		well

Next let's look at the *b* group of the same three adverbial subclasses — time, place, and manner.

	1		2		3		4		5
		He		will		play		tennis.	
Time:	Tomorrow		____		____		____		tomorrow
Place:	______		____		____		____		outside
Manner:	______		____		skillfully		____		skillfully

Here it is evident that each member of the group *a* adverbials of time, place, and manner has a distribution unlike that of its mate in group *b*. In other words we have positional sub-subclasses.

EXERCISE 203

★ You will find here two basic sentence patterns and illustrative sentences, with possible adverbial positions numbered above each pattern. Below each sentence are three potential adverbials. After each of these, write the numbers of the positions that it can occupy in the sentence without sounding un-English.

	1	2	3	4
Pattern 3:	N[1]	*be*	N[1]	
	Josephine	was	my	aid.

regularly ____________

always ____________

yesterday ____________

	1	2	3
Pattern 4:		N	InV
	The	picnickers	ate.

greedily ____________

soon ____________

there ____________

If we recall that there are nine basic sentence patterns and that there are more subclasses of adverbials than the three mentioned above, we can easily see how complex the matter of adverbial positions must be. There are, however, common adverbial positions that can be set forth:

1. Before the pattern, with or without juncture. (This slot, as we have seen, is also the habitat of the adjectival when occupied by an adjective or an adjective substitute.)

Really, you should know better.
Now it's time to go.

2. After the subject and before the verb.

She *actually* expects to marry him.

3. After the auxiliary or first auxiliary.

He would *seldom* make the effort.

4. After the verb in pattern 4 and after *be* in patterns 1, 2, and 3.

He drove *recklessly.*
She is *seldom* late.
She is *outside.*
My brother is *always* a gentleman.

5. After the complement of the verb (SC, OV, OC).

Hoskins will be quarterback *tomorrow.*
Hoskins will play football *tomorrow.*
Hoskins may be chosen captain *tomorrow.*

But this postcomplement position is also position 4 in pattern 7:

> They elected Monty *captain.*
> We considered her *lovely.*

There need be no trouble here. Since *captain* is a noun and *lovely* an adjective, we obviously have in these sentences a nominal and an adjectival, not adverbials. This positional overlap, however, can produce ambiguity, as in

> He considered the applicant *hard.*

Here *hard* may be looked at two ways. It is an adverbial at the end of pattern 5, as you can substitute for it an adverb, like *carefully.* But it is also an adjectival in pattern 7, as it permits a substitute like *unsuitable.* Hence the ambiguity.

In any of these five positions we can label a word an adverbial, unless we have an instance of positional overlap. In such cases the form-class that occupies a slot or that can be substituted will determine the positional classification. Here is an illustration of each case.

> He eats *doughnuts.*

The postverb position admits nominals, adjectivals, and adverbials. In this example the postverb slot is occupied by the form-class of noun (*doughnuts*) so that the word is positionally nominal. In the second illustration,

> He eats *fast,*

you can substitute the adverb *quickly* for *fast.* Thus *fast* is called an adverbial.

The passive transformation offers another test to distinguish nominals from adverbials in this postverbal position. If we compare

> He ate Wednesday.
> He ate sandwiches.

we see that the first cannot be made passive, for no one would say

> *Wednesday was eaten by him.

Hence *Wednesday* is not a nominal but an adverbial. But we can say

> Sandwiches were eaten by him.

Therefore, in "He ate sandwiches," the word *sandwiches* is a nominal.

Another way to spot adverbials is by their mobility. Most adverbials can be moved to one or more positions in the sentence without disturbing the sentence pattern or sounding un-English. In the illustrative "tennis" sentences, for instance, five of the six adverbials were movable.

As a last resort for identifying adverbials, try elimination. If the term in question is not a nominal, verbal, or adjectival — and not a structure word — then it is by elimination an adverbial.

It must never be forgotten that we are dealing with a positional class and that any form-class can be an adverbial, e.g.,

Noun:	He will come *Sunday.*
Verb:	They stood *eating.* (= thus)
Adjective:	They played *dirty.*
	Come *quick.*
Adverb:	Come *quickly.*
Uninflected word:	Come *back.*

In the word-stock of English there are many uninflected words often employed in adverbial positions, and it may be useful to you to inspect a sample of them before proceeding with the next exercise. Here they are:

1. Uninflected words used both as adverbials and prepositions: above, about, after, around, before, behind, below, down, in, inside, on, out, outside, since, to, under, up.

2. "-ward" series, with optional *-s:* afterward, backward, downward, forward, homeward, inward, northward, outward, upward, windward.

3. "Here" series: here, herein, hereby, heretofore, hereafter.

4. "There" series: there, therein, thereby, therefore, thereafter.

5. "-where" series: anywhere, everywhere, somewhere, nowhere.

6. "-ways" series: crossways, sideways; also, anyway.

7. "-time" series: meantime, sometime, anytime, sometimes.

8. Miscellaneous: today, tonight, tomorrow, yesterday, now, then, seldom, still, yet, already, meanwhile, also, too, never, not, forth, thus, sidelong, headlong, maybe, perhaps, instead, indeed, henceforth, piecemeal, nevertheless, downstairs, indoors, outdoors, offhand, overseas, unawares, besides, furthermore, always.

EXERCISE 204

★ Underline each one-word adverbial. In each blank of the first column write the number that shows which of the five numbered adverbial positions it occupies:

1. before the pattern, with or without juncture.
2. after the subject and before the verb.
3. after the auxiliary or the first auxiliary.
4. after the verb in pattern 4 and after *be* in patterns 1, 2, and 3.
5. after the complement of the verb (SC, OV, OC).

In each second blank identify the form-class of the adverbial by N (noun), V (verb), Adj (adjective), Adv (adverb), or UW (uninflected word).

1. Bob ran headlong into the fence. _____ _______
2. Indeed, bring him with you. _____ _______
3. He drove the car madly around the track. _____ _______
4. I certainly will. _____ _______
5. They entered singing. _____ _______
6. He frequently reads in bed. _____ _______
7. The deer was standing below. _____ _______
8. I'll see you afterward. _____ _______
9. I will eventually make a report. _____ _______
10. We usually stopped for tea. _____ _______
11. They stood around for ten minutes. _____ _______
12. Will you set the plant here? _____ _______
13. It is still a long distance to Albany. _____ _______
14. The vice-president had already signed the contract. _____ _______
15. The bus approached rapidly. _____ _______
16. We had seldom walked to the park. _____ _______
17. Meanwhile Giovanni started the fire. _____ _______
18. The ride was also tiresome. _____ _______
19. They rode Saturday. _____ _______
20. The ants were everywhere. _____ _______

Word groups as well as single words can occupy adverbial positions and thereby be classified as adverbials. Here are some illustrative groups in the five positions.

1. Before the pattern, with or without juncture.

With a sharp ax you can do wonders.
By using a little red here, you can balance your colors.
Unless you follow the printed directions, the set will not fit properly together.

2. After the subject and before the verb.

Angelina *in her own way* was a darling.

3. After the auxiliary or first auxiliary.

You may *in this way* be of great assistance.

4. After the verb in pattern 4 and after *be* in patterns 1, 2, and 3.

He drove *with abandon.*
She is *at any event* happy.
The wolf is *at the door.*
He is *without doubt* an expert.

When an infinitive (*to* + verb) follows the verb, it may be in one of two positions:

Adverbial, after verb in pattern 4, as in

They waited *to escape.*

Nominal, position 3 in pattern 5, as in

They expected *to escape.*

If *in order to* can be substituted for *to*, the infinitive is in the adverbial position: "They waited *in order to* escape." If a *that* or *it* can be substituted for the infinitive, it is in the nominal position: "They expected *that/it.*"

5. After the complement of the verb (SC, OV, OC).

My brother was a doctor *for twenty years.*
Tom put his watch *where he could find it in the dark.*
They believed the man crazy *after questioning him.*

A prepositional phrase after the object of the verb is not infrequently ambiguous:

They watched the hunter *with the binoculars.*
She spied the dog *on the corner.*

In these two sentences the prepositional phrase is either adjectival or adverbial.

EXERCISE 205

★ The adverbial word groups are italicized. In the blank indicate by number the adverbial position of each.

1. I'll dress *while you shave.* ___
2. *When the coffee is ready,* blow the whistle. ___
3. He might *under the circumstances* agree to the job. ___

4. Our guide split the log *with ease* ___

5. *Chewing his tobacco meditatively*, White Foot studied the blackening sky. ___

6. A hungry trout rose *to the surface.* ___

7. *By that time* the fish were no longer biting. ___

8. *To find the camp,* just follow the creek downstream. ___

9. *From the hilltop* you can see the sawmill. ___

10. Jake hunts *to make a living.* ___

11. You must hold the knife *this way.* ___

EXERCISE 206

★ This is a review of the four positional parts of speech. In the blanks identify each italicized element by N-al (nominal), V-al (verbal), Aj-al (adjectival), or Av-al (adverbial).

1. Last *Monday* was a holiday. ______________

2. The *Monday* washing is on the line. ______________

3. Mrs. Reed always washes *Mondays.* ______________

4. Won't you come *in?* ______________

5. The outs were angry with the *ins.* ______________

6. They stomped *upstairs.* ______________

7. They slept in the *upstairs* room. ______________

8. One can see the airport from *upstairs.* ______________

9. Jake was *wrestling* with his math. ______________

10. The *wrestling* roommates were exhausted. ______________

11. Juniper found *wrestling* exciting. ______________

12. They came in *wrestling.* ______________

13. The student movie is presented *weekly.* ______________

14. The student movie is a *weekly* occurrence. ______________

15. His *way* is the best. ______________

16. He had it *his way.* ______________

17. The mechanic ran the engine *full speed.* ______________

18. *By this means* he burned out the carbon. ______________

19. He raised the hood *because the engine was hot.* ______________

20. They found the cabin *just what they wanted.* ______________

EXERCISE 207

★ This is a review of the four form-class parts of speech. Classify the italicized words by writing in the blanks N (noun), V (verb), Adj (adjective), Adv (adverb) or UW (uninflected word). Remember to use derivational as well as inflectional criteria.

1. Minnie is fond of Siamese *cats.* ________
2. The island was *colonized* by the Northmen. ________
3. One of her *hose* is torn. ________
4. What *punishment* do you think should be administered? ________
5. Helen *always* says the wrong thing. ________
6. Her room was in a state of *chaos.* ________
7. We'll *gladly* refund your money. ________
8. The nurse puts a *disinfectant* on the cut. ________
9. Carl sleeps late *mornings.* ________
10. How *peaceful* the house seems today! ________
11. This dress must be *shortened.* ________
12. The salesman quietly turned *away.* ________
13. Our ladder is not *tall* enough. ________
14. The class listened to a *reading* from Shakespeare. ________
15. I don't know *offhand.* ________

I. Verb-Adverbial Composites

The form we are about to examine is, in its behavior, extraordinarily intricate. As you progress through the explanations, all may appear clear-cut and simple. But if you stray from this carefully laid-out path to inquire into instances of your own finding, you may meet with variations, exceptions, and impasses. So be warned that beneath the specious simplicity of what is to follow lies a tangle of complication.

A verb-adverbial composite consists of two words, a verb followed by an adverbial like *up, down, in, out, over*. There are two kinds, intransitive and transitive, each with partially different structural and transformational characteristics. We will begin with an example of an intransitive verb-adverbial composite, through which we can examine the characteristics of this genre.

1. He tûrned úp. (= appeared)

There are three matters to be noted here which are common to intransitive verb-adverbial composites.

a. The meaning of *tûrned úp* as a unit is different from the sum of the individual meanings of the two parts.

b. The adverbial element *up* has a primary stress. This is normal unless a following primary stress demotes the adverbial primary to a secondary, as in

He tûrned ûp súddenly.

c. The adverbial is not movable, for you would be unlikely to say "Up he turned."

The next example is of a different sort:

2. He clîmbed úp.

This is not a verb-adverbial composite but simply a verb and an adverbial. The differences are these:

a. The meaning is not different from the added total of *climbed* and *up*.

b. The *up* is movable:

Up he climbed.

The stress pattern, however, is the same in both.

EXERCISE 208

★ Classify the italicized words as VAC (verb-adverbial composite) or V + A (verb plus adverbial).

1. The two friends *fell out*. (= quarreled) ______

2. The two friends *walked out*. ______

3. England will always *carry on.* ________

4. Willard *went in.* ________

5. After drinking rapidly and heavily, he suddenly *passed out.* ________

In approaching the third example, we will begin with a simple statement containing a verb plus a prepositional phrase: "They laughed at him." If we turn this into the passive, it becomes

3. He was laughed at. (by them)*

Thus what at first sight might look like a verb-adverbial composite in sentence 3 above is really a passive with a suppressed *by* phrase. Prepositions in the passive, like the *at* here, take third stress, not the primary or secondary stress of adverbials.

EXERCISE 209

★ Classify the italicized words as VAC (verb-adverbial composite), V + A (verb plus adverbial), or P (passive).

1. This bed was *slept in.* ________

2. They *sat down.* ________

3. Harriet can be *depended on.* ________

---

* Some sentences of this type transform into a generally accepted passive: "We sent for the doctor" > "The doctor was sent for." Others are untransformable in this way: "He sat behind the desk" does not transform to "The desk was sat behind." Nor does "He entered with his sister" transform to "His sister was entered with." Between these two extremes are countless other sentences whose passives are doubtful: "He jumped from the cliff" > "The cliff was jumped from" and "He glanced through the window" > "The window was glanced through." These last two passives might be accepted by some native speakers and rejected by others. In short, with the passive transformation in this type of sentence we have a scale of grammaticality.

To witness for yourself this scale of grammaticality, you might try making these sentences passive and observe which passives you would consider grammatical, that is, natural English:

1. The hunter shot at the deer.
2. He waited for the bus.
3. He climbed up the tree.
4. He stood below the waterfall.
5. The prize came in the box.

All along the scale the word after the verb can be shown to be a preposition by transformation to a relative clause: "We sent for the doctor" > "The doctor for whom we sent" and "He sat behind the desk" > "The desk behind which he sat."

This difficulty with the passive will not trouble us here because we are working from the passive to the active; thus those structures which do not have a passive do not enter the picture.

4. The food finally *gave out.* ________

5. They *turned back.* ________

6. She will *make out.* ________

7. She is well *cared for.* ________

8. This sign has been *shot at.* ________

9. Why don't you kiss and *make up?* ________

10. If you are so sleepy, why don't you *turn in?* ________

We turn now to the transitive verb-adverbial composite, illustrated in

4. He tùrned dôwn the óffer.

A distinction must be made here between the verb-adverbial composite plus object of the verb, and the verb plus a prepositional phrase. Here is the second in contrast with example 4:

5. He tûrned dòwn the dríveway.

In sentences like 4 and 5 above we cannot use stress to distinguish adverbial from preposition because there are variations in the stress employed. Many persons, for example, would say *tûrned dôwn* in both sentences. Nor is meaning a completely reliable test, either with the transitive or the intransitive verb. But there remain three tests that are useful.

TEST 1. In a VAC sentence the adverbial can be placed after the object of the verb:

6. He turned the offer dówn.

This change is impossible with the preposition:

7. *He turned the driveway down.

Furthermore, when the object of the VAC is a personal pronoun, the adverbial must be placed after the pronoun object and only there:

8. He turned it dówn.

If one said

9. He turned dówn it

the last two words would be a preposition and its object.

When the adverbial is placed after the object in a VAC sentence, the stress is primary if the object is a pronoun, e.g.,

10. He brought it ín

But when the object is a noun, the stress is either primary or third:

11. He brought the cât ín.
12. He brought the cát ìn.

EXERCISE 210

★ Using test 1, classify the italicized words as VAC–O (verb-adverbial composite and object) or V–PP (verb and prepositional phrase).

1. I will *turn in the requisition.* ______
2. I will *turn in the street.* ______
3. We *called up the plumber.* ______
4. Mother *called up the stairs.* ______
5. He *broke in his new car.* ______
6. The windshield *broke in his new car.* ______

TEST 2. The verb-adverbial composite cannot be split by a modifier, but a modifier can occur between a verb and a prepositional phrase. For example,

13. VAC He *turned up* a new manuscript. (= discovered)
14. V–PP He *turned* (sharply) *up* the country road.

EXERCISE 211

★ Insert a modifier wherever you can after the verb. Then classify the italicized words as VAC or V–PP.

1. The wind *blew* (softly) *down* the valley. ______
2. The wind *blew down* the tree. ______
3. Jean *ran up* a bill. ______
4. Jean *ran* (quickly) *up* the hill. ______
5. Will you *turn on* the light in this room? ______
6. This car can *turn* (around) *on* a dime.* ______

* Compare

a. He knocked out his opponent.
b. He knocked his opponent (completely) out.

In some VAC's like *b*, the adverbial after the object may take a modifier.

TEST 3. The prepositional phrase following the verb can be transformed into a relative structure, but the VAC–O cannot be so treated. Two cases will illustrate.

15. V–PP She *ran down* the hill.

This can become "The hill down which she ran."

16. VAC–O She *ran down* her roommate. (= criticized adversely)

The relative transformation would be impossible: *"The roommate down whom she ran."

EXERCISE 212

★ Make a relative transformation below each sentence which permits it. Then label the italicized parts of each sentence as VAC–O or V–PP.

1. The police *ran in* the criminal. __________

   ____

2. They *ran in* a circle. __________

   ____

3. The teacher stood *drînking în* the móonlight. __________
   (= observing with pleasure)

   ____

4. The teacher stood *drînking ĭn* the móonlight. __________

   ____

5. Frank *called down* his son. (= reprimanded) __________

   ____

6. He *called down* the mountain. __________

   ____

Now an important point. If the verb plus O or PP in question passes any ONE of these three tests, it is deemed a VAC.

EXERCISE 213

★ Apply all three tests to each pair of italicized words. Indicate by number (1, 2, or 3) which tests show the item to be a VAC.

1. I *ran across* an old friend. ______
2. Marge *made up* her mind. ______
3. Marge *made up* the story. ______
4. She *turned over* the pancake. ______
5. Father *looked over* the evening paper. (= scrutinized) ______
6. The Senate *brought about* a change. ______
7. Ed always *turns out* a long term paper ______
8. The clerk *wrapped* the meat *up*. ______
9. Will you *take over* the job? ______
10. Willie soon *wore out* his shoes. ______

Some sentences of the kind we have been discussing seem to have two adverbials, as in

17. I won't *put up with* that child.

Such expressions are most simply analyzed as being composed of a VAC (or sometimes a verb plus adverbial) followed by a prepositional phrase. The stresses on the three words are variable, but we can say that the adverbial usually has a stronger stress than the preceding verb and the following preposition. The fact that you can substitute a single word, like *endure*, is irrelevant; for meaning, as you may have noticed in some of the exercise sentences, is an untrustworthy guide.

EXERCISE 214

★ This exercise merely brings to your attention a few examples of the kind of expression discussed immediately above and illustrates the variations in stress patterns. Place stress marks over the italicized words and add any primary stress that follows them.*

---

* The primary stress on the adverbial may be demoted to a secondary stress by a following primary in the same segment between terminals. For an example, see the answer to the first sentence.

1. She *looks up to* her mother. (= admires)
2. She *looks down on* her former friends. (= scorns)
   (Note that these two sentences can be interpreted literally with no change in stresses. For example,
   Sitting on the floor, the baby *looked up to* her mother.
   From the upper window she *looked down on* her former friends in the courtyard.)
3. *Look out for* the dog.
4. In case of an argument I'll *stand up for* you.
5. Will you *stand up for* me at the christening?
6. We'll *look in on* you. (= visit)
7. McBride *made off with* another man's wife.
8. The company will *make up for* your loss. (= repay)
9. After the quarrel we *made up with* them.
10. You must *get on with* the job.

J. Qualifiers

In our study of the parts of speech we have at this point completed our scrutiny of the four form-classes — noun, verb, adjective, and adverb — and their parallel positional classes. These form-classes are large and open groups, and we identified their members by means of inflectional and derivational affixes.

We now turn to parts of speech of a different kind known as structure classes. The structure classes are small and closed groups, seldom admitting new members. You have already studied three of these classes — auxiliaries, prepositions, and determiners. We recognize members of structure classes by position alone, since the members of each class have no characteristics of form in common; also, since the structure classes are small, varying from only one member to about fifty, and since most members do not have homophones in other classes, we get to know them individually, like Uncle Elmer. For example, we are never in doubt about *from.* We know that it is always a preposition and that its fellows are words like *at, of,* and *with.*

The fourth structure-class contains the qualifiers. The qualifier position is the one just before an adjectival or an adverbial, like the slots in these sentences:

The dinner was ________________ good.

She performed ________________ skillfully.

Thus it is evident that uninflected words like *very, quite,* and *rather* can be called qualifiers; and when an inflected word like *pretty* and *mighty* appears in the same position, consider it a qualifier by position. This is simple and clear enough. But this slot can also be filled by a number of adverbials like *fairly*, *moderately*, *awfully*, *really*, and *excessively*. We know such words to be adverbials for one or both of two reasons.

First, they may be adverbs by form, having as base an adjective, like *fair* or *excessive*, to which has been added the {-ly_1} suffix.

Second, they may occur in adverbial positions like

He played *fairly*.
He played the trumpet *awfully*.

These positions do not accept words of the *very* group, for we do not say

*He played *very*.
*He played the trumpet *quite*.

Hence the *very*, *quite* group must be a different positional class from the *fairly*, *awfully* group; and yet they share the same position in the first pair of sentences above. We get out of this quandary by simply acknowledging that the position before the adjectival and adverbial accepts both qualifiers and adverbials and by saying that words in this position will be termed qualifiers unless they can also be employed in adverbial positions.

EXERCISE 215

★ In the blanks write Q or Av-al to show whether the italicized words should be classified as qualifiers or adverbials.

1. That was *awfully* nice of you. ______
2. Professor Baldnoggin is *pretty* tough. ______
3. Dorothy was *rather* disappointed. ______
4. The novel proved *extremely* distasteful. ______
5. I feel *quite* fine, thank you. ______
6. You are *too* kind. ______
7. Are you *completely* happy with your courses? ______
8. My car is running *quite* nicely. ______
9. Bert has a *mighty* powerful jack there. ______
10. You played *very* acceptably in the second half. ______

Some qualifiers are not used before all adjectivals and adverbials but have a limited distribution. We shall not take the time to investigate all the vagaries of such distributions, but a glance at a few examples may prove instructive. Here are a few cases of qualifiers with restricted distribution:

stark naked	*far* up	*just* right
dead right	*bright* red	*almost* ready
clean out	*much* alive	*full* well
fresh out	*boiling* hot	*precious* little
right now	*fighting* mad	*jolly* hot
beastly cold	*great* big	*that* good

Sometimes noun clusters and idiomatic expressions are used in the position before adjectivals and adverbials and must therefore be regarded as qualifiers. Among the common ones are

a lot	kind of
a great deal	sort of
a little	a bit

With qualifiers of adjectivals and adverbials in the comparative degree, the description is a little different. As illustration, look at these sentences:

*I feel *much* good.
*I feel *very* better.

As a native speaker you know at once that these are un-English. Now, switch the qualifiers, and the sentences feel comfortable, like a well-tailored suit. The point is that the qualifiers used before a comparative are not quite the same as those before the positive degree.

EXERCISE 216

★ You are given below a list of words which are qualifiers when in the qualifier slot. Following the list are questions to answer.

a bit	a lot	enough
a good deal	awful	indeed
a great deal	a whole lot	just
almost	even	kind of
least	plenty	some
less	pretty	somewhat
lots	quite	sort of
mighty	rather	still
more	real	too
most	right	very
no	so	

You must remember that we are dealing with a positional class. So don't worry about words on this list which have homophones in other positional classes, e.g.,

Adjectival: It was the *most* fun.
What a *pretty* girl.
Adverbial: She is coming *too*.
Nominal: I've had *enough*.
He ate *a whole lot* of potatoes.

1. Which qualifier has a position after, not before, its head? ____________

2. Which qualifier can occur either before or after its head? ____________
3. Which qualifiers can occur in the slot below?

She is coming ____________ now. ____________
4. Which qualifiers can occur in the slot before comparatives, as in this sentence?

She is ____________ happier today. ____________

XVI.

Modification

THE nine basic sentence patterns that we studied in Chapter XIV were exemplified by somewhat skeletal sentences in order to reveal the structure without interference from unneeded parts. But in our actual speaking and writing we seldom use sentences so spare and bony. Instead we flesh out our sentences with many kinds of modifiers.

A modifier is a subordinate element in an endocentric structure.* It is

* An endocentric structure is a structure which has the same function as one of its parts or which is replaceable by one of its parts.

Structure	*Replacement*
those dirty dogs	dogs
extremely dirty	dirty
dog across the street	dog
dog which was howling	dog
reads rapidly	reads
reads to relax his mind	reads
often reads	reads
quite often	often

The replacing part is the head. The other words and word groups are the modifiers. The replacing part may retain a determiner from the endocentric structure because a certain class of nouns (count nouns) require a determiner in the singular:

Elmer bought *a shiny new bicycle.*
Replacement: Elmer bought *a bicycle.*

a word or word group that affects the meaning of a headword in that it describes, limits, intensifies, and/or adds to the meaning of the head. In the noun cluster *the blue shirt*, for example, the word *blue* describes the shirt; it limits by excluding other colors; and it adds to the plain meaning of *shirt*.

Modifiers may appear before or after the heads they modify, and sometimes they are separated from the head by intervening words. Here are some examples of modifiers with heads.

Modifier	*Head*	*Modifier*
dirty	dog	
that	dog	
	dog	there
	dog	across the street
	dog	barking angrily
	dog	to be feared
	dog	which was howling
extremely	dirty	
	reads	rapidly
	reads	standing
	reads	when he wants to relax
	reads	nights
	reads	to calm his mind
often	reads	
quite	often	

The position of a modifier sometimes shows the head that it modifies:

The ______________ flower

This slot, which we call adjectival, is the position of a modifier of the following noun, whether the slot is filled by an adjective (*lovely*), noun (*garden*), or a verb (*blossoming*). At times there is no positional cue to show what is modified:

A butterfly in the garden *which was fluttering among the flowers.*

In this sentence it is the meaning which reveals that the *which* group modifies *butterfly* and not *garden*. At other times we rely upon formal cues, not position or meaning, to keep the modification clear:

The flowers in the garden which *were* blossoming beautifully.
The flowers in the garden which *was* blossoming profusely.

When neither position nor formal signals reveal the modification, and when the meaning does not make it clear, we have an ambiguity, as in

A flower in the garden which was blossoming beautifully.

EXERCISE 217

★ Rewrite these sentences, replacing each italicized endocentric structure by its head. Retain the determiner when necessary.

1. His laughter was *extremely loud.*

   ____

2. *The jar on the shelf* is filled with dates.

   ____

3. McPherson was *a dour man who seldom smiled.*

   ____

4. The two *strolled through the park after they had finished work.*

   ____

5. The constable *laughed nastily.*

   ____

6. We heard *the loud rattling clank of the chain.*

   ____

7. *The angry squirrel in the pine* scolded the blue jays.

   ____

8. *The contract which he signed* had paragraphs of fine print.

   ____

9. The searchers found *the car lying on its side.*

   ____

10. Claribel *jumped into the pool.*

   ____

In the above exercise the parts that you left out were modifiers, both single-word and word-group modifiers. Take another look at these modifiers before going on to the next exercise.

EXERCISE 218

★ Write down the one-word heads that are modified by the italicized words.

1. A *noisy* motorcycle sputtered there. ______________
2. A noisy motorcycle sputtered *there.* ______________
3. The motorcycle *in the yard* had not been recently used. ______________
4. He stopped *for a second.* ______________

5. He stopped *to pick up the agate.* ______________
6. It was *very* nice of you. ______________
7. Walter came to the coffee shop *rather* often. ______________
8. He stopped *when the clock struck twelve.* ______________
9. That fellow *making his bed* is the supervisor. ______________
10. Gerald owned a long black whip, *which he could snap expertly.* ______________

The two exercises above illustrate modification. Modification is a function, and a word or word group which performs this function is a modifier. A modifier belongs not with the form-classes or the position-classes but with the function-classes, such as the subject of verb, direct object, indirect object, object complement, and object of preposition. Most words have a threefold classification — by form, by position, and by function. Here are two examples to make this clear:

The *jolly minstrel* sang a ballad.

In this sentence *minstrel* is classified as a noun by form, a nominal by position, and the subject of the verb by function; and *jolly* is called an adjective by form, an adjectival by position, and a modifier by function.

Now we are ready to look at modification systematically.

A. Sentence Modifiers

A sentence modifier is one which modifies, as its head, the entire rest of the sentence, and is often set apart by terminals — rising, sustained, or falling.

Example: Naturally he behaved at the party.

Here *naturally* modifies *he behaved at the party.* Compare this

He behaved naturally at the party.

In this sentence *naturally* modifies the verb *behaved,* and the meaning is different from that of the former sentence. Here are some examples of sentence modifiers:

1. *Luckily,* I knew how to swim.
2. *Since the door was closed,* we climbed in the back window.
3. *In fact,* the contract is invalid.
4. *The guests having departed,* we resumed the normal household routine.
5. *To keep dry in a tent,* you should be provided with a fly.
6. *Considering the circumstances,* he was lucky to escape alive.

Each of these, we note, is in initial sentence position, the most common one for sentence modifiers. However, sentence modifiers may appear in medial and final positions as well.

EXERCISE 219

★ Rewrite the six sentences above, placing the sentence modifiers in positions other than initial.

1. ____

2. ____

3. ____

4. ____

5. ____

6. ____

EXERCISE 220

★ Place above each juncture position separating the sentence modifier from the rest of the sentence an R, S, or F to show whether the juncture is rising, sustained, or fading. There will be considerable variation among different speakers at these points, so do not be disturbed if your answers do not accord with the key.

Example: In fact,^{R} he knew how to swim.

1. Apparently, the iron lung had been malfunctioning.
2. The iron lung, apparently, had been malfunctioning.
3. The iron lung had been malfunctioning, apparently.
4. Before frying the trout, the Indian guide greased the pan with raw bacon.
5. He spends his money, most of the time, on repairs for his car.
6. To be sure, the orchestra is not the best in the world.
7. The orchestra, to be sure, is not the best in the world.
8. The orchestra is not the best in the world, to be sure.
9. Unfortunately, she did not keep up her grades.
10. She did not keep up her grades, unfortunately.

It is not always possible to distinguish a sentence modifier from one which modifies a part of the sentence. At times there is a difference, often subtle, between the meaning of a sentence modifier and that of an identical expression which does not seem to be a sentence modifier. The next exercise will illustrate.

EXERCISE 221

1. In which sentence did Oliver die? Check one.

   a. Happily, Oliver did not die. ___

   b. Oliver did not die happily. ___

2. Write a synonym for *since*.

   a. I haven't seen my brother, since he moved away. ______________

   b. I haven't seen my brother since he moved away. ______________

3. Rewrite or rearrange these sentences to show the difference in meaning.

   a. He was anxious, to tell the truth.

   ____

   b. He was anxious to tell the truth.

   ____

4. In which sentence is Bernard going to the party?

   a. Bernard is not going to the party, because she will be there. ___

   b. Bernard is not going to the party because she will be there. ___

B. The Noun Cluster: Prenominal Modifiers

The noun cluster, you will recall, consists of a noun head together with all the modifiers that accompany it, before and after.

Example: All my many old school friends (NH) of other days who have passed away

We shall take up first those modifiers which precede the head. These are known as prenominal modifiers and constitute subclasses of the adjectival. Let us begin with the simple modification structure of determiner plus noun head, e.g.,

D NH
the fence

In case your memory has misted over, here are the determiners again:

Article	*Poss. Adj.*	*Poss. of Names*	*Demonstrative*
the	her	John's	this
a/an	his		that
	its		these
	my		those
	our		
	their		
	your		

Between the determiner and the noun is the position for adjectives:

D	*Adj*	*NH*
that	low	fence
your	sturdy	fence

The same position is also occupied by nouns which modify the noun head, e.g.,

D	*N*	*NH*
our	garden	fence
their	wire	fence

When an adjective and a noun both precede the noun head, the adjective precedes the modifying noun, thus:

D	*Adj*	*N*	*NH*
our	sturdy	garden	fence
that	low	wire	fence

EXERCISE 222

★ Make each list of words into a noun cluster following the pattern of *D Adj N NH.*

1. a, street, village, narrow ____________________
2. large, dormitory, college, this ____________________
3. players, tall, those, sophomore ____________________
4. photogenic, swimmer, that, girl ____________________
5. this, counselor, enthusiastic, senior ____________________
6. wool, blue, necktie, George's ____________________
7. leather, her, shoes, old ____________________
8. desk, hardwood, large, his ____________________
9. cheap, ballpoint, these, pens ____________________
10. typewriter, student, my, portable ____________________

This pattern of *D Adj N NH* is often ambiguous, as the adjective may modify either the first noun alone or the noun plus the noun head. Consider

a decent college graduate.

This cluster may mean either "graduate of a decent college" or "decent graduate of a college." The overlapping of superfixes may play a part in such ambiguities, as in

Those hôt cár dèals

Here we can say that *hôt* modifies the word-compound *cár dèals*, or that the *deals* are in *hôt cárs*, with the modifier plus noun-stress. Numerous ambiguous clusters have this stress pattern.

EXERCISE 223

★ Give two meanings for each of these ambiguous noun clusters.

1. A smâll árms fàctory a. ______________________

   b. ______________________

2. That grêasy kíd stùff a. ______________________

   b. ______________________

3. The bâsic bóok sèrvice a. ______________________

   b. ______________________

4. A fôreign lánguage tèacher a. ______________________

   b. ______________________

5. An ôld cár enthùsiast a. ______________________

   b. ______________________

We can now add to the prenominal modifiers another group which precede the determiners, and which are called predeterminers. This group consists of *all*, *both*, *half*, *double*, and a few others, as in

Pre D	*D*	*Adj*	*N*	*NH*
all	my	old	school	friends

EXERCISE 224

★ Make each list into a noun cluster, beginning with a predeterminer.

1. blocks, your, cement, half, new ______________________
2. long, copper, wires, all, the ______________________

3. engagement, both, lovely, her, rings ______________________

4. fresh, those, flowers, prairie, all ______________________

5. recalcitrant, both, coons, baby, my ______________________

The possessive of common nouns (not personal or geographical) appears between the determiner and the noun head. Let us examine its possible positions, using the pattern

D	*Adj*	*Noun*	*Noun Head*
the	red	garden	roses

We will use the noun possessive *summer's* and see where it fits.

D		*Adj*	*Noun Head*
the	summer's	red	roses

D	*Adj*		*Noun Head*
the	red	summer's	roses

D		*Noun*	*Noun Head*
the	summer's	garden	roses

D		*Adj*	*Noun*	*Noun Head*
the	summer's	red	garden	roses

All these sound like normal English. But we would not say

D	*Noun*		*Noun Head*
the	garden	summer's	roses

So it appears that the possessive of common nouns occurs anywhere between the determiner and the noun head, except between N and NH. Yet what about

D	*Noun*		*Noun Head*
a	cotton	man's	shirt ?

This too sounds English. It is likely that different subclasses of the noun or the noun possessive permit different positioning patterns. This is a matter that requires investigation. With this limitation in mind, we can say here that the possessive of common nouns can occur anywhere between the determiner and the noun head.

These noun possessives at times make for ambiguity in the noun cluster. For example, we can interpret *the late summer's roses* as "the roses of late summer" or "the late roses of summer." Such ambiguities in the written words may disappear in the spoken form because of the ability of the suprasegmentals to distinguish meanings. The cluster *camel's hair brush* is ambiguous to the eye, but the ear will distinguish between *câmel's háir brùsh* and *cámel's hàir brùsh.*

EXERCISE 225

★ Give two meanings for each of these noun clusters in their written form.

1. An old girl's bicycle a. ______________________

   b. ______________________

2. The world women's congress a. ______________________

   b. ______________________

3. A nice man's fur coat a. ______________________

   b. ______________________

4. A large woman's garment a. ______________________

   b. ______________________

5. An advanced learner's dictionary a. ______________________

   b. ______________________

The next step is to enlarge the class of determiners. The fourteen determiners you have learned can all be preceded by the predeterminers *all*, *both*, and *half*. But besides these fourteen there is a second set of determiners which are not preceded by predeterminers. There are twelve of these:

another	either	neither	what (a)
any	enough	no	which
each	much	some	whose

These belong in the determiner class because they precede adjectives and are mutually exclusive both with one another and with the members of the first set.* The first set we shall label the *the* determiners, subset A; and the others, the *another* determiners, subset B.

The order of the prenominal modifiers we have examined so far may be shown thus:

V	*IV*	*III*	*II*	*I*	*NH*
Pre D	Det A. *the* B. *another*	(Class yet to come.)	Adj	Noun	

* Don't be misled by cases like *this much cider*. Here *this* is not a prenominal modifier. It does not modify *much cider* or *cider;* it is a qualifier like *very* and merely modifies *much*.

EXERCISE 226

★ Place above each modifier the number of the class to which it belongs. In this and the following exercises, be careful about two successive nouns. They may be either a noun modifying a following noun, as in *côllege déan*, or a single compound noun, as in *cláss pìn*.

	IVB	II	I	NH
Example:	any	small	cloth	rag

1. Another huge glass ornament
2. Each happy farm duck
3. Some long winter vacations
4. All our friendly neighborhood dogs
5. Either short cotton dress
6. Enough college friends
7. Both my studious roommates
8. No cold cheese sandwich
9. Much evening enjoyment
10. Neither tired economics student

Above you noticed a blank Class III. This contains words which follow determiners and precede adjectives and which are called postdeterminers. The list is as follows:

ordinal numbers: first, second . . . last
cardinal numbers: one, two, three, through 99

every	most
few	other
less	same
little (quantity)	several
many (a)	single
more	such (a)

This is an untidy class. Not all postdeterminers follow all determiners, but each one follows at least one determiner. And within the group there are complicated orders of precedence. For example, ordinals usually precede cardinals, as in *the first three students*, but this order may be reversed, as in *the two first prizes*. If you try to plot the precedences of these postdeterminers, you will end with about six columns. This whole jungle of determiners and postdeterminers is a *terra incognita* that has not yet been mapped out with complete success. For our purpose it will suffice to recognize the class as a whole without exploring its internal complications.

EXERCISE 227

★ Place the class number — V, IV, III, II, or I — above each modifier.

1. The last three pickles
2. His every wish
3. Many fine university seniors
4. Some other bad newspaper reports
5. Much more white sand
6. Those same hungry ants
7. Both those two aimless fellows
8. Any such childish pranks
9. Harry's few acquaintances
10. What other foolish ideas

EXERCISE 228

★ Make each list of words into a noun cluster. Above each modifier, write the number of the class to which it belongs.

1. summer, several, flowers, pink ______________________
2. garden, both, old, his, hoes ______________________
3. junctures, three, these, all, terminal ______________________
4. bad, schedule, another, examination ______________________
5. two, silk, my, dresses, pretty ______________________

EXERCISE 229

★ Make each list into two noun clusters, and write above each modifier the number of the class to which it belongs.

1. truck, delivery, any, large ______________________

____

2. that, steel, heavy, construction ______________________

____

3. excellent, some, factory, parts ______________________

____

4. vacation, summer, long, student's, the ______________________

____

5. dog, first, good, her, house ______________________

____

One final class of prenominals remains, the restricters. This is a very small set of words like *just, only, even, especially, merely.* Like the other prenominals, these can modify the noun head alone —

just girls
even water
especially candy

or the noun head with its modifiers —

just college girls
just romantic college girls
just another romantic college girl.

These precede the predeterminers and are therefore in Column VI to the left of the noun head.

EXERCISE 230

★ Make a noun cluster of each list and write above each modifier its class number.

1. guests, all, our, especially ______________________
2. kitten, spotted, particularly, her ______________________
3. the, empty, even, box ______________________
4. white, socks, athletic, some, just ______________________
5. only, ten, minutes, short ______________________

A summary of the prenominal modifiers is given in the chart on page 244.

This brief look at the six classes of prenominals is perhaps enough to give you an inkling of the complexity of the modifications that we practice in our daily speech. We have left numerous questions of prenominal order unexplored, and we might take just a quick look to see what they are like. Here are a few:

1. What is the position of these classes?

a. **uninflected adjectivals:**	an *inside* look
b. {**-ing**} **verbs:**	an *approaching* stranger
c. {**-d**$_2$} **verbs:**	the *fallen* snow

2. In Class I which nouns precede which other nouns? For example, you would probably say "an iron garden gate" but not "a garden iron gate." What principle of precedence is operative here?

3. In Class II which adjectives precede which other adjectives? Would you say "a pink Chinese flower" or "a Chinese pink flower"? "A wonderful little book" or "a little wonderful book"? There are subclasses of adjectives in terms of precedence, e.g., those of color, nationality, and shape-size — and those inflected with *-er*, *-est* as opposed to those taking *more* and *most.* What orders of precedence do we as native speakers follow in using these different subclasses?

PRENOMINAL MODIFIERS

VI	*V*	*IV*	*III*	*II*	*I*	*Noun Head*
Restricter	*Predeterminer*	*Determiner*	*Postdeterminer*	*Adjective*	*Noun*	
		A. Articles	Cardinal numbers:	Examples:	Examples:	
especially	all	a/an	1, 2, 3, . . . 99	red	school	
even	both	the	Ordinal numbers:	blue	college	
just	half	Possessive adjs.	first, second	green	dormitory	
merely	double	her	. . . last	old	house	
only		his	every	new	garden	
particularly		its	few	young	fence	
		my	less	big	garage	
		our	little (quantity)	little (size)	door	
		their	many (a)	large	gate	
		your	more	small	summer	
		Poss. of names	most	high	rock	
		John's	other	low	wool	
		Demonstratives:	same	tall	silk	
		this	several	short	steel	
		that	single	thick	iron	
		these	such (a)	thin	clay	
		those	Poss. of common	intellectual	plastic	
		B. another	noun:	dogmatic	cloth	
		any	summer's	thoughtful	brass	
		each		commendable	copper	
		either		excellent	leather	
		enough		prevalent	nylon	
		much		Japanese	brick	
		neither		Chinese	cement	
				American	paper	

PRENOMINAL MODIFIERS

VI	*V*	*IV*	*III*	*II*	*I*	*Noun Head*
Restricter	*Predeterminer*	*Determiner*	*Postdeterminer*	*Adjective*	*Noun*	
		no some what (a) which whose		silken woolen wooden Poss. of common noun: summer's	shoe coat skirt Poss. of common noun: woman's	

C. The Noun Cluster: Postnominal Modifiers

Modifiers of the noun headword may be placed after the headword as well as before it.

Examples:
1. The apartment *downstairs*
2. The apartment, *large and empty*
3. The apartment *in front*
4. The apartment *standing empty*
5. The apartment *located in the rear*
6. The apartment *which is empty*
7. The apartment, *the present home of the Kallikaks*
8. An apartment *to inspect*
9. The apartment *where he lives*

EXERCISE 231

★ Each of the italicized expressions above has the function of modifying the headword, but each is different in form. In the sentences below, the noun modifiers are italicized. After each sentence place the number of the modifier above to which it corresponds.

1. We watched the brown river, *swollen with rain.* ___
2. I want to rent the bicycle *outside.* ___
3. It was a large outdoor swing, *the property of our neighbor.* ___
4. The fireworks were a sight *to behold.* ___
5. The hoe *leaning against the house* is dull. ___
6. The mountain top, *high and craggy,* was hidden in a cloud. ___
7. The building *which is near the library* is new. ___
8. The fan *in the corner* has only one speed. ___
9. I'll see you the day *before you go.* ___
10. Have you ever seen a woman *who loves toads?* ___

1. Word Adjectivals. Word adjectivals normally occur after the noun under two conditions:

1. When the word is not alone but is modified, e.g.,

The mailman, *exuberantly happy,* whistled merrily.
He had never seen a woman *more lovely.*

2. When more than one is employed, e.g.,

The mailman, *tired* and *wet*, trudged along in the rain.
A woman *old* and *gaunt* stood at the door.

EXERCISE 232

★ Underline the postnominal word adjectivals.

1. A new blossom, scarlet and exotic, excited his attention.
2. The emerald ring, inordinately expensive, was beyond his means.
3. There stood the quivering horse, stalwart and proud.
4. He tossed the bag, new and glossy, into the luggage compartment.
5. The problem, extremely complicated, would not yield to his operations.

Nouns may be modified by some of the uninflected words that are often adverbial (see page 215):

The apartment *downstairs*
The game *tomorrow*

An uninflected word in this position is called an adjectival. It usually has a place or time meaning and so may be replaced by *there* or *then*:

The apartment *there*
The game *then*

Occasionally a structural ambiguity will occur, like

The blue dress particularly interested her.

This happens because the postnominal adjectival position coincides with the preverbal adverbial position. In such cases the suprasegmentals usually show whether the word in the ambiguous position modifies the preceding noun or the following verb:

Thĕ blûe drêss partícularly→ínterested her.
Thĕ blûe dréss→particularly ínterested her.

EXERCISE 233

★ Underline each postnominal adjectival and encircle the noun it modifies. Insert primary stresses and juncture arrows.

Example: The (river) <u>belów</u>→wound through the górge.

1. The paragraph above is too long.

2. The students here are a courteous group.

3. This matter too must be discussed.

4. The party yesterday had a large attendance.

5. The weather outside is foul.

EXERCISE 234

★ The sentences below are ambiguous. For each put in the primary stress and the sustained juncture arrow that will indicate that the word in the ambiguous position goes with what follows it.

Example: The méetings→thereafter took place in the Georgian Lóunge.

1. My older brother especially likes to go fishing.
2. The discussion later was heated.
3. Her fiancé then was Elmer Jukes.
4. The rabbits also enjoyed our lettuce.
5. The members only were allowed to buy beer.

Some uninflected adjectivals like those in the last two exercises appear also in the prenominal position:

The above statement
An inside job
His off day

2. Phrase Adjectivals. A noun may be postmodified by the following kinds of phrases.

1. Prepositional phrase:

The bend *in the river*

2. Participial phrase, *-ing*:

The hawk, *spotting his prey*, swooped to the meadow.

3. Participial phrase, *-ed*:

The snow, driven by the wind, sifted through the cracks.

4. Infinitive phrase, *to* ——:

I have a lesson *to study*.

EXERCISE 235

★ Underline the phrases which modify nouns. In the blanks indicate by number the type of phrase.

1. The majority of the voters appeared satisfied. ___
2. There was Elaine, licking her ice-cream cone. ___
3. She gave him a sandwich to eat. ___
4. Johnny wanted the red scooter with the white trim. ___
5. We watched the fullback, urged on by the crowd, fight his way forward. ___
6. Do you have something to do? ___
7. The sailboat looked majestic, gliding across the bay. ___
8. On the river bank sat little Charles, covered with mud. ___
9. The roof of the garage was beginning to leak. ___
10. We saw the puppies tugging at the rope. ___

3. Relative Clause Adjectivals. A noun may be modified by a relative clause. In the examples which follow, the relative clauses are italicized.

1. The trees *that had mistletoe* were half dead.
2. The old carpenter, *who had been laying the floor*, stood up and straightened his back.
3. The partner *whom she selected* was a bashful, red-headed boy.
4. In the bargain basement he found his sister, *whom he had been looking for.*
5. It was the vice-president *to whom I sent the letter.*
6. The client *whose stock he was handling* died.
7. The boat *he wants* is a catamaran.
8. The success *that you become* depends on your initiative.

With the help of these examples we can easily learn to identify relative clauses, which have these characteristics:

1. A relative clause is introduced by a relative: *that, who, whom, whose, which,* and ø (= zero or omitted).

2. The relative has a function in its own clause. For instance, in sentences 1 and 2, *that* and *who* are subjects of the verb. In sentence 3, *whom* is the direct object. In sentences 4 and 5, *whom* is the object of a preposition. In sentence 6, *whose* is a modifier. In sentence 7 the relative is omitted. Such a zero relative can always be replaced by a *that* functioning as the direct object or subjective complement. In sentence 8, *that* is a subjective complement.

EXERCISE 236

★ Underline each relative clause, encircle the relative, and tell in the blank the function of the relative, using these abbreviations:

SV = subject of verb	SC = subjective complement
DO = direct object	M = modifier
OP = object of preposition	ø = relative omitted

1. The composer whom he studied with was Hindemith himself. ______
2. The doctor who performed the operation was Bernard Diamond. ______
3. That is the book I ordered. ______
4. The bait that Jack used was an old-fashioned spinner. ______
5. This is Roger Stuffy, whose mother is president of the PTA. ______
6. The old battered boathouse, which had long been our meeting place, was torn down. ______
7. She is not the woman that her mother was. ______
8. He was a young, blue-eyed pilot, who immediately won our hearts. ______
9. Another boy who helps me is Skunky Hooper. ______
10. The girl whom I met at the play disappeared during the intermission. ______

We shall next divide relative clauses into two kinds, a division that is useful for punctuation and for control of meaning. The two kinds are traditionally called restrictive and nonrestrictive clauses. Let's begin with examples:

Restrictive: He walked to the garage *which he liked best.*
Nonrestrictive: He walked to the garage, *which was a mile away.*

Do you sense the difference in the structural meaning of the two relative clauses? The first clause points out one garage out of many. Of all the garages, he walked to the particular one that he preferred. In the second sentence, however, there is only one garage, and as additional information, we learn that it is a mile away. In short, the restrictive clause restricts the meaning to part of the total, but the nonrestrictive clause makes no such limitation. This is the semantic way of distinguishing the two kinds of relative clauses.

Now we shall distinguish them structurally by means of the suprasegmentals. Look at these two cases:

2 3 2 2 3 1
Restrictive: The boy who úshers→is my latest stéady↓

2 3 2 2 3 2 2 3 1
Nonrestrictive: The bóy→who often úshers→has been rúshing me↓

The key is in the word which precedes the relative, in these examples the word *boy*. When the voice goes on smoothly and without change through the preceding word and the relative — *boy who* — the clause is restrictive, as in the first sentence. But one or more vocal events may happen to the preceding word:

1. It may take a primary stress.
2. It may rise to pitch level 3.
3. It may be followed by any one of the three terminal junctures, revealed by a lengthening of the word.

With a nonrestrictive clause, all three of these will usually occur at the word right before the relative, but the terminal MUST be present to identify a nonrestrictive clause. For example, the following clause is restrictive because it lacks a terminal after *hedge*.

2 3 1
They didn't like the hédge *which I planted*↓

EXERCISE 237

★ Above each relative clause and its headword place the symbols of primary stress, pitch, and juncture to show how you read the sentence aloud. At the end of each sentence place an *R* or an *NR* to indicate whether the relative clause is restrictive or nonrestrictive.

1. The blouse which she preferred was made of sea island cotton. ______
2. She wore an old blue blouse, which had always been her favorite. ______
3. The house that he built was of steel. ______
4. Marilyn, who is fond of dictionaries, bought the new *Webster's Third*. ______
5. The man whom I marry must have curly hair. ______
6. I'll take any man who wears pants. ______
7. The car I want is an MG. ______

8. The student whose purse he returned offered Dick a generous reward. ______

9. Have you a necktie which will match a brown suit? ______

10. Thomas bought a silk, red-and-grey striped necktie, which his roommate admired. ______

By this time you have probably noticed the relation between the type of relative clause and its punctuation: a nonrestrictive clause is set off by commas or a comma; a restrictive clause is not set off. And now you should have no trouble in punctuating them. But as a lagniappe here are a few practical hints:

1. A *that* clause is always restrictive.

2. A clause with a zero relative is restrictive.

3. If you can substitute *that* for *who, whom,* or *which* the clause is restrictive.

4. If the *whom* or *which* can be omitted, the clause is restrictive.

5. After a personal or geographical name, like Elmer Perkins or Brandy Branch, the clause is usually nonrestrictive.

Relative clauses may also begin with *when, where, why, after, before,* and similar words, e.g.,

The hour *when we leave* has not been decided.

EXERCISE 238

★ Underline the relative clause and write the relative in the blank at the right.

1. Do you know the reason why she deserted him? ______

2. The woods where we camp are filled with mushrooms. ______

3. The year after he enlisted was a momentous one. ______

4. Let me know the minute when he comes in. ______

5. I cannot find the place where I lost it. ______

We are now finished with relative clauses, except for a postscriptal caution. The relative *that* should not be confused with the subordinating conjunction *that.* The latter stands outside the sentence pattern of its clause and performs no function in it.

Example: I know *that* he is sick.

EXERCISE 239

★ Underline each relative and indicate its function. Encircle each subordinating conjunction.

1. The lawyer said that the will must be filed. __________
2. The lawyer that he chose was a shyster. __________
3. That he is competent cannot be doubted. __________
4. Are you sure that you returned the book? __________
5. The book that cost me a fine was *The Castle*. __________

4. Appositive Adjectivals. The final postnominal modifier that we shall study is the appositive. The two examples following will show what an appositive is.

2 3 2 2 3 2 2 3 1
The *Bailey Búgle*→a college néwspaper→appears wéekly↓

2 3 1 2 3 1
The top awards were won by two sísters↓ horsewomen in the ríding set↓

In these sentences the expressions *a college newspaper* and *horsewomen in the riding set* are the appositives. From these sentences we observe that:

1. An appositive is a noun cluster (infrequently a noun):

a college newspaper
horsewomen in the riding set

2. An appositive follows a noun cluster or noun:

The *Bailey Bugle*, a college newspaper
two sisters, horsewomen in the riding set

3. An appositive and the noun cluster or noun it follows have the same referent, that is, they refer to the same entity in the physical world. In our examples, the *Bugle* and *a college newspaper* are the same thing, and the *sisters* and *horsewomen* are the same persons.

4. Often, though not always, the appositive and the preceding noun head belong to the same substitute group:

Nouns	*Substitute Group*
Bugle, newspaper	3. it/ pl. they
sisters, horsewomen	2. she/ pl. they

But we also find combinations like

His *sister*, a *senior*, was an honor student.

In this we have

sister	2. she/pl. they
senior	4. he/she/pl. they

5. Appositives of this kind are set off by junctures — rising, sustained, or fading — in speech and by commas in writing.

Further relationships obtain between a noun cluster and the following appositive, those of gender, number, and class membership, but these five will be enough to enable us to understand a simple structure like the appositive.

EXERCISE 240

★ Underline each appositive. In the first blank write the noun or noun cluster which it modifies. In the next two blanks write the number and pronouns of the substitute group of the modified noun and of the appositive. The substitute groups are listed on page 146.

Example: Joseph, my cousin, plays chess.
Joseph 1. he 4. he/she

1. The new sophomore, a lumbering lad of two hundred pounds, appeared on the field for tryouts.

 ______________ ________ ________

2. The three puppies, offspring of registered parents, were taken to the veterinarian's office.

 ______________ ________ ________

3. We pushed off with the boat into the river, a sluggish, slowly winding stream.

 ______________ ________ ________

4. Her heart was set on Alpha Gamma Goopha, the crocheting sorority.

 ______________ ________ ________

5. Mary Evans, a graduate in journalism, became a feature writer for *Playgirl*.

 ______________ ________ ________

Occasionally an appositive occurs in a position other than after a noun or noun cluster, e.g.,

That was what he wanted, *a riding horse*.

A promising lad of eighteen, Harry was soon a favorite among his classmates.

Appositives may be divided into two kinds, restrictive and nonrestrictive, distinguished by the suprasegmentals which accompany them. Here they are:

2 3 1
Restrictive: We watched Colonel Kusack lead the pólo team↓

2 3 2 2 3 2 3 1
Nonrestrictive: We watched Kúsack,→the cólonel,→lead the pólo team↓

With the restrictive appositive there is no juncture between the noun cluster or noun and its following appositive, in our example between *Colonel* and *Kusack*. But with the nonrestrictive appositive there is a terminal juncture at this point, shown in writing by a comma. This terminal is usually a sustained → or a rising ↑ juncture. It is likely, however, to be a fading juncture ↓ if at this point the sentence pattern may be considered complete. For example,

2 3 2 2 3 2 2 3 1
The mótorcycle,→a secondhand contráption,→was in good shápe↓

2 3 1 2 3 1
They stopped before the hóuse,↓a decorated Victorian mánsion↓

EXERCISE 241

★ Above each sentence supply the primary stress, pitch, and juncture marks as far as the end of the appositive.

1. The scoutmaster, Longlegs, prepared the beans.
2. The pressman interviewed Scoutmaster Longlegs.
3. The play *Hamlet* will be presented next week.
4. We saw *Hamlet*, a play by Shakespeare.
5. She had always enjoyed the poem "Trees."
6. Her favorite poem, "Trees," was included in the new collection.
7. We inspected his new car, a long, sleek Humber.
8. The tulips, a hybrid variety from Holland, will bloom early.
9. A Republican from Vodka Valley, Ivanovitch sat at the speaker's table.
10. I felt what I always feel, a sense of frustration.

D. The Verb Cluster: One-Word Adverbials

A verb cluster, as you have already seen, consists of a verb and all the modifiers and complements that cluster around it. The one-word modifiers are the adverbials, which we studied in their characteristic positions. All adverbials in these positions are part of the verb cluster except those which serve the function of sentence modifiers. And we classified the three most common kinds of adverbials as expressing time, place, and manner, that is, as being replaceable by *then*, *there* or *thus*. Although these three categories account for the majority of adverbials, there are also other adverbials which are outside these classes, e.g.,

. . . will *perhaps* drive.
. . . should do it *anyway*.
. . . may dance *instead*.

Here a short review exercise may be salutary.

EXERCISE 242

★ Underline the one-word adverbials in these verb clusters. After each sentence classify them as T (time), P (place), M (manner), or ø (none of these).

1. . . . shouted angrily. ___
2. . . . often drove without her license. ___
3. . . . rarely drove carelessly. ___ ___
4. . . . felt fearfully in the drawer. ___
5. . . . never work Sunday. ___ ___
6. . . . was walking ahead to the bridge. ___
7. . . . could even smell him. ___
8. . . . had always lived alone. ___ ___
9. . . . kept looking backward. ___
10. . . . were happily chatting in the patio. ___
11. . . . may still snow. ___
12. . . . can't find it anywhere. ___
13. . . . cautiously looked sidewise. ___ ___
14. . . . read the story aloud. ___
15. . . . tasted the ginger timidly. ___
16. . . . works Saturdays. ___
17. . . . gnashes his teeth sleeping. ___

18. . . . ate seated. ___

19. . . . played cleaner than before. ___

20. . . . came prepared. ___

E. The Verb Cluster: Word-Group Modifiers

In the verb cluster we find various kinds of word groups operating to modify the verb headword. They are the following:

1. **Prepositional phrase adverbials:** eats *in the kitchen*
2. **Noun cluster adverbials:** eats *every hour*
3. **Subordinate clause adverbials:** eats *when he is hungry*
4. **Infinitive phrase adverbials:** eats *to satisfy his appetite*
5. **Participial phrases in -ing as adverbials:** eats *standing at the counter*
6. **Participial phrases in -ed as adverbials:** ate *seated at the counter*

1. Prepositional Phrase Adverbials. Prepositional phrases that modify the verb headword often come right after the verb, in adverbial position 4:

The car slid *into the garage.*

Two such modifying phrases may appear in succession, each modifying the verb:

The car slid *into the garage with its headlights on.*

Positions before the verb (position 2) and within the auxiliary-verb combination (position 3) are also possible:

Harry *at that time* was studying Akkadian.
Harry was *at that time* studying Akkadian.

And after the direct object one may often find a prepositional phrase modifying the verb head (position 5):

He put the chair *on the lawn.*

Two of the positions mentioned above are subject to ambiguity. You can guess which ones if you remember that in the noun cluster a prepositional phrase modifies an immediately preceding noun, e.g.,

The chair *on the lawn*
The garage *with the lights on*

They are the postnominal positions, of course — the one after the object of the preposition and the one after the direct object. Here is what can happen:

The car coasted into the garage with the lights on.
He found the chair on the lawn.

Each sentence is here structurally ambiguous.

EXERCISE 243

★ After each sentence write N if the italicized prepositional phrase modifies a noun headword, V if it modifies a verb headword, and A if it is structurally ambiguous.

1. He greeted the girl *with a smile.* ___
2. The child *in the blue rompers* ran *into the kitchen.* ___ ___
3. Jake was fishing *from the bridge* *for the first time.* ___ ___
4. The dog bit several people *in the crowd.* ___
5. We watched the game *on the front porch.* ___
6. We had never *until that time* visited the tomb. ___
7. She hurried *to the auditorium* *for her interview.* ___ ___
8. The flower *between the pages* was flat and dried. ___
9. She pressed the flower *between the pages.* ___
10. Georgia waited *in her room* *for the telephone call.* ___ ___

2. Noun Cluster Adverbials. Noun clusters are used as modifiers in the verb cluster to modify the verb head or the head with other words, as in

. . . held the hammer *that way.*
. . . will pay *the next time.*

EXERCISE 244

★ Underline the modifying noun clusters in these verb clusters.

1. . . . will see you this Friday.
2. . . . sold the cat the following day.
3. . . . had come the whole way.
4. . . . work a little while.
5. . . . return another time.

3. Subordinate Clause Adverbials. Subordinate clauses in this context are those word groups which have a subject and predicate and begin with words like *after*, *although*, *as*, *as if*, *as soon as*, *because*, *before*, *if*, *since*, *that*, *unless*, *until*, *when*, *where*, *in case* (*that*), *in order that*, *once*. These words are called subordinating conjunctions. Unlike the relatives, they have no function within the clause they introduce. They state a relationship, e.g., cause, time, condition, and make the clause a part of a larger grammatical structure. When such clauses are separated from the rest of the sentence by juncture, they are sentence modifiers, as we have learned. But when they occur in the verb cluster with no junctural separation, they are modifiers of the verb or of a larger group.

Examples· The terrified lad ran *until he was exhausted.*
Call *when you need me.*
I'll scream *unless you let go.*
She telephoned *as soon as she could.*
She looked at the toad *as if it were poisonous.*

EXERCISE 245

★ The modifying word groups in each verb cluster are italicized. Identify each one as PP (prepositional phrase), NC (noun cluster), or SC (subordinate clause.)

1. Come *as you are.* ________
2. Gerald has been working on his paper *the whole afternoon.* ________
3. I'll wait for you *where the road forks.* ________
4. I'll just sit *a while.* ________
5. The blue jay perched *on the eaves.* ________
6. Ellen has not written *since she left.* ________
7. Don't touch that wire *with your bare hands.* ________
8. Please mail this *before the post office closes.* ________
9. Bernie walks *two miles* to school *every day.* ________ ________
10. Let me know *if you need assistance.* ________
11. Why don't you come over *this evening?* ________
12. We must get home *before the sun rises.* ________
13. I'll write that letter *the first thing* in the morning. ________
14. You can't stop *once you have started.* ________
15. He will be at the office *until it closes.* ________

4. Infinitive Phrase Adverbials. It is necessary to distinguish between the infinitive phrase as modifier and as a direct object of the verb. The distinction can easily be made by substitution, as you learned in the chapter on adverbials. These sentences will remind you:

Modifier: He works *to* (= *in order to*) *succeed.*
Object: He wants *to succeed*(= *it/that*).

EXERCISE 246

★ In each blank label the italicized infinitive phrase as M (modifier) or OV (direct object of verb).

1. The children like *to gather hazelnuts.* ______
2. They waited *to see the result.* ______
3. O'Brian wanted *to be relieved of the office.* ______
4. O'Brian dieted *to reduce his weight.* ______
5. She studied long hours *to make an A in the course.* ______

5. Participial Phrases in* -ing *and in* -ed *as Adverbials. You have previously met participial phrases in *-ing* and *-ed* as modifiers of the noun. Their function as modifiers in the verb cluster is similar, as these sentences will show:

Modifier of noun: The girl *eating the sundae* is a freshman.
Modifier of verb: The girl sat *eating a sundae.*
Modifier of noun: The sonata *played at the recital* was Beethoven's *32nd.*
Modifier of verb: He returned *defeated by the weather.*

EXERCISE 247

★ The participial phrases are italicized. Point out what they modify by NM (modifier of noun) and VM (modifier of verb).

1. Mary came *laughing softly.* ______
2. He sat *entranced by the music.* ______
3. The girl *laughing at his sally* is a flatterer. ______
4. The pitcher arrived *broken to bits.* ______
5. She entered *singing a gay tune.* ______

EXERCISE 248

★ Underline the word group adverbials which function as modifiers in the verb cluster. Classify each as

1. Prepositional phrase
2. Noun cluster
3. Subordinate clause
4. Infinitive phrase
5. Participial phrase in *-ing*
6. Participial phrase in *-ed*

1. The patient lay prone on the operating table. ________
2. She labored to improve her flower garden. ________
3. We must send them a card this Christmas. ________
4. He lay crushed by the toppling rock. ________
5. Open your eyes when you hear the bell. ________
6. She swung holding the rope. ________
7. Bring a chair if you can. ________
8. Jim's work by that time had much improved. ________
9. You can do the problem either way. ________
10. She sat splashing the water. ________

XVII.

Constituents

A. Immediate Constituents

In our treatment of modification up to now, we have dealt with only first-level modifiers and their heads. For example, in a noun cluster like

> The man who stood on the corner of the street

we have pointed out that

> who stood on the corner of the street

is a relative clause modifying its head, *man*, but we have ignored the modifiers of modifiers and the modifiers of modifiers of modifiers, ad infinitum. Let us illustrate these by means of the noun cluster above. Within the modifying clause

> who stood on the corner of the street

we see that

> on the corner of the street

is an adverbial modifying its head, *stood*. And within

> on the corner of the street

it is apparent that

> of the street

is an adjectival modifying its head, *corner*. We might show these internal modifications in terms of levels, like this:

	The man who stood on the corner of the street
M level 1:	*who stood on the corner of the street*
M level 2:	*on the corner of the street*
M level 3:	*of the street*

Or we might use concentric boxes or circles to diagram this nesting characteristic of modifiers:

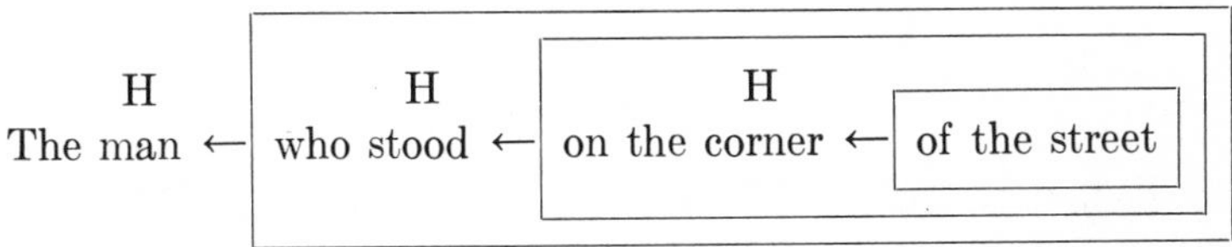

It is expedient, however, to deal with such levels or boxes of modification as part of a broader view of sentence structure known as immediate constituent analysis.

Grammatical structures in English, large and small, tend to be binary. This means that most structures can be divided into two parts and that native speakers of English show considerable agreement on the point of division. For example, where would you divide these structures into two parts?

1. The house on the hill was wrecked by the tornado
2. Standing near the tomb
3. All my college friends

It is likely that most of your class will divide after *hill, standing,* and *all.*

Each of the two parts into which any structure is divided is called an immediate constituent, abbreviated IC. In the complete IC analysis of a sentence we cut the sentence into two parts or IC's, then cut each of these two again into two, and so on until we have only individual words remaining as parts. Here is how such an analysis looks:

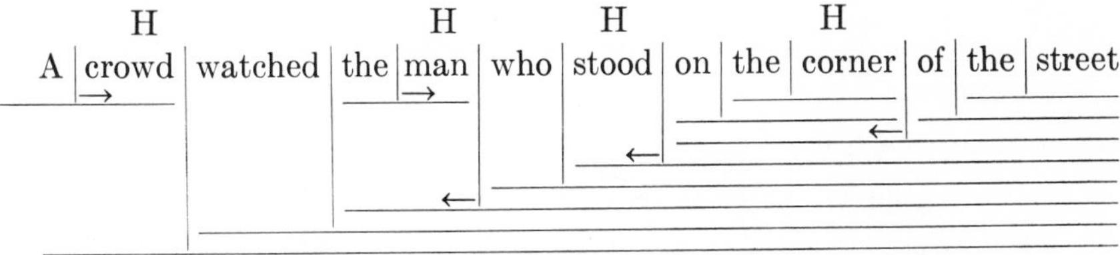

In this analysis an arrow points from each modifier to its head, and you can see here in graphic form the levels of modification amid the total pattern.

Now we shall see how various English structures are cut into IC's, recognizing, however, that not all sentences are amenable to this kind of analysis and that there is an element of arbitrariness in our procedure.

1. SENTENCES CONTAINING A SENTENCE MODIFIER. The first IC cut separates a sentence modifier from the rest of the sentence. Examples:

Of course | the money must be paid.

Unless you learn to swim | you cannot go on this trip.

To earn money | they organized a car wash.

Speaking earnestly | the lad convinced the dean.

I was sleeping | to tell the truth.

EXERCISE 249

★ Make the first IC cut in these sentences:

1. In fact, both tires are flat.
2. When the game is over, let's meet for a bite to eat.
3. I'll give you a hand, certainly.
4. To attract birds, one must provide shelter and food.
5. Smiling slightly, she gently rebuked him.

2. SENTENCE. In a sentence without a sentence modifier, the first cut is made between the noun cluster functioning as subject and the verb cluster functioning as predicate. Examples:

The canoe in the boathouse | had dried out during the winter.

The low-flying plane which roared above the trees | frightened the children.

EXERCISE 250

★ Make the first IC cut in these sentences.

1. The tulips in the flower bed drooped and died.
2. The striped Dutch tulips were gorgeous.
3. They soon had the boat in the water.
4. The lapping of the waves upon the shore lulled them to sleep.
5. The wine steward uncorked the bottle with a flourish.

EXERCISE 251

★ Make the first two IC cuts in these sentences.

Example: Unless you hurry, | we | shall be late.

1. Indeed, your first bullfight may not delight you.
2. Smoking a dainty pipe, Elaine remained pensive.
3. If I weren't afraid, I would pet him.
4. We will build the float tomorrow, notwithstanding their objections.
5. At long last, the letter of acceptance arrived.

3. SUBORDINATE CLAUSES. In a subordinate clause, the first IC cut is made after the subordinating conjunction, leaving as the two IC's the conjunction and a sentence.

Example: Although | it is growing late . . .

EXERCISE 252

★ Make your first IC cut in these subordinate clauses.

1. When Hubert plays his guitar
2. Unless you bring a bottle opener
3. Since the paddle is broken
4. If the motor begins to cough
5. Once this rain is over

4. RELATIVE CLAUSE. If the relative is a subject *who, which,* or *that,* the first IC cut is made after this relative.*

Example: . . . who | plays in the band.

EXERCISE 253

★ Make the first IC cut in these relative clauses.

1. . . . who was late for dinner.
2. . . . that inspired him.

* We shall bypass the relatives which function as object of the verb, object of the preposition, and subjective complement, but here is how they might be handled:

OV which | they | found

OP which | she | paid for

SC that | your mother | was

3. . . . which cost too much.
4. . . . which was chasing a rabbit.
5. . . . that caused my spine to tingle.

5. PREPOSITIONAL PHRASE. The first cut is right after the preposition.

Example: in | the box

EXERCISE 254

★ Make the first IC cut in these prepositional phrases.

1. under the fence
2. from the greenhouse
3. between the blue flowers
4. across the wide, sluggish river
5. to the flower-starred meadow

6. INFINITIVE PHRASE. The first IC cut is made after the *to.*

Example: to | raise the most luscious sweet corn

This is a reasonable though arbitrary cut. Some speakers may feel with justice that the division is after *raise.*

EXERCISE 255

★ Make the first IC cut in these infinitive phrases.

1. to lessen the tension
2. to depend on that rope
3. to repair the parachute
4. to haul in the sail
5. to avoid the black flies

7. NOUN CLUSTER. (a) Beginning at the end, cut off successively each postnominal modifier until you reach the noun head.

Example: The coeds (NH) | in the dormitory | who chatter all evening

Be careful about what goes with what in these postnominal modifiers.

Example: The coeds (NH) | who chatter (VH) all evening | in the dormitory

In this example you will note that *in the dormitory* does not modify *coeds*, but, as the arrow shows, modifies *chatter*.

Ambiguous postnominal modifiers offer more than one possibility of cutting.

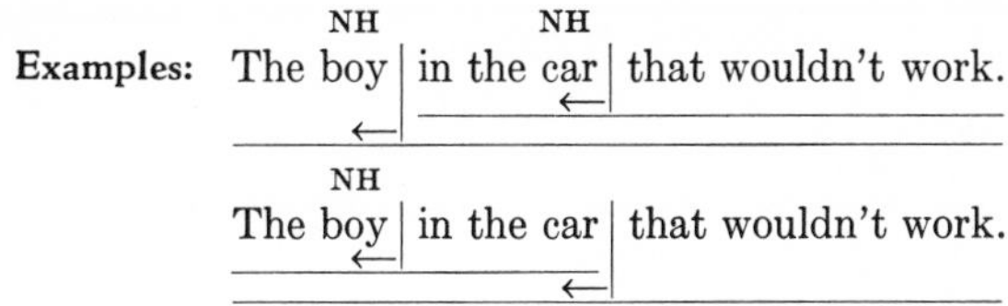

(b) After you have cut off the postnominal modifiers, begin at the front and cut off successively the prenominal modifiers until you reach the noun head.

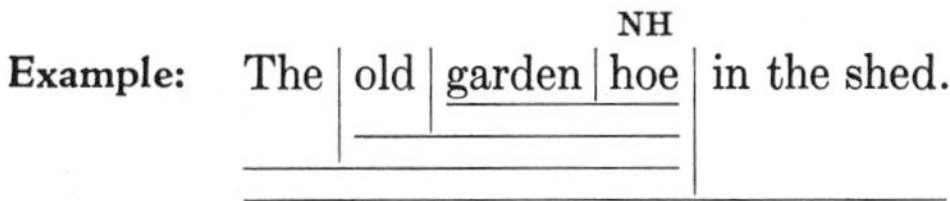

EXERCISE 256

★ Make all the IC cuts for the modifiers of the noun head in these noun clusters. Use arrows to show what modifies what. These you will have to copy on other sheets of paper.

1. The barking puppy in the kennel
2. Even the other girls who were making fudge in the kitchen
3. A ragged little urchin sitting forlornly on the fence
4. All the baby rabbits in the nest which were hungry
5. All the baby rabbits in the nest which was hidden from view
6. The forester with the pet bobcat which was always hungry
7. The forester with the pet bobcat who was always hungry
8. The young man accompanied by a girl who lost her temper
9. The young man accompanied by a girl who lost his temper
10. The driver of the bus which stopped at every corner
11. The driver of the bus who was drunk every Saturday afternoon
12. Her old-fashioned summer garden that we stopped to see
13. Those aluminum stakes which soon come loose
14. Many such stories in the book which she had drawn from the library
15. A gleaming sailboat in the middle of the lake

When two or more modifying word groups occur after a noun head, there is danger of ambiguity. Here are five examples:

1. The dog on the porch with the battered look
2. The young calf of the boy that was standing near the gate
3. The rooms of the house which seemed dirty
4. A dispute on drinking at the courthouse
5. A secondhand car that he later traded for a motorcycle which he loved to tinker with

Our English grammatical system provides us with at least five common means of avoiding such ambiguities:

1. Gender signals:

The dog on the porch with (his, its) battered look.

2. Person-thing signals:

The young calf of the boy (who, which) was standing near the gate.

3. Number signals:

The rooms of the house which (was, were) dirty.

4. Position:

A dispute at the courthouse on drinking.

5. Coordination:

A secondhand car that he later traded for a motorcycle and that he loved to tinker with.

EXERCISE 257

★ Using the grammatical means listed above, rewrite each noun cluster to remove its ambiguity.

1. The girl near the boy who was wearing a hat
2. A theater located near the business district which is crowded every night
3. The motorboat of the man that would not start
4. The spark plugs of the car which needed cleaning (Use *be in need of.*)
5. A new golf club that replaced his old one which he was very fond of

8. VERB CLUSTER
   a. Modifiers of the verb are cut off from the front, back to the verb head. There is seldom more than one before the verb.

Example: happily | jumped on the table

   b. After the preverbal modifiers have been cut off, one begins at the back and cuts off successive modifiers up to the verb head.

Examples: happily | jumped | on the table

soon | came | to her rescue | in a canoe

← ← →

EXERCISE 258

★ Make the successive IC cuts for modifiers of the verb. Use arrows to show modification. Use other paper for this exercise.

1. . . . reluctantly came to his mother when he heard the whistle
2. . . . never swam in cold water after a heavy meal
3. . . . at once ran to the coach upon seeing the hand signal
4. . . . often walked to the pool in his bathing suit
5. . . . eagerly grabbed at the gunwale to get a short rest

c. Auxiliaries are cut off successively up to the verb head.

Example: . . . may | have | been | eating

Adverbials embedded in the auxiliaries are taken in order.

Example: . . . could | never | have | survived

d. Complements after the verb are cut off successively, with adverbials, going from the end back to the verb head.

Examples: . . . put | a quarter | in the cup

. . . swung | the boy | lightly | into the boat

. . . made | his partner | a proposition | after the stock went down

EXERCISE 259

★ Make all the IC cuts required for the auxiliaries, adverbials, and complements in these verb clusters. Do not cut further into the phrases and clauses. Use arrows to show modification. Use other paper for this exercise.

1. . . . often had come to practice before the appointed time
2. . . . drove his car rapidly to the doctor's office
3. . . . should not have anchored the boat so close to the shore
4. . . . quickly made her way to the post office
5. . . . became a captain in the spring when promotions were announced

---

Now we are ready to try some IC analyses of entire sentences. Remember the order of cutting:

1. Cut off any sentence modifiers.
2. Cut between the subject noun cluster and the predicate verb cluster.
3. Cut these clusters into successive IC's, down to the individual words.

EXERCISE 260

★ Make an IC analysis of these sentences down to the individual words. For this purpose, copy the sentences on another sheet of paper.

1. If everyone is ready, we can begin to load the car.
2. Balancing on the edge of the board, he carefully poised himself for the dive.
3. All of the members had already paid their dues.
4. In those exciting pages, we followed the adventures of the swimmer who battled the waves.
5. After unloading the supplies, we hoisted the canoe on our shoulders for the long portage.

In doing IC analyses of complicated sentences, knotty problems may arise. These can be avoided if we confine such analysis to the basic sentences. Some grammarians, notably the transformationists, advocate that IC analysis be limited to kernel (= basic) sentences. By way of review let us put the nine basic sentences through their IC cuts. Here they are, padded out with a few modifiers. Copy the sentences on other sheets of paper.

EXERCISE 261

★ Make a complete IC analysis of each sentence. Use other paper for this exercise.

1. Your food is exceedingly good.
2. The girl from Skunk Hollow is here.
3. My oldest brother is the doctor in residence.
4. Many younger girls giggle outrageously.
5. The girl in the next house bought a silk dress at the auction.
6. The doting mother bought the girl a dress from the Smart Shop.
7. The basketball players chose Harry their captain for next year.
8. That muscular acrobat seems quite young.
9. My brother remained an outstanding student.

B. Coordination

In the chapter about modifiers, we were dealing with the phenomenon of subordination, for a modifier is always subordinate to its head. Now we turn to a related matter, coordination.

In English we have a small structure-class consisting of eight structure words called coordinating conjunctions. These are *and, but, for, nor, not, or, so, yet.* These conjunctions connect grammatical equivalents — form-classes or position-classes or structure-words or grammatical structures. A few cases will illustrate this connection of equivalents.

Connection of equivalent form-classes

Nouns	1. The library *and* the gymnasium are near by.
Adjectives	2. Fifi is beautiful *but* dumb.
Verbs	3. He studied hard, *yet* failed.
Adverbs	4. Arabella dances lightly *and* gracefully.

Connection of equivalent position-classes

Adjectivals	1. My business *and* academic friends . . .
	2. He was popular *and* in good health.
Adverbials	3. Is it upstairs *or* in the garage?
Nominals	4. He did what he pleased, *not* what was expected.
Verbals	5. We watched him rowing hard *but* getting nowhere.

Connection of equivalent structure-words

Auxiliaries	1. You can *and* should help your brother.
Prepositions	2. Was the witness walking to *or* from the scene of the accident?

Connection of equivalent grammatical structures

Prepositional phrases	1. You can sleep on the beach *or* in the woods.
Relative clauses	2. Bess was a girl who could swim *but* who was afraid to dive.

Connection of sentences

Ned began nodding *for* the room was hot.

All the coordinating conjunctions except *not* can occur between two sentences, changing them into a single sentence, but in other positions their distribution is limited. In other words, not all of them can be used to connect the same equivalents. For example, we do not use *for*, *nor*, or *so* to connect two adjectives.

In writing, these coordinating conjunctions are sometimes used to begin a sentence, as in

Jane was never on time. But that made no difference to Bob.

This would be uttered with a fading terminal juncture after *time* whether the punctuation mark were a comma, semicolon, or a period. Hence this way of beginning sentences can be considered simply as a writing convention that in no manner changes the classification of the coordinating conjunction.

EXERCISE 262

★ Underline each coordinating conjunction, and below each sentence identify the grammatical items that it connects.

Example: Samuel was equally happy hunting ducks <u>or</u> playing chess.
<u>participial phrases or -ing phrases</u>

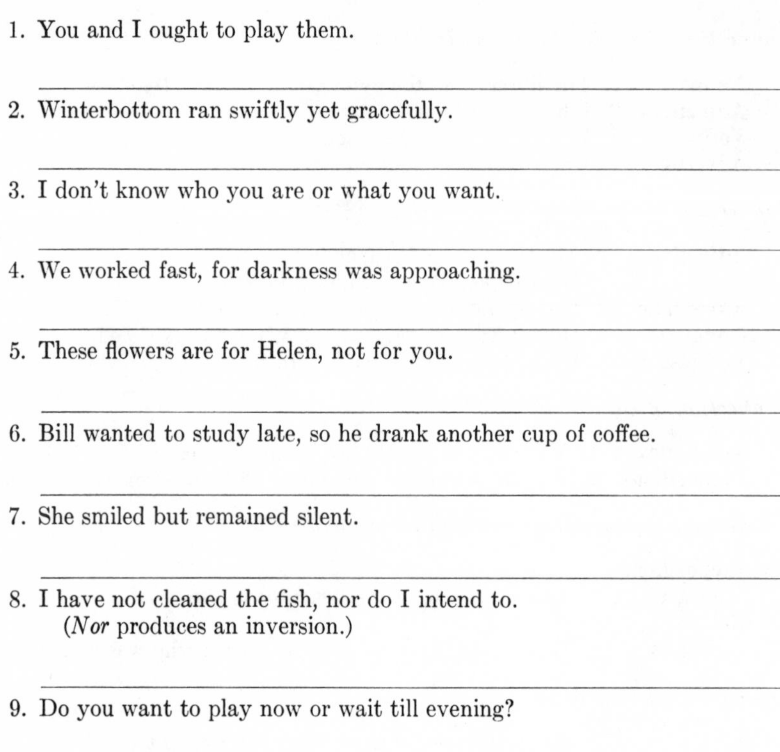

1. You and I ought to play them.

2. Winterbottom ran swiftly yet gracefully.

3. I don't know who you are or what you want.

4. We worked fast, for darkness was approaching.

5. These flowers are for Helen, not for you.

6. Bill wanted to study late, so he drank another cup of coffee.

7. She smiled but remained silent.

8. I have not cleaned the fish, nor do I intend to.
   (*Nor* produces an inversion.)

9. Do you want to play now or wait till evening?

10. Rising and stretching, Harry yawned and began to dress.

These conjunctions are sometimes doubled up, as in *and yet, and so, but yet,* and *but not.* Compare, for instance, these two sentences:

1. He was tired *but yet* he couldn't sleep.
2. He was tired *but* he couldn't sleep *yet.*

The first *yet* is a coordinating conjunction but the second is an adverbial with a different meaning.

In addition to the set of eight coordinating conjunctions, there is a second set that occurs in pairs:

either . . . or
both . . . and
neither . . . nor
not (only) . . . but (also)

These are a subclass of coordinating conjunctions known as correlative conjunctions.

EXERCISE 263

★ Underline the correlative conjunctions and below each sentence identify the grammatical items that are connected.

1. Either you leave or I will call the police.

   ____

2. They stood both in the aisles and on the platforms.

   ____

3. Jenkins had neither the time nor the energy to finish the job.

   ____

4. Our navigator was not only knowledgeable but careful not to make errors.

   ____

5. The main requirement for this position is not specialized knowledge but the ability to handle people tactfully.

   ____

C. Multiple Constituents

We are now in a position to account for coordinate items in an IC analysis. An illustration will show the procedure:

. . . enjoy | drama | and | opera

This verb cluster contains after the cut a multiple IC, the coordinate nouns *drama* and *opera*, but *and* is set off as a separate element and does not belong to either IC. Here are more examples:

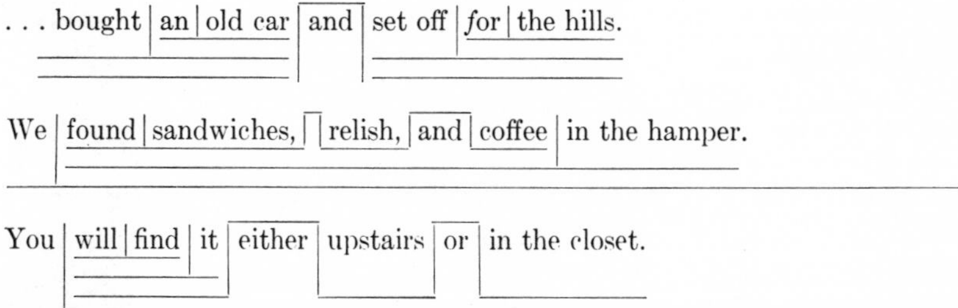

(Note here that though *upstairs* and *in the closet* are different in form, they are equivalent in that both are adverbials.)

EXERCISE 264

★ Make a complete IC analysis of each of these sentences. Use other paper for this exercise.

1. His favorite snack was fish and chips.
2. Both men and women may join the club.
3. The third problem is challenging but baffling.
4. You look attractive in either the blue sweater or the yellow.
   (After *yellow,* the word *sweater* can be said to be understood, since it has already been mentioned in the sentence. Thus the items following *either* and *or* may be considered grammatical equivalents.)
5. I will give you directions, but the rest is your responsibility.

XVIII.

Some Syntactic Details

In the foregoing pages of this section we have dealt chiefly with those matters that are central to an understanding of English syntax. Now we shall go back to examine a few concepts that were bypassed in the interest of a fast forward progression.

A. Complements

Complement of the Adjectival. One kind of completer that has not been mentioned yet is the complement of the adjectival, as in

I am happy *that you are here.*

Patterns 1 and 8, both of which contain predicate adjectives or adjectivals in the third position, can be extended by means of this particular complement, as these examples will show:

He was aware *that she suffered from insomnia.*
Jack appeared eager *to see her.*
My roommate became tired *of studying.*
She is indifferent *whether you come or not.*

It is commonly word groups that function as complement of the adjectival, though occasionally a single word might be said to function in this way:

This ball is worth *a dollar.*
He is like *his father.*

It is not always easy to make a clear-cut distinction between an adverbial and a complement of an adjectival. One can perhaps say that in natural speech the complement of the adjectival is not transposable but retains its position after the adjectival, whereas the adverbial is movable, e.g.,

Complement of the adjectival:

She was glad *that he was safe,*

but not

**That he was safe* she was glad.

Adverbial She was glad *when he arrived.*

and also

When he arrived she was glad.

EXERCISE 265

★ Underline the adjectival once, the complement of adjectival twice, and the adverbial three times.

1. We were reluctant to leave.
2. We were reluctant, to tell the truth.
3. Mrs. Hawkins is devoted to her daughter.
4. The child was interested in understanding the process.
5. The lad was afraid of venturing into the deep water.
6. They were hopeful that the weather would change.
7. Juliet became forgetful of her duties.
8. The dean was not angry with me.
9. Jane was conscious that something unpleasant had happened.
10. Mother will be happy if you can help.
11. Jim is doubtful if he can pass the course.
12. Joseph is fond of doughnuts.
13. Are you sure of it?
14. Penelope was delighted to receive the pillow.
15. Uncle Andrew was disturbed that the dogs had not been fed.

Internal Complements of the Verbal. The main verb, as we saw in the pattern sentences, can be complemented by an adjectival functioning as subjective complement and by a nominal functioning as subjective complement, direct object, indirect object, and object complement. These same kinds of complements can follow not only the main verb but other verbals in the sentence as well. A few examples will make this clear.

1. He | enjoys | playing golf.

Here the direct object of the main verb *enjoys* is the participial phrase *playing golf,* and within this phrase *golf* is the direct object of *playing.* Here is another:

2. We | wanted | to teach her a lesson.

In this example the direct object of *wanted,* as the IC cut shows, is the infinitive phrase *to teach her a lesson,* and within this phrase *to teach* has the indirect object *her* and the direct object *lesson.*

In the next sentence,

3. George asked her to drive the car,

we say that the infinitive phrase *her to drive the car* is the direct object of *asked* and that within this phrase *her* is the subject of *to drive* and *car* the direct object. In this kind of structure, an alternate analysis is to consider the slot before the verbal (e.g., ________ *to drive the car*) an indirect object and the rest the direct object. We shall adopt the former analysis because it is more in line with that which a transformational grammar would yield.

EXERCISE 266

★ In each sentence a verbal phrase is italicized. In the first blank indicate its function in the sentence by these abbreviations:

SV	subject of verb	DO	direct object
SCn	subjective complement, predicate nominal	IO	indirect object
		OC	object complement
SCa	subjective complement, predicate adjectival	OP	object of preposition
		RO	retained object

Next, underline the complement within the verbal phrase and show its function, using the same abbreviations, in the second blank.

1. She hated *to miss the party.* ________ ________

2. Peter tried *to remain calm.* ________ ________

3. *Shooting quail* takes a great deal of skill. _______ _______

4. I expect *you to be truthful.* _______ _______

5. *Finding the trail again* was no easy matter. _______ _______

6. Thank you for *washing dishes.* _______ _______

7. *Being a beauty queen* was exhilarating to Olga. _______ _______

8. I saw *them break the window.* _______ _______

9. The doctor advised *him to stop smoking.* _______ _______

10. We were requested *to leave the grounds.* _______ _______

***Complements in* -ing *and* to** __________. English verbs may be divided into three classes according to the form of the verbal complement that immediately follows them. The first class contains those followed by the *-ing* form of the verb but not by *to* plus a verb stem:

He enjoyed eating.
not *He enjoyed to eat.

Those of the second class are followed by *to* plus a verb stem but not by the *-ing* form:

He agreed to come.
not *He agreed coming.

Those of the third class are followed by either the *to* or the *-ing* form:

He preferred sleeping.
and He preferred to sleep.

There is no general principle that dictates which form to use immediately after a verb. As a native speaker you know from long experience with our language which forms are permitted with which verbs. But a non-native speaker must go through the arduous task of learning them one by one.

EXERCISE 267

★ Give the form of the verbal complement that immediately follows each verb by writing in the blank *-ing* or *to* or *both.*

1. refuse __________
2. miss __________
3. start __________
4. offer __________
5. postpone __________
6. continue __________

7. promise	______________	11. stop	______________
8. avoid	______________	12. decide	______________
9. hate	______________	13. risk	______________
10. try	______________	14. cease	______________

15. mention ______________

B. The Subjunctive Forms of the Verb

English has two verb forms, *were* and the stem of any verb, which have special uses.

1. The verb stem is used in certain nominal clauses in the slot of the present, as is shown by these sentences:

It is necessary that she *go* at once.
It is imperative that you *be* on time.
The boss insisted that Willard *arrive* at eight sharp.
She suggested that I *be* the cook.

2. The form *were* is used in subordinate contrary-to-fact clauses beginning with *if*, *as if*, and *as though*, and in nominal clauses after the verb *wish*, as in

If he *were* really my friend, he would get me a ticket.
Betty looks as if she *were* exhausted.
I wish I *were* in Italy.

In extremely formal English one sometimes hears *be* in *if* clauses, e.g.,

If that *be* the case . . . .

When these forms are used in the positions described, the verb is called subjunctive. Often these subjunctive forms are replaced by other forms or structures, as in

It is necessary *for her to go* at once.
It is necessary that she *should go* at once.
If he *was* really my friend, he would get me a ticket. (Informal usage)
I wish I *was* in Italy. (Informal usage)

EXERCISE 268

★ Underline the subjunctive forms of the verb in these sentences.

1. If she (was were) home, she would answer the phone.
2. I wish he (was were) with me now.

3. If that (is be) true, make the most of it.
4. The director asked that Elizabeth (stands stand) in the front row.
5. It is traditional that the table (is be) decorated.
6. It is advisable that a lawyer (writes write) the contract.
7. Rubenstein plays Chopin as though he (was were) inspired.
8. The rules required that they (are be) in uniform.
9. If I (was were) the pilot, I'd avoid that thunderstorm.
10. The invitation requested that she (answers answer) promptly.

C. Noun Subgroups

Nouns can be divided into different subclasses according to the grammatical purpose one has in mind. We have already met three such classes. The substitute-group and collective-noun classes were used to decide questions of number, and the animate-inanimate class was related to the choice between the $\{\text{-s}_1\}$ possessive and the *of* structure.

Now we shall take a look at three more noun subclasses, which are based on the ways nouns behave with determiners in conjunction with the singular and the plural. To these three classes belong the count noun, the mass noun, and the proper noun.

The count-noun class includes everything that is countable, like *beetles, books, sounds, concepts, minutes.* Count nouns have both singular and plural forms. In the singular they must always be preceded by a determiner, e.g.,

> *A* car drove by.
> *The* car drove by.

but not

> *Car drove by.

In the plural they may occur either with or without a determiner:

> *Cars* are dangerous on slippery roads.
> *Those cars* are dangerous on slippery roads.

The mass-noun class includes everything that is not countable, like *steam, music, justice, advice, water, bread, Latin, silk.* Mass nouns have no plural; they occur in the singular under these conditions:

Without a determiner:	*Information* is useful.
With *the*:	*The* information is useful.
But not with *a*:	**An* information is useful.

Many words may be mass nouns in one context and count nouns in a different context, e.g.,

Mass: *Beer* is refreshing in summer.
Count: They had *two beers.* (Remember that mass nouns have no plural.)
Mass: *Virtue* is its own reward.
Count: Her *virtues* were well known.
Mass: You have *egg* on your chin.
Count: *Eggs* were served for breakfast.

As a rule of thumb, it is worth remembering that count nouns can be modified by *many* and mass nouns by *much.*

EXERCISE 269

★ In the blanks write *count* or *mass* to classify the italicized words.

1. The *wines* of France are world-famous. ____________
2. The Thibaults drink *wine* with their meals. ____________
3. Hobson enjoys his *leisure.* ____________
4. There is *truth* in what he says. ____________
5. These *truths* you must never forget. ____________
6. Mrs. Lopez buys *coffee* every day at the market. ____________
7. Please bring me a *coffee.* ____________
8. Charles studied *Russian* in college. ____________
9. Today's world puts a high value on *knowledge.* ____________
10. We heard a *Russian* at the United Nations. ____________

Proper nouns are the names of particular, often unique, persons and things, e.g., *Wallace Anderson*, the *Mona Lisa*, the *Queen Mary* (ship), *Maine*, the *Rocky Mountains*, *Mount Washington.* They are considered a subclass of nouns because most of them conform in part to the noun paradigm, and they appear in nominal positions. Proper nouns are subdivided into four classes according to their grammatical number and their association with *the.*

1. Those which do not occur with *the.* These are singular.

Examples: *Margaret, Brussels, England, King George, Madison Square Garden, June, Easter, Chartres Cathedral, Pike's Peak, Lake Erie.*

2. Those which can occur in the plural with *the.*

Examples: the *Iowans,* the *Smiths,* the *Rembrandts,* the *Stuarts.*

Here the proper noun loses its uniqueness and might be considered a common noun, which is a class word.

3. Those that are always plural and always require *the.*

Examples: the *Netherlands,* the *West Indies,* the *Appalachians.*

4. Those that are always singular and always require *the.*

Examples: the *City of San Francisco* (train), the *Americana* (hotel), the *Maasdam* (ship), the *Rio Grande* (river), the *Atlantic Ocean,* the *Museum of Modern Art.*

EXERCISE 270

★ The proper names have been left uncapitalized. Classify the italicized nouns by *count, mass,* or *proper.*

1. Aunt tilda's favorite *month* is *may.* ________ ________
2. There is *dust* on the *mantelpiece.* ________ ________
3. The class had a *picnic* at *riverview park.* ________ ________
4. *Cotton* is more absorbent than *linen.* ________ ________
5. In the *alps* are many lovely *valleys.* ________ ________
6. Do you like *cream* in *coffee?* ________ ________
7. Numerous *injustices* were perpetrated by the *invaders.* ________ ________
8. Can one expect *justice* in this *court?* ________ ________
9. The *allens* are visiting us next *week.* ________ ________
10. They sailed on the *statendam* for the *canary islands.* ________ ________

part four

TRANSFORMATIONAL GRAMMAR

Note to the Instructor

The best theory of language is the one that makes the simplest, strongest, and most insightful assertions possible about language, consistent with all available information. As new insights are gained into language, the theory must be modified accordingly or even scrapped and a new one proposed. At present, new information about language is being made available and new concepts are emerging, thus new theories of language or modifications of old theories are being proposed.

The generative-transformational grammar in this chapter is presented primarily as a pedagogical not a theoretical work. Nevertheless, implicit in it is a theory of language, a theory that makes stronger assertions about language than do many generative-transformational models currently available in print. It is not a totally new theory by any means; rather, it is but a slight modification of the now familiar generative-transformational grammar of Noam Chomsky's *Syntactic Structures* (1957). The syntactical level of generative-transformational grammar is generally presented as a tripartite structure: a phrase structure grammar (sometimes called *constituent structure* grammar), which generates a finite number of strings; transformations, which are not selected within the phrase structure grammar; and morphophonemic rules. By contrast, the grammar presented here consists of five parts: (1) a phrase structure grammar, which includes recursive rules that generate an infinite number of strings and within which transformations are selected; (2) transformations; (3) morphophonemic rules; (4) a lexicon, whose logical structure is a kind of definition of "Lexical item," "Verb," and "Noun"; (5) Rules of Order. In addition to these rather broad differences, there are many differences of detail.

The purpose of this chapter on transformations is to give the student an introduction, simple and very limited in scope, to a generative-transformational grammar of English. Thus no theoretical discussions of grammaticality, criteria of adequacy, general theories of grammar, and the like are presented. Nor is there any discussion of recent work on phonology. In any introductory work of this type, instances of omission, simplification, and even slight distortion are likely to be encountered. Here are three examples of the many such instances in the present text. First, discussion of structural ambiguity, important as it is, is omitted altogether. Second, in the Rules of Order for Nonkernels, the impression is given that all transformations have a relative order of application; this is not true. Third, the comparison of structural and transformational grammar, the definitions of "phrase grammar rule," "transformation rule," and morphophonemic rule" are inadequate. Illustration is often substituted for rigorous explication. Despite such limitations, it is hoped that the student will emerge from his experience with transformational grammar with a fairly good idea of what its five parts are and how they fit together.

Most of the exercises are in semi-programmed form. In the beginning, some of the exercises have the purpose of forcing the student to become very well acquainted with the phrase grammar rules so that in the later exercises he will not need to be constantly turning back the pages. Only the last exercise of the book is difficult; it is constructed to make the student use almost all information previously presented in the text. But even this exercise is semi-programmed; the groundwork for it is the previous exercise; in addition, each sentence is prepared for by the immediately preceding sentence.

Although any work on generative-transformational grammar owes its greatest debt to its founder, Noam Chomsky, other linguists have made substantial contributions. In this chapter I have drawn on ideas from both published and unpublished materials of Robert P. Stockwell, Paul Schachter, Tommy Anderson, Robert Lees, and others. The model used as a basis for the lexical classification in this chapter is a modification of an idea first conceived by Tommy Anderson and later refined by Robert P. Stockwell and Paul Schachter in unpublished materials. The distinction between verb and noun is a modification of a suggestion by Noam Chomsky. Chomsky, in an informal meeting in 1963, reported that a similar though not identical model of lexical classification is being constructed by linguists at the Massachusetts Institute of Technology. Establishing the lexicon as a separate structure in the grammar resulted from my investigations into semantic theory. However, it was reported to me informally that a similar proposal is one of a number of alternatives being considered at M.I.T. The concept of the extended phrase structure grammar was suggested by various works in machine translation. The Rules of Order is an outgrowth of the suggestion put forward by Robert Lees and others that "traffic" rules may be needed within the transformational part of the grammar. Although the transformation formulas used in this chapter are not in customary form, they are but simplifications of formulas constructed by Noam Chomsky, Robert Lees, Robert Stockwell, Paul Schachter, and others.

I am particularly indebted to Norman Stageberg for his careful examination of this chapter and for his numerous suggestions, many of which have been incorporated.

To my wife I owe an enormous debt; I could not possibly have written this part in so short a time without her patience, encouragement, and time-consuming effort.

R.M.G.

XIX.

A Look at Transformational Grammar

A. Introduction

Up to this point you have been learning English grammar from a structural point of view. Now you will have a chance to observe another kind of grammar that is quite different — in its aims, its assumptions, and its procedures. This is called transformational grammar. In this chapter you will be presented with a bare minimum of this grammar, just enough to give you a sampling of it. It will be simplified in that only a few of its many rules will be given, and even details in these will be omitted. But you should emerge from this study with an idea of what this new and exciting grammar is like.

In Part III you analyzed raw text, that is, arbitrarily given sentences. Structural grammar attempts to give rules for automatically analyzing arbitrarily given sentences.* By contrast, transformational grammar gives rules for producing or *generating* sentences automatically. In so doing, it assigns each generated sentence an analysis. To understand the distinction between *analyzing an arbitrarily given sentence* and *generating a sentence*, let us first analyze and then generate the same sentence.

* This is true of some structural grammars. Structural grammars do other things as well; for example, many structural grammars give resultant analyses rather than rules for analysis.

Before we can analyze a sentence, we must first have a sentence to analyze. If, for example, this sentence is

Girls giggle.

one can make a structural analysis by means of using form, position, intonation, stress, and IC's.* *Girls* is seen to be a noun because it has a plural form and can take a possessive. It is the subject of the verb because of its position and because it is related to the verb by ties of agreement, that is to say, *girls giggle* and *a girl giggles*. The entire expression has a sentence contour of 231↓ and a stress pattern of ^′. The two IC's *girls|giggle* show the sentence to be divided into a subject and a predicate. This, then, is a simple structural analysis of our given sentence.

Now let us generate *girls giggle*. Instead of starting with the *arbitrarily* given sentence, *girls giggle*, we start with a set of *rewrite rules*. Here are two such rules:

RULE 1: *Sentence*

RULE 2: *Sentence*

↓

Noun Phrase + *Verb Phrase*

Rule 1, which is our starting point, says: Write down *Sentence*. This is interpreted to mean that all the following rules will generate all English sentences. Rule 2 says: Rewrite *Sentence* as *Noun Phrase* + *Verb Phrase*. The arrow means "Rewrite as." Rule 2 is interpreted to mean that *Noun Phrase* is the subject and *Verb Phrase* the predicate of all basic sentences. Later rules will specify the structure of the subject and predicate in more detail.

Here now are two more rewrite rules.

RULE 3: *Noun Phrase*

↓

girls, my brother, food

RULE 4: *Verb Phrase*

↓

giggle, is here, is good, is a doctor,
bought the dress

Rule 3 says: Rewrite *Noun Phrase* as *one* and *only one* of the expressions separated by commas. Rule 4 says: Rewrite *Verb Phrase* as one and only one of the expressions separated by commas. Commas always mean: Choose one and only one on a given application of the rule.

* See pages 262 ff. for a discussion of IC's.

A simple way of diagraming Rules 1 and 2 follows.

Sentence (corresponds to Rule 1)

Sentence ↙ ↘

Noun Phrase *Verb Phrase* (corresponds to Rule 2)

Whenever the rules are diagramed this way, two arrows will replace a plus sign.

Rule 3 is diagramed in one and only one of the following three ways:

Noun Phrase	*OR*	*Noun Phrase*	*OR*	*Noun Phrase*
↓		↓		↓
girls		my brother		food

EXERCISE 271

★ Diagram Rule 4 in the five possible ways using the word *OR* between diagrams as shown above.

Now we can put some of the diagrams of the four rules together to get diagrams for individual sentences. For example, here is the diagram for *girls giggle.*

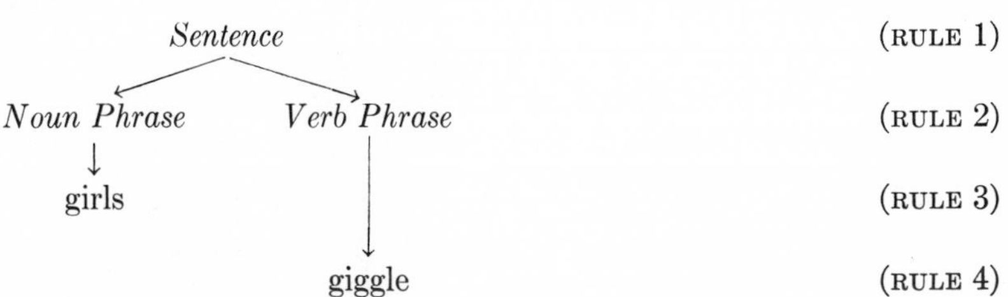

Note that we first followed Rule 1 and wrote down *Sentence;* then according to Rule 2 we divided *Sentence* into *Noun Phrase* and *Verb Phrase.* In Rule 3 we chose *girls,* one of the expressions set off by commas. Finally, in Rule 4, we chose *giggle,* again one of the expressions set off by commas. Thus by following the rules automatically, we have generated one of several possible sentences.

We could have generated different sentences by choosing different expressions from Rules 3 and 4. For example, we could have generated

My brother is a doctor.

Food is good.

These two sentences are diagramed as follows:

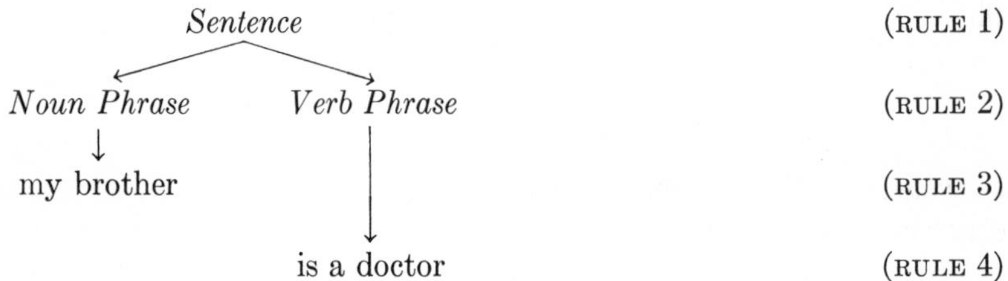

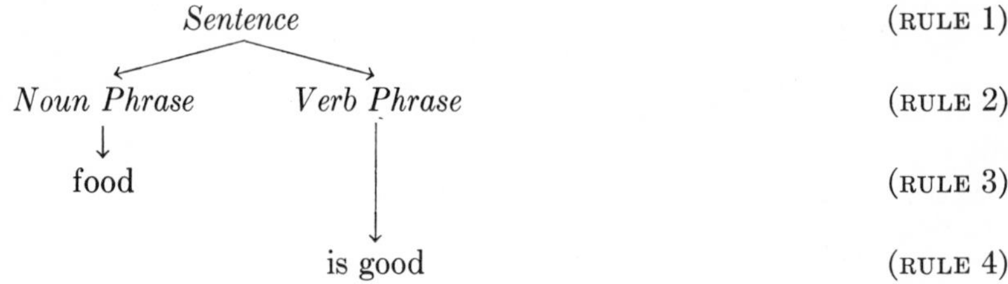

EXERCISE 272

★ Using the four rewrite rules, diagram the following sentences in the manner demonstrated above.

1. My brother bought the dress.

2. My brother is here.

3. My brother is good.

4. Food is here.

Let us now examine the process you went through in doing exercise 272. You did not analyze a sentence that you were given. Instead you did just the opposite; you followed a set of rules and the end result was a sentence. The fact that you knew the end result in advance does not contradict this assertion. You could have generated the same sentences, and others as well, even if you had not been guided by a knowledge of what you wanted to end up with.

EXERCISE 273

★ A. Using the four rewrite rules, generate at least two sentences. Do not think of any sentences in advance. You might end up with one of the ungrammatical or odd-sounding sentences listed in the answers. Note what the answer sheet has to say about such sentences. (Use separate paper.)

★ B. Do the four rules above generate all the sentences of English?

____

★ C. What rule would you amplify to include more subjects? __________

★ D. More predicates? __________ Note what the answer sheet has to say about a complete grammar.

This conclusion can be drawn from the above exercise: A complete grammar of English generates *all* and *only* the grammatical sentences of English.

We said that a transformational grammar does not analyze arbitrarily given sentences. Nevertheless, the sentences generated by the rules are given an analysis automatically. Let us see how. Here again is the diagram of *girls giggle*.

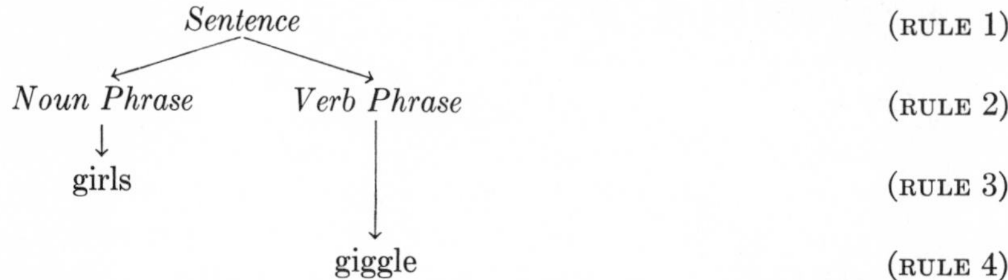

This diagram actually does represent an analysis. It tells us that *girls* is a noun phrase because the arrow leads from *Noun Phrase* to *girls*. Similarly it tells us that *giggle* is a Verb phrase. Because *girls* is first, it is the subject; because *giggle* is the only element in the verb phrase and comes second, it is the predicate. We can now make this generalization: to analyze an *arbitrarily* given sentence, which a structural grammar attempts to do, is not the same as to give an analysis for a generated sentence, which a transformational grammar does. In the first case we must actually have a sentence before us when we start; in the second case, the analysis is an automatic consequence of the manner in which a sentence is generated.

EXERCISE 274

★ Give the analysis of the sentence below by consulting your diagram in exercise 272 and the paragraph above.

My brother bought the dress. ______________________

____

____

____

____

____

In summary, we have seen that a structural grammar of English attempts to analyze arbitrarily given sentences, whereas a transformational grammar generates all and only the grammatical sentences automatically and in so doing assigns each generated sentence an analysis.

B. Phrase Structure Grammar

1

A transformational grammar consists of five parts:

a. Phrase structure grammar (abbreviation: PS)
b. The lexicon
c. Transformational rules
d. Morphophonemic rules
e. Rules of Order

In this section, only the PS grammar will be described.

The PS rules, of which those below are but a part, will generate all the basic or *kernel* sentences of English. A kernel sentence is a simple active declarative sentence whose grammatical structure falls into one of the basic sentence patterns. In Chapter XIV the nine most important basic sentence patterns were listed. Most kernel sentences will thus have one of the following grammatical structures. The example below each pattern is a kernel sentence.

1. *N*	*V*(be)	*Adj*	
Food	is	good.	
2. *N*	*V*(be)	*UW*	
The girl	is	here.	
3. *N*	*V*(be)	*N*	
My brother	is	a doctor.	
4. *N*	*InV*		
Girls	giggle.		
5. *N*	*TrV*	*N*	
The girl	bought	the dress.	
6. *N*	*TrV*	*N*	*N*
The mother	bought	the girl	a dress.
7. Not considered a basic pattern in transformational grammar.			
8. *N*	*LV*	*Adj*	
The acrobat	seems	young.	
9. *N*	*LV*	*N*	
My brother	remained	an outstanding student.	
10. Et cetera			

The item "Et cetera" is included to suggest that although the patterns above are the most important, there are other basic patterns as well. For example,

It	*InV*
It	rains.

might be considered a basic pattern different from pattern 4 because from sentences of this pattern we cannot derive questions like *What is raining?* whereas from sentences of pattern 4 we can derive questions like *Who giggles?*

In section A you were given four PS rules of English. The rules generated several different kinds of basic sentences but did not distinguish one kind from another. For example, they generated both *Girls giggle* and *The girl bought the dress*, but nowhere specified that the former was a sentence of pattern 4 and the latter a sentence of pattern 5. Let us now increase the number of rules in such a way that the grammar not only will generate more sentences of English but will clearly distinguish one basic sentence pattern from another. For convenience of comparison, the old rules of section A are written to the right of the new rules.

	NEW RULES	OLD RULES
RULE 1:	*Sentence* [*S*]	*S*
RULE 2:	*S* ↓ *Noun Phrase* [*NP*] + *Verb Phrase* [*VP*]	*S* ↓ *NP* + *VP*
RULE 3:	*NP* ↓ food, the girl, girls, my brother, my brothers, a doctor, the doctors, the dress, the dresses, the acrobat	*NP* ↓ girls, my brother, food
RULE 4:	*VP* ↓ *Verb* (+ *Complement*) [*Comp*]	*VP* ↓ giggle, is here, is good, is a doctor, bought the dress
RULE 5:	*Comp* ↓ { (*NP* +) *NP* / *Adverb* [*Adv*] / *Adjective* [*Adj*] }	
RULE 6:	*Adv* ↓ here, there, in the garden	

RULE 7: *Adj*

↓

good, bad, beautiful

RULE 8: *Verb*

↓

giggle, giggles, run, ran,
buy, bought, hit, is, are,
was, were, seems, remained

In these new rules, an abbreviation in brackets is given to the right of the first and only appearance of each nonabbreviated expression. Afterward only the abbreviation is used. For example, the nonabbreviated expression *Verb Phrase* occurs for the first and only time in New Rule 2; in New Rule 4 only the abbreviation *VP* is used.

Each expression in the rules, abbreviated or nonabbreviated, constitutes a single symbol called a *marker*. Thus Verb Phrase, or its abbreviation VP, is a marker. With respect to a given set of rules every marker that can be rewritten is called a *nonterminal marker*. Thus VP is rewritten in New Rule 4 and is therefore a nonterminal marker. With respect to a given set of rules every marker that cannot be rewritten is called a *terminal marker*. Thus *girls* in New Rule 3, *in the garden* in New Rule 6, *good* in New Rule 7, and *giggle* in New Rule 8 are terminal markers. Notice that *in the garden*, which consists of three words, is one and only one terminal marker, not three terminal markers.

EXERCISE 275

★ A. List all the terminal markers (there are twenty-nine).

1. ________	8. ________	15. ________	22. ________
2. ________	9. ________	16. ________	23. ________
3. ________	10. ________	17. ________	24. ________
4. ________	11. ________	18. ________	25. ________
5. ________	12. ________	19. ________	26. ________
6. ________	13. ________	20. ________	27. ________
7. ________	14. ________	21. ________	28. ________

29. ________

★ B. List all the nonterminal markers (there are seven).

1. __________ 3. __________ 5. __________ 7. __________

2. __________ 4. __________ 6. __________

Notice that New Rules 1, 2, 3 and Old Rules 1, 2, 3 are identical with this exception: New Rule 3 contains seven new terminal markers.

EXERCISE 276

★ A. How many diagrams can be made based on New Rule 3? __________

★ B. Diagram New Rule 3 in the ten possible ways, using the word *OR* between diagrams. See page 289 for diagrams of Old Rule 3.

★ C. Are there more noun phrases in English than those generated by New Rule 3? ____________________

★ D. Which rule would you amplify to increase the number of noun phrases the grammar will generate? ____________________

New Rule 4 specifies that we must rewrite VP as *one* and *only one* of the following:

1. Verb
2. Verb + Comp

Parentheses, such as you see in New Rule 4, mean *optional choice;* that is, you have the option of choosing the marker inside the parentheses or not, as you wish.

EXERCISE 277

★ Diagram New Rule 4 in the two possible ways, using the word *OR* between diagrams.

In New Rule 5, braces are used. Braces and commas both mean: Choose one and only one. Commas are employed between English words and expressions as in New Rules 3, 6, 7, and 8. Braces are used in other cases as here in Rule 5.

New Rule 5 specifies that Comp may be rewritten as one and only one of the following:

1. NP
2. NP + NP
3. Adv
4. Adj

Notice that 1 and 2 result from (NP +) NP, in which the parentheses mean that the first NP is optional. New Rules 6, 7, and 8 follow the same pattern as Old Rules 3 and 4 in that they require the selection of one and only one English expression.

EXERCISE 278

★ A. Diagram New Rule 5 in the four possible ways, using the word *OR* between diagrams.

★ B. Diagram New Rules 6, 7, and 8 in as many ways as possible, using the word *OR* between diagrams. (Use separate paper.)

★ C. Which rule would you amplify to increase the number of verbs?

____

★ D. Of adverbs? ____________________

★ E. Of adjectives? ____________________

Now we are ready to generate sentences with the new rules, which we shall henceforth refer to as *the* PS *rules*. Let us first generate *Girls giggle* and examine its diagram.

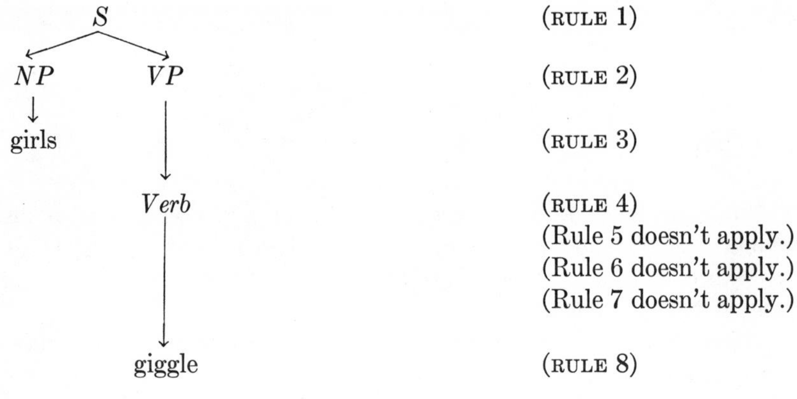

EXERCISE 279

★ A. Why doesn't Rule 5 apply? ____________________

____

★ B. Rule 6? ____________________

____

★ C. Rule 7? ____________________

____

EXERCISE 280

★ Diagram these two sentences. Follow the diagraming procedure illustrated above.

1. My brother giggles.
2. A doctor ran.

EXERCISE 281

★ A. In generating each of the above sentences did the diagrams specify which word was the noun phrase, and which the verb phrase? ______

★ B. How was this done for *A doctor ran?* (Use explanation on page 292 as a guide.) ______

★ C. Would you conclude from this that the generated sentences were each given a grammatical analysis? ______

Let us now generate *The doctors bought the dress.*

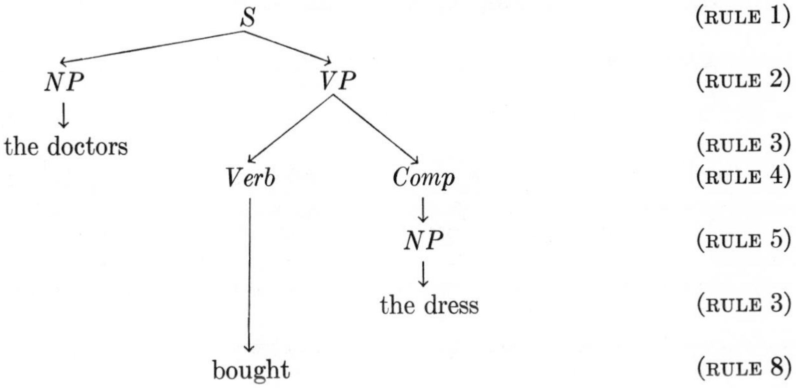

	S		(RULE 1)
NP	*VP*		(RULE 2)
↓ the doctors			(RULE 3)
	Verb	*Comp*	(RULE 4)
		↓ *NP*	(RULE 5)
		↓ the dress	(RULE 3)
	↓ bought		(RULE 8)

EXERCISE 282

★ A. What rules do not apply to the above diagram? ______

★ B. Why not? ______

★ C. Which rule was used more than once? ______

★ D. How many times? ______

★ E. How many choices does Rule 4 allow you? ______

★ F. What are they? ______

★ G. Which choice was selected? ______

EXERCISE 283

★ Diagram these sentences. (Use separate paper.)

1. My brother bought the dress.
2. The doctors bought food.

EXERCISE 284

★ A. Do the diagrams of the previous exercise specify which words are noun phrases? ______

★ B. How was this done in *The doctors bought food?* ______

★ C. What do the rules say the whole expression *bought food* is? Note the reason given in the answer. ______

★ D. Here is a tricky one. Do the rules say what the whole expression *The doctors bought* is? Note the reason given in the answer. ______

★ E. Which noun phrase is part of the verb phrase, *the doctors* or *food?*

★ F. Would you conclude from the previous exercise that the generated sentences were each given a grammatical analysis? ______

We now generate *My brother bought the girl the dress.*

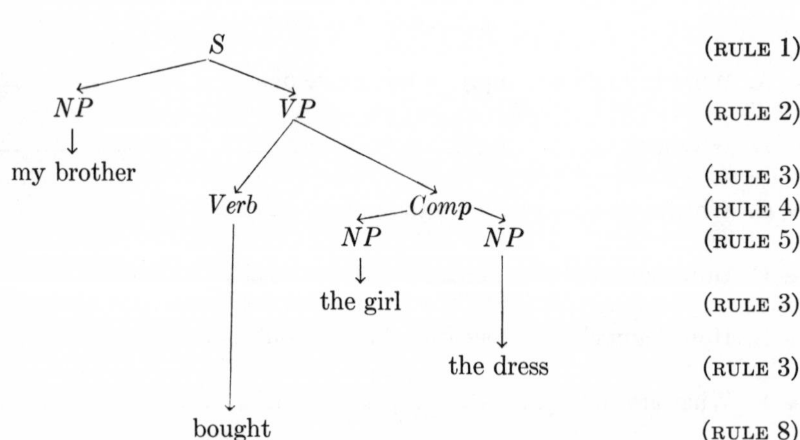

EXERCISE 285

★ A. What rules do not apply in the above diagram? ________________

★ B. Which rule was used more than once? ________________

★ C. How many times? ________________

★ D. How many choices does Rule 5 allow? ________________

★ E. What are they? ________________

★ F. Which choice was selected? ________________

EXERCISE 286

★ Diagram the following sentences. (Use separate paper.)

1. My brother bought the girl food.
2. My brothers buy the doctors food.

EXERCISE 287

★ A. What does your diagram of *My brothers buy the doctors food* say the whole expression *buy the doctors food* is? Note the reason in the answer.

____

★ B. Here is a tricky one. Do the rules say what the whole expression *my brothers buy* is? Note the reason in the answer. ________________

★ C. Would you conclude from the previous exercise that all the generated sentences were given a grammatical analysis? ________________

Finally, let us generate the following sentences:

1. Food is good.
2. The girl is here.
3. My brother is a doctor.
4. The acrobat seems good.
5. My brother remained a doctor.

1. **Food is good.**

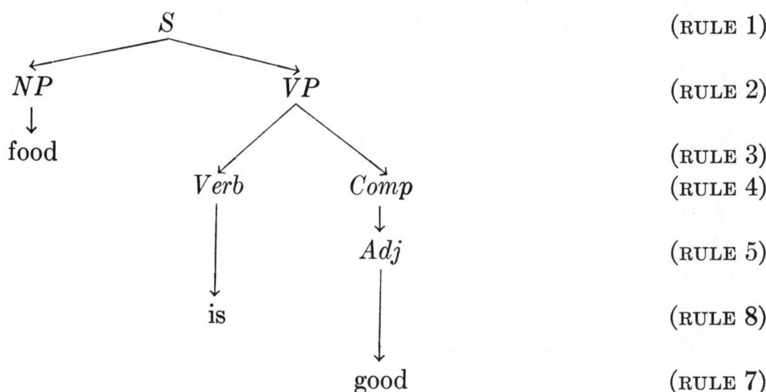

2. **The girl is here.**

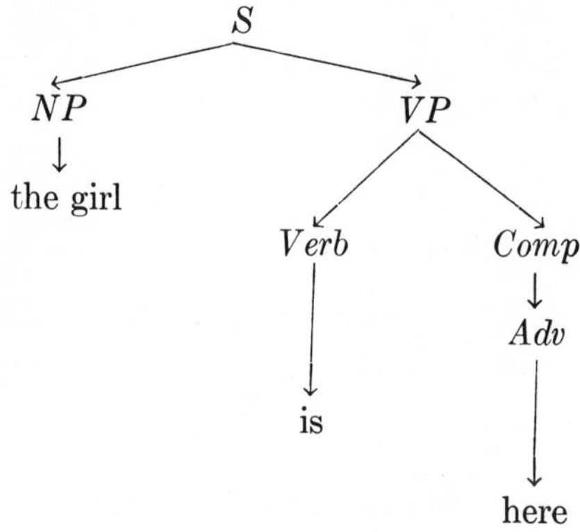

3. **My brother is a doctor.**

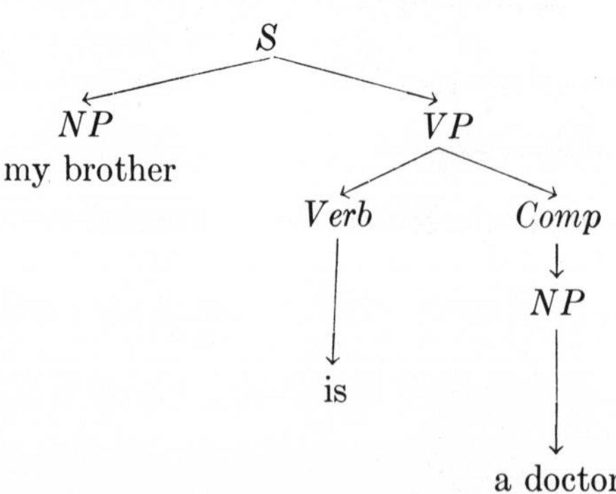

4. The acrobat seems good.

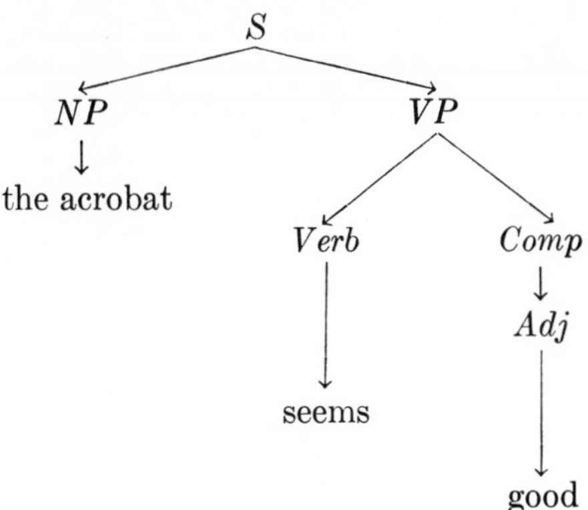

5. My brother remained a doctor.

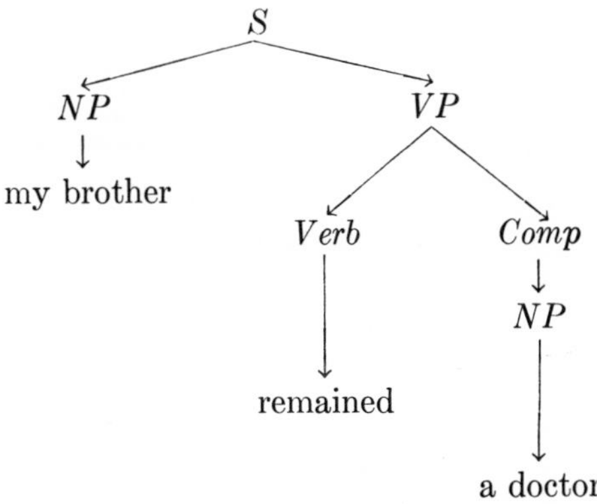

EXERCISE 288

★ A. In the above diagrams, do all the sentences use Rule 1? ________

★ B. If not, which ones do not? ________________________________

★ C. Do all use Rule 2? ____

★ D. If not, which ones do not? ________________________________

★ E. Do all use Rule 3? ____

★ F. If not, which ones do not? ________________________________

★ G. Do all use Rule 4? ______

★ H. If not, which ones do not? ______

★ I. Do all use Rule 5? ______

★ J. If not, which ones do not? ______

★ K. Do all use Rule 6? ______

★ L. If not, which ones do not? ______

★ M. Do all use Rule 7? ______

★ N. If not, which ones do not? ______

★ O. Do all use Rule 8? ______

★ P. If not, which ones do not? ______

EXERCISE 289

★ Diagram the following sentences. (Use separate paper.)

1. My brother is good.
2. Food is here.
3. The girl is a doctor.
4. The dress seems beautiful.
5. The girl remained a doctor.

2

Thus far we have generated sentences which exemplify all the basic patterns listed in Chapter XIV except pattern 7. But we did not explain how the PS grammar distinguishes these patterns from one another, or even whether it does distinguish all of them.

Basic sentence patterns are distinguished in the PS grammar by all the rules and markers except actual English expressions. Thus the markers *girls, giggle, good, in the garden,* and so on, which are English expressions, do not distinguish basic sentence patterns, whereas the markers NP, Verb, N, Adv, and so on, which are not English expressions, do.

To see this more clearly, let us remove those rules which contain English expressions, namely, Rules 3, 6, 7, and 8. To distinguish determiners (*the, a, this, that,* and so on) from nouns we will add a new Rule 3. Our shortened rules are as follows:

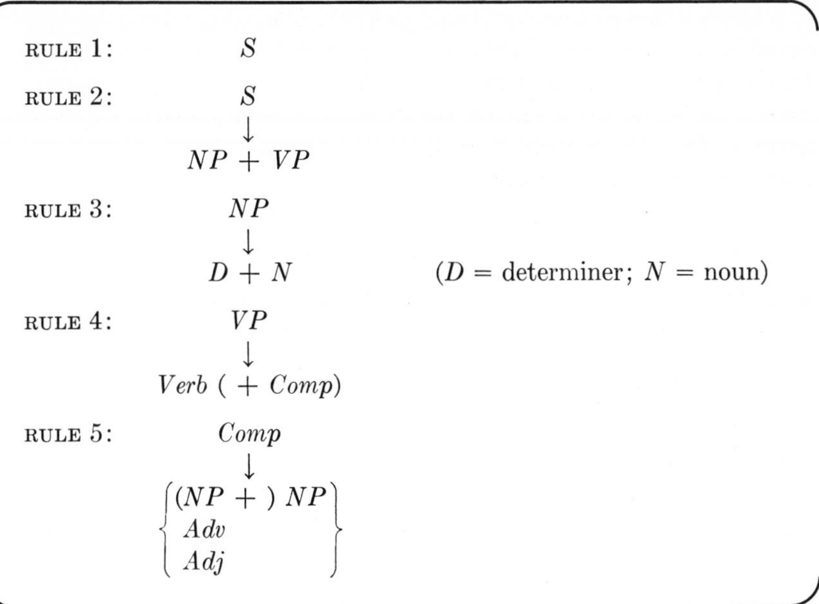

RULE 1: S
RULE 2: S → NP + VP
RULE 3: NP → D + N (D = determiner; N = noun)
RULE 4: VP → Verb (+ Comp)
RULE 5: Comp → {(NP +) NP / Adv / Adj}

EXERCISE 290

★ A. How many nonterminal markers are there in the shortened rules? (See definition of nonterminal markers on page 295.) _______________

★ B. List them. ____

★ C. How many terminal markers are there in the shortened rules? (See definition of terminal markers on page 295.) _____________________

★ D. List them. ____

Since all vocabulary or lexical items have been removed from these PS rules, can they generate sentences of English? Clearly, they cannot. They can, however, generate basic sentence patterns. Here is an illustration.

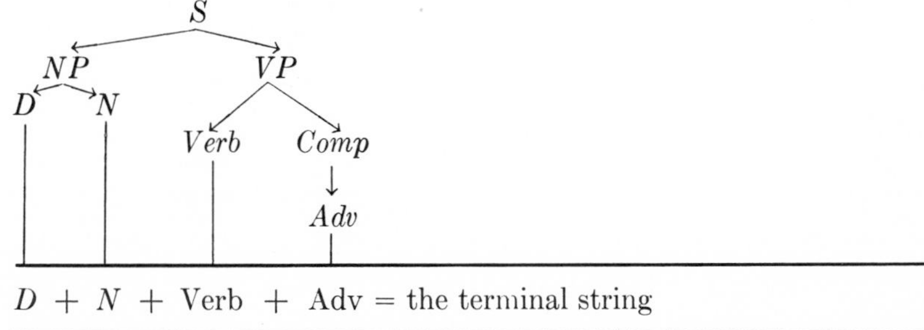

Any linear sequence of terminal markers resulting from our rules is called a *terminal string.* D + N + Verb + Adv is such a sequence and thus a terminal string. Every terminal string generated by rules that contain no lexical items can, for the moment, be considered a basic sentence pattern. Thus the terminal string D + N + Verb + Adv is a basic sentence pattern in our transformational grammar.

EXERCISE 291

★ A. Diagram the following terminal strings, that is, basic sentence patterns, by using the shortened rules. (Use separate paper.)

1. D + N + Verb + Adj
2. D + N + Verb + Adv
3. D + N + Verb
4. D + N + Verb + D + N
5. D + N + Verb + D + N + D + N

★ B. Will the shortened rules generate any terminal strings other than the five in this exercise? ____________

Now here are the five terminal strings of the last exercise and the basic patterns of Chapter XIV that correspond most closely to them.

Terminal String	Basic Patterns of Chapter XIV				
1. *D + N + Verb + Adj*	*N* Food	*V*(be) is	*Adj* good.		(PATTERN 1)
	N The acrobat	*LV* seems	*Adj* good.		(PATTERN 8)
2. *D + N + Verb + Adv*	*N* The girl	*V*(be) is	*UW* here.		(PATTERN 2)
3. *D + N + Verb*	*N* Girls	*InV* giggle.			(PATTERN 4)
4. *D + N + Verb + D + N*	*N* My brother	*V*(be) is	*N* a doctor.		(PATTERN 3)
	N The girl	*TrV* bought	*N* the dress.		(PATTERN 5)
	N My brother	*LV* remained	*N* a doctor.		(PATTERN 9)
5. *D + N + Verb + D + N + D + N*	*N* The mother	*TrV* bought	*N* the girl	*N* a dress.	(PATTERN 6)

Since nine basic patterns of Chapter XIV correspond to only five terminal strings generated by the PS rules, clearly, the PS grammar does not distinguish as many basic patterns as does Chapter XIV. For example, the terminal string D + N + Verb + Adj is distinguished as a basic pattern by the PS rules; but the PS rules do not distinguish between the basic patterns N V(*be*) Adj and N LV Adj since they do not distinguish between linking verbs and the verb *be*. Later we shall see how a transformational grammar can distinguish *all* the basic patterns.

EXERCISE 292

★ A. D + N + Verb + D + N is a terminal string; N TrV N, N LV N, and N V(*be*) N are three basic patterns of Chapter XIV that correspond to it. Why don't the PS rules distinguish between these three patterns? Be guided by the parallel explanation given above.

★ B. Diagram the *terminal strings* of the following kernel sentences using the shortened rules above. (Use separate paper.)

1. The doctors are good.
2. The dress seems beautiful.
3. The doctors remained good.
4. The acrobat remained a doctor.
5. My brother is my brother.
6. The doctors bought the dresses.
7. The dress is here.
8. My brother ran.
9. My brothers bought the girl the dress.

The shortened list of PS rules on page 305 will henceforth be the PS rules we shall employ. Rather than put English expressions back into the PS grammar, we will include them in the lexicon or dictionary to be discussed in the next section. Later we shall show how kernel sentences can be generated by using both PS rules and the lexicon.

3

On the basis of the content of the first two sections, we can make the following generalizations:

1. Transformational grammar generates all and only the grammatical sentences automatically.
2. Transformational grammar automatically assigns a grammatical analysis to each sentence generated.
3. Phrase structure grammar distinguishes between some but not all basic sentence patterns.

C. The Lexicon

1

Transformational grammar includes the lexicon of English as an integral part of the grammar of English.* A lexicon is necessary to transformational grammar because it specifies the pronunciation and grammatical classification of every item in the lexicon. Grammatical classification plays a very important role in co-occurrence and transformational rules. For example, it is necessary to know whether a noun is classified as a mass, count, or proper noun in order to determine what article, if any, can co-occur with it; it is necessary to employ a verb that is classified as allowing a passive transformation before a passive transformation can be applied.

Any good English dictionary will specify for each lexical item listed (1) its pronunciation, (2) its grammatical classification, and (3) its meaning or meanings. Similarly, a transformational grammar will specify for each item in its lexicon (1) its pronunciation in phonemic symbols, (2) its grammatical classifications, and (3) its meaning or meanings. In this chapter only pronunciation and grammatical classification will be treated; meaning will sometimes be referred to but not described in detail.

Here are some sample noun entries in the lexicon.

Lexical Item	*Pronunciation*	*Grammatical Classification*
1. milk	/mɪlk/	N—Mass
2. banana	/bənænə/	N—Count
3. Charles	/čarlz/	N—Proper

Entry 1 specifies that the word *milk* is pronounced /mɪlk/, that it is classified as a noun (represented by capital *N*), and that it is subclassified as a mass noun (represented by *Mass*).

EXERCISE 293

★ A. What does entry 2 specify? ______________________________

____

* How the grammar utilizes the lexicon will be made clear in part D3 on pages 335 ff.

★ B. Entry 3? ____

____

The grammatical classification of a word in the lexicon depends on the behavior of the word in various grammatical environments. We will illustrate this principle by classifying nouns, then verbs, and finally determiners.

2

Let us first consider the noun entries on page 308 as they occur in the following expressions.

1a. Milk is good. *Milks are good.
1b. The milk is good. *The milks are good.
1c. *A milk is good.

2a. Bananas are good.
2b. The banana is good.
2c. A banana is good.

3a. Charles is good.
3b. *The Charles is good.
3c. *A Charles is good.

An asterisk before a sentence means that it is ungrammatical. Notice that *milk* cannot be made plural (1a, 1b) and cannot be preceded by the indefinite article in the singular (1c); that *banana* can be made plural (2a) and can be preceded by the indefinite article in the singular (2c); and that *Charles* cannot be preceded by either the definite or the indefinite article (3b, 3c). Nouns that cannot be preceded by the indefinite article in the singular and cannot be made plural are called mass nouns; nouns that can be so preceded in the singular (but that cannot stand alone in the singular) and that can be plural are called count nouns; and nouns that can be preceded by neither the indefinite nor the definite article are called proper nouns.* Each noun *for a given meaning* will be classified as a mass, a count, or a proper noun.†

For example, *milk*, meaning "a white liquid," is a mass noun as in sentence 1a above; meaning "a bottle or other container of milk," it is a count noun, as in *Give me a milk. But whatever meaning a word has, its grammatical classification or classifications must ultimately rest on its grammatical behavior*. Thus *milk* here must be classified at least twice, once as

* The criteria for proper nouns are incomplete; for example, certain proper nouns can be preceded by *the* (*the Mississippi, the Alps*). Review pages 280 ff. on mass, count, and proper nouns.

† The stipulation *for a given meaning* is often very useful even though some words have more than one classification for a given meaning.

a count and once as a mass noun: When it can be preceded by the indefinite article it is a count noun; in the other case, a mass noun.

We can represent the three classifications of nouns so far introduced by the following chart:

N ┬ *Count*
  ├ *Mass*
  └ *Proper*

EXERCISE 294

★ Classify the following italicized nouns as either mass, count, or proper.

1. I saw a *fish*. ______________
2. I like to eat *fish*. ______________
3. Sincerity is an *abstraction*. ______________
4. Meat is a *food*. ______________
5. *Food* is necessary for life. ______________
6. Playing is *fun*. ______________
7. *Robert* enjoys life. ______________
8. A *thing* of beauty is a joy forever. ______________
9. *Chicago* is my home town. ______________
10. *Sincerity* is a virtue. ______________

Now consider these expressions.

1a. The girl who hit the boy giggled.
1b. The girl that hit the boy giggled.
1c. *The girl which hit the boy giggled.

2a. The rock which hit the boy was black.
2b. The rock that hit the boy was black.
2c. *The rock who hit the boy was black.

Notice that after *girl*, either *who(m)* or *that* may introduce a relative clause (1a, 1b), whereas after *rock*, either *which* or *that* may introduce a relative clause (2a, 2b). But *which* must not be used after *girl* (1c) nor *who* after *rock* (2c). Nouns that can be followed by *who(m)* in relative clauses are called human nouns; nouns that can be followed by *which* are called nonhuman nouns. Each noun *for a given meaning* will be classified as either human or nonhuman.* We can represent the two possibilities by a chart thus:

$$N \begin{cases} Hum \\ Nhum \end{cases}$$

EXERCISE 295

★ In the first blank in each sentence put either *who* or *which*. Then in the second blank indicate whether the italicized noun is human (*Hum*) or nonhuman (*Nhum*).

Examples:

This is the dog (*which*) won the blue ribbon. Nhum
This is my sister (*who*) is always hungry. Hum

1. It is *sincerity* ________ is a virtue. ________
2. *New York*, ________ is a large city, is on the eastern seaboard. ________
3. The *idea* ________ just occurred to me will make me rich. ________
4. *Man*, ________ invented the wheel, is resourceful. ________
5. The *man* ________ is drinking beer is an FBI agent. ________
6. This *table*, ________ I made myself, is solid oak. ________
7. *John*, ________ lives with his mother, will never grow up. ________

---

* The terms *human* and *nonhuman* are grammatical, not semantic, terms. Thus some nouns that denote animals are sometimes human nouns (for example, *This is my dog who is always hungry*). Another criterion for distinguishing human and nonhuman nouns is pronoun substitution, for example, *he/she* for human, *it* for nonhuman.

8. His *mother,* ______________________ John lives with, is a tyrant. ______________

9. *Bananas,* ______________________ are tropical fruit, are cheaper in the summer. ______________

10. My *doctor,* ______________________ is out of town, is an internist. ______________

By combining the mass-count-proper and human-nonhuman classification schemes, we can classify each noun as (1) either count, mass, or proper *and* (2) either human or nonhuman. Thus each noun will theoretically be classified as one of the following:

1. count *and* human
2. count *and* nonhuman

3. mass *and* human
4. mass *and* nonhuman

5. proper *and* human
6. proper *and* nonhuman

We can represent these possibilities by a chart thus:

N — { *Count* / *Mass* / *Proper* } A
N — { *Hum* / *Nhum* } B

To get any one of the six possible classifications we must choose one and only one classification from the part labeled A *and* one and only one classification from the part labeled B.

Here are some sample entries employing this classification scheme:

1. man	/mæn/	*N*—*Count*, *Hum*	(A man who works . . .)
2. man	/mæn/	*N*—*Mass*, *Hum*	(*Man*, who invented the wheel . . .)
3. banana	/bənænə/	*N*—*Count*, *Nhum*	(A *banana* which tastes good . . .)

4. food	/fud/	*N*—[*Mass*, *Nhum*]	(*Food* which is necessary . . .)
5. John	/ǰan/	*N*—[*Proper*, *Hum*]	(*John*, who works . . .)
6. New York	/nu yɔrk/	*N*—[*Proper*, *Nhum*]	(*New York*, which is a big city . . .)

EXERCISE 296

★ Using the above lexical entries as a guide classify the italicized nouns:

1. *Woman*, who is man's helpmeet, is creative.

2. I saw a *woman* who wore red suspenders.

3. This is a *dog* which won a blue ribbon.

4. This is a *dog* who is always friendly.

5. Here is a *fish* which is swimming rapidly.

6. Here is *fish* which is ready to eat.

7. A *diet* which is healthful will keep you slim.

8. *Chicago*, which is a midwestern city, is my home town.

9. *Harry*, who chases girls, works with me.

10. A *girl* who wears red suspenders will attract attention.

Finally consider these sentences:

1. a. The man is good.
   b. The men are good.

2. a. The news is good.
   b. *The news are good.

3. a. *The police is good.
   b. The police are good.

We observe in these sentences that *man* can be either singular or plural; that *news* must always be singular and *police* always plural. These sentences illustrate another kind of noun classification. Each noun *for a given meaning* will be classified according to whether (1) it may be either singular or plural, (2) it is always singular, or (3) it is always plural.

By adding this classification scheme to that introduced above, we can now classify each noun as (1) either count, mass, or proper *and* (2) either human or nonhuman *and* (3) either always singular, always plural, or either singular or plural. This gives us eighteen theoretical possibilities.

We can represent these possibilities by the following chart:

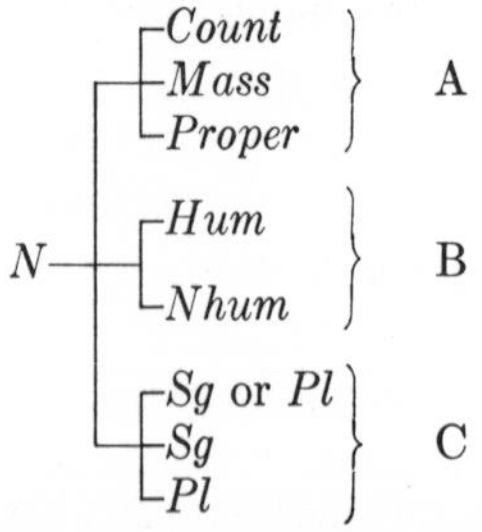

```
       ┌─┬─Count      ┐
       │ ├─Mass       ├  A
       │ └─Proper     ┘
       │
       │ ┌─Hum        ┐
  N────┼─┤            ├  B
       │ └─Nhum       ┘
       │
       │ ┌─Sg or Pl   ┐
       └─┼─Sg         ├  C
         └─Pl         ┘
```

To get any one of the eighteen possible classifications, we must choose one and only one classification from the part labeled A *and* one and only one classification from the part labeled B *and* one and only one classification from the part labeled C.

Here are some sample entries in our lexicon employing this classification scheme:

man	/mæn/	N	*Count* *Hum* *Sg* or *Pl*	(A *man* who is . . . , *Men* who are . . .)
police	/pəlis/	N	*Count* *Hum* *Pl*	(*Police* who are . . .)
news*	/nuz/	N	*Mass* *Nhum* *Sg*	(*news* which is . . .)
John	/ǰan/	N	*Proper* *Hum* *Sg*	(*John*, who is . . .)

EXERCISE 297

★ Using the entries above as a guide, classify the italicized nouns:

1. *People* who are strong exercise a lot.

2. *Milk*, which is a good food, comes from a cow.

3. A *baby* which is crying is usually hungry. *OR*
   Babies which are crying make a lot of noise.

4. An *abstraction* which is hard to understand requires you to think. *OR*
   Abstractions which are difficult require much thought.

5. *Fish* which are swimming are difficult to catch. *OR*
   A *fish* which is swimming looks very graceful.

---

* Since mass nouns are always singular, Sg could be omitted from the lexical entries of mass nouns and replaced by a more general rule.

6. *Fish*, which tastes good, is a wholesome food.

7. *Harry*, who is my friend, is very tall.

8. *Sincerity*, which is a virtue, is appreciated.

9. A *table* which is made of oak is heavy. *OR*
   Tables which are made of oak are expensive.

10. *Fun*, which children enjoy, sometimes gets them into trouble.

In this subsection we have classified nouns according to their grammatical behavior; that is, according to how they behave with articles, with relative clauses, and with plural and/or singular morphemes.

3

Turning now to the classification of verbs in the lexicon, we find that verbs are classified by two criteria:

a. by whether or not they occur with particular markers; and
b. by what transformations they allow.

To illustrate these criteria, a classification scheme for verbs will now be given.

First consider these sentences:

1. They vanished.
2. John is hammering nails.
3. John is hammering.
4. John tabled the motion.

Vanish, as in sentence 1, is classified as intransitive because it cannot be followed by an NP (direct object) in the PS grammar. *Hammer*, as in sentences 2 and 3, is classified as transitive because it *may* be followed by an NP in the PS grammar. *Table*, as in sentence 4, is also classified as transitive because it *must* be followed by an NP in the PS grammar.

In general, intransitive verbs cannot be followed by an NP in the PS grammar, whereas transitive verbs either *may* or *must* be followed by an

NP. Every verb *for a given meaning* is classified as either transitive or intransitive.*

Instead of employing the terms *transitive* and *intransitive,* we shall employ the symbols vNP and vø, respectively. A vNP verb is one that *may* or *must* be followed by an NP; a vø verb is one that cannot be followed by an NP. We can represent the two possible verb classifications thus:

V —┬ *vNP*
     └ *vø*

Here are two sample lexical entries which employ this classification scheme.

hammer	/hæmər/	*V–vNP*	(He *hammered* the nail, He *hammered*)
vanish	/vænɪsh/	*V–vø*	(He *vanished*)

EXERCISE 298

★ Using the two sample lexical entries above as a guide, classify the italicized verbs as vNP or as vø.

1. He *knew. OR* He *knew* it. ________

2. They *feasted.* ________

3. He *disappeared* into the woods. ________

4. He *saw* the ship go sailing by. ________

5. She *bought* the dress for her mother. ________

6. He *brought* the paper home. ________

7. He *went* away. ________

8. He *ran* the factory efficiently. ________

9. He *rose* quickly. ________

10. He *smoked* a pipe. ________

---

* The difference of meaning between a transitive verb followed by an NP and the same verb not followed by an NP is the same for a great many verbs. For example, the difference of meaning of the verbs in pairs of sentences such as *He hammered the nail: He hammered, He spoke the words: He spoke,* and *He smoked the pipe: He smoked* is that the verbs of the first members of each pair do not emphasize the nature of the action whereas the verbs of the second members do. For purposes of classifying verbs for a given meaning, we can disregard these differences since they are predictable.

Consider now these sentences.

1. a. My brother is a doctor.
   b. My brother is good.
2. a. *My brother seems a doctor.
   b. My brother seems good.

The verb *be* can be followed by either an NP or Adj (1a, 1b); the verb *seem*, only by an Adj (2b). Verbs like *be* will be called vNP/Adj verbs; verbs like *seem*, vAdj verbs. Thus far, then, each verb *for a given meaning* will be classified as either a vNP, vø, vAdj, or vNP/Adj verb.

We can now represent the four possible classifications in this chart:

```
   ┌vNP
   ├vø
V──┤
   ├vAdj
   └vNP/Adj
```

To get the classification of any one verb, we choose one and only one of the classifications listed on the chart.

Here are some sample entries using the classification scheme for verbs thus far developed in the lexicon.

hammer	/hæmər/	*V–vNP*	(He *hammered* the nail, He *hammered*)
disappear	/dɪsəpɪr/	*V–vø*	(He *disappeared*)
seem	/sim/	*V–vAdj*	(He *seems* happy)
be	/bi/	*V–vNP/Adj*	(He *is* a man, He *is* happy)

EXERCISE 299

★ Using the above sample entries as a guide, classify the italicized verbs:

1. He *sat* down. ____________________
2. He *remained* a doctor. *OR* He *remained* happy. ____________________
3. He *violated* the law. ____________________
4. He *looked* miserable. ____________________
5. He *smelled* the roast.* ____________________
6. The roast *smelled* good.* ____________________

* Verbs like *smell, taste,* and so on, can be analyzed as basically vNP verbs (*He smelled the roast, He tasted the roast*); the vAdj verbs *smell, taste* (*The roast smelled good, The roast tasted good*) could then be derived (by transformations) from their vNP counterparts.

7. He *told* a story. ____________________
8. He is *lying*. ____________________
9. He *weighed* the bananas. ____________________
10. He *heard* music. ____________________

Now consider these sentences:

1. The girl gave her mother a dress.
2. *The girl saw her mother a dress.

Certain vNP verbs like *give* can be followed by two NP's, the first an indirect and the second a direct object (sentence 1). Other vNP verbs like *saw* can be followed by only one NP. (Sentence 2 is ungrammatical.) Those that can be followed by two NP's are designated vNPNP verbs; those that can be followed by only one are designated vøNP verbs. In the symbol vøNP, the ø indicates the absence of the indirect object. Each vNP verb *for a given meaning* will be further classified as either a vNPNP or a vøNP verb.

On the basis of the classification scheme thus far developed each verb can now be classified as one and only one of the following:

1. vNPNP as a subclass of vNP
2. vøNP as a subclass of the same vNP
3. vø
4. vAdj
5. vNP/Adj

We can represent these five possible classifications by this chart:

```
                  ┌vNPNP
    ┌vNP──────────┤
    │             └vøNP
    ├vø
V───┤
    ├vAdj
    │
    └vNP/Adj
```

To get any of the five possible classifications we must first choose either vNP, vø, vAdj, or vNP/Adj. If we choose vNP we must then choose either vNPNP or vøNP. To state these choices in more familiar terms, we must first choose a classification that is either transitive, intransitive, linking, or copulative (= vNP/Adj). If we choose a transitive classification, we must then choose either an indirect-plus-direct-object, or a direct-object-only classification.

On the following page are some examples of lexical entries using the classification scheme above.

give	/gɪv/	*V–vNP–vNPNP*	(He *gave* her the flowers)
hammer	/hæmər/	*V–vNP–vø*NP	(He *hammered* the nail, He *hammered*)
disappear	/dɪsəpɪr/	*V–vø*	(He *disappeared*)
seem	/sim/	*V–vAdj*	(He *seems* happy)
be	/bi/	*V–vNP/Adj*	(He *is* a man, He *is* happy)

EXERCISE 300

★ Using the entries above as a guide, classify the italicized verbs.

1. *Tell* me a story. ______________
2. He *met* her. ______________
3. He *asked* her a question. ______________
4. The girls *listened.* ______________
5. She *made* John a hearty meal. ______________
6. He *threw* her the ball. ______________
7. He *taught* her a lesson. ______________
8. It *tasted* good. ______________
9. *Bake* me a cake. ______________
10. He *became* dissolute. *OR* He *became* a lawyer. ______________

Now consider these sentences:

Active:	1. a.	Boys hit girls.
Passive:	b.	Girls are hit by boys.
Active:	2. a.	The suit fit John.
Passive:	b.	*John was fitted by the suit.

Such vNP verbs as *hit* can be made passive (1a, 1b); vNP verbs like *fit* cannot (2a, 2b). All vNP verbs that allow a passive transformation will be classified as Tpas verbs; others will be classified as $\overline{\text{Tpas}}$. The line above $\overline{\text{Tpas}}$ here means "not." All vNP verbs *for a given meaning* will be classified as either Tpas or $\overline{\text{Tpas}}$.

Now let us chart the classification of the verb up to this point.

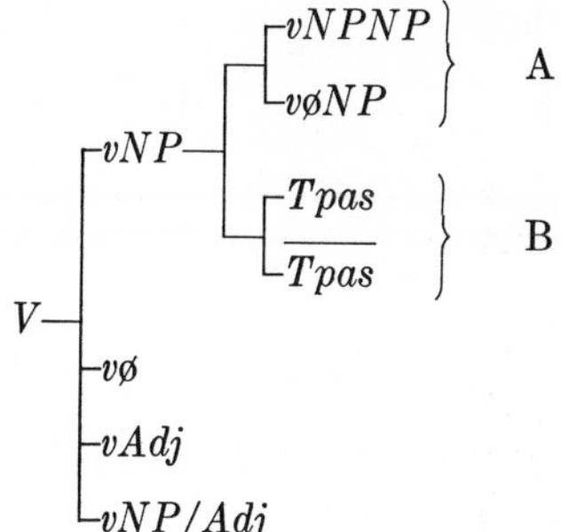

To classify a verb, we must first choose either vNP, vø, vAdj, or vNP/Adj. If we choose vNP we must then choose (1) either vNPNP or vøNP from the part labeled A *and* (2) either Tpas or $\overline{\text{Tpas}}$ from the part labeled B.

Here are some examples of entries in the lexicon using the classification scheme thus far developed.

give	/gɪv/	*V–vNP–* *vNPNP* *Tpas*	(He *gave* her the flowers, The flowers were *given* her)
smoke	/smok/	*V–vNP–* *vøNP* *Tpas*	(He *smoked* a cigar, A cigar was *smoked*)
fit	/fɪt/	*V–vNP–* *VøNP* $\overline{Tpas}$	(The suit *fit* John)
giggle	/gɪgəl/	*V–vø*	(Girls *giggle*)
seem	/sim/	*V–vAdj*	(He *seems* happy)
be	/bi/	*V–vNP/Adj*	(He *is* a man, He *is* happy)

EXERCISE 301

★ Using the sample lexical entries above as a guide, classify the italicized verbs.

1. This box *contains* a cake.

2. He *baked* the lady a cake. *OR* A cake was *baked* for the lady.

3. It *happened* yesterday.

4. He *resembles* a monkey.

5. He *weighed* the meat. *OR* The meat was *weighed* by him.

6. He *grew* sleepy.

7. He *stayed* a general. *OR* He *stayed* thin.

8. He *gave* her the money. *OR* The money was *given* to her.

9. His face *went* pale.

10. He *went* yesterday.

Finally, consider these sentences:

1. a. The girl knows that the boy is here.
   b. The girl knows where the boy is.

2. a. *The man tabled that the motion is bad.
   b. *The man tabled where the motion is bad.

The verb *know* as in 1a and 1b can be followed by a factive clause; the verb *table* as in 2a and 2b cannot. A factive clause is one that (a) begins with *that* or a question word such as *where, when* or *how* and that (b) substitutes for the direct object.* Such vNP verbs as *know* are Tfac verbs;

* In the sentence *The man tabled what he was told to table*, the clause *what he was told to table* is not a factive clause. *What* is analyzed as *that* plus *which, that* being the direct object and *which* the introducer of the relative clause *which he was told to table.*

vNP verbs such as *hit* are $\overline{\text{Tfac}}$ verbs, the raised line again meaning "not." Each vNP verb *for a given meaning* will be classified as either a Tfac or a $\overline{\text{Tfac}}$ verb.

Now to the classification scheme already given, we can add another choice, Tfac or $\overline{\text{Tfac}}$; hence our chart can be amplified.

- *V*
  - *vNP*
    - A: *vNPNP* / *vøNP*
    - B: *Tpas* / $\overline{Tpas}$
    - C: *Tfac* / $\overline{Tfac}$
  - *vø*
  - *vAdj*
  - *vNP/Adj*

Here are some examples of entries using the classification scheme above.

know	/no/	*V–vNP* — *vøNP*, *Tpas*, *Tfac*	(He *knew* the man; The man was *known* by him; The girl *knows* that the boy is here, The girl *knows* where the boy is)
tell	/tɛl/	*V–vNP* — *vNPNP*, *Tpas*, *Tfac*	(I *told* her a story; A story was *told* her; I *told* her that John was here, I *told* her where John was)
esteem	/ɛstim/	*V–vNP* — *vøNP*, *Tpas*, $\overline{Tfac}$	(Boys *esteem* girls, Girls are *esteemed* by boys)
give	/gɪv/	*V–vNP* — *vNPNP*, *Tpas*, $\overline{Tfac}$	(He *gave* her the flowers, The flowers were *given* her)
fit	/fɪt/	*V–vNP* — *vøNP*, $\overline{Tpas}$, $\overline{Tfac}$	(The suit *fit* John)
giggle	/gɪgəl/	*V–vø*	(Girls *giggle*)
seem	/sim/	*V–VAdj*	(He *seems* happy)
be	/bi/	*V–vNP/Adj*	(He *is* a man, He *is* happy)

EXERCISE 302

★ Using the entries above as a guide, classify the italicized verbs.

1. I *believe* it. *OR* It was *believed. OR* I *believe* that he will go.

2. He *remembered* the book. *OR* The book was *remembered OR* He *remembered* that he had the book.

3. He *taught* her a lesson. *OR* A lesson was *taught* her. *OR* He *taught* that politicians learn by history.

4. I *have* a dollar.

5. He *tasted* the soup. *OR* The soup was *tasted.*

6. He *lay* down.

7. He *felt* happy.

8. Donald *continued* my friend, despite our differences. *OR* Donald *continued* constant despite our differences.

9. The author *continued* the book. *OR* The book was *continued* by the author.

10. He *enjoyed* the party. *OR* The party was *enjoyed* by him.

In this subsection we have classified verbs according to (1) what markers they can or cannot occur with in the PS grammar; for example, NP and/or Adj, and (2) what transformations they allow, for example, passive or factive. Notice that verbs are classified, in part, on the basis of their occurrence or nonoccurrence with nouns. Nouns, however, are not classified on the basis of their occurrence or nonoccurrence with verbs.*

4

Determiners will be classified in the lexicon according to whether they are (1) articles, demonstratives, or neither articles nor demonstratives and (2) always singular, always plural, or either singular or plural. We can represent these possibilities by the chart on the following page.

* A more detailed study of verbs suggests that verbs can be classified in accordance with their occurrence or nonoccurrence with various subclasses of nouns, adjectives, and adverbs. For example, *surprise* is classified as a verb that takes only human and animate nouns since we can say *The event surprised John* or *The event surprised the dog*, but not **The event surprised the rock*.

```
            ┌─Art        ┐
         ┌──┼─Dem        ├  A
         │  └─Other      ┘
    D────┤
         │  ┌─Sg or Pl   ┐
         └──┼─Sg         ├  B
            └─Pl         ┘
```

Here are some example entries:†

a	/ə/	*D*—*Art*, *Sg*	(*A* book)
the	/ðə/	*D*—*Art*, *Sg* or *Pl*	(*The* book, *the* books)
this	/ðɪs/	*D*—*Dem*, *Sg*	(*This* book)
these	/ðiz/	*D*—*Dem*, *Pl*	(*These* books)
my	/mai/	*D*—Other, *Sg* or *Pl*	(*My* book, *my* books)

EXERCISE 303

★ Using the entries above as a guide classify the following determiners:

1. your

2. an

† This classification is simplified and does not specify many underlying relationships among subgroups of determiners.

3. his

4. that

5. those

6. her

7. the

8. its

9. our

10. their

Although adjectives, adverbs and prepositions must be subclassified, we shall not do so in this chapter.* Instead, adjective, adverb, and preposition entries in the lexicon will simply indicate the part of speech. Here are three examples:

good	/gud/	Adj
here	/hɪr/	Adv
by	/bai/	Prep

* Adjectives are, in part, subclassified in terms of their environment and the transformations they allow. Prepositional phrases that are adverbs are, in part, subclassified in terms both of the kinds of nouns and the kinds of prepositions they consist of.

EXERCISE 304

★ Using the above two entries as a guide classify the italicized words as Adj, Adv, or Prep.

1. They are *bad.* ____________________
2. They are *there.* ____________________
3. She seemed *beautiful.* ____________________
4. She is *here.* ____________________
5. He walked *fast.* ____________________
6. His mind is *quick.* ____________________
7. The boy was hit *by* the girl. ____________________

5

For convenience of reference here now are the shortened PS rules, given on page 305, summary classification charts for nouns, verbs, and determiners, and the sample lexicon to be employed in some of the exercises of the remainder of the chapter.

I. PS RULES

RULE 1: S

RULE 2: $$S \rightarrow NP + VP$$

RULE 3: $$NP \rightarrow D + N$$

RULE 4: $$VP \rightarrow Verb\ (+\ Comp)$$

RULE 5: $$Comp \rightarrow \begin{Bmatrix} (NP +)\ NP \\ Adv \\ Adj \end{Bmatrix}$$

II. NOUN CLASSIFICATION CHART

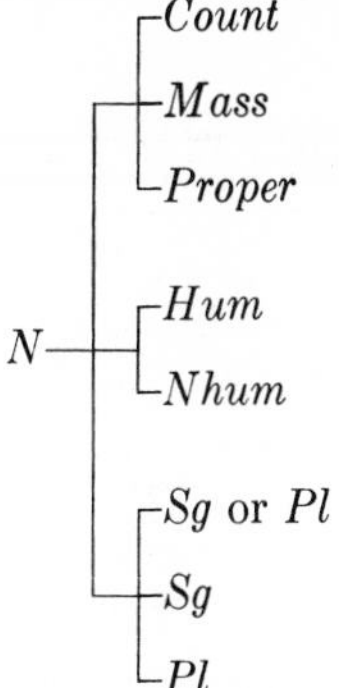

III. VERB CLASSIFICATION CHART

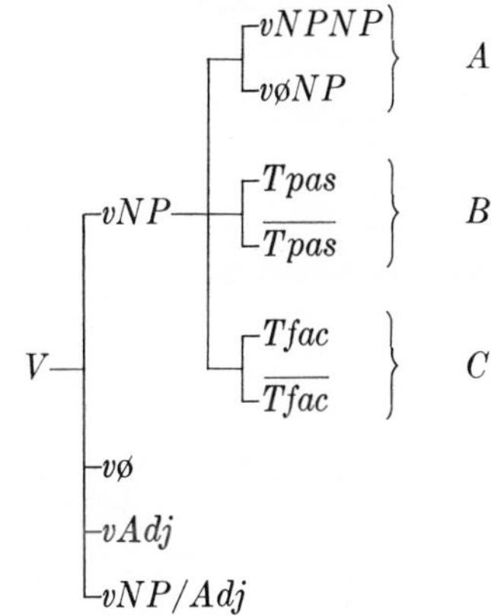

IV. DETERMINER CLASSIFICATION CHART

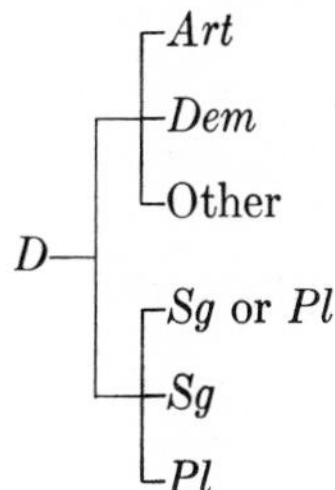

V. SAMPLE LEXICON

Determiners

the /ðə/ *D*—{*Art*, *Sg* or *Pl*}

this	/ðɪs/	*D*—*Dem* *Sg*
that	/ðæt/	*D*—*Dem* *Sg*
those	/ðoz/	*D*—*Dem* *Pl*

Nouns

boy	/bɔi/	*N*—*Count* *Hum* *Sg* or *Pl*
cat	/kæt/	*N*—*Count* *Nhum* *Sg* or *Pl*
cow	/kau/	*N*—*Count* *Nhum* *Sg* or *Pl*
dog	/dɔg/	*N*—*Count* *Nhum* *Sg* or *Pl*
girl	/gərl/	*N*—*Count* *Hum* *Sg* or *Pl*
milk	/mɪlk/	*N*—*Mass* *Nhum* *Sg*
police	/pəlis/	*N*—*Count* *Hum* *Pl*

Robert /rabərt/ N — [*Proper*, *Hum*, *Sg*]

water /wɔtər/ N — [*Mass*, *Nhum*, *Sg*]

Adjectives

brown	/braun/	*Adj*
good	/gʊd/	*Adj*
happy	/hæpi/	*Adj*

Adverb

here /hɪr/ *Adv*

Preposition

by /bai/ *Prep*

Verbs

be /ar/ $V{-}vNP/Adj$
(= present, plural)

give /gɪv/ $V{-}vNP$ — [$+vNPNP$, $+Tpas$, $-\overline{Tfac}$]

hit /hɪt/ $V{-}vNP$ — [$v\phi NP$, $Tpas$, $\overline{Tfac}$]

know /no/ $V{-}vNP$ — [$v\varnothing NP$, $Tpas$, $Tfac$]

laugh /læf/ $V{-}v\varnothing$

like /laik/ $V{-}vNP$ — [$v\varnothing NP$, $Tpas$, $\overline{Tfac}$]

seem /sim/ $V{-}vAdj$
vanish /vænɪš/ $V{-}v\varnothing$

6

In summary, the lexicon is an integral part of transformational grammar. It consists of entries for all the words of English, with their pronunciation, meanings (which were not discussed), and grammatical classifications.

D. Morphophonemic Rules and Rules of Order

1

The PS rules and lexicon taken by themselves will not generate kernel sentences. To generate kernel sentences we also need both morphophonemic rules and a set of Rules of Order. Let us now take up the morphophonemic rules, abbreviated Mph rules. Roughly speaking, a Mph rule gives directions for rewriting certain morphemic elements phonemically. The Mph rules given here are a preparation for the Rules of Order to follow directly. No attempt will be made to explain in detail the role of phonology in a transformational grammar.

2

The Mph rules to be described here will concern the following grammatical problems:

1. plural of nouns (review pages 29-30)
2. third person singular for verbs (review page 30)
3. past tense for verbs (review pages 30-31)
4. present and past tense of the verb *be*

Rule 1: Plurals. The Mph rules for plurals are as follows:

A. 1. man + *Pl* ⟶ /mɛn/
   2. child + *Pl* ⟶ /čɪldrɨn/
   3. police + *Pl* ⟶ /pəlis/

B. *N* + *Pl* ⟶ /N/ + {
/ɨz/ when preceded by /s/, /z/, /š/, /ž/, /č/, /ǰ/
/z/ when preceded by other voiced sounds
/s/ when preceded by other voiceless sounds
}

/N/ = phonemic representation of nouns given in the lexicon that take a regular plural. How elements like *Pl* (also *Sg* and *past*) are introduced into grammatical strings will be made clear in the Rules of Order, pages 335 ff.

The arrow means "Rewrite as." The rules of A apply to nouns that take an irregular plural; rule B applies to nouns with regular plurals. To operate Rule B, it is necessary to look up in the lexicon the phonemic representation of each lexical item being rewritten.

Applying Rule B to specific cases, we get:

1. boy + *Pl* ⟶ /bɔiz/
2. cat + *Pl* ⟶ /kæts/
3. kiss + *Pl* ⟶ /kɪsɨz/

EXERCISE 305

★ Rewrite the following combinations of elements using the above Mph rules. To get the phonemic representation of the nouns below, refer to the partially specified lexicon on page 335.

1. banana + *Pl* ⟶
2. mass + *Pl* ⟶
3. book + *Pl* ⟶
4. dog + *Pl* ⟶
5. pod + *Pl* ⟶

Rule 2: Third Person Singular for Verbs. The Mph rules for third-person singular verbs are as follows:*

$$V + Sg \rightarrow /V/ + \begin{cases} /\text{ɨz}/ \text{ when preceded by } /s/, /z/, /\check{s}/, /\check{z}/, /\check{c}/, /\check{j}/ \\ /z/ \text{ when preceded by other voiced sounds} \\ /s/ \text{ when preceded by other voiceless sounds} \end{cases}$$

/V/ = phonemic representation of any verb in the sample lexicon other than *be*.

To apply this rule, it is necessary to look up in the lexicon the phonemic representation of each item being rewritten.

Applying this rule to specific cases, we get:

1. play + *Sg* ⟶ /plez/
2. bat + *Sg* ⟶ /bæts/
3. kiss + *Sg* ⟶ /kɪsɨz/

EXERCISE 306

★ Rewrite the combinations on page 334 using the above Mph rule. To get the phonemic representation of the verbs given, refer to the partially specified lexicon on page 335.

* This rule and the preceding one on plurals can be written as a single rule. For pedagogical reasons they have been separated.

1. know + *Sg* ⟶
2. hit + *Sg* ⟶
3. miss + *Sg* ⟶
4. like + *Sg* ⟶
5. sing + *Sg* ⟶

Rule 3: Past Tense of Verbs. The Mph rules for the past tense of verbs are as follows:

A. 1. know + *past* ⟶ /nu/
   2. hit + *past* ⟶ /hɪt/

B. *V* + *past* ⟶ /V/ + { /ɨd/ when preceded by /t/ or /d/; /d/ when preceded by other voiced sounds; /t/ when preceded by other voiceless sounds }

The rules in A apply to verbs with irregular past tenses; those in B apply to verbs with regular past tenses. Applying Rule B to specific cases, we get:

1. play + *past* ⟶ /pled/
2. kiss + *past* ⟶ /kɪst/
3. bat + *past* ⟶ /bætɨd/

EXERCISE 307

★ Rewrite the following combinations of elements using the Mph rules above. To get the phonemic representation of the verbs below, refer to the partially specified lexicon on page 335.

1. smile + *past* ⟶
2. match + *past* ⟶
3. like + *past* ⟶
4. taste + *past* ⟶
5. seem + *past* ⟶

***Rule 4: The Verb* be.** The verb *be* is an irregular verb requiring special treatment. The Mph rules for *be* are as follows:

A. be + *Sg* ⟶	/æm/ /ar/ /ɪz/	(1st-, 2nd-, and 3rd-person singular, present tense)
B. be + *past* ⟶	/wər/	(plural, past tense)
C. be + *Sg* + *past* ⟶	/wər/ /wəz/	(2nd-, 1st- and 3rd-person singular, past tense)

Partially Specified Lexicon for Exercises 305, 306, and 307

Nouns		*Verbs*	
banana	/bənænə/	hit	/hɪt/
book	/bʊk/	know	/no/
dog	/dɔg/	like	/laik/
mass	/mæs/	match	/mæč/
pod	/pad/	miss	/mɪs/
		seem	/sim/
		sing	/sɪŋ/
		smile	/smail/
		taste	/test/

3

Now we are ready to generate kernel sentences. To do this we need to follow a set of Rules of Order for Kernels which primarily specify the order in which elements and rules are to be selected and applied. In some cases, however, these rules actually introduce new elements into the grammar. This latter function is necessary for generating sentences since one must know what markers and lexical items must co-occur (or go together) to make each generated sentence grammatical.

As you study each rule, examine the corresponding parts of the two illustrations which follow on pages 338 and 339.*

RULES OF ORDER

First (Terminal String Selection)

Generate a terminal string with associated diagram.

Second (Noun Selection)

a. Select a noun from the lexicon (page 330) for each N marker in the terminal string. Select basic entry form, not phonemic form.

b. For each noun selected that is classified Sg *or* Pl (page 330), choose Sg or Pl; if Pl is chosen, add the element Pl to the right of the appropriate noun.

* The Rules of Order in conjunction with the PS grammar and lexicon already given, and also various rules to follow later, will generate a number of types of ungrammatical sentences. This cannot be helped since these rules are incomplete (see page 382 for a few illustrations of ungrammatical sequences produced by this grammar).

c. For nouns classified as Pl, add Pl to the right of the appropriate noun.

Third (Determiner Selection; that is, Agreement of Noun and Determiner)

a. 1. If the noun selected is classified Mass, or Count with Pl added to it, the determiner before it may optionally be omitted. Omit D before the appropriate noun if desired.

2. If a noun is classified as Proper, omit D before it.

b. If D is chosen, then

1. if noun is classified Mass, do not select *a* or *an*.

2. if Pl follows noun selected, select a determiner classified as either Pl, or Sg *or* Pl (page 329).

3. Otherwise select a determiner classified as either Sg, or Sg *or* Pl (page 329).

Fourth (Adjective and Adverb Selection)

Select adjectives and adverbs from the lexicon for each marker Adj or Adv, respectively (page 331).

Fifth (Verb Selection)

a. Select appropriate kind of verb from the lexicon (page 331) by observing the structure of the diagram:

1. if the verb has one NP following it, select either a vNP or vNP/Adj verb.

2. if the verb has two NP's following it, select a vNPNP verb.

3. if the verb has Adj following it, select either a vAdj or vNP/Adj verb.

4. if verb has Adv or nothing following it, select a vϕ verb or a vNP/Adj verb (e.g., *be*, which can be followed by certain adverbs).

b. Select past or present.

1. If present is selected, leave the verb as it is.

2. If past is selected add the element *past* to the right of the verb.

Sixth (Subject-verb Agreement)

a. If verb is in the present tense (doesn't have *past* added to it) and the NP preceding it, which is the subject, is singular (doesn't have Pl added to it), add the element Sg to the right of the verb.

b. If verb is *be* (past or present) and the NP preceding it is singular, add Sg to the right of *be*.

Seventh (LX Terminal String)

Bring down resultant string and place LX in front of it. This is called the *lexical terminal string* or, briefly, the *LX terminal string*. The LX terminal string is not yet a kernel sentence (see page 342 immediately following the two illustrations for an explanation of LX terminal strings).

Eighth (Kernel Sentence)

a. Apply the Mph rules on pages 332, 333, 334, and 334 to get noun plural forms, third-person singular forms, past-tense forms, and forms of *be*.

b. Additional agreement rules for the verb *be* (on page 334). Note: present plural form /ar/ is given in lexicon, page 331.

For *be* + Sg

1. If subject is *I*, select /æm/ from the Mph rule A.
2. If subject is *you* and singular, select /ar/ from the Mph rule A.
3. Otherwise, select /ɪz/ from the Mph rule A.

For *be* + Sg + Past

4. If subject is *you*, select /wər/ from the Mph rule C.
5. Otherwise, select /wəz/ from the Mph rule C.

c. Substitute phonemic symbols given in the lexicon for the remainder of the lexical items.

Example 1 of Application of Rules of Order

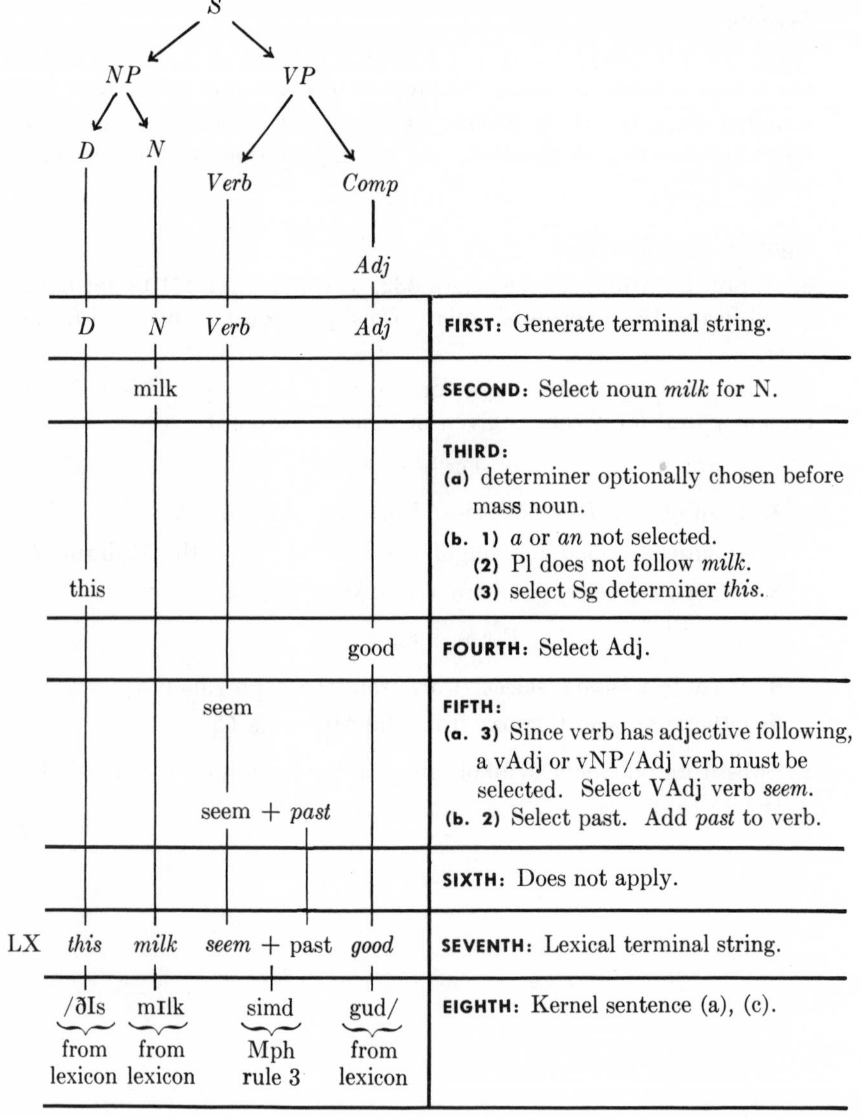

S
NP
VP
D
N
Verb
Comp
Adj
D N Verb Adj
milk
this
good
seem
seem + past
LX this milk seem + past good
/ðIs mIlk simd gud/
from lexicon
from lexicon
Mph rule 3
from lexicon
FIRST: Generate terminal string.
SECOND: Select noun milk for N.
THIRD:
(a) determiner optionally chosen before mass noun.
(b. 1) a or an not selected.
(2) Pl does not follow milk.
(3) select Sg determiner this.
FOURTH: Select Adj.
FIFTH:
(a. 3) Since verb has adjective following, a vAdj or vNP/Adj verb must be selected. Select VAdj verb seem.
(b. 2) Select past. Add past to verb.
SIXTH: Does not apply.
SEVENTH: Lexical terminal string.
EIGHTH: Kernel sentence (a), (c).

Example 2 of Application of Rules of Order

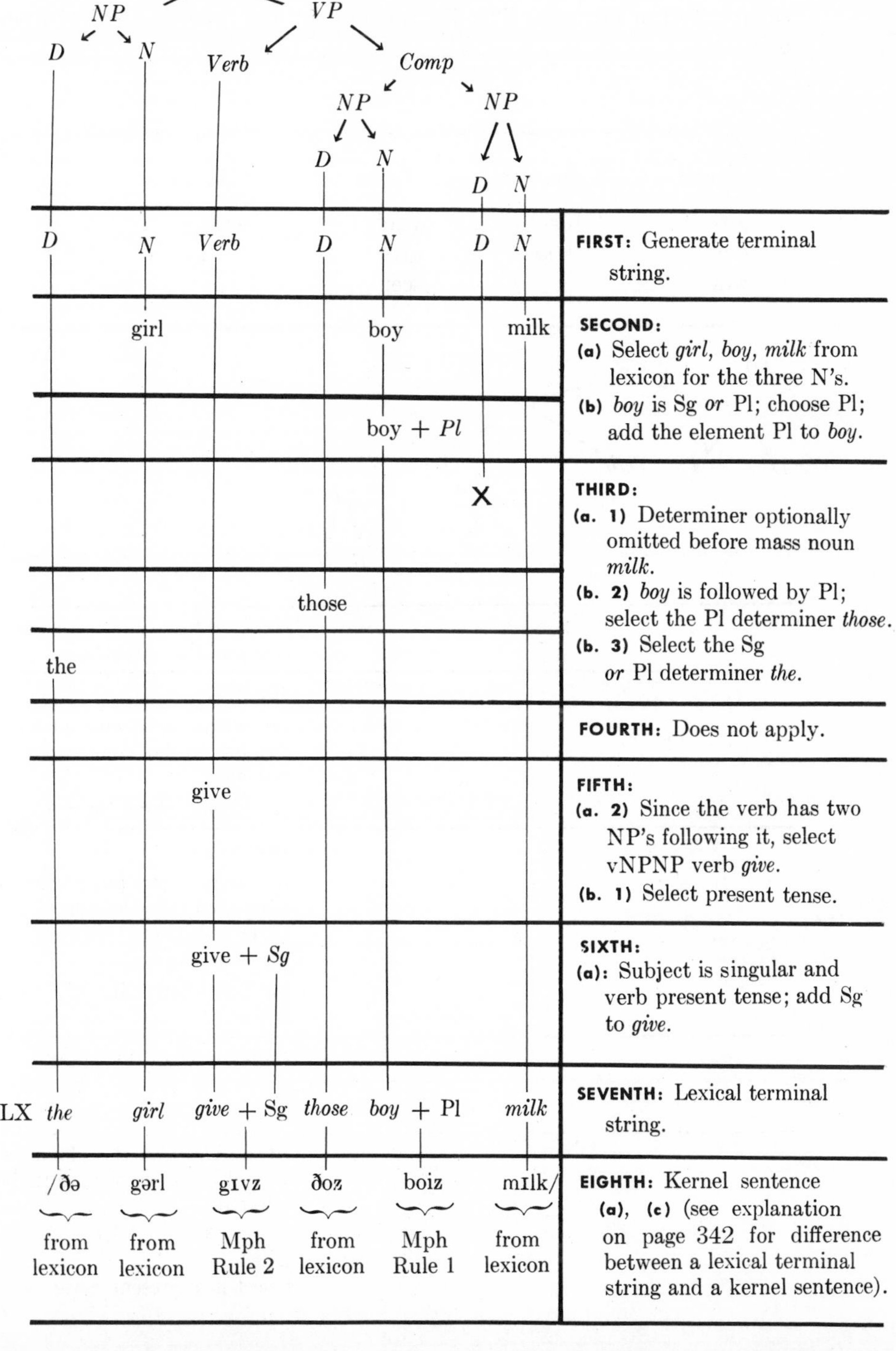

S
NP
VP
D
N
Verb
Comp
NP
NP
D
N
D
N
D N Verb D N D N
FIRST: Generate terminal string.
girl boy milk
SECOND:
(a) Select girl, boy, milk from lexicon for the three N's.
boy + Pl
(b) boy is Sg or Pl; choose Pl; add the element Pl to boy.
X
THIRD:
(a. 1) Determiner optionally omitted before mass noun milk.
those
(b. 2) boy is followed by Pl; select the Pl determiner those.
the
(b. 3) Select the Sg or Pl determiner the.
FOURTH: Does not apply.
give
FIFTH:
(a. 2) Since the verb has two NP's following it, select vNPNP verb give.
(b. 1) Select present tense.
give + Sg
SIXTH:
(a): Subject is singular and verb present tense; add Sg to give.
LX the girl give + Sg those boy + Pl milk
SEVENTH: Lexical terminal string.
/ðə gərl gɪvz ðoz boiz mɪlk/
from lexicon
from lexicon
Mph Rule 2
from lexicon
Mph Rule 1
from lexicon
EIGHTH: Kernel sentence (a), (c) (see explanation on page 342 for difference between a lexical terminal string and a kernel sentence).

EXERCISE 308

★ A. Generate three sentences following the directions given. Use the sample lexicon on pages 329–331 but employ the following lexical items only:

Nouns	*Determiners*	*Verbs*	*Adjective*
girl	this	vanish	happy
dog	those	give	
water		seem	

1.

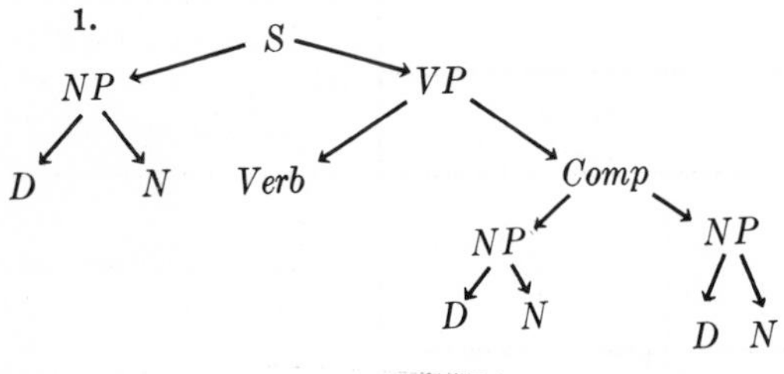

( ) **FIRST:** Write down terminal string in the parentheses.

SECOND:

(a) Write down *girl* for first, *dog* for second, and *water* for last noun.

(b) Choose plural for *dog*.

THIRD:

(a) Omit determiner before mass nouns; use lexicon to discover which of the above nouns are mass nouns.

(b) Select determiners for other nouns.

FOURTH: Does this apply?

____

FIFTH: What is the classification of the verb that must be selected?

____

Select it in present tense.

SIXTH: Make subject and verb agree.

SEVENTH: Write down LX terminal string.

EIGHTH: Write down kernel sentence.

2.

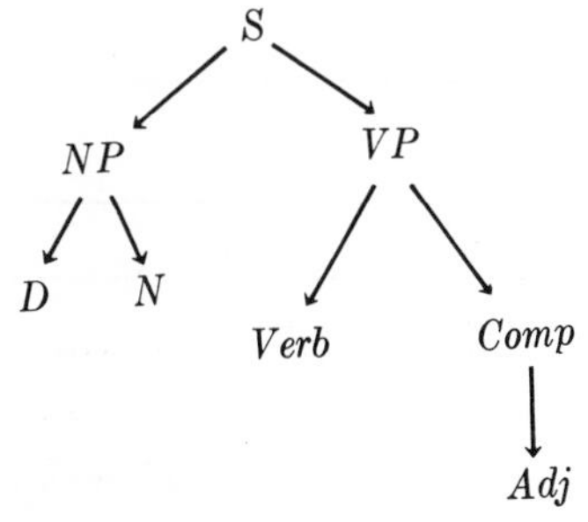

( ) **FIRST:** Write down the terminal string in the parentheses.

SECOND: Write down *girl* for N. Don't select plural.

THIRD: Select determiner.

FOURTH: Select adjective.

FIFTH: What is (are) the classification(s) of the verb that must be selected:

____

Select it in past tense.

SIXTH: Does this apply?

____

SEVENTH: Write down LX terminal string.

EIGHTH: Write down the kernel sentence.

3.

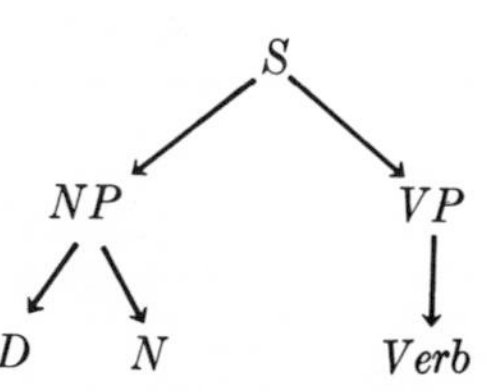

( ) **FIRST:** Write down the terminal string in the parentheses.

SECOND: Write down *milk* for N.

THIRD: Select determiner.

FOURTH: Does this apply? ______________________

FIFTH: Does (a) apply? __________________________

What classification? ____________________________
Select past tense.

SIXTH: Does this apply? _________________________

SEVENTH: Write down LX terminal string.

EIGHTH: Write down the kernel sentence.

★ B. Generate the following kernel sentences giving the number and subnumber [e.g., Eighth Rule (b. 4)] of the rules in the Rules of Order for Kernels for each step. Refer to the sample lexicon on pages 329-331. (Use separate sheets of paper.)

1. Those boys are here.
2. Robert was happy.
3. The cats were brown.
4. Police like milk.

4

The lexical terminal string is represented primarily by a sequence of spelled lexical items preceded by the symbol *LX*. For example, the LX terminal string

LX *this milk seem* + past *good*

consists of four spelled items, namely, *this*, *milk*, *seem*, *good.* Each such item actually represents (1) the grammatical classifications listed under it in the lexicon, (2) the pronunciation listed under it in the lexicon, and (3) the meaning(s) listed under it in the lexicon. Using spelled items is a simple way of representing more complex-looking LX terminal strings. Leaving meaning aside, if fully expanded the above LX terminal string would be written as follows:

$$\text{LX}\left\{\begin{matrix} D\begin{cases} Dem \\ Sg \end{cases} \\ /\text{ðɪs}/ \end{matrix}\right\} + \left\{\begin{matrix} N\begin{cases} Mass \\ Nhum \\ Sg \end{cases} \\ /\text{mɪlk}/ \end{matrix}\right\} + \left\{\begin{matrix} V\text{–}vAdj \\ /\text{sim}/ \end{matrix}\right\} + past + \left\{\begin{matrix} Adj \\ /\text{gʊd}/ \end{matrix}\right\}$$

A kernel sentence is a sequence of phonemic symbols that is derived from an LX terminal string by

1. applying the morphophonemic rules required and
2. substituting for each remaining item its phonemic representation.

For the sake of simplicity, kernel sentences will be written using spelling instead of phonemic symbols. These are easily distinguished from LX terminal strings since kernel sentences (a) are not preceded by the symbol *LX* and (b) begin with a capital letter.

EXERCISE 309

★ On separate paper write the LX terminal strings corresponding to kernel sentences in each of the following. Use the fully expanded example above as a guide. Be sure to use the sample lexicon on pages 329–331.

1. /ðə kæt noz ðə dɔg/ (In spelling: The cat knows the dog.)
2. /ðoz gərlz læft/ (In spelling: Those girls laughed.)
3. /ðə mɪlk simd gʊd/ (In spelling: The milk seemed good.)

5

As a preliminary to working with transformations, we need to understand the nature and variety of strings. A *string* is any linear sequence of symbols generated by the lexicon, by the PS grammar, by the Rules of Order, by the morphophonemic rules, and by the transformational rules which have yet to be discussed. A *PS string* is a linear sequence of symbols generated by all rules other than transformational rules. All ten strings below are examples of PS strings.

1. S
2. $NP + VP$
3. $D + N + VP$
4. $D\text{–}Art + N + VP$
5. $D\begin{cases} Art \\ Sg \text{ or } Pl \end{cases} + N + VP$
6. $D + N\text{–}Hum + VP$
7. $NP + V\text{–}Tfac + NP$
8. $D\begin{cases} Art \\ Sg \text{ or } Pl \end{cases} + N\begin{cases} Count \\ Hum \\ Sg \text{ or } Pl \end{cases} + V\text{–}vNP\begin{cases} v\emptyset NP \\ Tpas \\ Tfac \end{cases} + D\begin{cases} Art \\ Sg \text{ or } Pl \end{cases} + N\begin{cases} Count \\ Nhum \\ Sg \text{ or } Pl \end{cases}$
9. LX the man like + *past* the play.
10. $D + N + Verb + D + N$

Note that 1, 2, 3, 4, 5, 6, and 7 are PS strings containing nonterminal markers, for example, NP and VP. Of these, strings 3, 4, 5, and 6 contain terminal markers, for example, D and N. Numbers 4, 6, and 7 contain partially specified subclassifications for determiner, noun, and verb, respectively, that is, D–Art, N–Hum, and V–Tfac. Number 5 contains a completely specified classification for the determiner, and number 8, completely specified classifications for each element.

Number 9 is a lexical terminal string; number 10, a PS terminal string.

Strings, such as 1, 2, or 3 above, for example, are used in transformation formulas (pages 347 ff.) in which each specifies a kind of grammatical *domain*, a domain which includes an entire set of grammatical structures. Each such structure can be derived from a string by carrying out all operations on the string that will result in a full diagram with completely specified classifications substituted for all terminal markers. These operations include rewriting all nonterminal markers, adding all higher level markers (markers higher up in the diagram), and substituting a completely specified classification for each terminal marker. That is, a completely specified determiner classification is substituted for each D, a completely specified noun classification for each N, and so on. The resulting diagram represents one grammatical structure in the domain specified by the string. For example, one of the many grammatical structures specified by string 3 above is represented by the following diagram:

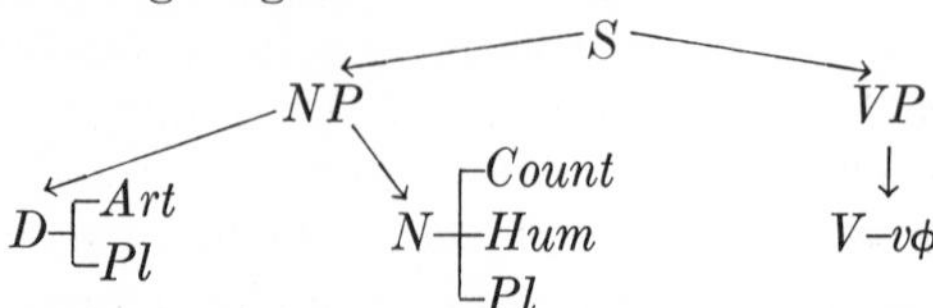

Note that the nonterminal marker VP in string 3 is rewritten, that all higher level markers (NP, S) have been added, and that all terminal markers (D, N, Verb) have completely specified classifications substituted for them. Other diagrams belonging to the domain specified by string 3 include different kinds of noun classifications substituted for N; still others include direct and indirect objects since these are included in some rewritings of VP.

Strings composed entirely of nonterminal markers specify a larger domain — that is, a domain that includes a larger set of grammatical structures — than strings composed entirely of terminal markers. These in turn specify domains larger than strings composed entirely of fully specified classifications. Thus string 3 specifies a larger grammatical domain than string 10, and string 10 a larger domain than string 8.

EXERCISE 310

★ A. Specify whether each string contains one or more of the following, using for your answers the letters a, b, c, d, and/or e.

a. Nonterminal marker(s)
b. Terminal marker(s)
c. Classifications fully specified
d. Classifications partially specified
e. Lexical item(s)

1. S __________

2. NP + VP __________

3. D + N + VP __________

4. NP + Verb + Adj __________

5. D + N + Verb + Adj __________

6. D + N + Verb + D + N + D + N __________

7. D–Art + N–Mass + V–vNP + D–Dem + N–Count __________

8. NP + V–vNP + D–Dem + N—{Count, Nhum, Sg} __________

9. NP + V–vNP—{vøNP, Tpas, Tfac} + D + N __________

10. D + N + V–vNP—{vøNP, Tpas, Tfac} + D + N __________

11. LX the + cow + jump + *past* + over + the + moon __________

12. LX the + cow + jump + *past* + over + D + N __________

13. D + N + V–vNP + D + N __________

14. D + N + V–vNP + D–Art + N–Count __________

★ B. 1. Which of the above strings specifies the largest grammatical domain: 1, 3, 5, or 7? _____ 2. Which of 13 and 14? _____

6

At the end of section B (pages 306 ff.), we specified that the five terminal strings of our PS grammar could be considered as five basic sentence patterns. There we listed the nine patterns from Chapter XIV that most closely corresponded to these terminal strings. For convenience we list the correspondences again on page 346.

1. *D + N + Verb + Adj*	*N*	*V*(be)	*Adj*	(PATTERN 1)
	Food	is	good.	
	N	*LV*	*Adj*	(PATTERN 8)
	The acrobat	seems	good.	
2. *D + N + Verb + Adv*	*N*	*V*(be)	*UW*	(PATTERN 2)
	The girl	is	here.	
3. *D + N + Verb*	*N*	*InV*		(PATTERN 4)
	Girls	giggle.		
4. *D + N + Verb + D + N*	*N*	*V*(be)	*N*	(PATTERN 3)
	My brother	is	a doctor.	
	N	*TrV*	*N*	(PATTERN 5)
	The girl	bought	the dress.	
	N	*LV*	*N*	(PATTERN 9)
	My brother	remained	a doctor.	
5. *D + N + Verb + D + N + D + N*				
	N	*TrV*	*N N*	(PATTERN 6)
	The mother	bought	the girl a dress.	

It was noted earlier that the PS grammar does not distinguish pattern 1 from pattern 8 (number 1 above), nor patterns 3, 5, and 9 (4 above), from each other. That is, the PS grammar does not distinguish between *be* and linking verbs such as *seem*, nor between *be*, transitive verbs such as *buy*, and verbs such as *remain*. We can now show that all these distinctions except that between patterns 3 and 9 can be made by using both the PS grammar and the following part of the classification of verbs.

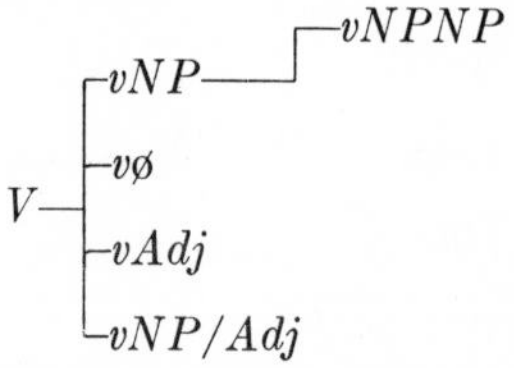

V
- *vNP*
  - *vNPNP*
- *vø*
- *vAdj*
- *vNP/Adj*

Using PS strings other than terminal strings we can get the following strings corresponding to eight of the basic patterns of Chapter XIV.

Pattern Number PS String			
1. *NP + V–vNP/Adj + Adj*	*N*	*V*(be)	*Adj*
	Food	is	good.
2. *NP + V–vNP/Adj + Adv*	*N*	*V*(be)	*UW*
	The girl	is	here.
3. *NP + V–vNP/Adj + NP*	*N*	*V*(be)	*N*
	My brother	is	a doctor.
4. *NP + V–vø*	*N*	*InV*	
	Girls	giggle.	
5. *NP + V–vNP + NP*	*N*	*TrV*	*N*
	The girl	bought	the dress.

6. *NP + V–vNP–NPNP + NP + NP*	*N* The mother	*TrV* *N* *N* bought the girl a dress.	
7. Not considered a basic pattern in transformational grammar.			
8. *NP + V–vAdj + Adj*	*N* The acrobat	*LV* seems	*Adj* good.
9. Same as number 3.	*N* My brother	*LV* remained	*N* a doctor.

Because PS strings are many and various, more patterns than the seven patterns listed above are possible. It therefore becomes difficult to distinguish those PS strings that might be considered "basic" patterns from those that might be considered less basic. The PS string S is the most general type of pattern, the PS string NP + V less general, and finally, the PS string LX *the + man + hit + past + the + ball* as specific as one can get. For practical purposes, linguists introduce strings, which they call basic sentence patterns, that are neither too general nor too specific.

7

In summary, after generating a terminal string, entries from the lexicon are selected for the various terminal symbols according to a set of Rules of Order. This selection results in an LX terminal string from which kernel sentences are derived.

E. Transformations

1

By following the rules of the grammar given thus far, you have drawn labeled PS diagrams such as those illustrated in the answers to exercise 292. A diagram represents a grammatical analysis in which the labels (e.g., S, NP, VP, N) representing grammatical categories are placed at points in the diagram in accordance with correspondences to the PS rules. These correspondences have been made by you in all exercises in which you were required to draw diagrams.

In addition to the grammatical analyses based on PS rules, you have studied the grammatical structure of lexical items, the underlying patterns of which are summarized on page 329. For purposes of labeled diagram analysis, these lexical classifications can be considered to be extensions added to the bottom of the diagrams, extensions constructed by substituting a lexical classification for each terminal marker as was done in the diagram on page 344.

Finally, in the Rules of Order, you have added the elements Sg, Pl, and *past* to the total grammatical description. These elements can also be considered as extensions to the bottom of labeled diagrams more or less on a par with lexical classifications. The following is one such diagram:

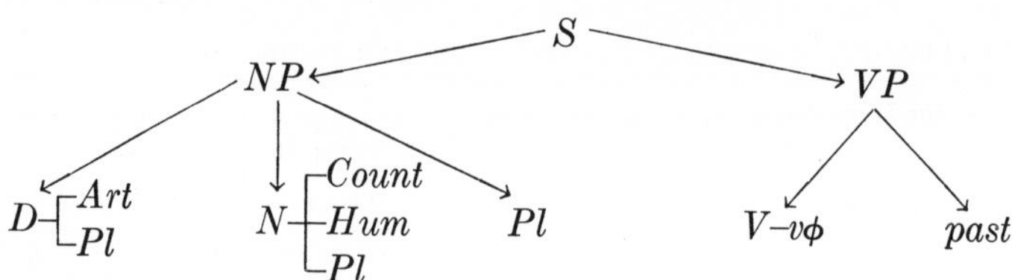

Note that this diagram contains lexical classifications substituted for terminal markers and also two elements added by the Rules of Order, namely, Pl and *past*.

In a complete grammar, the PS rules together with all rules that yield extensions to the bottom of labeled PS diagrams specify all the fundamental syntactic classes and their relations that underlie the structure of all English sentences. This idea is not really new to you. You will remember that when you learned the nine patterns of Chapter XIV, you were told that these patterns were the basic patterns, that is, the basic designs on which all other sentences are built. Similarly, the total grammatical structure presented thus far is a sample of the basic design of English.

To specify how this basic design is modified and expanded to generate longer and/or more complex sentences, new rules are needed, among them transformations. A transformation operates on a string which specifies the domain of the set of labeled diagrams with extensions, as explained above, and with expansions, as will be explained later, to which the transformation applies (review page 344). By performing a transformation, we derive a new string which specifies the domain of the set of derived labeled diagrams to which still other transformations may possibly apply.

In its operation, a transformation may perform one *or more* of the following functions (the sample strings are only rough approximations):

a. It may rearrange elements in a string.

Example: **String:** NP + V + Adv = The man walked slowly.
Transform: NP + Adv + Verb = The man slowly walked.
(Adv and Verb are rearranged.)

b. It may add elements to a string.

Example: **String:** NP_1 + V + NP_2 = The man hit the ball.
Transform: NP_2 + *be* + V + *by* + NP_1 = The ball was hit by the man.
(*Be* and *by* are added; also, the NP's are rearranged.)

c. It may delete elements.

Example: **String:** *You* + *will* + V = You will go.
Transform: V = Go.
(*You* and *will* are deleted.)

d. It may "combine" two or more strings.

Example: **String:** 1. $NP_1 + V_1$ = John walks.
2. $NP_1 + V_2$ = John giggles.
Transform: $NP_1 + who + V_2 + V_1$ = John, who giggles, walks.

(Strings 1 and 2 are combined; NP_1 of string 2 is deleted; *who* is added to replace NP_1 of string 2.)

Example: **String:** 1. NP + V = John knows.
2. S = The world is round.
Transform: NP + V + *that* + S = John knows that the world is round.

(Strings 1 and 2 are combined; *that* is added.)

EXERCISE 311

★ The following sentences have been generated by using transformations. Determine which of the following changes they involve; more than one may be involved in a single sentence.

a. rearrangement of elements
b. addition of elements
c. deletion of elements
d. combination of strings

Use a, b, c, or d, or a combination of these in your answers.

1. Quickly, John looked up. ________

2. The girl was spanked by her mother. ________

3. The lion that roared loudly was gentle. ________

4. The lion that loudly roared was gentle. ________

5. The elephant remembered that the water hole was dry. ________

Just on the basis of the sentences in exercise 311, you can derive a fundamental assumption of transformational grammar. The infinite number of possible sentences of English are all either kernel sentences or, in effect, one or more of these:* (1) rearrangements of kernel sentences, (2) additions to kernel sentences, (3) deletions from kernel sentences *and/or* (4) combinations of kernel sentences. With this conception clearly in mind, let us now describe a few transformations in more detail.

* The expression "in effect" signifies that nonkernel sentences do not really result from a combination or modification of kernels but rather result from a combination or modification of grammatical structures that underlie kernels.

2

First, we shall describe the passive transformation. But before doing so, we need to expand the phrase structure grammar to include one new element. Here now is the expanded phrase structure grammar, abbreviated EPS.

RULE 1: *S*

RULE 2: *S* → *NP* + *VP*

RULE 3: *NP* → *D* + *N*

RULE 4: *VP* → *Verb* (+ *Comp*)

RULE 5: *Comp* → $\left\{\begin{array}{l} (NP +)\ NP\ (Tpas) \\ Adv \\ Adj \end{array}\right\}$

Rule 5 of this slightly expanded phrase structure grammar includes the new element *Tpas*, called a T-marker. The T-marker Tpas is enclosed in parentheses and is therefore optional. If selected, it requires that the passive transformation be applied. Here is an LX terminal string that includes a Tpas marker.

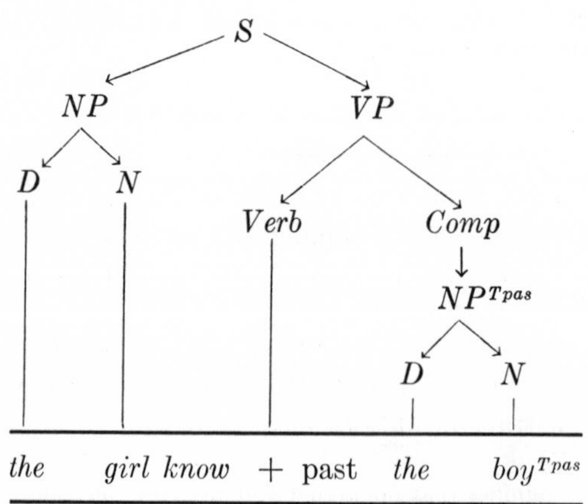

Notice that in the LX terminal string, the Tpas marker is placed above the NP to be made the subject in the transformed sentence.*

The passive transformation is as follows.† The explanation of this formula is given immediately below.

$$NP_1 + Verb\text{–}Tpas + [past] + NP_2^{Tpas} \rightarrow NP_2 + \text{be} + [past] + Verb\text{–}Tpas + pp \ (+ \text{by} + NP_1)$$

The arrow means "rewrite as"; the parentheses mean that *by* + NP_1 is optional. The *pp* on the right side of the arrow stands for the past participle morpheme. The element *past* in brackets is optional; but if it is selected for the string on the left, it must follow *be* in the transformed string on the right. The string on the left ends with the T-marker Tpas, which means: Apply the passive transformation.

Transformations alone do not generate completed sentences. Rather, they transform the string on the left of the arrow, which specifies the domain of the set of underlying grammatical structures (See again page 344.) to which the transformations apply, to the string on the right of the arrow, which both specifies the changes that must be made to these underlying structures and the domain of the set of resultant grammatical structures to which other transformations may apply. Transformations actually apply to labeled diagrams rather than merely to strings as such. (Review pages 347 and 348.) To generate completed sentences, Mph rules and Rules of Order must be applied.

The Mph rule needed for this transformation in our illustrative LX string is this:‡

know + *pp* ⟶ /non/

Applying the passive transformation to the LX terminal string we generated above, we get:

Formula: $\text{NP}_1 + \text{Verb–Tpas} + \text{past} + \text{NP}_2^{Tpas} \longrightarrow$
$\text{NP}_2 + \textit{be} + \text{past} + \text{Verb–Tpas} + \text{pp} \ (+ \textit{by} + \text{NP}_1)$

---

* A more complete grammar would specify that in a grammatical string containing both a direct and an indirect object, the Tpas marker may be applied to either one, to account for the fact that two passives are possible. T-markers may be given a semantic interpretation in a semantic theory.

† This formula has been simplified and will not account for all passives, for example, those with auxiliary verbs.

‡ The following Mph rule applies to verbs that take regular past participial endings:

Verb + *pp* ⟶ /V/ + { /ɨd/ when preceded by /t/ or /d/; /d/ when preceded by other voiced sounds; /t/ when preceded by other voiceless sounds }

The verb *know* is irregular and is thus handled by a special rule.

Example: LX *the girl* + *know* + past + *the boy*$^{T_{pas}}$ ⟶
LX *the boy* + *be* + past + *know* + pp (+ *by* + *the girl*)

Applying the Mph rule just above to the transformed string, we get

LX *the boy* + *be* + past + /non/ (+ *by* + *the girl*)

Finally, applying the remainder of the rules, we can generate these sentences:*

/ðə bɔi wəz non bai ðə gərl/
/ðə bɔi wəz non/

Although completely generated sentences are given in phonemic symbols, for reasons of simplicity we shall continue to use spelling instead of phonemic symbolization in our examples of completed sentences. Such examples will readily be recognized as sentences rather than LX strings since they will begin with a capital and will not be preceded by the symbol *LX*.

EXERCISE 312

★ Apply the passive transformation and the following Mph rule to the LX terminal string below. Do not generate a completed sentence.

Mph rule: hit + *pp* ⟶ /hɪt/

LX *the girl hit* + past *the boy*$^{T_{pas}}$

* We will henceforth assume that all necessary Rules of Order are being followed. The complete set of such rules will be presented later.

3

For the restrictive clause and nonrestrictive clause transformations, we need to expand our EPS grammar to include more T-markers and to include S in rules other than Rules 1 and 2. Let us first expand our grammar by adding two S's to Rule 3 thus:

RULE 1: S

RULE 2:
$$S \\ \downarrow \\ NP + VP$$

RULE 3:
$$NP \\ \downarrow \\ \begin{Bmatrix} D + N \ (+ S) \\ S \end{Bmatrix}$$

RULE 4:
$$VP \\ \downarrow \\ Verb \ (+ Comp)$$

RULE 5:
$$Comp \\ \downarrow \\ \begin{Bmatrix} (NP +) \ NP \ (+ Tpas) \\ Adv \\ Adj \end{Bmatrix}$$

These rules are the same as those on page 350 except for the addition of two S markers to Rule 3. Rule 3 may now be rewritten in three different ways:

a. D + N
b. D + N + S
c. S

The first is familiar to you; the second and third are new. The marker S (= Sentence) in (b) and (c) is the same marker S that appears in Rules 1 and 2. This means that the S in (b) and (c) may be rewritten as NP + VP according to Rule 2; both NP and VP would then be rewritten in the usual way, and so on.

Let's generate an LX terminal string choosing D + N + S from Rule 3.

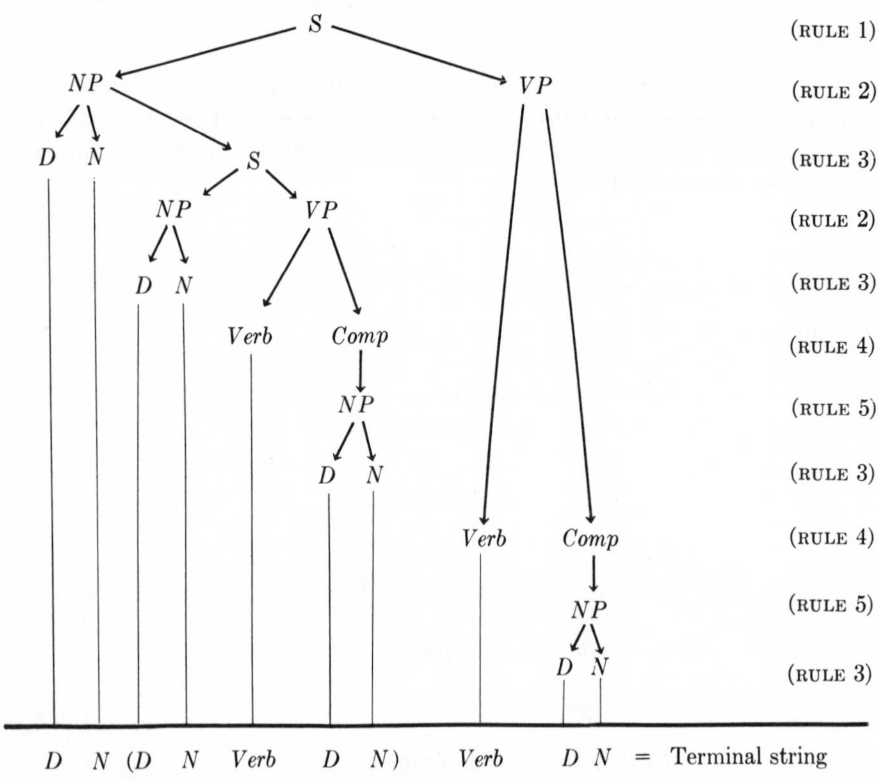

LX *The girl* (*the girl hit* + past *that boy*) *know* + past *the boy* = LX Terminal string

Later we shall see that this LX terminal string can be transformed into *The girl who hit that boy knew the boy;* this sentence is, in effect, a combination of the two kernel sentences *The girl knew the boy* and *The girl hit that boy.**

Notice that the portion of the LX terminal string in parentheses, namely, *LX the girl hit* + past *that boy*, is itself an LX terminal string since it is a rewriting of the marker S. For each appearance of S in a diagram based on the EPS grammar, a new terminal string must be generated and hence a new LX terminal string. Thus, since there are two S's in the EPS diagram above, two LX terminal strings must be generated. The two strings are these:

1. LX *the girl* (*the girl hit* + past *that boy*) *know* + past *the boy.*
2. LX *the girl hit* + past *that boy.*

* To refresh your mind on the difference between an LX terminal string and a kernel sentence, refer to page 342.

But we can discover still another LX terminal string even though only two S's appear in the EPS diagram, namely, the LX terminal string that results when we remove the parenthetical expression from (1) above; this string results from rewriting the first or higher S in the diagram and then removing the second or lower S and all its rewritings. It is this:

3. LX *the girl know* + past *the boy.*

Both (2) and (3) are LX terminal strings that can be generated by our previous PS rules alone (page 328) and thus can result in *kernel* sentences. By contrast, (1) cannot be generated by the previous rules but only by the EPS rules given immediately above and cannot become a *kernel* sentence. In general, though an S may be rewritten to yield expanded strings, there is for each S in a diagram an associated LX string that underlies a kernel sentence.

EXERCISE 313

★ For the following diagrams write down all the LX terminal strings that would result in *kernel* sentences.

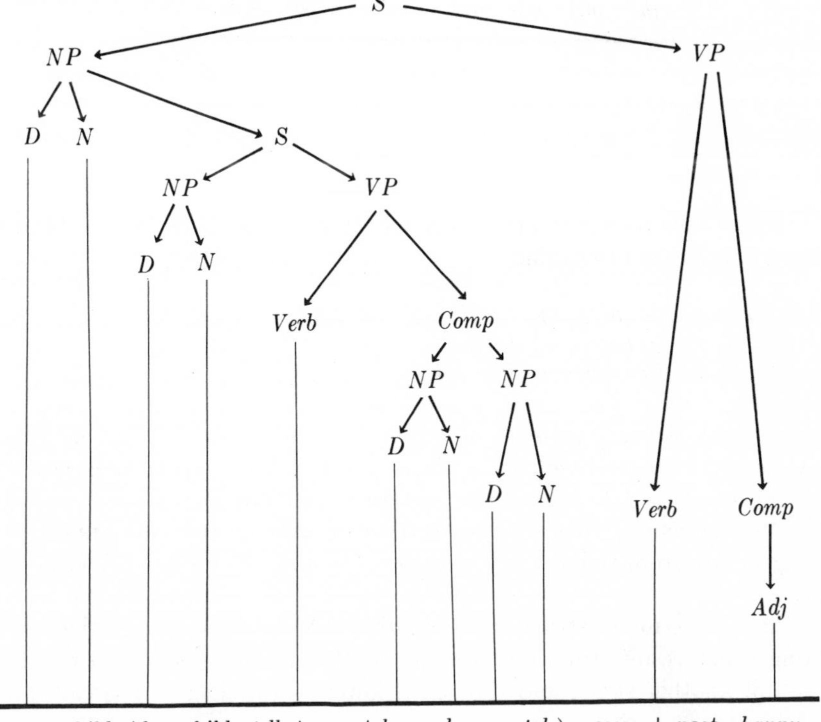

★A Write the answer here: ______________________________

____

____

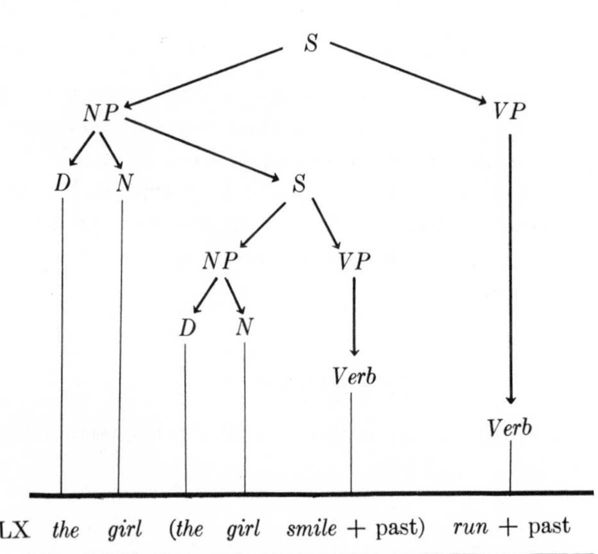

★B Write the answer here: ______________________________

____

Let us now review the three LX terminal strings listed in the example above. Here they are again:

1. LX *the girl* (*the girl hit* + past *that boy*) *know* + past *the boy*
2. LX *the girl hit* + past *that boy*
3. LX *the girl know* + past *the boy*

Notice that string 1 consists of string 2 inside string 3. That is, when *LX the girl hit + past that boy* is placed inside *LX the girl know + past the boy* the result is *LX the girl* (*the girl hit + past that boy*) *know + past the boy*. As said before, when the proper transformational rules are applied we can generate from string 1 the sentence *The girl who hit that boy knew the boy*.

An LX terminal string inside another LX terminal string (that is, a string which results from rewriting an S other than the first S in the diagram of another string and thus an S lower in the diagram) is called an *embedded LX terminal string*, or an *embedded string*. Thus *LX the girl hit + past that boy* is an embedded LX terminal string, or an embedded string.

An LX terminal string that includes another LX terminal string is called an embedding *LX terminal string*, or an *embedding string*. Thus *LX the girl know + past the boy* is an embedding LX terminal string, or an embedding string.

An LX terminal string that is a composite of two or more LX terminal strings is called an *expanded LX terminal string*, or an *expanded string*. Thus *LX the girl* (*the girl hit + past that boy*) *knew + past the boy* is an expanded LX terminal string, or an expanded string.

The briefer expressions will be employed only when no confusion results from their use. The reason for using the longer expressions is to distinguish LX terminal strings from other EPS strings. Other EPS strings may also be embedded, embedding, and expanded.

EXERCISE 314

★ A. Specify whether the italicized strings are one of the following:

a. en embedded string
b. an embedding string
c. an expanded string
d. none of the above (a string resulting from rules on page 328 ff).

Use the letters a, b, c, or d in your answers.

1. LX *John watch + past the lion.* ________
2. LX *John be + past afraid.* ________
3. LX John (*John be + past afraid*) watch + past the lion. ________
4. LX *John* (John be + past afraid) *watch + past the lion.* ________
5. LX *John* (*John be + past afraid*) *watch + past the lion.* ________
6. LX *John know + past something.* ________
7. LX *Jack fail + past the test.* ________
8. LX John know + past (*Jack fail + past the test*). ________
9. LX *John know + past* (Jack fail + past the test). ________
10. LX *John know + past* (*Jack fail + past the test*). ________

★ B. For the two LX expanded strings above (numbers 5 and 10) specify a sentence that could be generated when the proper transformation is applied.

1. For sentence 5 ______________________________

2. For sentence 10 ______________________________

EXERCISE 315

★ Using the diagram for *LX the girl* (*the girl hit* + *past that boy*) *know* + *past the boy* as a guide (page 354), diagram the following expanded strings. (Use separate sheets of paper.)

1. LX the boy (the boy be + past afraid) watch + past the lion.
2. LX the boy (the boy watch + past the lion) be + past afraid.
3. LX the girl (the girl buy + past her mother a dress) be + past here.
4. LX the girl (the girl be + past here) buy + past her mother a dress.

EXERCISE 316

★ For each of the expanded strings you generated in the previous exercise specify a sentence that could be generated when the proper transformation is applied.

For string 1 ______________________________

For string 2 ______________________________

For string 3 ______________________________

For string 4 ______________________________

On page 359 is a diagram of a still more complex LX expanded terminal string.

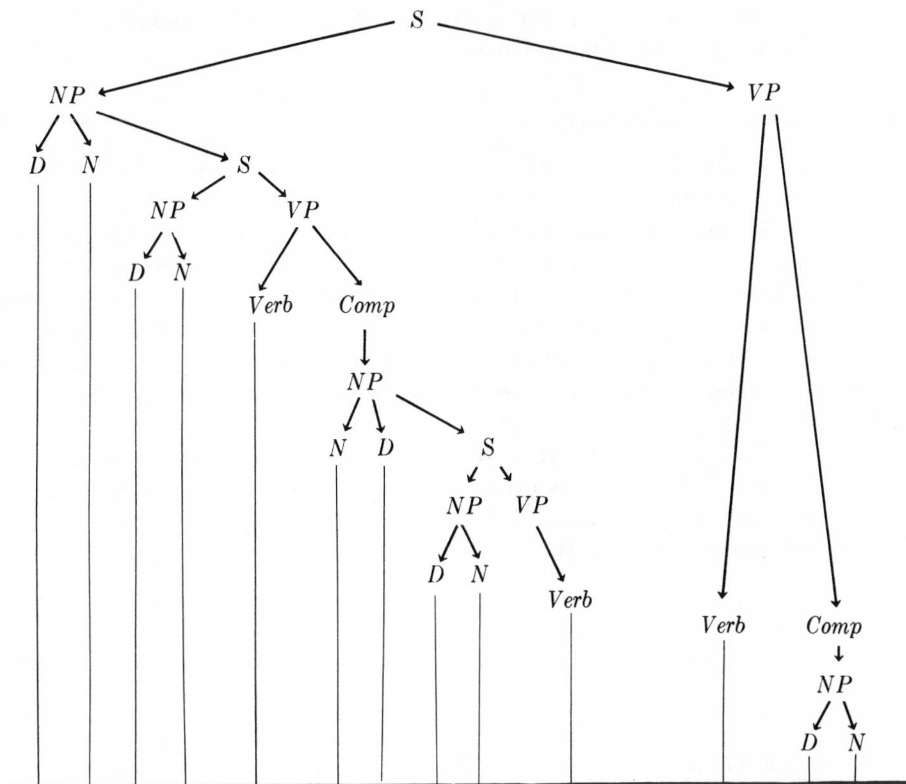

LX *the girl* [*the girl hit* + past *that boy* (*that boy laugh* + past)] *know* + past *the boy* =

LX terminal string

Later we shall see that this expanded string will yield the sentence *The girl who hit that boy who laughed knew the boy.* This sentence is, in effect, a combination of three kernel sentences: *The girl knew the boy, The girl hit that boy,* and *That boy laughed.*

The first thing to notice about the expanded string is that its diagram contains three S markers and thus results in three LX terminal strings which underlie kernel sentences. Here they are:

1. LX *the girl know* + past *the boy*
2. LX *the girl hit* + past *that boy*
3. LX *that boy laugh* + past

The part enclosed in brackets is an expanded terminal string since it contains the following two LX terminal strings, one of which is embedded.

a. LX *the girl hit* + past *that boy* (embedding string)
b. LX *that boy laugh* + past (embedded string)

But the bracketed part is itself an embedded LX terminal string in the following larger expanded string.

c. LX *the girl* [*the girl hit* + past *that boy* (*that boy laugh* + past)] *know* + past *the boy*

Notice also that there are two embedding strings in (c): (1) and (2) above. The embedding string 2 is part of the embedded string in brackets.

We now see that embedded strings may themselves have embedded strings. In fact, these in turn may have embedded strings, and so on *ad infinitum*. Thus by using a single relatively small set of rules, we can get infinitely many strings which will result in infinitely many sentences, each sentence, being, in effect, a kernel or a combination of two or more kernel sentences. A well-known illustration is the "house that Jack built" sentences.

To apply restrictive and nonrestrictive clause transformations, we need to add T-markers other than the T-marker Tpas of Rule 5. Here once more is the EPS grammar of page 353 expanded still further to include restrictive and nonrestrictive T-markers.

RULE 1: S

RULE 2:
$$\begin{array}{c} S \\ \downarrow \\ NP + VP \end{array}$$

RULE 3:
$$\begin{array}{c} NP \\ \downarrow \\ \left\{ \begin{array}{c} D + N\ (+\ S^{Tres}_{Tnres}) \\ S \end{array} \right\} \end{array}$$

RULE 4:
$$\begin{array}{c} VP \\ \downarrow \\ Verb\ (+\ Comp) \end{array}$$

RULE 5:
$$\begin{array}{c} Comp \\ \downarrow \\ \left\{ \begin{array}{l} (NP +)\ NP\ (Tpas) \\ Adv \\ Adj \end{array} \right\} \end{array}$$

Rule 3 now contains two T-markers, namely, *Tres* and *Tnres*. Each time the S adjacent to these T-markers is selected from Rule 3, one and only one of these T-markers must be selected. A T-marker specifies what transformation must be applied to the string that results from rewriting the adjacent S.

A selection of Tres means that a restrictive clause transformation *must* be applied to the string that results from rewriting the adjacent S. A selection of Tnres means that a nonrestrictive clause transformation *must* be applied to the string that results from rewriting the adjacent S.

In general, Rule 3 specifies that when we select the markers D + N, we have the option of selecting what is in parentheses, namely S^{Tres}_{Tnres}. If we decide to select S^{Tres}_{Tnres}, we *must* select (1) the marker S *and* (2) either the T-marker Tres or the T-marker Tnres but not both.

Here is an informal example of a restrictive transformation. By applying the restrictive transformation to the LX terminal string *LX the girl (the girl hit + past that boy) know + past the boy,* we can generate the sentence

The girl who hit that boy knew the boy.

This sentence has one restrictive clause, namely, *who hit that boy,* which modifies *the girl.*

Let us now generate an LX terminal string that includes the marker Tres.

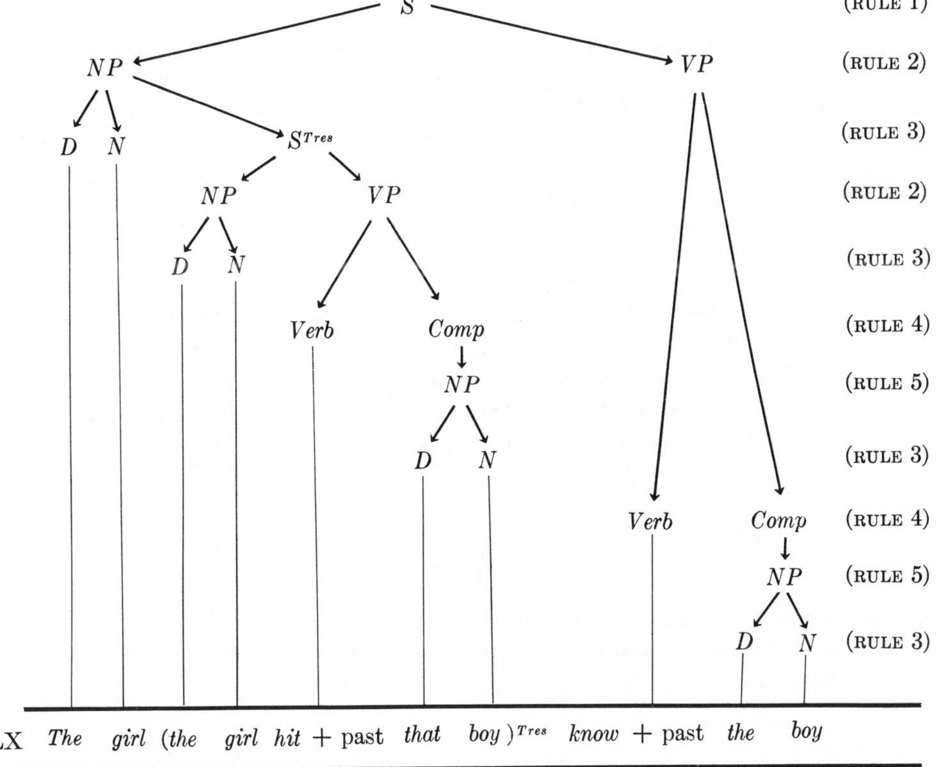

The above diagram requires a restrictive clause transformation. Notice that in the LX terminal string, the T-marker Tres is written above and after the second parenthesis. This means that the transformation specified by the T-marker must apply to the LX terminal string in parentheses.

Here now is the restrictive transformation formula. X, Y, and Z are symbols that stand for unstated material, that is, for one or more markers or for none at all.*

$$X + D + N\,(D + N + Y)^{Tres} + Z \longrightarrow X + D + N + wh_{res} + D + N + Y + Z$$

Condition:

For this transformation, the D + N in the embedded string left of the arrow must be the same as the D + N of the embedding string.

Let us apply the restrictive transformation rule to the LX terminal string above.

Formula: X + D + N + (D + N + Y $)^{Tres}$
Example: LX {nothing} + *the* + *girl* + (*the* + *girl* + *hit* + past *that boy*)^{Tres}
\+ Z
\+ *know* + past + *the* + *boy*

X + D + N + wh_{res} + D + N + Y
LX {nothing} + *the* + *girl* + wh_{res} + *the* + *girl* + *hit* + past *that boy*
\+ Z
\+ *know* + past *that boy* = transformed string

First, notice that in each part X stands for nothing since nothing precedes this LX terminal string being transformed, that Y stands for the whole expression *LX hit* + past *that boy* and Z for the whole expression *LX know* + past *the boy*. Second, notice that the D + N's of both embedded and embedding strings are the same.

EXERCISE 317

★ Using the above example as a guide, apply the indicated transformations to the LX terminal strings given on the top of page 363. (Use separate paper.)

* This transformation is simplified and will not generate expressions like *whom the boy hit* since the D + N of the embedded sentence is the subject of the verb only, not the object of the verb.

1. LX the painter (the painter draw + past a picture)$^{T_{res}}$ be + past happy.
2. LX the cow (the cow kick + past the milkmaid)$^{T_{res}}$ moo + past.

To generate a completed sentence from the LX transformed string, *LX {nothing} + the + girl +* wh_{res} *+ the + girl + hit + past + that + boy + know + past + the + boy,* we must first apply the following Mph rule:

$$wh_{res} + NP_{Hum} \longrightarrow \left\{ \begin{matrix} /\text{hu}/ \\ /\text{ðæt}/ \end{matrix} \right\}$$

NP_{Hum} signifies that the noun in the NP is a human noun as specified by the lexicon.

Applying this rule to this LX transformed string we get these strings:

a. LX {nothing} + the girl + /hu/ + hit + past that boy + know + past the boy
b. LX {nothing} + the girl + /ðæt/ + hit + past that boy + know + past the boy

Notice that /hu/ in (a) and /ðæt/ in (b) both result from applying the Mph rule since *girl* is a N-Hum as specified by the lexicon.

To generate the sentences themselves, we follow out the remainder of the rules to get the following:

a. /ðə gərl hu hɪt ðæt bɔi nu ðə bɔi/
b. /ðə gərl ðæt hɪt ðæt bɔi nu ðə bɔi/

EXERCISE 318

★ Using separate paper, apply the restrictive clause transformation and the required Mph rules to the following LX terminal strings. *Cow,* which is listed in the lexicon as a nonhuman noun, requires the following Mph rule:

$$wh_{res} + NP_{Nhum} \longrightarrow \left\{ \begin{matrix} /\text{wɪč}/ \\ /\text{ðæt}/ \end{matrix} \right\}$$

1. LX the cow (the cow kick + past the milkmaid)$^{T_{res}}$ moo + past.
2. LX the girl (the girl be + past happy)$^{T_{res}}$ know + past the boy.

4

To get attributive adjectives before the noun, we employ the attributive transformation. This transformation is not selected in the EPS rules; that is, there is no T-marker that specifies that the attributive transformation must be applied at any point in the EPS rules. Unlike the other transformations described above, which are chosen in the EPS rules as optional choices, this transformation is optional within the transformations themselves. In general, transformations that produce stylistic variants are not selected in the EPS rules.

Using the restrictive clause transformation, we can generate LX strings such as the following:

1. a. LX the girl that be + past happy know + past the boy
2. a. LX the rock that be + past large fall + past
3. a. LX the pipe that be + past brown be + past old

The attributive transformation can (optionally) change the above strings into the following:

1. b. LX the happy girl know + past the boy
2. b. LX the large rock fall + past
3. b. LX the brown pipe be + past old

Here is the attributive transformation formula:

$$X + D_1 + N_1\ (wh_{res} + D + N + be + Y + Adj) + Z \longrightarrow X + D_1 + Adj + N_1 + Z$$

Note that the entire string on the left of the arrow results from having applied the restrictive clause transformation to a string of the following type:

$$X + D + N\ (D + N + \text{be} + Y + Adj)^{T_{res}} + Z$$

Thus the attributive transformation must be applied *only after* the restrictive clause transformation has been applied. Applying this transformation to the string underlying string 1a above we get the following:

$X + D_1 + N_1\ (wh_{res} + D + N + \text{be} + Y + Adj) + Z$
LX {nothing} the + girl (wh_{res} + the + girl + be + *past* + happy) + know + *past* the boy

→ $X + D_1 + Adj + N_1 + Z$
LX {nothing} the + happy + girl + know + *past* the boy

EXERCISE 319

★ Using the above illustration as a guide, apply the attributive transformation to the following LX terminal strings. (Use separate paper.)

1. LX the rock (wh_{res} + the rock + be + past + large) + fall + past.
2. LX the pipe (wh_{res} + the pipe + be + past + old) + be + past brown.

5

The next two transformations that we shall scrutinize require that we add two new T-markers to the EPS rules. The following rules contain these two additions.

RULE 1: S

RULE 2:
$$S \downarrow NP + VP$$

RULE 3:
$$NP \downarrow \begin{Bmatrix} D + N\ (+\ S^{Tres}_{Tnres}) \\ S^{Tfac\text{-}that}_{Tfac\text{-}q\text{-}word} \end{Bmatrix}$$

RULE 4:
$$VP \downarrow Verb\ (+\ Comp)$$

RULE 5:
$$Comp \downarrow \begin{Bmatrix} (NP +)\ NP\ (Tpas) \\ Adv \\ Adj \end{Bmatrix}$$

The T-markers Tfac-that and Tfac-q-word have been added to Rule 3. The selection of Tfac-that means that a factive-that transformation must be applied; the selection of Tfac-q-word means that a factive question-word transformation must be applied.

Let us first illustrate the result of applying these two transformations. By applying a factive-that transformation to the LX terminal string *LX the girl know + past (the boy be + past here)* we could generate either

a. The girl knew that the boy was here.
b. The girl knew the boy was here.

By applying a factive question-word transformation (so called because the clause in the transformed sentence begins with a question word like *where*) we can generate

c. The girl knew where the boy was.

In all three sentences, the clause after the verb *knew* is a substitute for the direct object. In (a) and (b), *that* or the absence of *that* is used to introduce the clause; in (c), the question word *where* is used to introduce the clause.

Now let us generate two terminal strings, one including a Tfac-that marker and one a Tfac-q-word marker.

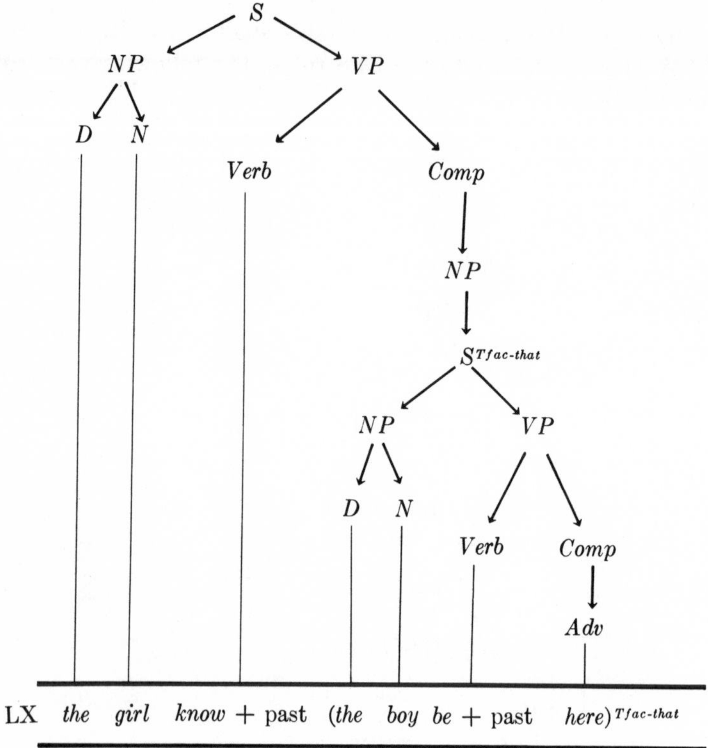

The T-marker written above the second parenthesis in the illustration above and in the one on the next page means in each case that the transformation specified by the T-marker changes the LX terminal string inside the parentheses to a nominal clause.

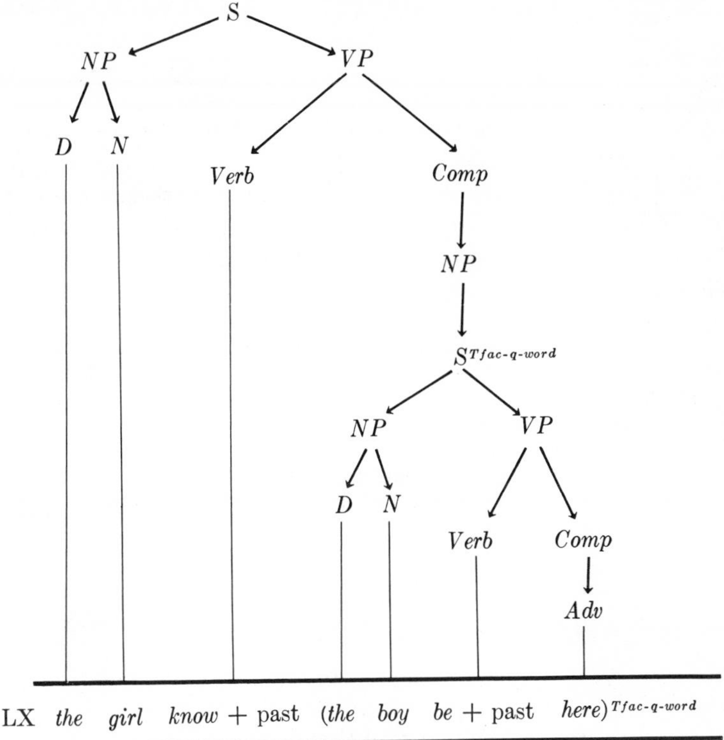

EXERCISE 320

★ Using the diagrams on page 366 and above as models, diagram on separate paper the following LX terminal strings.

1. LX Robert remember + past (John be + past here)$^{Tfac\text{-}that}$
2. LX Robert remember + past (John be + past here)$^{Tfac\text{-}q\text{-}word}$.

Let us now apply Tfac-that and Tfac-q-word transformations to the LX terminal strings illustrated on page 366 and above. On page 368 are the two transformation formulas and an associated Mph rule.*

---

* Related transformations can generate sentences like *That the boy was here is obvious.* Verbs that allow this transformation are *be, seem, appear,* and the like.

1. $X + Verb\text{-}Tfac + S^{Tfac\text{-}that} \longrightarrow X + Verb\text{-}Tfac(+/\text{ðæt}/)+S$
2. $X + Verb\text{-}Tfac + (Y + \text{Adv})^{Tfac\text{-}q\text{-}word} \longrightarrow X + Verb\text{-}Tfac + wh + Adv + Y$

Mph rule: * $wh + Adv \rightarrow$ /wɛr/

In formula 1 the parentheses enclosing /ðæt/ on the right of the arrow mean that /ðæt/ may optionally be chosen. *Verb-Tfac* is a partially specified symbol and states that the verb required for these transformations is a factive verb. The lexicon will specify which verbs are factive verbs.

We now apply these rules to the LX terminal strings generated above as follows:

1. X + *Verb-Tfac* + $S^{Tfac\text{-}that}$
LX *the girl* + *know* + past + (*the boy be* + past *here*)$^{Tfac\text{-}that}$

→ X + *Verb-Tfac* + (/ðæt/) + S
LX *the girl* + *know* + past + (/ðæt/) + *the boy be* + past *here.*

2. X + *Verb-Tfac* + (Y + *Adv*)$^{Tfac\text{-}q\text{-}word}$
LX *the girl* + *know* + past + (*the boy be* + past + *here*)$^{Tfac\text{-}q\text{-}word}$

→ X + *Verb-Tfac* + *wh* + *Adv* + Y
LX *the girl* + *know* + past + wh + *here* + *the boy be* + past.

Applying the Mph rule above to the transformed string of (2) we get:

LX *the girl* + *knew* + /wɛr/ + *the boy be* + past

By following the remainder of the rules, we can generate these sentences:

1. a. /ðə gərl nu ðæt ðə bɔi wəz hɪr/
   b. /ðə gərl nu ðə bɔi wəz hɪr/
2. /ðə gərl nu wɛr ðə bɔi wəz/

EXERCISE 321

★ Apply the indicated transformation to the following strings. Use the Mph rule above but do not represent the final strings phonemically.

* This Mph rule is actually one of a number of similar rules that are rewritten as /wɛr/, /wɛn/, /hau/, /wai/, and so on. Adverb subclassification is necessary before exact specification of this rule and related rules can be given.

1. T-fact-that transformation

LX Robert remember + past (John be + past here)$^{Tfac\text{-}that}$

2. Tfac-q-word transformation
LX Robert remember + past (John be + past here)$^{Tfac\text{-}q\text{-}word}$

6

We will now generate an LX terminal string that is, in a sense, a combination of these two LX terminal strings:

LX *the girl* [*the girl hit* + past *that boy* (*that boy laugh* + past)] *know* + past *the boy*.
LX *the girl know* + past (*the boy be* + past *here*).

This LX terminal string is introduced (1) to illustrate how a fairly complex string can be generated and (2) to supply an illustration for the Rules of Order which follow.

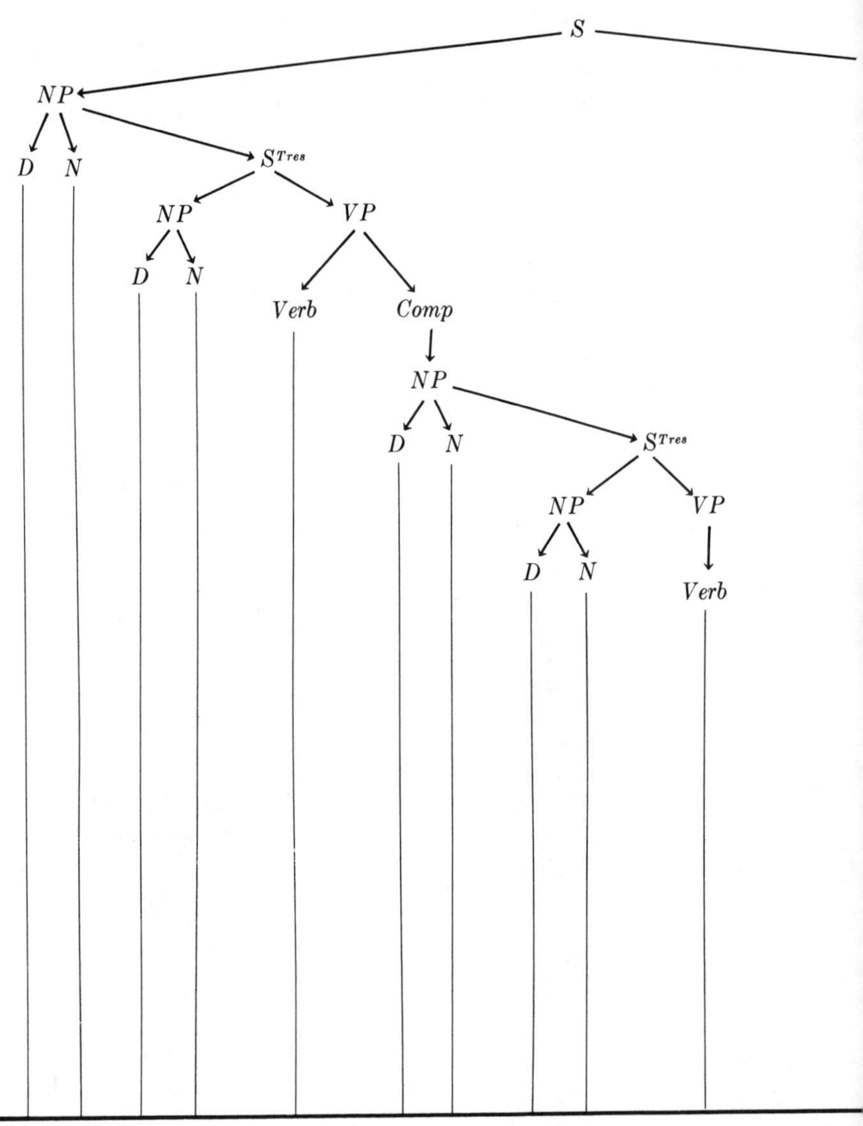

LX *the girl* [*the girl hit* + past *that boy* (*that boy laugh* + past)^{Tres}]^{Tres}

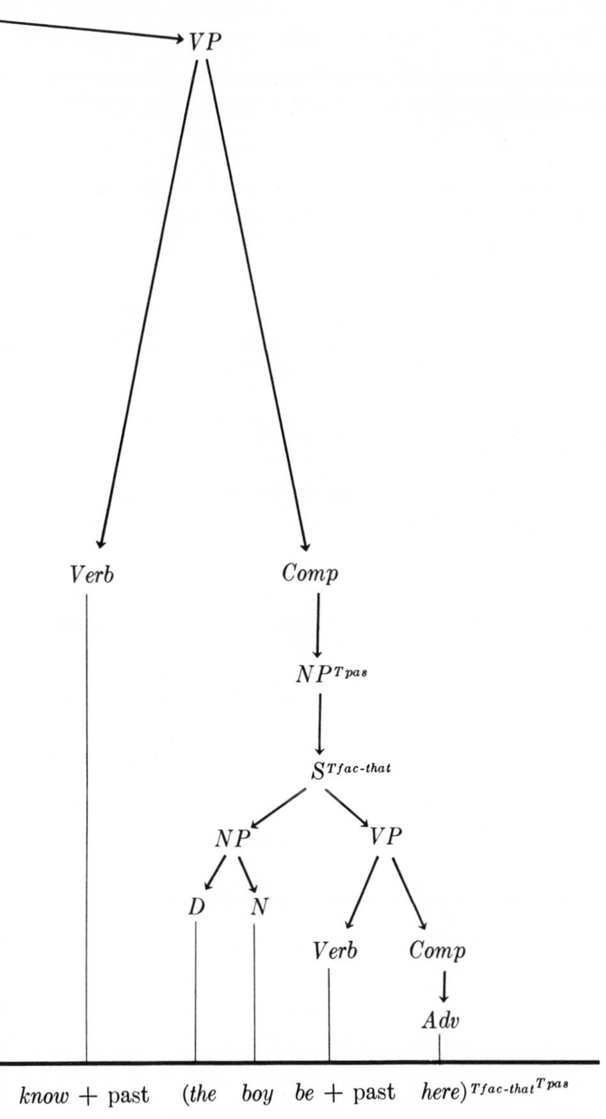
VP
Verb
Comp
NP^Tpas
S^Tfac-that
NP
VP
D
N
Verb
Comp
Adv
know + past (the boy be + past here)^Tfac-that^Tpas

EXERCISE 322

★ A. Following the diagram just above as a guide, generate the following LX terminal string. (Use a separate sheet of paper.)

> LX *the painter* [*the painter draw* + past *the picture* (*the picture be* + past *beautiful*)^{Tres}]^{Tres} *believe* + past (*the picture be* + past *good*)$^{Tfac\text{-}that\,Tpas}$

★ B. Specify a sentence that will be generated when the proper transformations are applied to the LX terminal string of exercise A.

In the LX string at the bottom of the diagram on pages 370-371 it is important to know what each of the T-markers *applies to.** The first Tres, which is in

> (*that boy laugh* + past)^{Tres},

applies to the string in parentheses and will in the end transform this string into a restrictive clause modifying the first *that boy.* The second Tres, which is in

> [*the girl . . .* past]^{Tres},

applies to the string in brackets and will make this string a restrictive clause modifying the preceding *the girl.* The third T-marker, Tfac-that, applies to the entire string in that it will make

> (*the boy . . . here*)$^{Tfac\text{-}that}$

into a necessary part of the sentence, a nominal clause functioning as the object of the verb *knew.* The fourth T-marker, Tpas, also applies to the entire string and will make the closing nominal clause the subject of the sentence by a passive transformation. The resultant sentence is the answer to the second part of exercise 322.

F. Rules of Order for Nonkernels

In the illustrations in section E, Rules of Order were followed implicitly but not explicitly, partly because doing so simplified exposition and partly because a more complete set of Rules of Order than those given on pages 335 ff. is needed. In addition to the Rules of Order for Kernels, a set of Rules of Order for Nonkernels specifying the order of application of EPS, lexical, and transformational rules is necessary. These will now be presented.

---

* The general rule specifying what strings T-markers apply to is not given in this chapter.

As you make your way through these Rules of Order, you may find the passage thorny; but there is no escape, for the application of the rules requires a certain sequence or order.

RULES OF ORDER FOR NONKERNELS

First Rule (EPS Terminal String Selection)

Generate expanded terminal string with associated diagram.

Application of First Rule

On page 374 is an EPS diagram and terminal string:

Note that the Tpas marker in the diagram (look at the diagram, not the terminal string) is adjacent to the NP that becomes the subject when the passive transformation is performed (review page 351). The NP in this particular case has the form D + N + Verb + Adv, which is a rewriting of the S below NP^{Tpas} in the diagram (and labeled "A" in the terminal string).

Second Rule (Rules Second through Fifth in the Rules of Order for Kernels, with Additions)

For each string, follow Rules SECOND through FIFTH in the Rules of Order for Kernels, placing an LX before resultant string. Add the following to Rule FIFTH, part a:

5. If Tpas applies to the string, select a Tpas verb from the lexicon.
6. If Tfac-that or Tfac-q-word applies to the string, select a Tfac verb from the lexicon.

(See page 372 for discussion of *applies to*.)

Application of Second Rule for Nonkernels to Strings A1 and A (page 374)

A1	A
LX that boy laugh + *past*	LX the boy be + *past* here

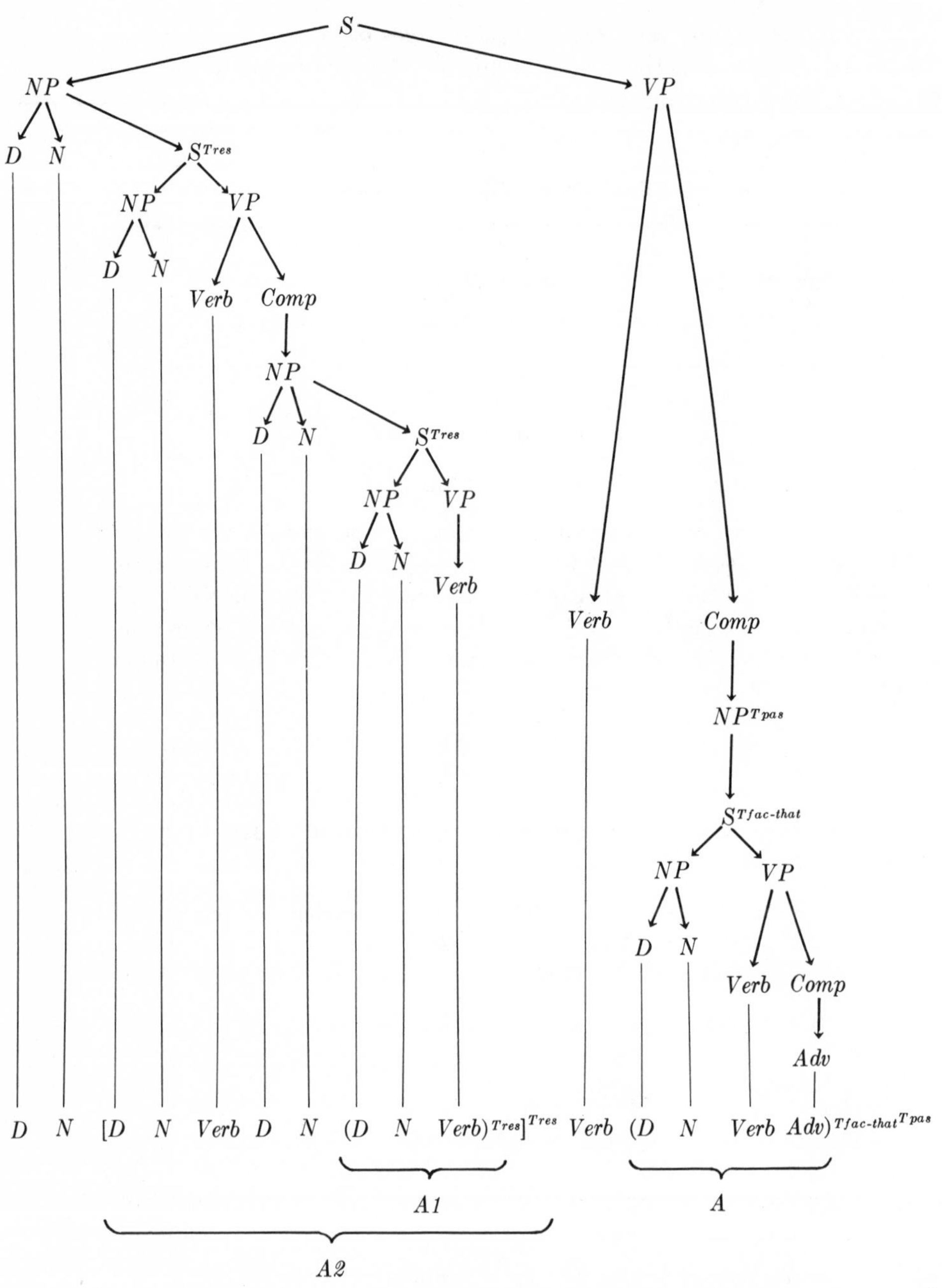
S
NP
VP
D N
S^Tres
NP VP
D N
Verb Comp
NP
D N
S^Tres
NP VP
D N
Verb
Verb Comp
NP^Tpas
S^Tfac-that
NP VP
D N
Verb Comp
Adv
D N [D N Verb D N (D N Verb)^Tres]^Tres Verb (D N Verb Adv)^Tfac-that^Tpas
A1
A
A2

Neither a Tpas, a Tfac-that, nor a Tfac-q-word marker applies to these strings. Thus only the Rules of Order for Kernels SECOND through FIFTH need be applied to A and A1. Having done this, we get the LX terminal strings just above. (We can get other similar strings as well, of course, depending on the choices of lexical items and other elements we make.)

Application of Second Rule to String A2

EPS Terminal String

A2

A1

$[D + N \;\; Verb \;\; D + N \quad (D + N \;\; Verb)^{Tres}]^{Tres}$

LX Terminal String

A2

A1

LX [the girl hit + *past* that boy (that boy laugh + *past*)^{Tres}]^{Tres}

Neither a Tpas, a Tfac-that, nor a Tfac-q-word applies to string A2. Thus (a. 5) and (a. 6) under the SECOND rule do not apply. Having applied rules SECOND through FIFTH to the EPS terminal string above, we get the LX terminal string above.

Application of Second Rule to String A3

EPS Terminal String

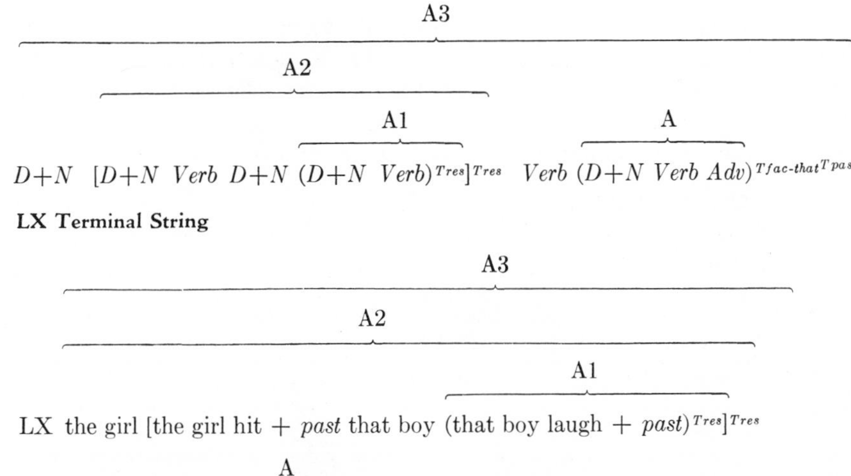

know + *past* (the boy be + *past* here)$^{Tfac\text{-}that\,Tpas}$.

Both a Tpas and a Tfac marker apply to string A3, requiring that we choose a Tpas-Tfac verb; we choose *know*, which, according to the lexicon, is both a Tpas and a Tfac verb. Having applied also Rules SECOND through FIFTH to the EPS terminal string above, we get the LX terminal string above.

General Instructions for Third Rule

For each S in the EPS diagram, there will be an associated EPS string which is a result of rewriting S and all nonterminal symbols therefrom. This is the order in which these associated EPS strings are worked on:

If an EPS string A1 is embedded in an EPS string A2 which itself is embedded in an EPS string A3, and so forth, apply the THIRD rule (immediately below) to A1 first, then to A2, then to A3, and so forth.*

Application of These General Instructions

By referring to the EPS illustrative diagram on page 374, we can see the relation of one string to another.

I. String A embedded in string A3

II. String A1 embedded in string A2
String A2 embedded in string A3

As a result of the above relationships the THIRD rule just below would in theory first be applied to strings A or A1. Notice that both A and A1 are embedded in A3 independently; that is, the relationships expressed in I above are treated as completely separate from the relationships in II. For this reason, we could, in theory, first apply the THIRD rule either to

1. A and A1 at the same time, or to
2. A first, or to
3. A1 first.

These three theoretical possibilities would pertain to our illustration only if T-markers applied to both A and A1. Since, in fact, no T-marker applies to A (see page 372), we apply the THIRD rule to the strings listed in II.

* Precision has to some extent been sacrificed here and in the illustrations below for pedagogical reasons; in particular, the exact nature of the embedding relationships is obscured. Refer to page 357 for a definition of "embedded" (the definition there is not precise but it is sufficient for application to the problems in exercise 324).

This means that after we apply the THIRD rule to A1, we apply it next to A2, and finally to A3. After having applied it to A3 we automatically will have applied it to all the strings of I as well as of II. We are then done with the THIRD rule.

Third Rule (Order of Transformations)

Apply transformations in the following order for each string that requires the application of more than one transformation.* Make sure the structure of the string to be transformed has the structure specified by the transformation to be applied.

a. Factive-that or factive-question word
b. Passive
c. Restrictive (or nonrestrictive)
d. Attributive

Application of Third Rule to String A1

The following string is the LX terminal string A3:

A2

A1

LX the girl [the girl hit + *past* that boy (that boy laugh + *past*)$^{T_{res}}$]$^{T_{res}}$

A

know + *past* (the boy be + *past* here)$^{T_{fac\text{-}that} T_{pas}}$

Applying the restrictive transformation to string A1 of the above LX terminal string, we get the following transformed string:

A2

A1

I. LX The girl [the girl hit + *past* that boy wh_{res} + that boy laugh + *past*]$^{T_{res}}$

A

know + *past* (the boy be + *past* here)$^{T_{fac\text{-}that} T_{pas}}$

* This order of application is designed for the specific grammar given here. Order of application of transformations will probably apply to types of transformations rather than to specific transformations.

Note that there is a wh_{res} and only one *Tres* marker in transformed string I.

Application of Third Rule to String A2

We now apply the restrictive transformation to A2 of transformed string I above. Here, now, is the resultant transformed string:

A2

A1

II. LX The girl wh_{res} + the girl hit + *past* that boy wh_{res} + that boy laugh + *past*

A

know + *past* (the boy be + *past* here)$^{Tfac\text{-}that\,Tpas}$

Note that a second element wh_{res} has been added and that no Tres markers remain. Notice also that string II is a transformed string derived from a transformed string, namely string I.

Application of Third Rule to String A3

Notice that both the passive and factive transformations must now be applied to string A3. The order of precedence in the THIRD rule requires that we apply the factive before the passive transformation.

Applying the factive transformation to transformed string II we get the following:

A2

A1

III. LX the girl wh_{res} + the girl hit + *past* that boy wh_{res} + that boy laugh + *past*

A

know + *past* /ðæt/ the boy be + *past* here^{Tpas}

Notice that transformed string III would, if we were to apply no passive transformation, result in the following sentence:

A

1. The girl who hit that boy who laughed knew that the boy was here.

We shall now see how, by a passive transformation, we get a string that will result in the following sentence:

A

2. That the boy was here was known by the girl who hit that boy who laughed.

The passive transformation is applied to III as follows:

A

IV. LX /ðæt/ the boy be + *past* here be + *past* know + *pp* by the girl

A2

A1

wh_{res} the girl hit + *past* that boy wh_{res} + that boy laugh + *past*

Fourth Rule (Subject-Verb Agreement for Third-Person Singular)

Apply subject-verb agreement rules as in the SIXTH rule of the Rules of Order for Kernels with this addition: If the subject is a clause and the verb present tense or *be* (past or present), add Sg to the right of the verb. The subject is now defined as the first NP preceding the verb in each string that results from the application of all the above rules.

Application of Fourth Rule

The subject of the above resultant String IV is:

LX /ðæt/ *the boy be + past here* (agreement required for the *be* which follows this clause)

The subject of *LX the boy be + past here* is *the boy* (agreement required for *be*).

The subject of *LX the girl hit + past that boy* is *that girl* (no agreement)
The subject of *LX that boy laugh + past* is *that boy* (no agreement)

Applying these rules to (IV), we get:

A

V. LX /ðæt/ the boy be + *Sg* + *past* here be + *Sg* + *past* know + *pp* by the girl

A2

A1

wh_{res} + the girl hit + *past* that boy wh_{res} + that boy laugh + *past*

Fifth Rule (Nonkernel Sentence)

(*This rule applies after all the above rules have been applied to each string.*) Apply EIGHTH rule of Rules of Order for Kernels.

Application of Fifth Rule

a. Applying Mph rules and agreement rules for *be* to transformed String V, we get:

LX /ðæt/ the boy /wəz/ here /wəz/ /non/ by the girl /hu/ /hɪt/ that boy /hu/ /læft/

b. Substituting phonemic symbols given in the lexicon for the remainder of the lexical items, we get:

/ðæt ðə bɔi wəz hɪr wəz non bai ðə gərl hu hɪt ðæt bɔi hu læft/

RÉSUMÉ OF RULES OF ORDER FOR NONKERNELS

First Rule (EPS Terminal String Selection)

Generate expanded terminal string with associated diagram.

Second Rule (Rules First through Fifth in the Rules of Order for Kernels, with Additions)

For each string, follow rules FIRST through FIFTH in the Rules of Order for Kernels, placing an LX before resultant string. Add the following to rule FIFTH, part (a):

5. If Tpas applies to the string, select a Tpas verb from the lexicon.
6. If Tfac-that or Tfac-q-word applies to the string, select a Tfac verb from the lexicon.

If an EPS string A1 is embedded in an EPS string A2 which itself is embedded in an EPS string A3, and so forth, apply the THIRD rule (immediately below) to A1 first, then to A2, then to A3, and so forth.

Third Rule (Order of Transformations)

Apply transformations in the following order for each string that requires the application of more than one transformation.

a. Factive-that or factive-question word
b. Passive
c. Restrictive (or nonrestrictive)
d. Attributive

Fourth Rule (Subject-Verb Agreement for Third-Person Singular)

Apply subject-verb agreement rules as in the SIXTH rule of the Rules of Order for Kernels with this addition: If the subject is a clause and the verb present tense or *be* (past or present), add Sg to the right of the verb. The subject is now defined as the first NP preceding the verb in each string that results from the application of all the above rules.

Fifth Rule (Nonkernel Sentence)

(*This rule applies after all the above rules have been applied to each string.*) Apply EIGHTH rule of Rules of Order for Kernels.

PAGE REFERENCE CHART OF RULES

EXERCISE 323

★ Generate the following kernel sentences following the Rules of Order for Kernels. Number each step as you proceed. (Use separate sheets of paper.)

1. Robert knows cows.
2. Robert likes cows.
3. Cows liked Robert.
4. Cows are brown.
5. The cows were here.

EXERCISE 324

★ Generate the following nonkernel sentences following the Rules of Order for nonkernels. Number each step as you proceed. Follow the procedure illustrated in the text above. (Use separate sheets of paper.)

1. Robert who likes cows knows cows.
2. Robert was liked by cows.
3. Robert who was liked by cows knows cows.
4. Robert who was liked by brown cows knows cows. (Note that *brown* is an attributive adjective; apply restrictive before attributive transformation.)
5. Robert who was liked by brown cows knows where the cows were.
6. Where the cows were was known by Robert who is liked by brown cows.

The rules of the grammar in this chapter will not always generate grammatical sentences since they are incomplete. Here are five instances of weakness in the rules given above; these are not the only weaknesses, however.

1. Two Tres (or nTres) markers can now be selected in the EPS rules so that they apply to the same noun. For example, the rules allow an expression such as **The cow which which mooed kicked vanished* from a string such as LX *the cow* [*the cow* (*the cow moo* + *past*)^{Tres} *kick* + *past*]^{Tres} *vanish* + *past.**

2. In a string to which both a Tpas and a Tfac-that apply, the optional element "/ðæt/" must be selected to avoid generating **The cows were here was known by Robert.*

3. In the present grammar, we can generate a sentence like *He is hammering nails,* but not *He is hammering.*

4. The rules will generate a string like

$S^{Tfac\text{-}that} + Verb + S^{Tfac\text{-}that} + S^{Tfac\text{-}that}$

A properly constructed grammar will either not generate such strings, or not allow such strings to be the basis of English sentences.

5. The rules will not generate sentences like *The boy whom the girl hit laughed* in which *whom* is a direct object.

Note that it is possible to generate strings to which the indicated transformation cannot be applied [for example, LX *the girl* (*Robert like* + *past cow* + Pl)^{Tres} *laugh* + *past*]. Such strings would not yield sentences and are thus stopped in their tracks, so to speak.

---

* A lexical string such as this (though with predicate adjectives following *be*) is a possible underlying structure for generating a sequence of prenominal modifiers. This problem was ignored in presenting the attributive transformation.

By relatively simple modifications and/or additions to the rules, the first three problems above can be eliminated. We leave it to you to think what they may be.

2

In summary, the EPS grammar rules, the lexicon, the transformational rules, and the morphophonemic rules are applied in an order given by the Rules of Order for Kernel and Nonkernel sentences.

G. Conclusion

In this chapter we have examined a sample of transformation grammar as it is applied to the English language. But the theory of grammar proposed by transformationalists normally encompasses language in general, not merely a single language. This theory specifies the logical structure common to all languages. For example, it sets down for language in general the logical structure of each of the five major divisions we have studied: the PS grammar, the lexicon, the transformational rules, the morphophonemic rules, and the Rules of Order.

Here is a specific illustration of one difference between the *logical structure* of the PS grammar and of the lexicon. In the PS grammar we have *either-or* choices, that is, choices such as this: *either* A *or* B *or* C *or* . . . . In the lexicon we have both *either-or* and *and* choices, that is, choices such as this: *either* A *or* B *or* C *or* . . . **and** *either* A1 *or* B1 *or* C1 *or* . . . . For example, in the PS grammar, Comp is subclassified as *either* NP *or* NP + NP *or* Adv *or* Adj. But in the lexicon a vNP verb is classified as *either* vNPNP *or* vϕNP **and** *either* Tpas *or* $\overline{\text{Tpas}}$ **and** *either* Tfac *or* $\overline{\text{Tfac}}$.

Although this illustration deals with English, transformationalists might theorize that this distinction between PS grammar and the lexicon is the same for all languages. Of course, it must be realized that this theory is offered as a hypothesis, and as a hypothesis, it is subject to verification or modification.

ANSWERS TO EXERCISES

IMPORTANT: At times your answer may be correct and yet not agree with the answer given here. In the phonology this will happen because there are many variations of pronunciation, both dialectal and idiolectal, in American English, and your pronunciation may be one of these. In other parts of the grammar your "wrong" answer may represent a variant usage or a different but legitimate way of viewing a particular form or structure. Therefore, whenever you are in doubt about an answer, do not hesitate to bring up the matter in class.

Also, you should use these answers intelligently. Suppose, for example, that you are asked to find an English word that begins with the sounds /gw-/. If your own mental resources, aided by a desk dictionary, do not yield the answer in a reasonable time, don't spend further effort on it but look at the answer, and then go on with the assignment.

EXERCISE 1

The nasals are the final sound in *rim, bin, sing, trim, pain, wrong.* The other final sounds are orals.

EXERCISE 2

The voiced sounds are the final sound in *hum, pin, among, fin,* and *song.* The other final sounds are voiceless.

EXERCISE 3

The first sound in each of these words is voiced: *vine, then, zeal, late,* and *rate.* The other initial sounds are voiceless.

EXERCISE 4

The first sound in each of these words is voiced: *bin, dime,* and *goon.* The initial sound in each of the other three words is voiceless.

EXERCISE 5

1. p	b	6. r	t	11. d	t
2. b	d	7. f	v	12. d	k
3. l	r	8. z	t	13. l	m
4. p	k	9. h	g	14. t	n
5. g	s	10. s	w	15. n	ŋ

EXERCISE 6

1. pæk
2. kep
3. pit
4. pɪt
5. pet
6. pɛt
7. pæt
8. kip
9. kɪd
10. kæt
11. bik
12. bɪg
13. det
14. dɛt
15. kɪk
16. kæp
17. pɛk
18. pɪk
19. pik
20. gæd
21. gɛt
22. get
23. gæt
24. bæk
25. bek
26. tæp
27. tep
28. tɪp

EXERCISE 7

1. fud
2. fʊt
3. fo
4. fɔt
5. šu
6. šo
7. ðo
8. θɔ
9. sup
10. ɔt
11. vudu
12. šʊk
13. hu
14. ho
15. zon
16. zu
17. θɔt
18. ðoz
19. oθ
20. vɪžən

EXERCISE 8

(Here particularly, your pronunciation may not be that of the key.)

1. dɪnər
2. sɪstər
3. čɪldrɨn
4. rozəz
5. rozɨz
6. θisɨs
7. startɨd
8. foldɨd
9. rigard
10. dɨgri
11. hæbɨt
12. ǰəǰɨz

EXERCISE 9

1. ərǰ
2. stap
3. kət
4. sofə
5. rəg
6. əbəv
7. bərd
8. rəst
9. rən
10. čərč
11. ližər
12. ərbɨn
13. ad
14. əfɛkt
15. əfɛkt
16. pakɨt
17. tɨde
18. kəbərd
19. ǰərni
20. hat

EXERCISE 10

1.	si̱t	1
2.	ɪ̱nfɛ̱kt	2
3.	pe̱pə̱r	2
4.	dɪ̱sɪ̱nčæ̱nt	3
5.	ə̱nɔ̱stɨ̱nte̱šə̱s	5

EXERCISE 11

1. mai
2. tɔi
3. hau
4. tai
5. kau
6. ǰɔi
7. čaivz
8. ðau
9. šai
10. rai
11. hai
12. auč
13. maiti
14. rɔil
15. kɔi
16. trai
17. straip
18. raudi
19. kɪlrɔi
20. dɨstrɔi

EXERCISE 12

(Numerous variations are possible here.)

1. wɪr
2. bɪr
3. ðɛr
4. ðɛr
5. kɛr
6. mɛri
7. mɛri
8. mɛri
9. barǰ
10. mɔrnɪŋ
11. mɔrnɪŋ
12. nɔrθ
13. nɔrðərn
14. flɔr
15. hɪr
16. tur
17. hɔrs
18. hɔrs
19. pɛr
20. peər
21. stɛr
22. steər
23. mɛr
24. meər
25. spərɪŋ
26. sprɪŋ
27. kər
28. kraud
29. pər
30. praud
31. bər
32. brɛd
33. šʊr, šər
34. šuər
35. dair
36. daiər

[Exercise 13 omitted]

EXERCISE 14

1. pɪp
2. bɪb
3. tat
4. did
5. kok
6. gæg
7. stapt
8. stapgæp
9. hɪkəp
10. səbpɔint
11. fæst
12. fæsɨn
13. uzd
14. hænd
15. hænz
16. lɪkər
17. sɪks
18. gɛst
19. kip
20. kup

EXERCISE 15

The /k/ of *coop* is far back because the /u/ of *coop* is in the back. The /k/ of *keep* is further front because of the influence of the front vowel /i/ in *keep*.

EXERCISE 16

1. ɨnəf
2. waif
3. waivz
4. fɪfθ
5. sauθ
6. səðərn
7. wɪð
8. sɛnt
9. klos
10. kloz *or* kloðz
11. nuz
12. nuspepər
13. haus
14. həzbənd
15. ləkšəri
16. ləgžəriəs
17. mɛžər
18. həmbəl
19. anɨst
20. amɨǰ
hamɨǰ

EXERCISE 17

1. baind
2. bes
3. bol
4. məs
5. dim
6. ǰæm
7. lərk
8. ædər
9. sæŋ

EXERCISE 18

1. lɪtərəčər
2. čæmpiən
3. šæmpen
4. solǰər
5. ǰəǰ
6. saləm
7. nəmoniə
8. siŋər
9. lɪŋgər
10. strɔŋ
11. strɔŋgər
12. ɪlužən
13. fok
14. mɪlk
15. yuz
16. əpɪnyən
17. trai
18. wɛr
19. hwɛr
20. bɨret, biret

[Exercise 19 omitted]

EXERCISE 20

1. frog
2. sorry
3. why
4. room
5. room
6. pretty
7. woman
8. women
9. chiefs
10. lives
11. sense
cents
scents
12. sense
cents
scents
13. pounds
14. across
15. affect
effect
16. wash
17. wash
18. wash
19. horse
hoarse
20. horse
hoarse
21. something
22. language
23. contact
24. contact
25. Tuesday

1. Let me go.
2. I'm going to cry.
3. Who asked you?
4. I told him.
5. We told them.
6. I should think he would.
7. She's pretty cheeky.
8. They could have bought them.
9. I'll miss you.
10. I'll treat you.

EXERCISE 21

1. lɛd̳ər
bad̳əl
dərd̳i
2. sauθ
səð̳ərn
3. ɪt
ɪd̳ɪz
4. wərθ
wərð̳i
5. gat
aiv gad̳ɪt
6. kəp
kəb̳ərd
7. gus
guz̳bɛri
8. šət
šəd̳əp
9. hæv
ai hæf̳tə fɪš
ai hæv tu fɪš*
hau mɛni gɛs wɪl yə hæf̳tə fid
hau mɛni gɛs wɪl yə hæv tə fid
10. yuzd
hi yus̳tə dæns
hi yuzd tu ɛgz

---

* your /hæv/ may sound like this: [hævf].

EXERCISE 22

	Singular	*Plural*		*Singular*	*Plural*
1.	stap	staps	11.	sən	sənz
2.	rait	raits	12.	sɔŋ	sɔŋz
3.	kek	keks	13.	dal	dalz
4.	məf	məfs	14.	fɪr	fɪrz
5.	brɛθ	brɛθs	15.	glæs	glæsɨz
6.	mab	mabz	16.	roz	rozɨz
7.	raid	raidz	17.	dɪš	dɪšɨz
8.	frɔg	frɔgz	18.	gəraž	gəražɨz
9.	wev	wevz	19.	dɪč	dɪčɨz
10.	səm	səmz	20.	ɛǰ	ɛǰɨz

Answer to question 1: The three forms of the plural are /s/, /z/, and /ɨz/ or /əz/.

Answer to question 2: A singular form ending in an s-like sound — /s/, /z/, /š/, /ž/, /č/, /ǰ/ — is followed by /ɨz/ or /əz/. As for the remaining, /s/ follows a voiceless sound and /z/ follows a voiced sound.

EXERCISE 23

	Present	*Past*		*Present*	*Past*
1.	pæs	pæst	11.	həg	həgd
2.	læf	læft	12.	rev	revd
3.	map	mapt	13.	mɪl	mɪld
4.	bæk	bækt	14.	stər	stərd
5.	rəš	rəšt	15.	rat	ratɨd
6.	rɛnč	rɛnčt	16.	lod	lodɨd
7.	rab	rabd	17.	sit	sitɨd
8.	sim	simd	18.	sad	sadɨd
9.	lon	lond	19.	nid	nidɨd
10.	rɔŋ	rɔŋd	20.	ripit	ripitɨd

The answers are just what you expected:

1. the -ed suffix has three forms: /t/, /d/, and /ɨd/ or /əd/.
2. The /ɨd/ or /əd/ follows a /t/ or /d/. The /t/ follows other voiceless sounds and /d/ follows other voiced sounds.

EXERCISE 24

1. strɛnθ	/ŋ/ becomes /n/ because of /θ/. Both are dentals or interdentals.
2. ðɪšʊgər	/s/ becomes identical with /š/. They are adjacent sounds.
3. græmpə	/nd/ becomes /m/ because of /p/. Both are bi-labials.
4. græmə	/nd/ becomes /m/ because of /m/. Both are bi-labials.
5. hæŋkərčɪf	/nd/ becomes /ŋ/ because of /k/. Both are velars.
6. wɪtθ	/d/ becomes /t/ because of /θ/. Both are voiceless.

7. brɛtɵ	/d/ becomes /t/ because of /ɵ/. Both are voiceless.
8. kaŋkər	/n/ becomes /ŋ/ because of /k/. Both are velars.
9. wəžər	/z/ + /y/ move together in position, becoming /ž/.
10. hi lɛfɵə taun	/t/ is lost because of difficulty of articulation. /ð/ becomes /ɵ/ because of /f/. Both are voiceless.
11. ǰəsɵɪŋk	/t/ lost because of difficulty of articulation.
12. dɪǰə	/d/ + /y/ move together in position, becoming /ǰ/.
13. ðə mos fən	/t/ lost because cluster /stf/ is difficult to say.

EXERCISE 25

1. The assimilated /mp/, with two bilabials juxtaposed, is easier to say.
2. *Emplane* is more likely to become the standard form, for reason given in answer above.
3. *Condemn* contains the alveolar /n/ because the next sound, /d/, is also alveolar. *Congress* contains the velar /ŋ/, because the next sound, /g/, is also velar.
4. The intervocalic /t/ of *writing* is often voiced, becoming /d/.
5. The /n/, which is alveolar, is assimilated to the /p/, bilabial, becoming /m/, also bilabial.
6. The /t/ of *patrem* is between two voiced sounds and thus becomes voiced as /d/.

EXERCISE 26

1. Old English *brid,* young bird
2. Old English *thridda,* third
3. Old English *gærs* and *græs,* grass
4. Middle English *clapsen,* clasp. Middle English already has the metathesized form *claspen.*
5. Middle English *drit*

EXERCISE 27

1. Yes. The Middle English original of *glimpse* was *glimsen;* and the Old English original of *empty* was *ǣmtig,* which in Middle English became *emti* and *empti.* Old English and especially Middle English spellings were variable, so do not be disturbed at differences in etymologies among different dictionaries.
2. *Sampson* and *Thompson.* Both *p*'s are epenthetic.
3. These words are sometimes heard with an excrescent /p/: *comfort, warmth, Tomkins, dreamt.*

EXERCISE 28

1. *Lend.* Epithetic /d/. Middle English *lenen,* to lend.
2. *Bound.* Epithetic /d/. Middle English *boun,* ready, prepared.
3. *Against.* Epithetic /t/. Middle English *agenes* and *ageinst.*
4. *Midst.* Epithetic /t/. Middle English *middes.*
5. *Amongst.* Epithetic /t/. Middle English *amonges.*

EXERCISE 29

a. 1. /s/
2. /z/
3. /š/
4. /ž/
5. /ø/ = none

b. 6. /s/
7. /k/
8. /š/

c. 9. /i/
10. /ε/
11. /ɪ/
12. /ɨ/
13. /a/

EXERCISE 30

a. 1. shame
2. machine
3. ocean
4. suspicious
5. schist
6. conscience
7. sure
8. nausea
9. tension
10. attention
11. issue
12. mission

b. 1. dote
2. oh
3. coat
4. foe
5. soul
6. mow
7. yeoman
8. hautboy
9. sew
10. beau
11. dough

EXERCISE 31

a. 1. /lit/
2. /vek/
3. /zait/
4. /nok/
5. /fub, fyub/
6. /θit/
7. /nut/
8. /dit/
9. /pot/
10. /bo/

b. 1. dit
2. tet
3. jat
4. zot
5. chut
6. zale, zail
7. omect, omeked
8. bamthum, bamthem
9. sile
10. thoot, thute

EXERCISE 32

/ɪn/		/æt/		/at/	
pɪn	pin	pæt	pat	pat	pot
bɪn	bin	bæt	bat	bat	bot
tɪn	tin	tæt	tat	tat	tot
dɪn	din	kæt	cat	dat	dot
kɪn	kin	gæt	gat	kat	cot
gɪn	gin	fæt	fat	gat	got
fɪn	fin	væt	vat	šat	shot

/ɪn/		/æt/		/at/	
θɪn	thin	ðæt	that	hat	hot
sɪn	sin	sæt	sat	ǰat	jot
šɪn	shin	hæt	hat	nat	not
čɪn	chin	čæt	chat	lat	lot
ǰɪn	gin	mæt	mat	rat	rot
mɪn	min	næt	gnat	yat	yacht
lɪn	lin	læt	lat	wat	watt
rɪn	rin	ræt	rat		
wɪn	win				

In comparing the three lists of spelled words, we find a high degree of correspondence between the consonant phonemes and the letters that represent them.

EXERCISE 33

a. In subset *a,* a one-syllable word ending in a silent *e* drops the *e* before a suffix beginning with a vowel.
b. In subset *b,* a one-syllable word ending in a single consonant preceded by a single vowel doubles the consonant before a suffix beginning with a vowel.

EXERCISE 34

When a suffix is added to words ending in a silent *e,* the *e* is retained before a suffix beginning with a consonant but dropped before a suffix beginning with a vowel.

EXERCISE 35

1. ænθəni	Tony	toni	
2. θiədɔr	Ted	tɛd	
3. dɔrəθi	Dot	dat	
4. arθər	Art	art	
5. ilɪzəbɛθ	Betty	bɛti	bɛdi
6. mæθyu	Mat	mæt	
7. nəθæniəl	Nate	net	

The /t/ of the nicknames has come down by oral tradition from the time when the *th* was pronounced /t/. The /θ/ of the full names is a spelling pronunciation.

Thomas and *Esther* have resisted spelling pronunciation.

EXERCISE 36

Answers cannot be given for this exercise because it is *your* pronunciation that you are investigating. But frequent spelling pronunciations are:

1. bričɪz
2. blækgard
3. kəmptrolər
4. ælmənd
5. nɛfyu
6. kakswen
7. grinwɪč
8. fælkən
9. pɔl mɔl
10. arktɪk

EXERCISE 37

1. kəm
hom
2. muv
šəv
3. frɛnd
find
sɪv
4. swɔr
sɔrd
5. hɔrnɨt, hɔrnɛt
aur
6. haus
kərauz
feməs
7. kɔr
ailənd
dɛt
savərn, savrən
numædɪk
8. kərnəl

EXERCISE 38

1. defér
2. díffer
3. pervért (verb)
4. pérvert (noun)
5. conflíct (verb)
6. cónflict (noun)
7. évil
8. supérb
9. románce, or rómance
10. detáil, or détail
11. reséarch, or réesearch
12. defénse, or défense

EXERCISE 39

1. díctionàry
2. sécretàry
3. sèparátion
4. íntellèct
5. fùndaméntal
6. àviátion
7. pèrpendícular
8. àcadémic
9. ùnivérsity
10. àbsolútely

EXERCISE 40

1. áccènt
2. aùstére
3. ámbùsh
4. hùmáne
5. bláckbìrd
6. fòrgíve
7. ìráte
8. páthòs
9. díphthòng
10. phónème

EXERCISE 41

1. ìntĕlléctŭăl
2. désĭgnàte
3. èdŭcátĭon
4. búsўbòdў
5. ìntĕrrúptĭon
6. hùmànĭtárĭăn
7. sócĭalìzed
8. cérĕmònў
9. mílĭtàrў
10. ùnĭnspíred

EXERCISE 42

1. remárkable
2. remârkable invéntion
3. tíresome
4. tîresome jób
5. cóntract (noun)
6. côntract brídge
7. práiseworthy
8. prâiseworthy remárk
9. académic
10. acadêmic procéssion
11. blôoming
12. blôoming plánt

EXERCISE 43

1. îdèal gírl	
2. îdéal	
3. ôvernìght gúests	òverníght
4. cût-glàss bówl	cùt-gláss
5. înlaìd tíles	ìnlaíd
6. âlmòst kílled	àlmóst
7. òverséas	ôversèas jób
8. Chìnése	Chînèse ármy
9. foùrtéen	fôurtèen yéars
10. lêft-hànded pítcher	lèft-hánded

EXERCISE 44

1. bláckbòard
2. hótbèd
3. pálefàce
4. máilmàn
5. shórtcàke
6. róundhoùse
7. páperbàck
8. rócking chàir
9. spínning whèel
10. flýing òfficer

EXERCISE 45

1. hôt hóuse
2. dârk róom
3. blâck bírd
4. têndei fóot
5. hândy mán
6. rêd skín
7. fûnny bóne
8. dâncing téacher
9. môwing máchine
10. hûmming bírd

EXERCISE 46

1a. a chair that is high	1b. a special chair for babies
2a. a fish that is game, plucky	2b. a fish that may be taken as game
3a. a book that is blue	3b. an examination booklet
4a. a house that is green	4b. a glass-covered building where green things are raised
5a. two u's	5b. the 23rd letter in the alphabet
6a. a horse which is racing	6b. a horse for purposes of racing
7a. a room that is smoking	7b. a room that is for smoking
8a. any man who is traveling	8b. a commercial salesman who travels in his business
9a. any girl who is dancing	9b. a girl whose profession is dancing
10a. a lotion that feels cool	10b. a lotion for cooling
11a. a teacher who is French	11b. a teacher who teaches French
12a. a hand which is not short	12b. writing by hand as opposed to typing

EXERCISE 47

1. vêry tíred
2. râther óld
3. qûite háppily
4. môre sophísticated
5. tôo béautiful
6. prêtty bád
7. mîghty háppy
8. âwfully glád
9. rêally sórry
10. rêal sórry

EXERCISE 48

1. Someone is running horses against one another.
2. They are horses for racing.
3. He likes to run or race greyhounds.
4. He raises greyhounds for racing.
5. On the stove they have apples which are being cooked.
6. These apples are for cooking.
7. Turkeys which have been raised for smoking are more expensive than others.
8. If you smoke turkeys you will make money.

EXERCISE 49

1. She abhors dogs which are scratching.
   She doesn't like to scratch dogs.
2. Books which are emotionally stirring always disturbed him.
   When anyone moved books he was always disturbed.
3. We enjoy visitors who provide us entertainment.
   We like to entertain visitors.
4. Those reports encourage us.
   They encourage reports.
5. Oil which was burning frightened him.
   Whenever anyone burned oil he became frightened.

EXERCISE 50

1. júmp ròpes
2. jûmp rópes
3. wâsh rágs
4. wásh ràgs
5. mâp róutes
6. máp ròutes
7. flâsh líghts
8. fláshlìghts
9. wâtch dógs
10. wátchdògs

EXERCISE 51

1. cûtting úp
2. cútùp
3. hânded óut
4. hándòuts
5. hêld óver
6. hóldòver
7. côme dówn
8. cómedòwn
9. cómeòn
   câme ón

EXERCISE 52

1. Sàint Pául
2. Grèat Brítain
3. ròast béef
4. lòudspéaker
5. òld-tímer
6. íce crèam
7. pàrched córn
8. hèadmáster
9. fòurth-gráder
10. lèft wíng

EXERCISE 53

1. The literary form called a short story is not necessarily short in length.
2. A spinster is not necessarily old.
3. The town of Clear Lake is not a lake that is clear.
4. An inhabitant of New York is not an inhabitant of York who is new in town.
5. The town of Long Prairie is not a prairie which is long.

EXERCISE 54

1. hizəǰə̂st mæn
2. ǰɨ̆stə mɪnɨt, ǰə̆stə
3. ár
4. ðe ə̆r gɔn
5. dipóz
6. dɛpə̆zɪšən
7. hǽv
8. hi məstə̆v lɛft
9. ɔ́r
10. wɪl ɪt bi wɪnd ə̆r ren
11. hi kǽn bədi wont
12. hi kɨ̆n du ɪt
13. ðí
14. ðə̆ bɛst wən
15. æ̂z yu si, æ̂žu si
16. ǰəst ə̆z gʊd
17. lɛ́nt
18. sailɨ̆nt
19. bí
20. bɨ̆kəz

EXERCISE 55

2 **3 1**
1. He walked to the láb ↓

2 **3 1**
2. Get out of my síght ↓

2 **3 1**
3. Where is my nécktie ↓

2 **3 3**
4. She won't be home till twélve ↑

2 **3 3**
5. Are you going to the game eárly ↑

2 **3 3 2** **3 1**
6. To tell the trúth, ↑ I haven't learned to dánce ↓

2 **3 3 2** **3 1**
7. Unless you take the cár, ↑ I won't gó ↓

EXERCISE 56

2 **3 1**
1. When do we éat ↓

2 **3 2**
2. If you'll wáit, → or ↑

2 **3** **2**
3. For the móst part, → or ↑

2 **3** **2**
4. He's very hándsome, → or ↑ (but)

3 **2**
5. Géorge, → (come home at once.)

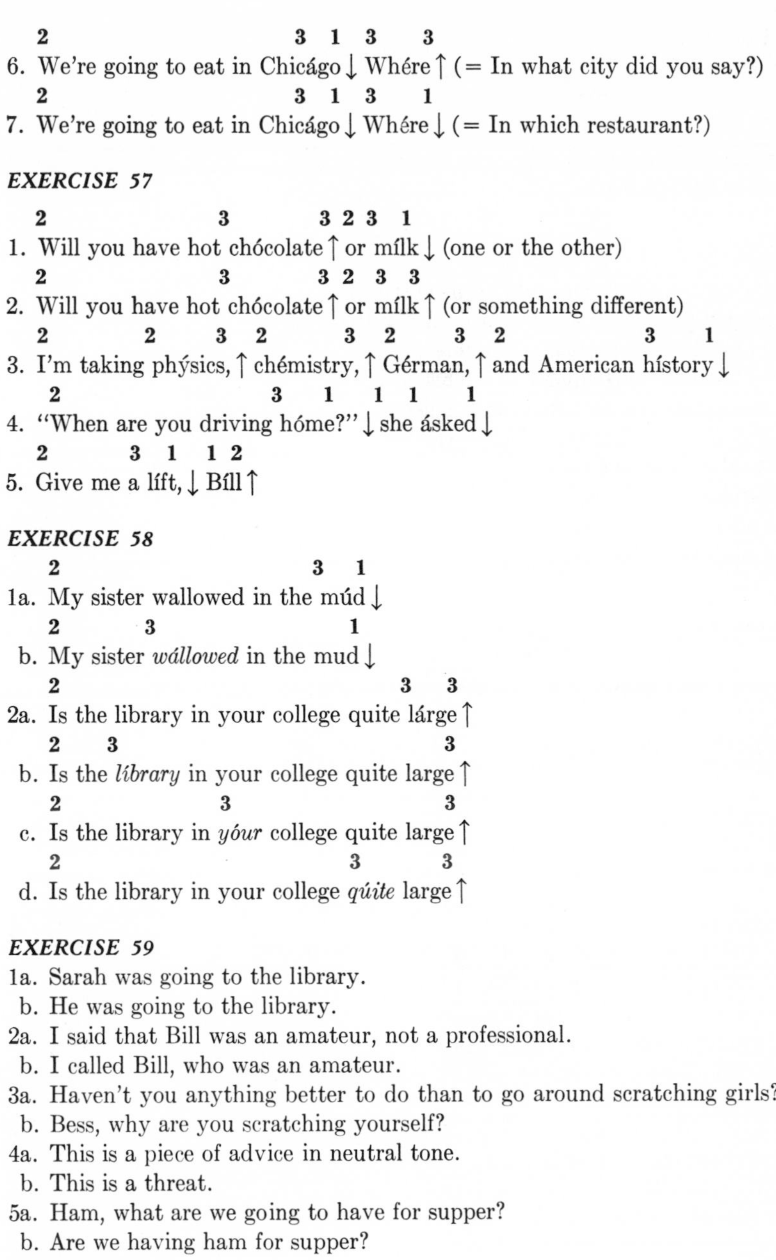

2 3 1 3 3
6. We're going to eat in Chicágo ↓ Whére ↑ (= In what city did you say?)
2 3 1 3 1
7. We're going to eat in Chicágo ↓ Whére ↓ (= In which restaurant?)

EXERCISE 57

2 3 3 2 3 1
1. Will you have hot chócolate ↑ or mílk ↓ (one or the other)
2 3 3 2 3 3
2. Will you have hot chócolate ↑ or mílk ↑ (or something different)
2 2 3 2 3 2 3 2 3 1
3. I'm taking phýsics, ↑ chémistry, ↑ Gérman, ↑ and American hístory ↓
2 3 1 1 1 1
4. "When are you driving hóme?" ↓ she ásked ↓
2 3 1 1 2
5. Give me a líft, ↓ Bíll ↑

EXERCISE 58

2 3 1
1a. My sister wallowed in the múd ↓
2 3 1
b. My sister *wállowed* in the mud ↓
2 3 3
2a. Is the library in your college quite lárge ↑
2 3 3
b. Is the *líbrary* in your college quite large ↑
2 3 3
c. Is the library in *yóur* college quite large ↑
2 3 3
d. Is the library in your college *qúite* large ↑

EXERCISE 59

1a. Sarah was going to the library.
b. He was going to the library.
2a. I said that Bill was an amateur, not a professional.
b. I called Bill, who was an amateur.
3a. Haven't you anything better to do than to go around scratching girls?
b. Bess, why are you scratching yourself?
4a. This is a piece of advice in neutral tone.
b. This is a threat.
5a. Ham, what are we going to have for supper?
b. Are we having ham for supper?

EXERCISE 60

1a. fâir crówd
b. fáir cròwd
2a. gîrl húnter
b. gírl hùnter

3a. a récord sàle
b. a rêcord sále
4a. a sécondary ròad prògram
b. a sêcondary róad prògram
5a. They're wáding pòols
b. They're wâding póols.

EXERCISE 61

1a. Every dáy → passengers enjoy a meal like thís.
b. Everyday pássengers → enjoy a meal like thís.
2a. The blue dréss → particularly ínterested her.
b. The blue dress partícularly → ínterested her.
3a. French pláne → with twenty-four cráshes.
b. French plane with twenty-fóur → cráshes.
4a. I consider thése → érrors.
b. I consider these érrors.
5a. The sóns → raise méat.
b. The sun's ráys → méet.

EXERCISE 62

2
1. . . . for a lake that . . .
2 3 1 2
2. . . . to Clèar Láke ↓ which . . .
2
3. . . . the freshmen who . . .
2 3 2 2
4. The incoming fréshmèn → who . . .
2
5. . . . the canoe that . . .
2 3 1 2 2 3 3 2
6. . . . Smíth ↓ who . . . or . . . Smíth ↑ who . . .
2
7. . . . students who . . .
2 3 1
8. . . . the shrúbs which . . .
2 3 1 2
9. . . . French lílacs ↓ which . . .
2 3 2 2
10. Dr. Blóom → who . . .

EXERCISE 63

2 3 1 2 3 1
1. . . . Harry Bóulder ↓ a promising júnior ↓
3 2 2 3 2 →
2. Hóskins → a first-string quárterback. . . .

2 3 2 3 2→
3. *Typhóon* → a well-known nóvel . . .

2 3 1
4. . . . the novel *Typhóon* ↓

2 3 1 2 3 1
5. . . . silk nécktie ↓ a hand-painted béauty ↓

2 3 2→
6. . . . sister Káren. . . .

2 3 2 2 3 2→
7. . . . Káren → my younger síster . . .

2 3 1 2 3 1
8. . . . Elk Válley ↓ a county séat ↓

2 3 1 2 3 1
9. . . . *Cármen* ↓ a work by Bizét ↓

2 3 2
10. . . . opera *Cármen* . . . →

EXERCISE 64

1a. A strip artist who is funny dies.
b. An artist who produces comic strips dies.
2a. He accidentally drowns a man who is wanted.
b. He, a wanted man, accidentally drowns.
3a. Automatic collectors of the bridge toll. (That is, machines)
b. Toll collectors for the automatic bridge.
4a. A story editor who is not tall.
b. An editor of the literary form known as the short story.
5a. Wow!
b. Come here, kid.
6a. The body works that belong to George.
b. George's body engages in work.
7a. I love the out-of-doors.
b. I do my loving outdoors.
8a. A reading course that is good.
b. A course in good reading.
9a. He gave the books belonging to the library.
b. He gave books to the library.
10a. The Women's Institute of the village of Ugley.
b. The institute of the Ugley women.

EXERCISE 65

1a. ai + skrim
b. ais + krim

In *a* the /ai/ and the /s/ are both longer than in *b*, indicating that they are respectively prejunctural and postjunctural. In *a* the /k/ has only slight aspiration, indicating that it is a post-/s/ /k/. In *b* the /k/ has strong aspiration, showing that it is a postjunctural /k/.

2a. nait + ret
b. nai + tret

In *a* the /r/ is voiced, showing it is postjunctural. In *b* the /t/ has strong aspiration, showing that it is postjunctural. In *b* the /r/ may be devoiced, showing that it follows /t/ directly without an intervening juncture.

3a. ðæt + stəf
b. ðæts + təf

In *a* the /s/ has the greater length of a postjunctural /s/, and the /t/ has the lack of aspiration of a /t/ that follows directly an /s/. In *b* the /s/ has the shortness of a prejunctural /s/, and the /t/ has the strong aspiration of a postjunctural /t/.

4a. sim + ebəl
b. si + mebəl

The greater length of /m/ in *b* tells our ears that it is postjunctural. (We should expect the prejunctural /i/ of *see* to be longer than the /i/ of *seem*, but laboratory experiment seems to show that the difference is not within the limits of human perception. Perhaps the /m/ following the /i/ serves to lengthen it. Compare for example the length of /i/ in *seat* and *seam*.)

5a. ɪts + lɪd
b. ɪt + slɪd

In *b* the greater length of /s/ shows that it is postjunctural, and the /l/ may be partly or wholly voiceless, showing that it directly follows /s/ without intervening juncture. In *a* the /l/ with normal voicing indicates that it is postjunctural.

6a. nu + dil
b. nud + il

The longer /u/ of /nu/ shows that it is prejunctural. The longer /d/ of /dil/ shows that it is postjunctural.

7a. ɪt + sprez
b. ɪts + prez

In *a* the /sprez/ has the longer /s/ characteristic of postjunctural /s/, and the unaspirated /p/ of the /sp/ combination. In *b* the /s/ is shorter and the /p/ is aspirated, indicating a prejunctural /s/ and a postjunctural /p/.

EXERCISE 66

ME form	*Process*
1. a naddre	became "an adder"
2. a napron	became "an apron"
3. a nauger	became "an auger"
4. an ekename	became "a nickname"
5. a noumpere	became "an umpire"

EXERCISE 67

1. fîne + jób
2. môst ŏf thĕ tíme
3. ă sôlo + ŏf + Jím's
4. thĕ párty
5. thât + párty
6. tâlk + wísely
7. sòme ŏf thĕ + inspîred + ártìsts
8. Jâne + lôves + cándy
9. stône + fénce
10. bîrd ĭn thĕ búsh
11. óut + lòok
12. Lòng + Îsland, Lòng Islánd

EXERCISE 68

The answers are in the text.

EXERCISE 69

1. splash
2. spread
3. spew
4. string
5. stupid
6. sclerosis
7. screech
8. skewer
9. squeak

EXERCISE 70

a. 1. spider
   2. stuff
   3. skate

b. 1. please
   2. prey
   3. pew
   4. trash
   5. clean
   6. crazy
   7. cute
   8. quiet
   9. twig

c. 1. slam
   2. sweet
   3. suit

d. 1. lute (Cf. loot)

EXERCISE 71

1. snow
2. smoke
3. bleed
4. breeze
5. beauty
6. dream
7. dew
8. dwell
9. gleam
10. grass
11. gules
12. sphere
13. music
14. news
15. flame
16. fresh
17. feud
18. thread
19. thews
20. thwack
21. shred
22. view
23. whinny
24. huge
25. chew
26. juice

EXERCISE 72

1. pueblo
2. Buena Vista
3. guava
4. moire
5. noir
6. svelte
7. spitz
8. shtetl
9. shkotzim
10. Schlitz
11. Schmidt
12. Schneider
13. schwa
14. tsetse
15. Vladivostok
16. Vries
17. voyageur
18. zloty
19. Zwingli
20. joie

EXERCISE 73

1. /ŋ/ 2. /ž/

EXERCISE 74

1. s 1	5. tə 2	9. ŋkə 3	13. lftə 4
2. sk 2	6. mpt 3	10. kst 3	14. ksts 4
3. skt 3	7. nts 3	11. rst 3	15. kstəs 5
4. ltə 3	8. nts 3	12. kstə 4	16. lftəs 5

In 12, 13, 15, and 16 the /t/ is questionable.

EXERCISE 75

1. it
2. ɪt
3. et
4. ɛvri
5. æt
6. This is rare in initial position. It may occur in words like *ill* /ɨl/ and *irrupt* /ɨrəpt/.
7. ərǰ
8. əbəv
9. ar
10. uz
11. ʊmlaut
12. ozon
13. ɔfəl

EXERCISE 76

/u/	/ʊ/
uz	ʊmpf
udəlz	ʊrdu
ups	
uləŋ	

EXERCISE 77

1. si
2. se
3. sər
4. sofə
5. ša
6. du
7. ho
8. lɔ

EXERCISE 78

1. 1	4. 2	7. 2	10. 1	13. 2	16. 2	19. 2
2. 2	5. 1	8. 1	11. 2	14. 1	17. 1	20. 1
3. 1	6. 1	9. 2	12. 1	15. 1	18. 2	

EXERCISE 79

1. before
2. again
3. like
4. one who
5. not
6. marked by
7. most
8. not
9. not
10. bad

EXERCISE 80

1. speak*er*
2. king*dom*
3. phonem*ic*
4. idol*ize*
5. select*ive*
6. deliver*y*
7. *inter* *vene*
8. *re* *vise*
9. dream*ed*
10. *un*done

EXERCISE 81

1. *woman*ly
2. en*dear*
3. *fail*ure
4. *fam*ous
5. in*fam*ous
6. *light*en
7. en*light*en
8. *friend*ship
9. be*friend*
10. *Boston*ian
11. un*like*ly
12. pre*war*
13. sub*way*
14. *fals*ify
15. unen*liv*ened

EXERCISE 82

1. hear
2. kill
3. mouth, speak
4. water
5. dead, death
6. body
7. hold
8. hang
9. hand
10. throw

EXERCISE 83

1.	see	devise
2.	say	dictate
3.	go	progress
4.	come	convene
5.	seize	apprehend
6.	run	current
7.	look	spectacles
8.	place, put	depose
9.	breathe	respire
10.	gnaw	erode
11.	carry	report
12.	break	erupt
13.	year	annuity
14.	flesh	carnage
15.	marriage	polygamy

EXERCISE 84

Here is a sizable list which probably includes your answers, though you may have found some words that the author missed. Note the irregularities. English has *entertainment* but not *pertainment, deceptive* but not *conceptive, acceptance* but not *receptance,* and many others.

1. *-tain*
   contain, containment, container, containable
   detain, detainer, detainee, detainment, detainingly
   entertain, entertainment, entertainer
   (*Enter-* is a form of *inter-* though you could not be expected to know this.)
   pertain
   retain, retainer

2. *-ceive, -cept, -ceit*
   accept, acceptance, acceptable, acceptability, acceptableness, accepter
   conceive, conceivable, conception, conceit, conceiver
   deceive, deceivable, deception, deceiver, deceptive
   perceive, perceivable, perception, perceiver, perceptive
   receive, receivable, reception, receiver, receptive, except
3. *-fer*
   confer, conferee, conferment, conferrable, conference, conferral, conferrer
   defer, deference, deferent, deferential, deferment, deferrable, deferentially
   infer, inferable, inferrer, inference, inferential, inferentially
   prefer, preferrer, preferable, preferability, preferably, preference, preferential, preferentially, preferment
   refer, referable, referrer, referee, reference, referendum, referent, referential, referentially, referral
   transfer, transferable, transferal, transferrer, transferase, transferee, transference, transferential, transferor
4. *-clude*
   conclude, concluder
   exclude, excludable, excluder, excludability
   include, includable
   preclude
5. *-port*
   comport, comportment
   deport, deportable, deportation, deportee, deportment
   disport
   export, exportable, exportation, exporter
   import, importable, importation, importer, important, importance, importancy, importantly
   report, reportable, reportage, reporter
   support, supportable, supportableness, supportably, supporter, supportive
   transport, transportable, transportability, transporter, transportation, transportational

EXERCISE 85

1. against	anticlimax
2. around	circumference
3. with	cocurricular
	collide
	comply
	convoke
	correlate
4. against	contravene
5. do the opposite of	deactivate
6. remove	dehorn
7. reduce	degrade
8. absence of, or opposite	disaffection

9. not	dishonest
10. not	incompetent
	impossible
	illegal
	irreplaceable
11. in, on	inscribe
	impale
12. between	intercede
13. within	intravenous
14. against, opposite	obstacle
	oppress
15. before	preconceive
16. after	postmortem
17. forward	progress
18. backward	retrogress
19. half	semisoft
20. under	substandard
21. over	superhuman
22. not	unattractive
23. do the opposite of	unfold

EXERCISE 86

1. 2
2. 3
3. 2
4. 3
5. 2
6. 2
7. 2
8. 2
9. 2
10. 3

EXERCISE 87

1. enlivened
2. terminating
3. moralizers
4. provincialisms
5. gruesomely
6. workability
7. innermost
8. marriageability
9. gangsterdom
10. affectionately

EXERCISE 88

1. happiness
2. friendship
3. girlhood
4. composure
5. shrinkage
6. activity
   activism
   activation
   activeness
7. supremacy
   supremeness
8. trueness
   truth
   truism
9. paganism
10. discovery

EXERCISE 89

1.	V (N)	N	14.	N (V)	A
2.	V (N)	A (N)	15.	N (V)	N
3.	V	N	16.	N (A)	N
4.	V	N	17.	N	A (N)
5.	A (N)	V	18.	V	A
6.	A	V	19.	V	A
7.	N	A	20.	V	A
8.	N (V)	A	21.	N	A (N)
9.	N (V)	N	22.	N (V)	A
10.	V (N)	N	23.	A	V
11.	V	N	24.	A	N
12.	N	A	25.	V	N
13.	N (V)	N			

EXERCISE 90

1. reasonableness
2. formality
3. organization
4. purification
5. puristic

EXERCISE 91

1. kindnesses
2. beautified
3. quarterlies
4. popularized
5. depths
6. pressures
7. extemporaneously
8. orientated
9. friendlier
10. loudly

No words can be formed by adding another inflectional suffix to the above words.

EXERCISE 92

1. sinful, sinfulness, sinless, sinlessness, sinner
2. kindly, kindliness, kindless, kindness, unkind, unkindly, unkindliness, unkindness
3. alive, aliveness, lively, liveliness, livelihood, liven, enliven, unenliven, unlively, unliveliness
4. transportable, transportability, transporter, transportation, transportational
5. audibility, auditory, auditive, audile, audio, audit, auditor, auditorium, audience, audition

EXERCISE 93

Unlawful is wrongly cut because the first cut leaves *unlaw*, which is not a free form.

EXERCISE 94

1. item | ize | d
2. pre | pro | fess | ion | al
3. news | paper | dom
4. counter | de | clar | ation
5. mal | con | struc | tion
6. contra | dict | ory
7. dis | en | throne
8. mid | after | noon
9. Ice | land | ic
10. super | natur | al
11. un | com | fort | able
12. fest | iv | al
13. en | gag | ing
14. ex | press | ion | ism
15. mis | judg | ment

or mis | judg | ment

EXERCISE 95

The two forms *a/an* have the same meaning and are in complementary distribution, *a* occurring before consonants and *an* before vowels.

EXERCISE 96

1. {wide} = /waid/ ~ /wɪd-/
2. {broad} = /brɔd/ ~ /brɛd-/
3. {wolf} = /wʊlf/ ~ /wʊlv-/
4. {able} = /ebəl/ ~ /əbɪl-/
5. {supreme} = /səprim/ ~ /səprɛm-/
6. {divine} = /dəvain/ ~ /dəvɪn-/
7. {fame} = /fem/ ~ /fəm-/
8. {vise} = /vɪž-/ ~ /vaiz/
9. {sun} = /sən/
10. {atom} = /ǽtəm/ ~ /ətám-/

EXERCISE 97

1. sənz
2. næps
3. pæsɨz
4. hɔgz
5. sæks
6. fɪzɨz
7. dɪšɨz
8. gəražɨz
9. hoz
10. stæfs
11. čərčɨz
12. gɔrǰɨz
13. səmz
14. hiθs
15. gɔŋz

Plural -es = /s/ ~ /z/ ~ /ɨz/

CD: /ɨz/ after /s/, /z/, /š/, /ž/, /č/, /ǰ/.
/s/ after other voiceless sounds.
/z/ after other voiced sounds.

EXERCISE 98

be {-d_1} = /wəz/ ∞ /wər/

EXERCISE 99

1. /sɔ/ = /si/ + /i > ɔ/
2. /bigæn/ = /bigɪn/ + /ɪ > æ/
3. /bɪt/ = /bait/ + /ai > ɪ/
4. /gev/ = /gɪv/ + /ɪ > e/
5. /gru/ = /gro/ + /o > u/
6. /rod/ = /raid/ + /ai > o/
7. /graund/ = /graind/ + /ai > au/
8. /tʊk/ = /tek/ + /e > ʊ/
9. /tɔr/ = /tɛr/ + /ɛ > ɔ/
10. /spok/ = /spik/ + /i > o/

EXERCISE 100

1. meat
   meet
   mete
2. might (noun)
   mite
   might (aux.)
3. you
   yew
   ewe
4. pear
   pare
   pair
5. its
   it's
6. to
   two
   too (= also)
   too (= more than should be)

EXERCISE 101

1. W
2. NW
3. W
4. W
5. NW
6. W
7. NW
8. W
9. NW
10. NW

EXERCISE 102

1.	knave	S
2.	knav|ish	C–FB
3.	graph	S
4.	tele|graph	C–FB
5.	merge	S
6.	e|merge	C–FB
7.	moron	S
8.	demo|cracy	C–BB
9.	pur|ist	C–FB
10.	comic|al	C–FB
11.	philosophic|al	C–FB
12.	sophist|ic	C–FB
13.	sopho|more	C–BB
14.	miso|gynist	C–BB
15.	refus|al	C–FB
16.	carn|al	C–BB
17.	en|able	C–FB
18.	mete	S
19.	mete|r	C–FB
20.	chrono|meter	C–FB

EXERCISE 103

1. C
2. GS
3. C
4. GS
5. C
   GS
6. C
7. GS
8. C
9. C
10. GS
11. C
12. GS
13. (ambiguous) {C / GS}

EXERCISE 104

1.	sharpshooter	WCP
2.	a sharp shooter	GS
3.	act	S
4.	react	C–FB
5.	storekeeper	WCP
6.	passbook	WCP
7.	apparatus	S
8.	detain	C–BB
9.	recur	C–BB
10.	current	C–BB
11.	unearth	C–FB
12.	referee	C–FB
13.	solve	S
14.	dissolve	C–FB
15.	solvent	C–FB
16.	búll's-éye (of target)	WCP
17.	bûll's éye (of bull)	GS
18.	highlander	C–FB
19.	biochemical	C–FB
20.	inaccessible	C–FB

EXERCISE 105

1.	{-d_1}	past tense
2.	{-s_2}	noun plural
3.	{-s_3}	present third-person singular
4.	{-s_1}	noun possessive
5.	{-s_2}	noun plural
	{-s_1}	noun possessive
6.	{-ing_1}	present participle
7.	{-er_1}	comparative
8.	{-d_1}	past tense
9.	{-est_1}	superlative
10.	{-d_2}	past participle
11.	{-ly_1}	adverb
12.	{-d_1}	past tense
13.	{-ing_1}	present participle
14.	{-s_2}	noun plural
15.	{-s_3}	present third-person singular

EXERCISE 106

1. 1
2. 3
3. 2
4. 1
5. 3

EXERCISE 107

1. A
2. V
3. A
4. V
5. V
6. A
7. V
8. A
9. A
10. A

EXERCISE 108

1. V
2. A
3. A
4. V
5. V
6. V
7. V
8. A
9. A
10. A

EXERCISE 109

1. a. It was a completed job.
   b. It was an artistic (perfected, polished) job.
2. a. My fiancée is quiet, reticent.
   b. My fiancée is kept in reserve, set aside, for me. Keep away from her!

EXERCISE 110

1. 1
2. 2
3. 2
4. 1
5. 2
6. 2
7. 1
8. 2
9. 2
10. 2

EXERCISE 111

1. IS
2. DS
3. DS
4. IS
5. IS
6. DS
7. Amb
8. DS
9. DS
10. DS
11. IS
12. DS
13. DS
14. DS
15. IS
16. Amb
17. DS
18. DS
19. DS
20. DS

EXERCISE 112

	Possessive	*Plural*	*Possessive + Plural*
1.	carpenter's	carpenters	carpenters'
2.	woman's	women	women's
3.	brother's	brothers brethren	brothers'
4.	cloud's (probably infrequent)	clouds	clouds' (probably infrequent)
5.	________	cattle	cattle's
6.	duck's	ducks duck	ducks'
7.	________	Japanese	________

8. ________	means	________
9. athletics'	________	________
10. ________	________	________

(There are differences of usage among the noun forms, particularly with the possessive.)

EXERCISE 113

1. them P
2. it S
3. it S
4. them P
5. them P
6. them P
7. it S
8. them P
9. it S
10. it S

EXERCISE 114

1. few
2. that
3. its
4. their
5. both

EXERCISE 115

1. was
2. were
3. is
4. are
5. has

EXERCISE 116

1. S
2. P
3. P
4. S
5. S
6. P
7. P
8. S
9. S
10. P

EXERCISE 117

1. child, children
   /čɪldrɨn/ = /čaild/ + /ai > ɪ/ + /-rɨn/
2. herring, herring
   /hɛriŋ/ = /hɛriŋ/ + /ø/
3. foot, feet
   /fit/ = /fʊt/ + /ʊ > i/
4. leaf, leaves
   /livz/ = /lif/ + /f > v/ + /-z/
5. wolf, wolves
   /wʊlvz/ = /wʊlf/ + /f > v/ + /-z/

EXERCISE 118

One allomorph	*Two allomorphs*
grief	scarf
chief	truth
belief	wharf
waif	wreath
	staff
	sheath

EXERCISE 119

1. /a/ > /i/
2. /-z/ or /ə > i or ai/
3. /-ɨz/ or /s > ərə/
4. /-ɨz/ or /ɪks > əsiz/
5. /əm > ə/
6. /ɪs > iz/
7. /-z/ or /-ɪm/
8. /ø/ or /-ɨz/
9. /-z/ or /əm > ə/
10. /əs > i or ai/
11. /-z/ or/əm > ə/
12. /-z/ or /o > i/ or /so > zi/
13. /-ɨz/ or /əs > ai/
14. /ɨs > iz/
15. /-z/ or /əm > ə/

EXERCISE 120

1. 4
2. 3
3. 2
4. 6
5. 5
6. 3
7. 5
8. 4
9. 3, 1
10. 5

EXERCISE 121

There are no right answers, as this is an investigation of the usage of the class.

EXERCISE 122

1. Pauline
2. chanteuse
3. protégée
4. czarina
5. songstress
6. majorette
7. heiress
8. equestrienne
9. Angelina
10. empress
11. laundress
12. proprietress
13. waitress
14. trickster

EXERCISE 123

1. N	6. N	11. —
2. —	7. N	12. N
3. N	8. N	13. N
4. —	9. —	14. N
5. —	10. —	15. —

EXERCISE 124

Pres. 3rd Sg.	*Pres. P.*	*Past T.*	*Past Part.*	
1. bids	bidding	bid, bade	bid, bidden	3, 4, or 5
2. bites	biting	bit	bit, bitten	4 or 5
3. keeps	keeping	kept	kept	4
4. freezes	freezing	froze	frozen	5
5. sets	setting	set	set	3
6. sells	selling	sold	sold	4
7. puts	putting	put	put	3
8. rises	rising	rose	risen	5
9. teases	teasing	teased	teased	4
10. sleeps	sleeping	slept	slept	4

EXERCISE 125

Past T.	*Past P.*	*Past T.*	*Past P.*
1. stəŋ	stəŋ	8. ræŋ	rəŋ
2. krɛpt	krɛpt	9. kɛpt	kɛpt
3. drov	drɪvɨn	10. dɛlt	dɛlt
4. sæŋ	səŋ	11. swæm	swəm
5. rod	rɪdɨn	12. spən	spən
6. rot	rɪtɨn	13. wən	wən
7. kləŋ	kləŋ	14. spræŋ	sprəŋ

Class 1: sting, cling, spin, win	{-d$_1$} = /ɪ > ə/
	{-d$_2$} = /ɪ > ə/
Class 2: creep, keep, deal	{-d$_1$} = /i > ɛ/ + /t/
	{-d$_2$} = /i > ɛ/ + /t/
Class 3: drive, ride, write	{-d$_1$} = /ai > o/
	{-d$_2$} = /ai > ɪ/ + /ɨn/
Class 4: sing, ring, swim, spring	{-d$_1$} = /ɪ > æ/
	{-d$_2$} = /ɪ > ə/

EXERCISE 126

1. 2
2. 2
3. 3
4. 0
5. 2

EXERCISE 127

1. QA
2. MA
3. QA
4. MA
5. QA

EXERCISE 128

1. <u>must</u> <u>be</u>
2. <u>ought</u> . . . <u>have</u>
3. <u>could</u> <u>have</u>
4. <u>could</u> <u>have</u> <u>been</u>
5. <u>might</u> <u>have</u>

(No checks needed)

EXERCISE 129

1.	Neg.	He was not eating.	Aux
	Q.	Was he eating?	
2.	Neg.	He did not quit eating.	V
	Q.	Did he quit eating?	
3.	Neg.	The worker was not killed.	Aux
	Q.	Was the worker killed?	
4.	Neg.	The worker did not get killed.	V
	Q.	Did the worker get killed?	
5.	Neg.	We must not hurry.	Aux
	Q.	Must we hurry?	
6.	Neg.	We did not have to hurry.	V
	Q.	Did we have to hurry?	
7.	Neg.	They are not going.	Aux
	Q.	Are they not going?	
8.	Neg.	They did not keep going.	V
	Q.	Did they keep going?	
9.	Neg.	He might not have been sleeping.	Aux
	Q.	Might he have been sleeping?	
10.	Neg.	He didn't use to play.	V
	Q.	Did he use to play?	

EXERCISE 130

1. N
2. NV
3. V
4. N
5. N
6. V
7. NV
8. V
9. N
10. NV
11. N
12. V
13. NV
14. N
15. N
16. NV
17. N
18. V
19. NV
20. V

EXERCISE 131

With some of these forms there is variation in usage both among different speakers and in the speech of a single individual. The answers here are the forms that the author would generally use, and yours may be different.

1.	angrier	angriest
2.	healthier	healthiest
3.		bitterest
4.	commoner	commonest
5.	crueler	cruelest
6.		foolishest
7.	handsomer	handsomest
8.		
9.	mellower	mellowest
10.	pleasanter	pleasantest
11.	quieter	quietest
12.	remoter	remotest
13.		severest
14.		solidest
15.		stupidest
16.	nobler	noblest
17.	dustier	dustiest
18.	dirtier	dirtiest
19.	livelier	liveliest
20.	gentler	gentlest

EXERCISE 132

1.		oftener	oftenest
2.	No		
3.	No		
4.	No (But cf. Tennyson's		

Music that gentlier on the spirit lies
Than tired eyelids upon tired eyes.)

5.		later	latest
6.	No		
7.	No		
8.	No		
9.	No		
10.		slower	slowest
11.	No		
12.		nearer	nearest
13.	No		
14.		farther	farthest
		further	furthest
15.		quicker	quickest
16.	No		

17.	louder	loudest
18. No		
19.	higher	highest
20.	lower	lowest

EXERCISE 133

1. better	best
2. worse	worst
3. less	least
littler	littlest
4. more	most
5. older	oldest
elder	eldest

EXERCISE 134

1. A	6. NA
2. NA	7. A
3. A	8. A
4. NA	9. NA
5. NA	10. A

EXERCISE 135

1. √	6. √
2. —	7. √
3. √	8. —
4. —	9. —
5. √	10. √

EXERCISE 136

1. who	H
2. who	H
3. which	NH
4. who, which	H, NH
5. which	NH

EXERCISE 137

1. *my*	PP
2. *mine*	SP
3. *his*	PP
4. *ours*	SP
5. *Hers*	SP
6. *yours*	SP
7. *your*	PP
8. *Their*	PP
9. *ours*	SP
10. *her*	PP

EXERCISE 138

1. 2
2. 1
3. 7
4. 6
5. 5
6. 11
7. 10
8. 8
9. 3
10. 9
11. 7
12. 2
13. 1
14. 4
15. 5
16. 6
17. 8
18. 4
19. 3
20. 11

EXERCISE 139

1. advertisement
2. gasoline
3. taximeter
4. cabriolet
5. fraternity
6. photograph
7. geneva
8. brandywine
9. curiosity
10. memorandum
11. Frederick
12. Albert, Alfred, Alvin
13. Thomas
14. Joseph
15. Philip

EXERCISE 140

1. disport
2. turnpike
3. omnibus
4. violoncello
5. raccoon
6. periwig
7. acute
8. Eugene
9. Elizabeth
10. Albert

EXERCISE 141

1. American Indian
2. maître d'hôtel
3. European Asian
4. newspaper boy
5. Medicare

EXERCISE 142

1. Women's Army Corps
2. master of ceremonies
3. United Nations Educational, Scientific, and Cultural Organization
4. dichlorodiphenyltrichloroethane
5. long-range navigation
6. absent without leave
7. galvanized iron; mistakenly, general issue
8. very important person
9. GP = general purpose
10. National Association of Manufacturers

EXERCISE 143

1. smoke fog
2. television broadcast
3. motorist hotel
4. electro execute
5. splash spatter

EXERCISE 144

1. happenstance
2. autobus
3. escalator
4. blurt
5. squawk

EXERCISE 145

1. need needy
   speed speedy
   seed seedy
   bead beady
2. televise
3. donate
   orate

EXERCISE 146

1. bootlegger
2. typewriter
3. coronation
4. resurrection
5. baby-sitter
6. advance registration
7. lazy
8. jelly
9. escalator
10. reminiscence

EXERCISE 147

1. D
2. NS
3. D
4. D
5. NS
6. D
7. D
8. D
9. D
10. D
11. NS
12. D
13. D
14. D
15. D

EXERCISE 148

1. Police raid a gathering
2. Complete the faculty at State
   A complete faculty at State
3. Rule the book not obscene
4. A clean model house
   Clean the model house
5. A girl shows top baby beef

EXERCISE 149

1. The car stopped ăt the station.
2. He came frŏm the farm.
3. This is the farm he came fròm. NO
4. These roses are fŏr you.
5. The chimpanzee ĭn the cage was yawning.
6. The lad stood ŏn the barrel.
7. The plumber washed ĭn the basin.
8. This basin has been washed ìn. NO
9. He objected tŏ the last paragraph.
10. The part he objected tò was the last paragraph NO

EXERCISE 150

Dissyllabic prepositions have a primary stress when the object is a personal pronoun and weak and third stresses when the object is a noun.

EXERCISE 151

1. belów
2. bĕlòw
3. néar
4. nèar
5. òff
6. óff
7. áfter
8. àftĕr
9. sínce
10. sĭnce yesterday

(Prepositions usually take third and weak stresses.)

EXERCISE 152

1. Barring
2. following
3. following
4. regarding
5. regarding
6. Considering
7. including
8. including
9. beginning
10. concerning

EXERCISE 153

1. ahead of
2. on account of
3. up at
4. Contrary to
5. with reference to
6. on behalf of
7. instead of
8. in lieu of
9. In spite of
10. with respect to

EXERCISE 154

1. fence
2. fence
3. fence
4. fence
5. fence
6. fence
7. putter
8. putter
9. car
10. swings

EXERCISE 155

1. The small study table
2. Any great European opera
3. That somber evening sky
4. My roommate's dirty tennis shoes
   My dirty roommate's tennis shoes
5. All the other white linen handkerchiefs
6. A soft pat on the head
7. A hard blow which staggered him
8. That broken ski lying in the basement
9. A junior with a lame leg who was walking on crutches
10. The girl in the front row whose books he was carrying

EXERCISE 156

Here are a few samples of the kinds of modifiers you might use.

1. The sailboats on the bay are beautiful to watch.
2. They sailed under the wooden bridge near the lighthouse.
3. He makes exquisite jewelry which is bought by collectors.

EXERCISE 157

1. Stepped
2. Stepped
3. stepped
4. Stepped
5. shouted
6. shouted
7. watching
8. eaten
9. driven
10. Spoke

EXERCISE 158

1. Sold
2. Sold
3. Appeared
4. chose
5. remained
6. gave
7. paid
8. called
9. was
10. returned

EXERCISE 159

1. pony . . . | galloped
2. students | attended
3. senior . . . | will be honored
4. pipes . . . | pounded
5. choir . . . | sang

EXERCISE 160

Here are samples of what you might do.

1. The tiny leak in the hose soon became enlarged.
2. The canoe that he wanted was a narrow, aluminum model.
3. The pie had a rich, flaky crust.
4. The steaming apple pie made her mouth water.
5. The passenger in the front seat who was watching the speedometer became nervous.

EXERCISE 161

Here are samples of what you might do.

1. Emil later regretted his decision.
2. The lad with the freckled nose came after his dog when school was over.
3. The summer vacationers will soon return to college.
4. That gloomy grind always seemed to have a complaint to make.
5. The mountaineer merrily swung the heavy pack on his back to begin the long hike.

EXERCISE 162

1. 1
2. —
3. 1
4. —
5. 1
6. —
7. 1
8. 1
9. —
10. —

EXERCISE 163

1. 1
2. both
3. 2
4. 1
5. 2
6. both
7. 1
8. 1
9. both
10. 1

EXERCISE 164

1. 2
2. 1
3. 1
4. 2
5. 2
6. 2
7. 2
8. 2
9. 1
10. 2

EXERCISE 165

1. 3
2. 2
3. 1
4. 3
5. 3
6. 3
7. 1
8. 1
9. 2
10. 3

EXERCISE 166

1. The cat purrs.
2. The student studies.
3. The house deteriorates.
4. The vase breaks.
5. The visitor departs.

EXERCISE 167

1. Cats prowl.
2. Musicians play.
3. Professors teach.
4. Buses wait.
5. Comedians laugh.

EXERCISE 168

1. purposes make
2. leader selects
3. one maintains
4. difference appears
5. troublemakers were

EXERCISE 169

1. The patients are being watched.
2. The janitors have waxed the floor.
3. The wrestlers do not smoke.
4. The cars have been stolen.
5. The ships were disappearing beyond the horizon.

EXERCISE 170

1. cat sleeps cats sleep
2. cat sleeps cats sleep
3. junior refuses juniors refuse
4. milkman delivers milkmen deliver
5. paper goes papers go

EXERCISE 171

1. They found out who I am. I
2. We are eager to know who he is. he
3. The police could not discover who they are. they
4. The auditor asked what the amount was. amount
5. Can you tell which one is yours? one
   Can you tell which one yours is? yours

EXERCISE 172

1. InV
2. InV
3. InV
4. —
5. InV
6. —
7. InV
8. —
9. InV
10. —

EXERCISE 173

1. it
2. him
3. them
4. her, him
5. it
6. it
7. it
8. her
9. it, him, her
10. them

EXERCISE 174

1. TrV 5
2. InV 4
3. be 3
4. TrV 5
5. InV 4
6. TrV 5
7. be 1
8. TrV 5
9. InV 4
10. TrV 5

EXERCISE 175

1. The window was opened (by the maid).
2. The dice were rolled (by him).
3. Dancing is liked (by most adolescents).
4. The mountains were chosen (by us) for our vacation.
5. *King Lear* has never been read (by Jim).
6. Wood was burned in the fireplace (by the tourists).
7. His sheep were counted (by the shepherd).
8. The game was begun (by us) at four o'clock.
9. A new house on the river was built (by the Smiths).
10. A pileated woodpecker was spotted (by the nature club).

EXERCISE 176

1. was killed

   The terrier killed the rat.
2. were turned

   The cook turned the pancakes.
3. is raised

   Farmers raise much corn in Iowa.
4. was heard

   We heard an early folk tune.
5. been washed

   Mavis has washed the dishes.
6. was had

   All had a good time.
7. was teased

   Her boy friend teased Jane.
8. been lowered

   The sergeant had lowered the flag.
9. were stopped

   The traffic officer stopped the motorcycles.
10. is played

    A carillonneur plays a carillon concert at 7:45 in the morning.

EXERCISE 177

1. The librarian found the pamphlet for me.
2. He assigned the toughest job to Jack.
3. The spaniel brought the stick to his master.
4. Susie fed some juicy worms to the baby robins.
5. Her mother sent a new laundry box to her.

EXERCISE 178

1. He was given a dirty look (by her).

   A dirty look was given him (by her).
2. The manager was made a fine offer (by the company).

   A fine offer was made the manager (by the company).
3. I was dealt a bad hand (by the dealer).

   A bad hand was dealt me (by the dealer).
4. His roommate was offered the car (by him).

   The car was offered his roommate (by him).
5. She was asked a question (by the instructor).

   A question was asked her (by the instructor).

EXERCISE 179

See answers to Exercise 178.

EXERCISE 180

1. She played a trick.	6
2. We appointed George.	7
3. You threw a curve.	6
4. The student body elected Arabella.	7
5. The faculty chose Sieverson.	7
6. We found a sandwich.	6
7. The dealer sold an air mattress.	6
8. She fed the pablum.	6
9. The city elected Mouchy.	7
10. He named his new boat.	7

EXERCISE 181

1. outside	uninflected word
2. yellow	adjective
3. elected	past participle
4. bad	adjective
5. fit	adjective

EXERCISE 182

1. 8	6. 4
2. 4	7. 4
3. 4	8. 8
4. 8	9. 8
5. 8	10. 4

EXERCISE 183

1. 4	6. 8
2. 8	7. 8
3. 8	8. 4
4. 4	9. 8
5. 8	10. 8

EXERCISE 184

1. 9	6. 9
2. 9	7. 5
3. 5	8. 9
4. 9	9. 5
5. 5	10. 9

EXERCISE 185

1. 1	6. 7	11. 9	16. 8
2. 2	7. 3	12. 7	17. 9
3. 6	8. 5	13. 5	18. 2
4. 3	9. 7	14. 2	19. 9
5. 4	10. 6	15. 7	20. 7

EXERCISE 186

1. 6	7		6. 5	6
2. 5	9		7. 1	3
3. 4	8		8. 4	5
4. 3	5		9. 4	5
5. 5	6		10. 5	7

EXERCISE 187

1. president . . . plan.	3	3
2. janitors . . . umbrella.	2	3
3. counselor . . . approach.	3	3
4. aunt . . . son.	3	3
5. Mother's cake.	1	3

EXERCISE 188

1. failure	fail	-ure
2. payment	pay	-ment
3. assistant	assist	-ant
4. device	devise	-/s/
5. catcher	catch	-er
6. collision	collide	-ion
7. leakage	leak	-age
8. Reformation	reform	-ation
9. discovery	discover	-y
10. amusement	amuse	-ment
11. sickness	sick	-ness
12. refusal	refuse	-al
13. width	wide	-th
14. sincerity	sincere	-ity
15. freedom	free	-dom
16. Childhood	child	-hood
17. beautician	beauty	-ician
18. scholarship	scholar	-ship
19. fragrance	fragrant	-ce
20. intimacy	intimate	-cy

EXERCISE 189

1. comp. SV
2. noun SV
3. UW OP
4. verb OV
5. noun SC
6. pr. SC
7. UW OV
8. noun OC
9. UW SV
10. comp. RO

EXERCISE 190

1. OV
2. SC
3. OC
4. IO
5. OP

EXERCISE 191

1. that SV
2. your seat OP
3. that woman, my aunt OP
4. it IO
5. that SV
6. a star, that SC
7. that OV
8. it OV
9. it, her beauty SV
10. that OC

EXERCISE 192

1. what we said OV
2. What you do SV
3. what I thought too SC
4. what you have OP
5. whoever came there IO
6. whatever his grandfather wishes OC
7. paying cash OP
8. whichever is the most durable OV
9. to bring the coffee OV
10. mailing the letter OV

EXERCISE 193

1. met 4 4
2. swept 4 5
3. leave 4 1
4. spreading 3 3
5. eaten 5 5
6. eats 5 2
7. set 3 4
8. lying 5 3
9. bought 4 5
10. sank 5 4

EXERCISE 194

1.	besieged	siege	be-
2.	personifies	person	-ify
3.	prove	proof	-ve
4.	weaken	weak	-en
5.	liberalized	liberal	-ize
6.	enrich	rich	en-
7.	idolize	idol	-ize
8.	bewitched	witch	be-
9.	clothes	cloth	-the
10.	enraptured	rapture	en-

EXERCISE 195

1. have been making
2. is being made
3. was established
4. has . . . been beaten
5. is waiting
6. Have . . . repaired
7. missed, seeing
8. offered . . . delay
9. Being . . . put
10. lost . . . playing

EXERCISE 196

	-er	*-est*	*-ly*	*-ness*
1.	closer	closest	closely	closeness
2.	icier	iciest	icily	iciness
3.	sweeter	sweetest	sweetly	sweetness
4.	sadder	saddest	sadly	sadness
5.	higher	highest	highly	highness
6.	sunnier	sunniest	sunnily	sunniness
7.	gentler	gentlest	gently	gentleness
8.	smaller	smallest	—	smallness
9.	littler	littlest	—	littleness
10.	faster	fastest	—	fastness
11.	holier	holiest	holily	holiness
12.	longer	longest	—	longness
13.	friendlier	friendliest	—	friendliness
14.	iller worse	illest worst	illy	illness
15.	—	—	naturally	naturalness

(Some of the words that might fit the blanks above, like *holily,* are listed in current dictionaries but are probably of low frequency. The use of some others, like *friendlily* and *naturaler,* is a matter of dialect or idiolect.)

EXERCISE 197

1.	gold	-en
2.	help	-less
3.	love	-ly
4.	mess	-y
5.	peace	-ful
6.	consul	-ar
7.	nerve	-ous
8.	fragment	-ary
9.	repent	-ant
10.	affection	-ate
11.	fool	-ish
12.	rhythm	-ic
13.	region	-al
14.	tire	-ed
15.	separate /et/	/ət/
16.	recur	-ent
17.	instruct	-ive
18.	perish	-able
19.	meddle	-some
20.	congratulate	-ory
21.	please	-ant
22.	good	-ly
23.	live	-ly

EXERCISE 198

1.	A *clêan* ápron	A
2.	An *êvening* párty	N
3.	A *prêtty* nécklace	A
4.	The *clâss* dánce	N
5.	A *hôpeful* sígn	A
6.	Their *bâck* yárd	UW
7.	Those *nêighborhood* cáts	N
8.	Sally's *nêw* rádio	A
9.	That *pâper* bóok	N
10.	A *fîghting* róoster	V
11.	These *brôken* bóxes	V
12.	An *ûpstairs* róom	UW
13.	Their *garâge* dóor	N
14.	The *ôffice* týpewriter	N
15.	Our *schôol* príncipal	N
16.	The *abôve* státement	UW
17.	That *fûnny* hát	A
18.	A *scênic* dríve	A
19.	Those *châttering* gírls	V
20.	His *glâss* éye	N

EXERCISE 199

1. pink
2. dark
3. afraid
4. asleep
5. alive
6. tall
7. —
8. dewy
9. —
10. hostile

EXERCISE 200

1.	alone	UW	
2.	cheering	V	
3.	shining and smooth	V	A
4.	today	UW	
5.	homeward	UW	
6.	afterward	UW	
7.	prim	A	
8.	floating	V	
9.	aboard	UW	
10.	ajar	UW	

EXERCISE 201

(Word-group adjectivals are set in regular type; words they modify are set in italics.)

1. *day* to remember
2. *chap* sitting in that cubicle
3. *size* I ordered
4. *drugstore* on the corner
5. *week* when I was housecleaning
6. *girl* spoiled by her mother
7. *time* convenient to yourself
8. *head* of this club
9. *book* I lent you
10. *sight* to behold

EXERCISE 202

1.	Adv	adj
2.	UW	
3.	Adv	noun
4.	Adj	
5.	Adv	adj
6.	Adv	adj
7.	Adj	
8.	Adv	adj
9.	UW	
10.	UW	
11.	Adv	adj
12.	Adv	noun
13.	Adv	noun
14.	Adv	adj
15.	Adv	adj

EXERCISE 203

regularly	3	4	
always	2	3	4
yesterday	1	4	
greedily	2	3	
soon	1	2	3
there	1	3	

EXERCISE 204

1.	headlong	4	UW
2.	Indeed	1	UW
3.	madly	5	Adv
4.	certainly	2	Adv
5.	singing	4	V
6.	frequently	2	Adv
7.	below	4	UW
8.	afterward	5	UW
9.	eventually	3	Adv
10.	usually	2	Adv
11.	around	4	UW
12.	here	5	UW
13.	still	4	UW
14.	already	3	UW
15.	rapidly	4	Adv
16.	seldom	3	UW
17.	Meanwhile	1	UW
18.	also	4	UW
19.	Saturday	4	N
20.	everywhere	4	UW

EXERCISE 205

1. 4
2. 1
3. 3
4. 5
5. 1
6. 4
7. 1
8. 1
9. 1
10. 4
11. 5

EXERCISE 206

1. N–al
2. Aj–al
3. Av–al
4. Av–al
5. N–al
6. Av–al
7. Aj–al
8. N–al
9. V–al
10. Aj–al
11. N–al
12. Av–al
13. Av–al
14. Aj–al
15. N–al
16. Av–al
17. Av–al
18. Av–al
19. Av–al
20. N–al or Aj–al

EXERCISE 207

1. N
2. V
3. UW
4. N
5. UW
6. UW
7. Adv
8. N
9. N
10. Adj
11. V
12. UW
13. Adj
14. N
15. UW

EXERCISE 208

1. VAC
2. V + A
3. VAC
4. V + A
5. VAC

EXERCISE 209

1. P
2. V + A
3. P
4. VAC
5. V + A
6. VAC
7. P
8. P
9. VAC
10. VAC

EXERCISE 210

1. VAC–O
2. V–PP
3. VAC–O
4. V–PP
5. VAC–O
6. V–PP

EXERCISE 211

1. V–PP
2. VAC
3. VAC
4. V–PP
5. VAC
6. V–PP

EXERCISE 212

1. The police *ran in* the criminal. VAC–O
2. They *ran in* a circle. V–PP
   The circle in which they ran
3. The teacher stood *drînking în* the móonlight. VAC–O

4. The teacher stood *drînking ĭn* the móonlight. V–PP
   The moonlight in which the teacher stood drinking.
5. Frank *called down* his son. (= reprimanded) VAC–O
6. He *called down* the mountain. V–PP
   The mountain down which he called.

EXERCISE 213

1. 3
2. 1 2 3
3. 1 2 3
4. 1 2 3
5. 1 2 3
6. 1 2 3
7. 1 2 3
8. 1 2 3
9. 1 2 3
10. 1 2 3

EXERCISE 214

1. She *lôoks ûp tò* her móther. (= admires)
2. She *lôoks dôwn òn* her former fríends. (= scorns)
3. *Lôok ôut fòr* the dóg.
4. In case of an argument I'll *stând úp fòr* you.
5. Will you *stând úp fòr* me at the christening?
6. We'll *lôok ín òn* you. (= visit)
7. McBride *mâde ôff wĭth* another man's wífe.
8. The company will *mâke ûp fòr* your lóss. (= repay)
9. After the quarrel we *mâde úp wĭth* them.
10. You must *gêt ôn wĭth* the jób.

EXERCISE 215

1. Av—al
2. Q
3. Q
4. Av–al
5. Q
6. Q
7. Av–al
8. Q
9. Q
10. Q

EXERCISE 216

1. enough
2. indeed, still
3. just, right, even
4. a bit, a good deal, a great deal, almost, a whole lot, even, indeed, lots, much, no, some, somewhat, still. A few of the others are possible if not likely.

EXERCISE 217

1. His laughter was loud.
2. The jar is filled with dates.
3. McPherson was a man.
4. The two strolled.
5. The constable laughed.

6. We heard the clank.
7. The squirrel scolded the blue jays.
8. The contract had paragraphs of fine print.
9. The searchers found the car.
10. Claribel jumped.

EXERCISE 218

1. motorcycle
2. sputtered
3. motorcycle
4. stopped
5. stopped
6. nice
7. often
8. stopped
9. fellow
10. whip

EXERCISE 219

1. I knew how to swim, luckily.
2. We climbed in the back window, since the door was closed.
3. The contract is, in fact, invalid.
4. We resumed the normal household routine, the guests having departed.
5. You should be provided with a fly, to keep dry in a tent.
6. He was lucky, considering the circumstances, to escape alive.

EXERCISE 220

R
1. Apparently

R R
2. The iron lung, apparently,

F
3. malfunctioning, apparently.

R
4. Before frying the trout,

R R
5. He spends his money, most of the time,

R-F
6. To be sure,

R R
7. The orchestra, to be sure,

F-R
8. not the best in the world,

R
9. Unfortunately,

F
10. She did not keep up her grades,

EXERCISE 221

1b. x
2a. because
b. after

3a. To tell the truth, he was anxious.
b. He wished to tell the truth.
4b. x

EXERCISE 222

1. a narrow village street
2. this large college dormitory
3. those tall sophomore players
4. that photogenic girl swimmer
5. this enthusiastic senior counselor
6. George's blue wool necktie
7. her old leather shoes
8. his large hardwood desk
9. these cheap ballpoint pens
10. my portable student typewriter

EXERCISE 223

1. a. An arms factory that is small
   b. A factory for small arms
2. a. That stuff for greasy kids
   b. That kid stuff which is greasy
3. a. The service for basic books
   b. The book service that is basic
4. a. A language teacher who is foreign
   b. A teacher of a foreign language
5. a. A car enthusiast who is old
   b. An enthusiast about old cars

EXERCISE 224

1. Half your new cement blocks
2. All the long copper wires
3. Both her lovely engágement rìngs
4. All those fresh prairie flowers
5. Both my recalcitrant baby coons

EXERCISE 225

1. a. A girl's bicycle that is old
   b. A bicycle for an old girl
2. a. The congress of world women
   b. The women's congress of the world
3. a. A man's fur coat that is nice
   b. A fur coat of a nice man
4. a. A garment of a large woman
   b. A woman's garment that is large
5. a. A dictionary for advanced learners
   b. An advanced dictionary for learners

EXERCISE 226

IVb II I
1. Another huge glass ornament

IVb II
2. Each happy fárm dùck

IVb II I
3. Some long winter vacations

V IVa II I
4. All our friendly neighborhood dogs

IVb II I
5. Either short cotton dress

IVb I
6. Enough college friends

V IVa II
7. Both my studious roommates

IVb II I
8. No cold cheese sandwich

IVb I
9. Much evening enjoyment

IVb II
10. Neither tired ecońomics stùdent

EXERCISE 227

IVa III III
1. The last three pickles

IVa III
2. His every wish

III II I
3. Many fine university seniors

IVb III II
4. Some other bad néwspaper repòrts

IVb III II
5. Much more white sand

IVa III II
6. Those same hungry ants

V IVa III II
7. Both those two aimless fellows

IVb III II
8. Any such childish pranks

IVa III
9. Harry's few acquaintances

IVb III II
10. What other foolish ideas

EXERCISE 228

III II I
1. Several pink summer flowers

V IVa II I
2. Both his old garden hoes

V IVa III II
3. All these three terminal junctures

IVb II
4. Another bad examinátion schèdule

IVa III II I
5. My two pretty silk dresses

EXERCISE 229

IVb II
1. Any large delívery trùck

IVb II
Any large trúck delìvery

IVa II I
2. That heavy steel construction

IVa II
That heavy constrúction stèel

IVb II
3. Some excellent párts fàctory

IVb II
Some excellent fáctory pàrts

IVa III II I
4. The student's long summer vacation

IVa III II
The student's long vacátion sùmmer

IVa III II
5. Her first good hóuse dòg

IVa III II
Her first good dóg hòuse

EXERCISE 230

VI V IVa
1. Especially all our guests

VI IVa II
2. Particularly her spotted kitten

VI IVa II
3. Even the empty box

VI IVb II
4. Just some white athlétic sòcks

VI III II
5. Only ten short minutes

EXERCISE 231

1. 5
2. 1
3. 7
4. 8
5. 4
6. 2
7. 6
8. 3
9. 9
10. 6

EXERCISE 232

1. scarlet . . . exotic
2. expensive
3. stalwart . . . proud
4. new . . . glossy
5. complicated

EXERCISE 233

1. The *paragraph* abóve → is too lóng.
2. The *students* hére → are a cóurteous group.
3. This *matter* toó → must be discússed.
4. The *party* yésterday → had a large atténdance.
5. The *weather* outsíde → is fóul.

EXERCISE 234

1. My older bróther →
2. The discússion →
3. Her fiancé →
4. The rábbits →
5. The mémbers →

EXERCISE 235

1.	of the voters	1
2.	licking her ice-cream cone	2
3.	to eat	4
4.	with the white trim	1
5.	urged on by the crowd	3
6.	to do	4
7.	gliding across the bay	2
8.	covered with mud	3
9.	of the garage	1
10.	tugging at the rope	2

EXERCISE 236

1.	*whom* he studied with	OP
2.	*who* performed the operation	SV
3.	I ordered	ø
4.	*that* Jack used	DO
5.	*whose* mother is president of the PTA	M
6.	*which* had long been our meeting place	SV
7.	*that* her mother was	SC
8.	*who* immediately won our hearts	SV
9.	*who* helps me	SV
10.	*whom* I met at the play	DO

EXERCISE 237

2 3 2
1. The blouse which she preférred → was made of sea island cotton. R

2 3 1 2 3 1
2. She wore an old blue blóuse, ↓ which had always been her fávorite. ↓ NR

2 3 2
3. The hóuse that he built → was of steel. R

3 2 2 3 2
4. Márilyn, → who is fond of díctionaries, → bought the new *Webster's Third.* NR

2 3 2
5. The man whom I márry → must have curly hair. R

2 3 1
6. I'll take any man who wears pánts. ↓ R

2 3 1
7. The car I want is an MǴ. ↓ R

2 3 2
8. The student whose púrse he returned → offered Dick a generous reward. R

2 3 3
9. Have you a necktie which will match a brown súit? ↑ R

2 2 3 2 3 1
10. Thomas bought a sílk, ↑ red-and-grey striped nécktie, ↓
2 3 1
which his roommate admíred. ↓ NR

EXERCISE 238

1. why she deserted him — why
2. where we camp — where
3. after he enlisted — after
4. when he comes in — when
5. where I lost it — where

EXERCISE 239

(Relatives are set in regular type; subordinating conjunctions are set in italics.)

1. *that* —
2. that DO
3. *That* —
4. *that* —
5. that SV

EXERCISE 240

1. lad
The new sophomore 4. he/she 1. he
2. offspring
The three puppies 7. he/she/it 7. he/she/it

3. stream

   the river 3. it 3. it

4. sorority

   Alpha Gamma Goopha 3. it 3. it

5. graduate

   Mary Evans 2. she 2. he/she

EXERCISE 241

2 3 2 3 2
1. The scóutmaster, → Lónglegs, → prepared the beans.

2 3 1
2. The pressman interviewed Scoutmaster Lónglegs ↓

2 3 2
3. The play *Hámlet* → will be presented next week.

2 3 1 2 3 1
4. We saw *Hámlet* ↓ a play by Shákespeare ↓

2 3 1
5. She had always enjoyed the poem "Trées" ↓

2 3 2 3 2
6. Her favorite póem, → "Trées," → was included in the new collection.

2 3 1 2 3 1
7. We inspected his cár, ↓ a long, sleek Húmber ↓

2 3 2 2 3 2
8. The túlips, → a hybrid variety from Hólland, → will bloom early.

2 3 2
9. A Republican from Vodka Válley, → Ivanovitch sat at the speaker's table.

2 3 1 2 3 1
10. I felt what I álways feel, ↓ a sense of frustrátion ↓

EXERCISE 242

1. . . . angrily M
2. . . . often T
3. . . . rarely . . . carelessly T M
4. . . . fearfully M
5. . . . never . . . Sunday T T
6. . . . ahead P
7. . . . even ø
8. . . . always . . . alone T M
9. . . . backward P
10. . . . happily M
11. . . . still ø–T
12. . . . anywhere ø–P
13. . . . cautiously . . . sidewise M P
14. . . . aloud M
15. . . . timidly M

16. . . . Saturdays T
17. . . . sleeping ϕ–T
18. . . . seated ϕ–M
19. . . . cleaner M
20. . . . prepared ϕ

Did you notice how imprecise these three categories of meaning are? For example, in sentences 2 and 3, do *often* and *rarely* really indicate time or do they indicate some unnamed category of meaning? In 9 does *backward* show place or manner or something else? In 12 is *anywhere* a place? In 17 is *sleeping* expressive of time or not? In 20 does *prepared* show manner?

EXERCISE 243

1. A
2. N V
3. V V
4. A
5. A
6. V
7. V V
8. N
9. A
10. V V

EXERCISE 244

1. . . . this Friday
2. . . . the following day
3. . . . the whole way
4. . . . a little while
5. . . . another time

EXERCISE 245

1. SC
2. NC
3. SC
4. NC
5. PP
6. SC
7. PP
8. SC
9. NC NC
10. SC
11. NC
12. SC
13. NC
14. SC
15. SC

EXERCISE 246

1. O
2. M
3. O
4. M
5. M

EXERCISE 247

1. VM
2. VM
3. NM
4. VM
5. VM

EXERCISE 248

1. on the operating table 1
2. to improve her flower garden 4
3. this Christmas 2
4. crushed by the toppling rock 6
5. when you hear the bell 3
6. holding the rope 5
7. if you can 3
8. by that time 1
9. either way 2
10. splashing the water 5

EXERCISE 249

1. In fact, | both tires are flat.
2. When the game is over, | let's meet for a bite to eat.
3. I'll give you a hand, | certainly.
4. To attract birds, | one must provide shelter and food.
5. Smiling slightly, | she gently rebuked him.

EXERCISE 250

1. The tulips in the flower bed | drooped and died.
2. The striped Dutch tulips | were gorgeous.
3. They | soon had the boat in the water.
4. The lapping of the waves upon the shore | lulled them to sleep.
5. The wine steward | uncorked the bottle with a flourish.

EXERCISE 251

1. Indeed, | your first bullfight | may not delight you.
2. Smoking a dainty pipe, | Elaine | remained pensive.
3. If I weren't afraid, | I | would pet him.
4. We | will build a float tomorrow, | notwithstanding their objections.
5. At long last, | the letter of acceptance | arrived.

EXERCISE 252

1. When | Hubert plays his guitar
2. Unless | you bring a bottle opener
3. Since | the paddle is broken
4. If | the motor begins to cough
5. Once | this rain is over

EXERCISE 253

1. . . . who | was late for dinner.
2. . . . that | inspired him.
3. . . . which | cost too much.
4. . . . which | was chasing a rabbit.
5. . . . that | caused my spine to tingle.

EXERCISE 254

1. under | the fence
2. from | the greenhouse
3. between | the blue flowers
4. across | the wide, sluggish river
5. to | the flower-starred meadow

EXERCISE 255

1. to | lessen the tension
2. to | depend on that rope
3. to | repair the parachute
4. to | haul in the sail
5. to | avoid the black flies

EXERCISE 256

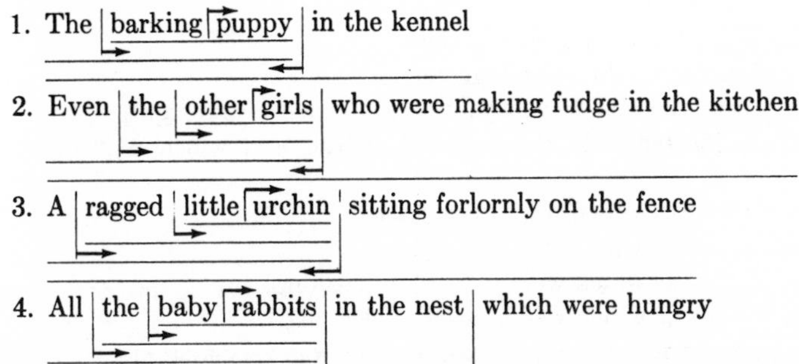

1. The barking puppy in the kennel
2. Even the other girls who were making fudge in the kitchen
3. A ragged little urchin sitting forlornly on the fence
4. All the baby rabbits in the nest which were hungry

5. All | the | baby | rabbits | in the nest which was hidden from view

6. The | forester | with the pet bobcat which was always hungry

7. The | forester | with the pet bobcat | who was always hungry

(Since *forester* belongs to the *he* substitute group and *bobcat* to the *he/she/it* group, the *who* is ambiguous in that it may refer to either *forester* or *bobcat.* In the sentence above the cuts show *who* referring to *forester*. In the sentence below, the cuts show *who* referring to *bobcat.*)

The | forester | with the pet bobcat who was always hungry

8. The | young | man | accompanied by a girl who lost her temper

9. The | young | man | accompanied by a girl | who lost his temper

10. The | driver | of the bus which stopped at every corner

11. The | driver | of the bus | who was drunk every Saturday afternoon

12. Her | old-fashioned | summer | garden | that we stopped to see

13. Those | aluminum | stakes | which soon come loose

14. Many | such | stories | in the book which she had drawn from the library

15. A | gleaming | sailboat | in the middle of the lake

EXERCISE 257

1. The girl near the boy who was wearing his hat.
   (Note that *her* before *hat* would be ambiguous.)
2. A theater located near the business district and crowded every night.
   A theater which is located near the business district and which is crowded every night.
3. The motorboat of the man which would not start.
   The motorboat of the man who would not start.
4. The spark plugs of the car which were in need of cleaning.
   The spark plugs of the car which was in need of cleaning.
5. A new golf club that replaced his old one and that he was very fond of.
   A new golf club which replaced his old one and which he was very fond of.

EXERCISE 258

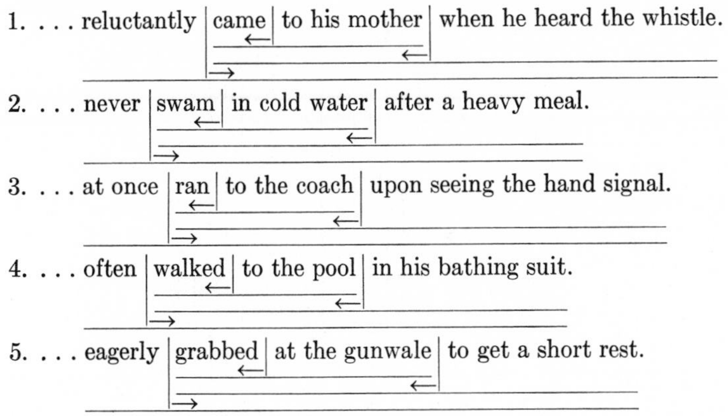

1. . . . reluctantly | came | to his mother | when he heard the whistle.

2. . . . never | swam | in cold water | after a heavy meal.

3. . . . at once | ran | to the coach | upon seeing the hand signal.

4. . . . often | walked | to the pool | in his bathing suit.

5. . . . eagerly | grabbed | at the gunwale | to get a short rest.

EXERCISE 259

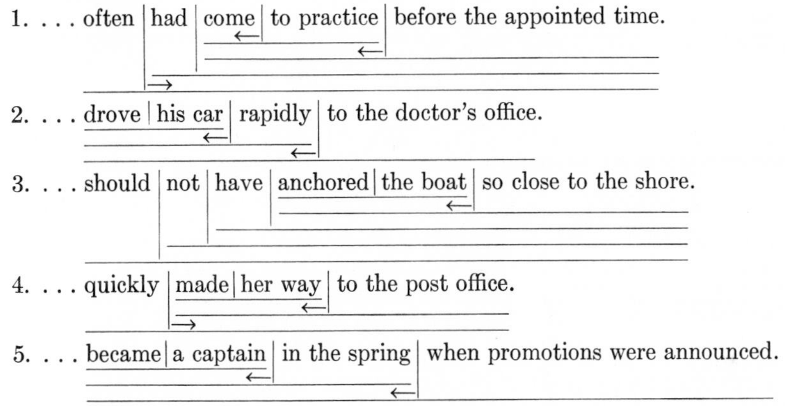

1. . . . often | had | come | to practice | before the appointed time.

2. . . . drove | his car | rapidly | to the doctor's office.

3. . . . should | not | have | anchored | the boat | so close to the shore.

4. . . . quickly | made | her way | to the post office.

5. . . . became | a captain | in the spring | when promotions were announced.

EXERCISE 260

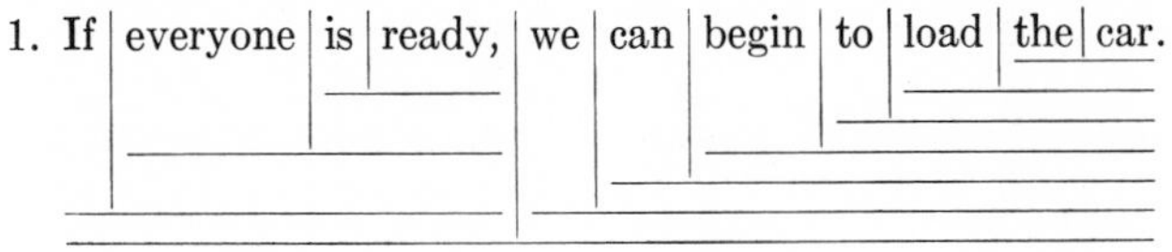

1. If | everyone | is | ready, | we | can | begin | to | load | the | car.

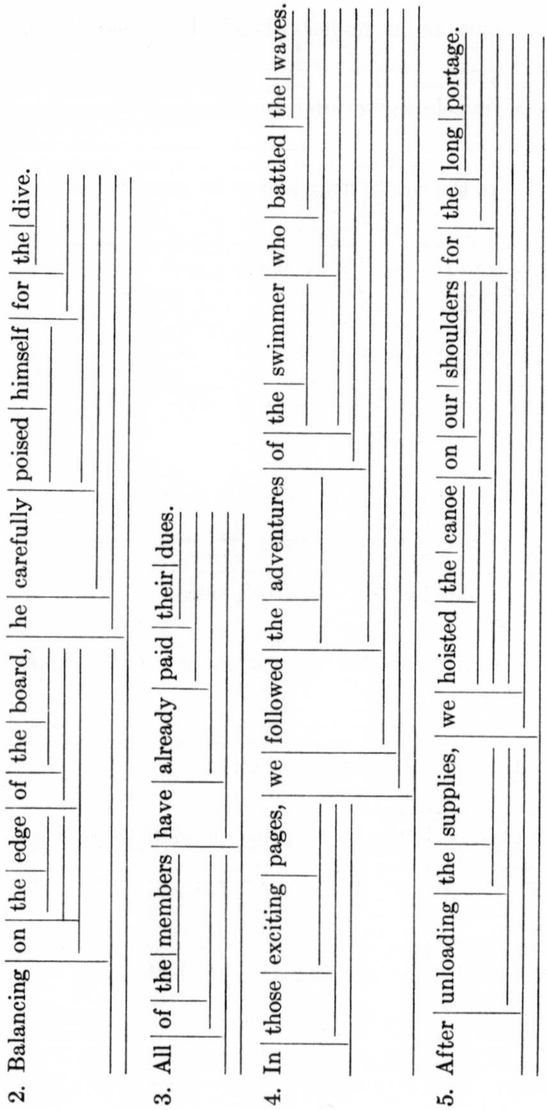

2. Balancing | on | the | edge | of | the | board, | he | carefully | poised | himself | for | the | dive.

3. All | of | the | members | have | already | paid | their | dues.

4. In | those | exciting | pages, | we | followed | the | adventures | of | the | swimmer | who | battled | the | waves.

5. After | unloading | the | supplies, | we | hoisted | the | canoe | on | our | shoulders | for | the | long | portage.

EXERCISE 261

1. Your | food | is | exceedingly | good.
2. The | girl | from | Skunk | Hollow | is | here.
3. My | oldest | brother | is | the | doctor | in | residence.
4. Many | younger | girls | giggle | outrageously.
5. The | girl | in | the | next | house | bought | a | silk | dress | at | the | auction.
6. The | doting | mother | bought | the | girl | a | dress | from | the | Smart | Shop.
7. The | basketball | players | chose | Harry | their | captain | for | next | year.
8. That | muscular | acrobat | seems | quite | young.
9. My | brother | remained | an | outstanding | student.

EXERCISE 262

1. and
   personal pronouns
2. yet
   adverbs
3. or
   nominal clauses
4. for
   sentences
5. not
   prepositional phrases
6. so
   sentences
7. but
   verbs
8. nor
   sentences

9. or
 infinitives
10. and
 present participles verbs

EXERCISE 263

1. Either . . . or
 sentences
2. both . . . and
 prepositional phrases
3. neither . . . nor
 nouns
4. not only . . . but
 adjectives
5. not . . . but
 nouns

EXERCISE 264

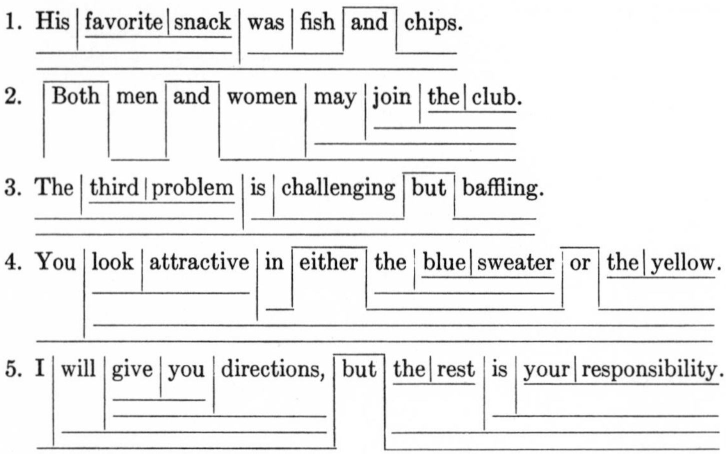

1. His | favorite | snack | was | fish | and | chips.

2. Both | men | and | women | may | join | the | club.

3. The | third | problem | is | challenging | but | baffling.

4. You | look | attractive | in | either | the | blue | sweater | or | the | yellow.

5. I | will | give | you | directions, | but | the | rest | is | your | responsibility.

EXERCISE 265

1. We were reluctant to leave.
2. We were reluctant, to tell the truth.
3. Mrs. Hawkins is devoted to her daughter.
4. The child was interested in understanding the process.
5. The lad was afraid of venturing into the water.
6. They were hopeful that the weather would change.
7. Juliet became forgetful of her duties.
8. The dean was not angry with me.

9. Jane was conscious that something unpleasant had happened.
10. Mother will be happy if you can help.
11. Jim is doubtful if he can pass the course.
12. Joseph is fond of doughnuts.
13. Are you sure of it?
14. Penelope was delighted to receive the pillow.
15. Uncle Andrew was disturbed that the dogs had not been fed.

EXERCISE 266

1. She hated *to miss the party.*	DO	DO
2. Peter tried *to remain calm.*	DO	SCa
3. *Shooting quail* takes a great deal of skill.	SV	DO
4. I expect *you to be truthful.*	DO	SCa
5. *Finding the trail* again was no easy matter.	SV	DO
6. Thank you for *washing dishes.*	OP	DO
7. *Being a béauty quèen* was exhilarating to Olga.	SV	SCn
8. I saw *them break the window.*	DO	DO
9. The doctor advised *him to stop smoking.*	DO	DO
10. We were requested *to leave the grounds.*	RO	DO

EXERCISE 267

1. to
2. -ing
3. both
4. to
5. -ing
6. both
7. to
8. -ing
9. both
10. both
11. -ing
12. to
13. -ing
14. both
15. -ing

EXERCISE 268

1. were
2. were
3. be
4. stand
5. be
6. write
7. were
8. be
9. were
10. answer

EXERCISE 269

1. count
2. mass
3. mass
4. mass
5. count
6. mass
7. count
8. mass
9. mass
10. count

EXERCISE 270

1.	count	proper
2.	mass	count
3.	count	proper
4.	mass	mass
5.	proper	count
6.	mass	mass
7.	count	count
8.	mass	count
9.	proper	count
10.	proper	proper

EXERCISE 271

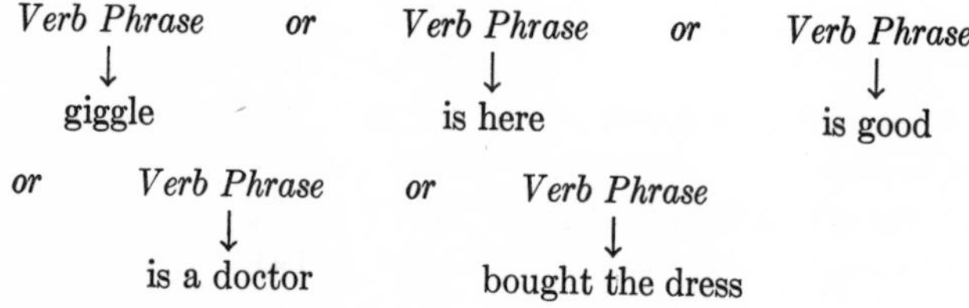

EXERCISE 272

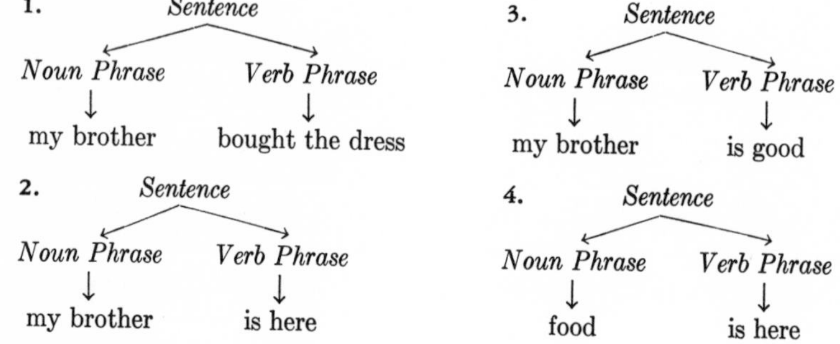

EXERCISE 273

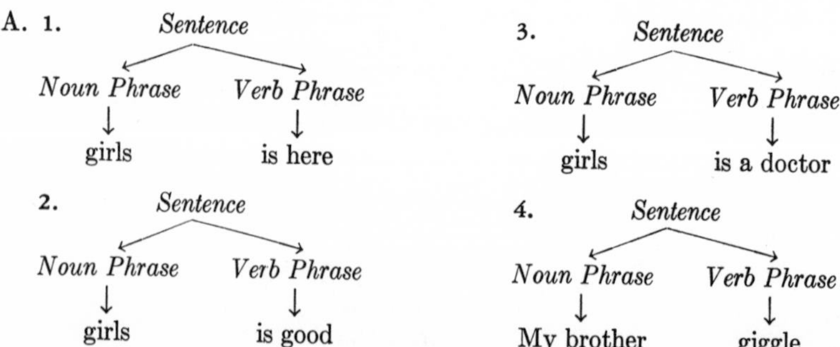

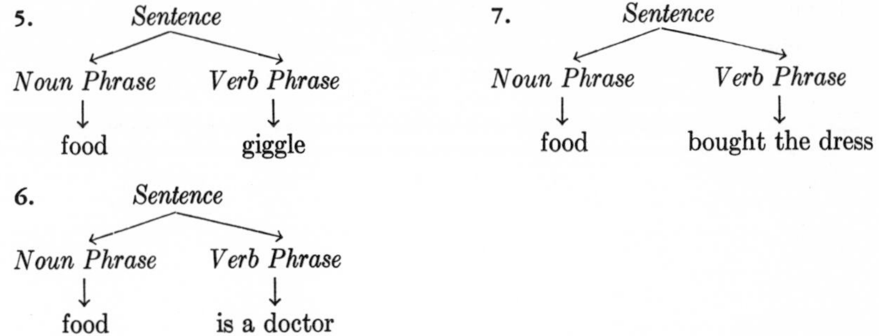

The grammar of English generates only the grammatical sentences of English. But notice that sentences 1, 2, 3, 4, and 5 are ungrammatical because the subject and verb do not agree. This means that the rules above are inadequate and incomplete and must be modified to include rules of agreement. Notice also that though sentences 6 and 7 are not ungrammatical, they are nonsensical. A grammar will generate nonsense sentences because grammar does not account for all the semantic features of a language. There are, in fact, *degrees* of grammatical and semantic deviation which must be accounted for in a complete theory of language.

B. No.

C. Rule 3.

D. Rule 4.

A complete grammar of English will generate not only *some* of the grammatical sentences of English but *all* the grammatical sentences, and these are infinite in number, as you will see later.

EXERCISE 274

My brother is a noun phrase because an arrow leads from *Noun Phrase* to *my brother*. Similarly, *bought the dress* is a verb phrase because an arrow leads from *Verb Phrase* to *bought the dress*. Because *my brother* is first, it is the subject; because *bought the dress* is the only element in the verb phrase and comes second, it is the predicate.

EXERCISE 275

A. 1. food
2. the girl
3. girls
4. my brother
5. my brothers
6. a doctor
7. the doctors
8. the dress
9. the dresses
10. the acrobat
11. here
12. there
13. in the garden
14. good
15. bad
16. beautiful
17. giggle
18. giggles
19. run
20. ran

21. buy
22. bought
23. hit
24. is
25. are
26. was
27. were
28. seems
29. remained

B. 1. S
2. NP
3. VP
4. Comp
5. Adv
6. Adj
7. Verb

EXERCISE 276

A. Ten

B. 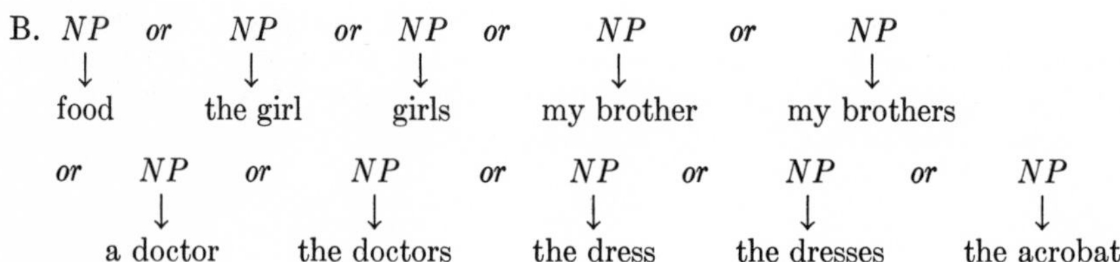

C. Yes.

D. Rule 3.

EXERCISE 277

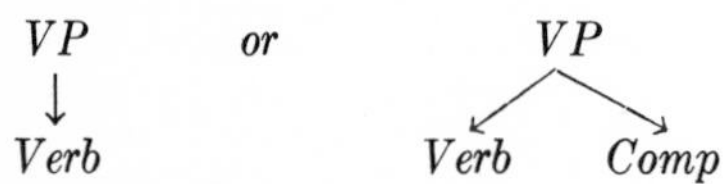

EXERCISE 278

A. 

B. *Rule 6*

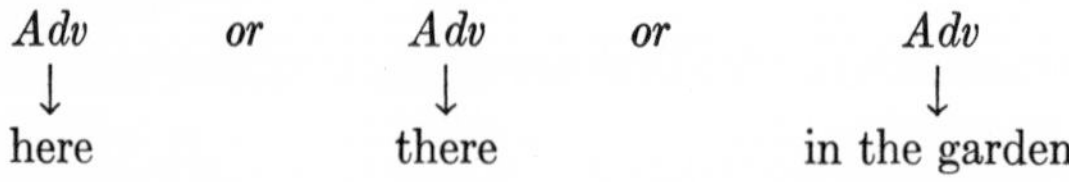

Rule 7

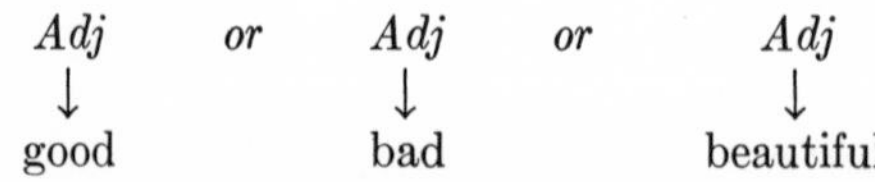

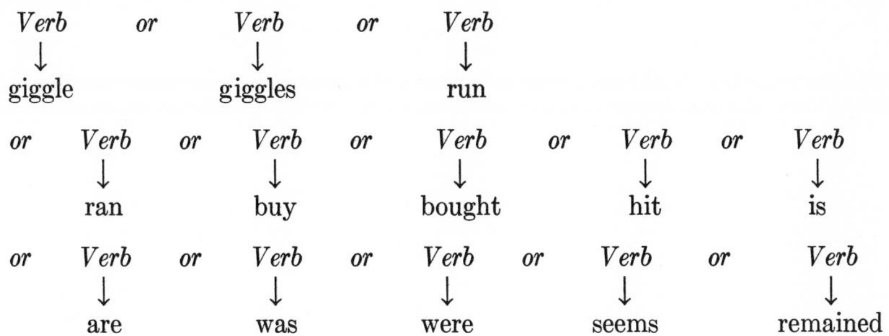

C. Rule 8.

D. Rule 6.

E. Rule 7.

EXERCISE 279

A. Because *Girls giggle* doesn't have a complement; that is, it doesn't have an NP, NP + NP, Adv, or Adj following the verb.

B. Because *Girls giggle* doesn't have an adverb.

C. Because *Girls giggle* doesn't have an adjective.

EXERCISE 280

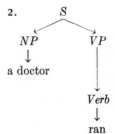

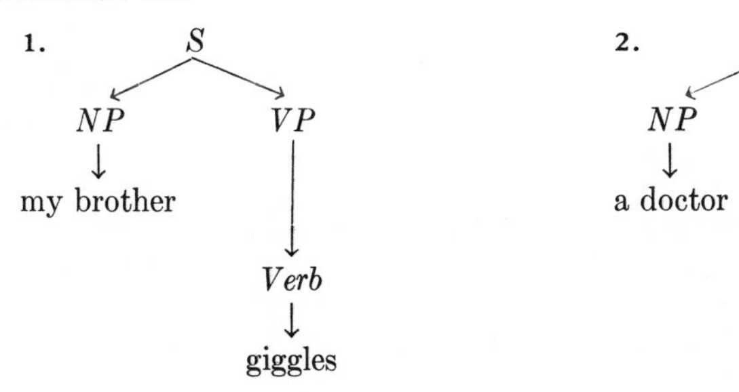

EXERCISE 281

A. Yes.

B. The arrow from NP leads to *a doctor*.
The arrow from VP points to Verb, which leads to *ran*.

C. Yes.

EXERCISE 282

A. Rules 6 and 7.

B. *The doctors bought the dress* has no adverbs (Rule 6) and no adjectives (Rule 7).

C. Rule 3.

D. Twice.

E. Two.

F. Verb and Verb + Comp.

G. Verb + Comp.

EXERCISE 283

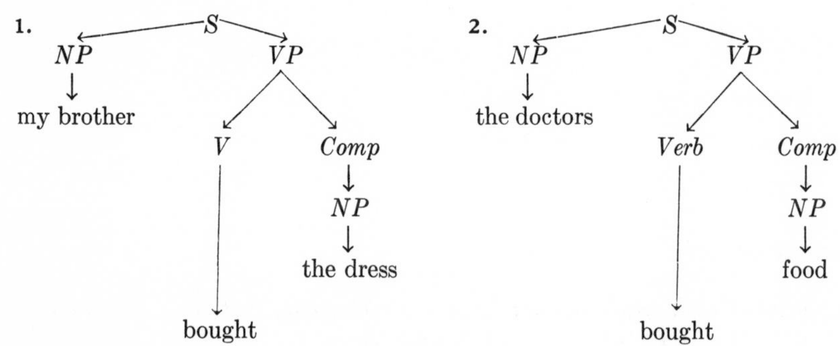

EXERCISE 284

A. Yes.

B. The arrow from one NP leads to *the doctors;* the arrow from the other NP leads to *food.*

C. Verb Phrase. Because the marker VP has arrows that eventually lead to *bought food* (by first leading to Verb + Comp with Verb leading to *bought* and Comp leading to *food*).

D. No. Because no single marker has arrows that eventually lead to *the doctors bought.* This shows that *the doctors bought* is not a grammatical unit such as noun phrase, verb phrase, noun, or verb; it shows that the IC structure of a sentence like *The doctors bought food* is *NOT The doctors bought|food* but rather *The doctors|bought food.*

E. *Food.*

F. Yes.

EXERCISE 285

A. Rules 6 and 7.

B. Rule 3.

C. Three times.

D. Four.

E. NP, NP + NP, Adj, and Adv.

F. NP + NP.

EXERCISE 286

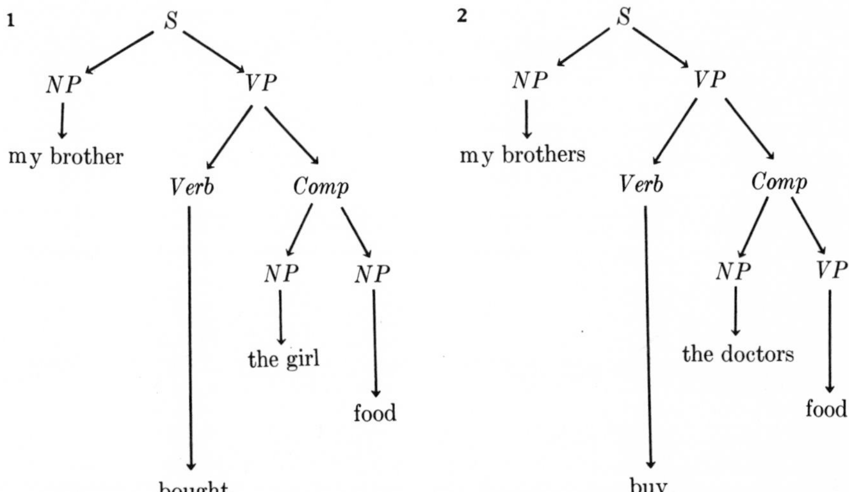

EXERCISE 287

A. Verb Phrase. Because the arrows leading from VP lead eventually to *buy the doctors food* (see parallel explanation in answer C in exercise 284).

B. No. Because no marker has arrows that eventually lead to *My brothers buy* (see answer to exercise 284D).

C. Yes.

EXERCISE 288

A. Yes.

B. ______

C. Yes.

D. ______

E. Yes.

F. ______

G. Yes.

H. ______

I. Yes.

J. ______

K. No.

L. 1, 3, 4, 5.

M. No.

N. 2, 3, 5.

O. Yes.

P. ______

EXERCISE 289

1

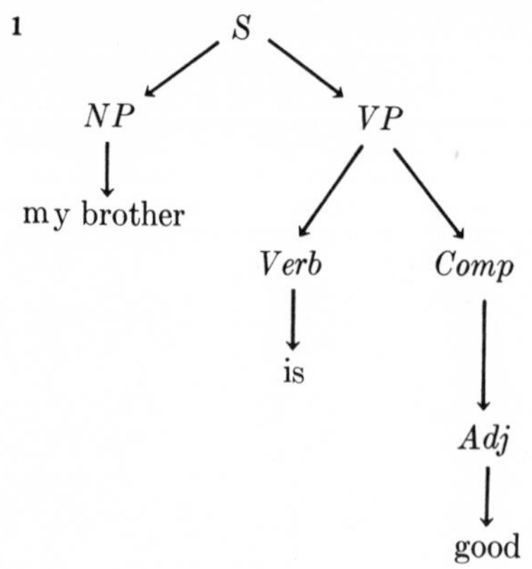

2

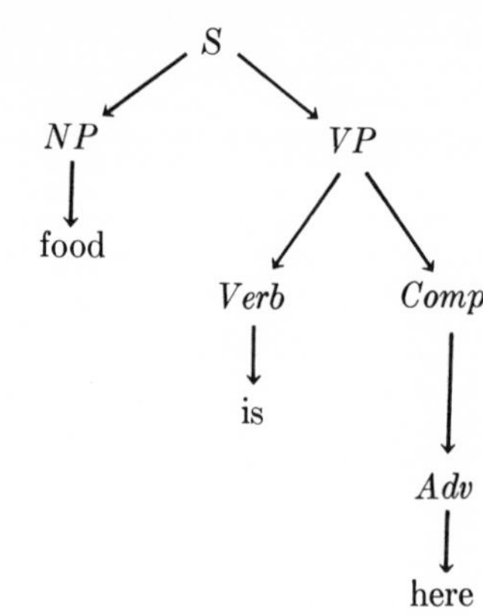

3

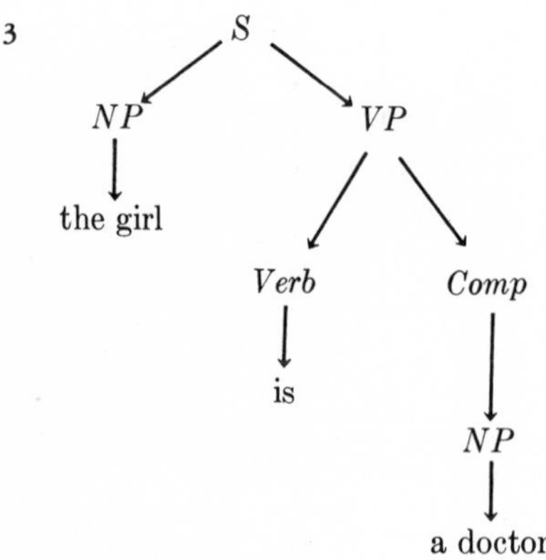

4

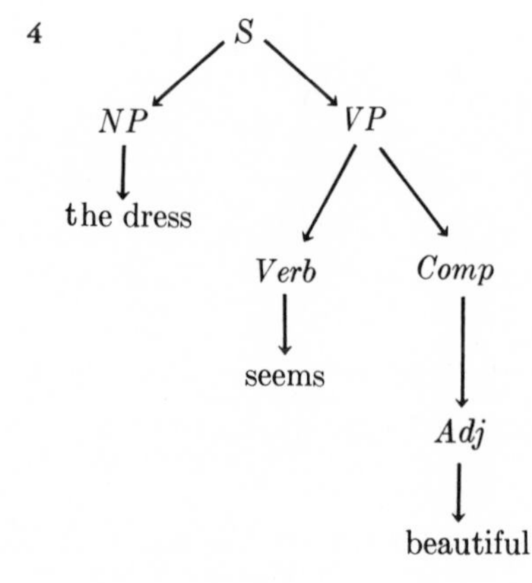

5

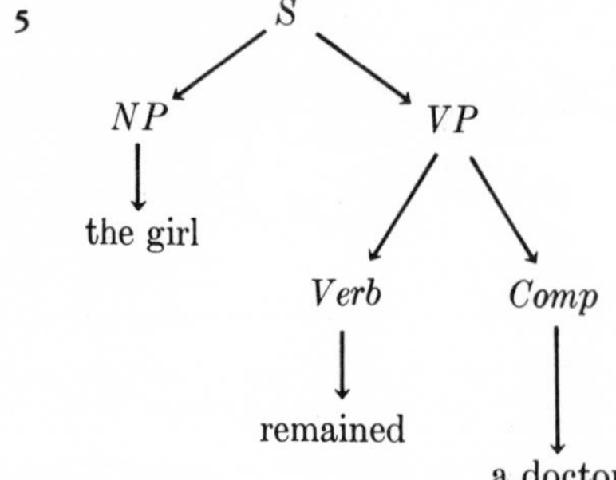

EXERCISE 290

A. Four.

B. S, NP, VP, Comp.

C. Five.

D. D, N, Verb, Adv, Adj.

EXERCISE 291

A.

1

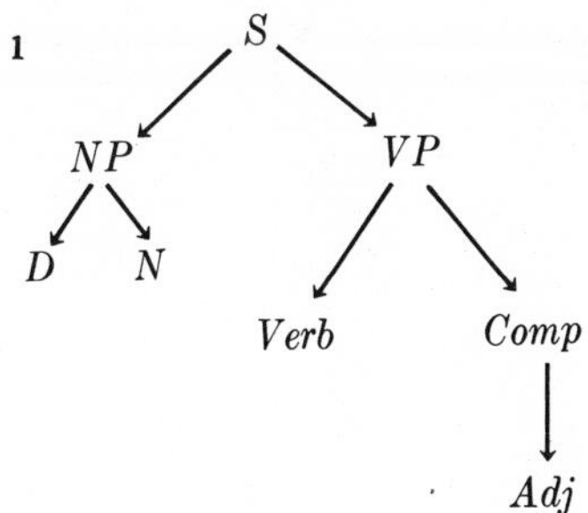

2

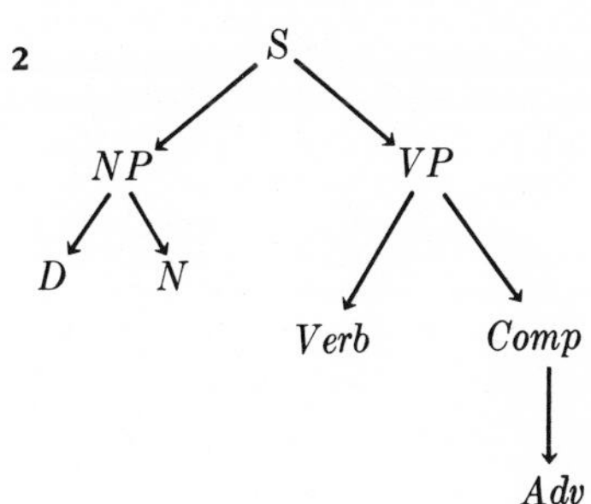

3

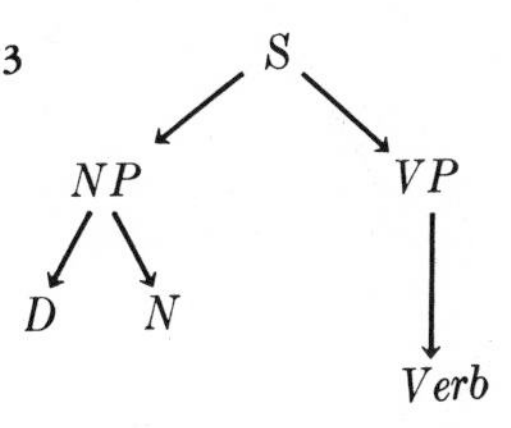

4

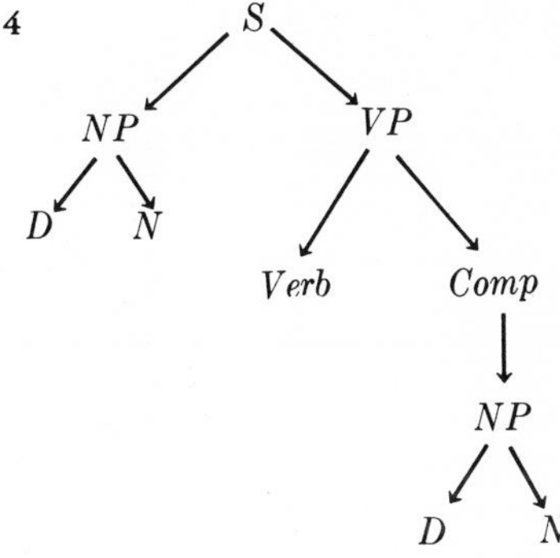

5

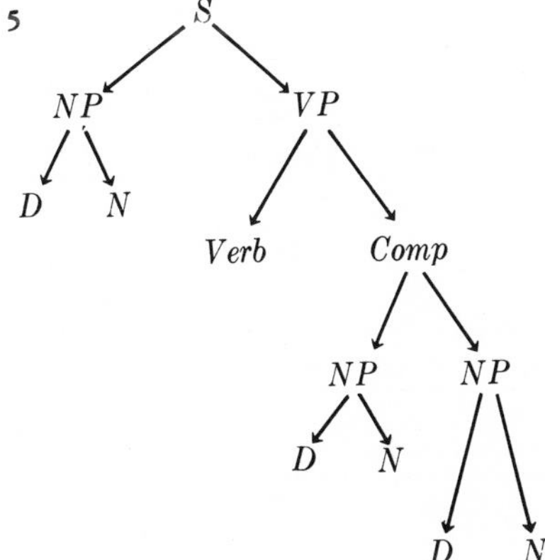

B. No.

EXERCISE 292

A. Because the PS rules do not distinguish between transitive verbs, linking verbs and *be*.

B.

1

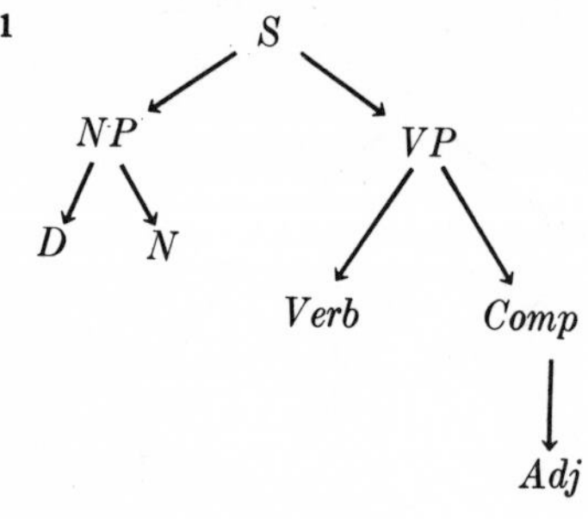

S
NP
VP
D
N
Verb
Comp
Adj

2

S
NP
VP
D
N
Verb
Comp
Adj

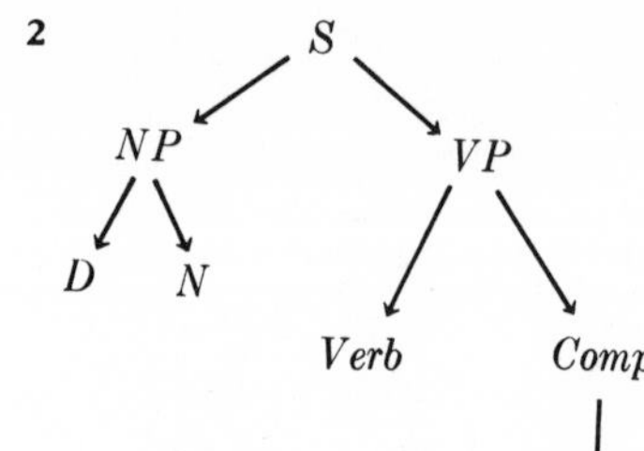

3

S
NP
VP
D
N
Verb
Comp
Adj

4

S
NP
VP
D
N
Verb
Comp
NP
D
N

5

S
NP
VP
D
N
Verb
Comp
NP
D
N

6

S
NP
VP
D
N
Verb
Comp
NP
D
N

7

S
NP
VP
D
N
Verb
Comp
Adv

8

S
NP
VP
D
N
Verb

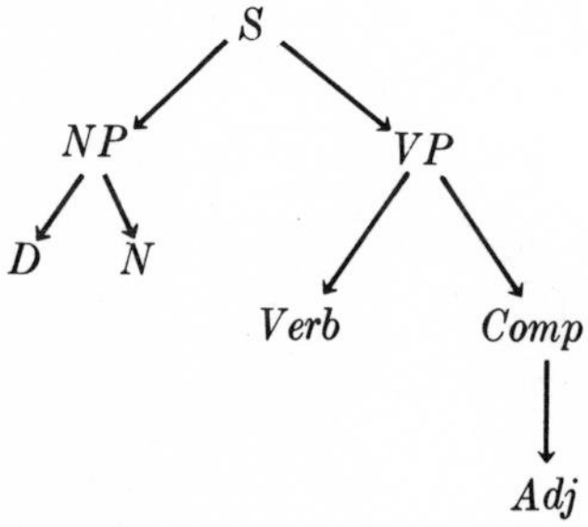

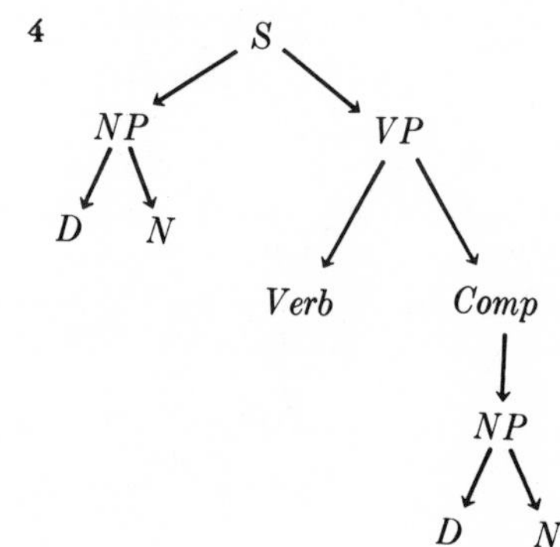

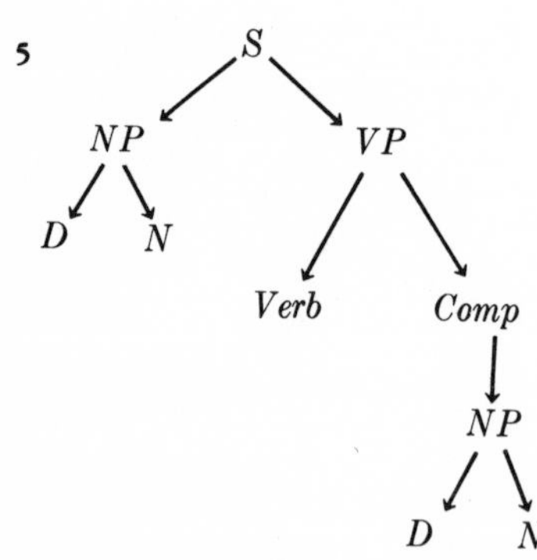

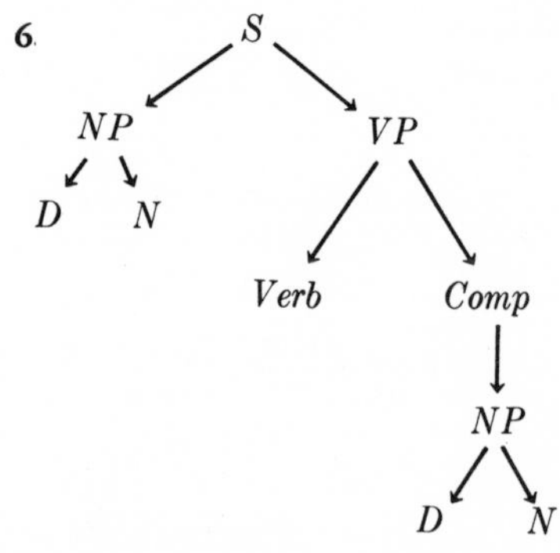

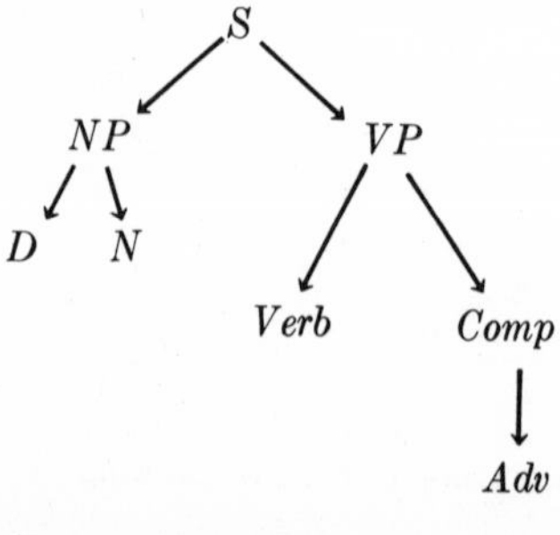

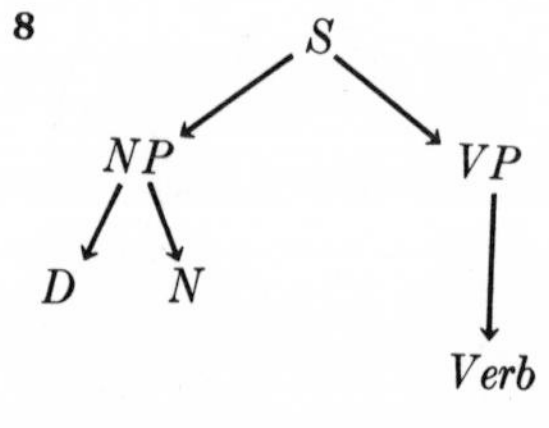

9

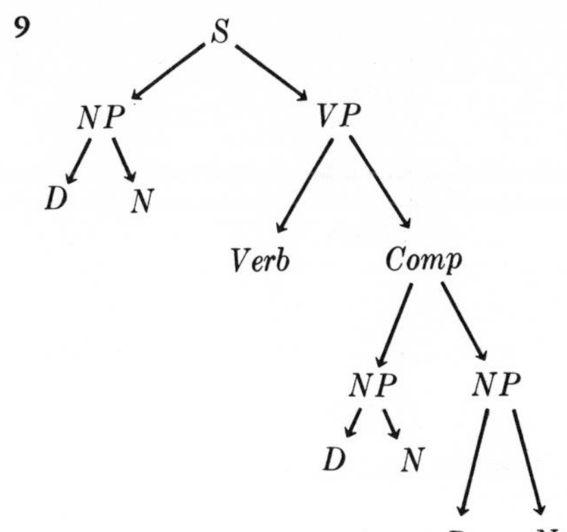

EXERCISE 293

A. It specifies that *banana* is pronounced /bənænə/, that it is classified as a noun and subclassified as a count noun.
B. It specifies that *Charles* is pronounced /čarlz/, that it is classified as a noun, and subclassified as a proper noun.

EXERCISE 294

1. Count
2. Mass
3. Count
4. Count
5. Mass
6. Mass
7. Proper
8. Count
9. Proper
10. Mass

EXERCISE 295

1. which: Nhum
2. which: Nhum
3. which: Nhum
4. who: Hum
5. who: Hum
6. which: Nhum
7. who: Hum
8. who(m): Hum
9. which: Nhum
10. who: Hum

EXERCISE 296

1. $N-\left[\begin{array}{l}\textit{Mass}\\ \textit{Hum}\end{array}\right.$
2. $N-\left[\begin{array}{l}\textit{Count}\\ \textit{Hum}\end{array}\right.$
3. $N-\left[\begin{array}{l}\textit{Count}\\ \textit{Nhum}\end{array}\right.$
4. $N-\left[\begin{array}{l}\textit{Count}\\ \textit{Hum}\end{array}\right.$
5. $N-\left[\begin{array}{l}\textit{Count}\\ \textit{Nhum}\end{array}\right.$
6. $N-\left[\begin{array}{l}\textit{Mass}\\ \textit{Nhum}\end{array}\right.$

7. *N*—{*Count*, *Nhum*}

8. *N*—{*Proper*, *Nhum*}

9. *N*—{*Proper*, *Hum*}

10. *N*—{*Count*, *Hum*}

EXERCISE 297

1. *N*—{*Count*, *Hum*, *Pl*}

2. *N*—{*Mass*, *Nhum*, *Sg*}

3. *N*—{*Count*, *Nhum*, *Sg* or *Pl*}

4. *N*—{*Count*, *Nhum*, *Sg* or *Pl*}

5. *N*—{*Count*, *Nhum*, *Sg* or *Pl*}

6. *N*—{*Mass*, *Nhum*, *Sg*}

7. *N*—{*Proper*, *Hum*, *Sg*}

8. *N*—{*Mass*, *Nhum*, *Sg*}

9. *N*—{*Count*, *Nhum*, *Sg* or *Pl*}

10. *N*—{*Mass*, *Nhum*, *Sg*}

EXERCISE 298

1. *V–vNP*
2. *V–vø*
3. *V–vø*
4. *V–vNP*
5. *V–vNP*
6. *V–vNP*
7. *V–vø*
8. *V–vNP*
9. *V–vø*
10. *V–vNP*

EXERCISE 299

1. *V–vø*
2. *V–vNP/Adj*
3. *V–vNP*
4. *V–vAdj*

5. *V–vNP*
6. *V–vAdj*
7. *V–vNP*
8. *V–vø*
9. *V–vNP*
10. *V–vNP*

EXERCISE 300

1. *V–vNP–vNPNP*
2. *V–vNP–vøNP*
3. *V–vNP–vNPNP*
4. *V–vø*
5. *V–vNP–vNPNP*
6. *V–vNP–vNPNP*
7. *V–vNP–vNPNP*
8. *V–vAdj*
9. *V–vNP–vNPNP*
10. *V–vNP/Adj*

EXERCISE 301

1. $V\text{–}vNP\text{—}\left[\begin{array}{l} v\emptyset NP \\ \hline Tpas \end{array}\right.$
2. $V\text{–}vNP\text{—}\left[\begin{array}{l} vNPNP \\ Tpas \end{array}\right.$
3. *V–vø*
4. $V\text{–}vNP\text{—}\left[\begin{array}{l} v\emptyset NP \\ \hline Tpas \end{array}\right.$
5. $V\text{–}vNP\text{—}\left[\begin{array}{l} v\emptyset NP \\ Tpas \end{array}\right.$
6. *V–vAdj*
7. *V–vNP/Adj*
8. $V\text{–}vNP\text{—}\left[\begin{array}{l} vNPNP \\ Tpas \end{array}\right.$
9. *V–vAdj*
10. *V–vø*

EXERCISE 302

1. $V\text{–}vNP\text{—}\left[\begin{array}{l} v\emptyset NP \\ Tpas \\ Tfac \end{array}\right.$
2. $V\text{–}vNP\text{—}\left[\begin{array}{l} v\emptyset NP \\ Tpas \\ Tfac \end{array}\right.$
3. $V\text{–}vNP\text{—}\left[\begin{array}{l} vNPNP \\ Tpas \\ Tfac \end{array}\right.$
4. $V\text{–}vNP\text{—}\left[\begin{array}{l} v\emptyset NP \\ \hline Tpas \\ \hline Tfac \end{array}\right.$
5. $V\text{–}vNP\text{—}\left[\begin{array}{l} v\emptyset NP \\ Tpas \\ \hline Tfac \end{array}\right.$
6. *V–vø*
7. *V–vAdj*
8. *V–vNP/Adj*

9. $V\text{–}vNP \left[\begin{array}{l} v\text{ø}NP \\ Tpas \\ \overline{Tfac} \end{array}\right.$

10. $V\text{–}vNP \left[\begin{array}{l} v\text{ø}NP \\ Tpas \\ \overline{Tfac} \end{array}\right.$

EXERCISE 303

1. $D \left[\begin{array}{l} \text{Other} \\ Sg \text{ or } Pl \end{array}\right.$

2. $D \left[\begin{array}{l} Art \\ Sg \end{array}\right.$

3. $D \left[\begin{array}{l} \text{Other} \\ Sg \text{ or } Pl \end{array}\right.$

4. $D \left[\begin{array}{l} Dem \\ Sg \end{array}\right.$

5. $D \left[\begin{array}{l} Dem \\ Pl \end{array}\right.$

6. $D \left[\begin{array}{l} \text{Other} \\ Sg \text{ or } Pl \end{array}\right.$

7. $D \left[\begin{array}{l} Art \\ Sg \text{ or } Pl \end{array}\right.$

8. $D \left[\begin{array}{l} \text{Other} \\ Sg \text{ or } Pl \end{array}\right.$

9. $D \left[\begin{array}{l} \text{Other} \\ Sg \text{ or } Pl \end{array}\right.$

10. $D \left[\begin{array}{l} \text{Other} \\ Sg \text{ or } Pl \end{array}\right.$

EXERCISE 304

1. Adj
2. Adv
3. Adj
4. Adv
5. Adv
6. Adj
7. Prep

EXERCISE 305

1. /bənænəz/
2. /mæsɨz/
3. /bʊks/
4. /dɔgz/
5. /padz/

EXERCISE 306

1. /noz/
2. /hɪts/
3. /mɪsɨz/
4. /laiks/
5. /sɪŋz/

EXERCISE 307

1. /smaild/
2. /mæčt/
3. /laikt/
4. /testɨd/
5. /simd/

EXERCISE 308

A. 1.

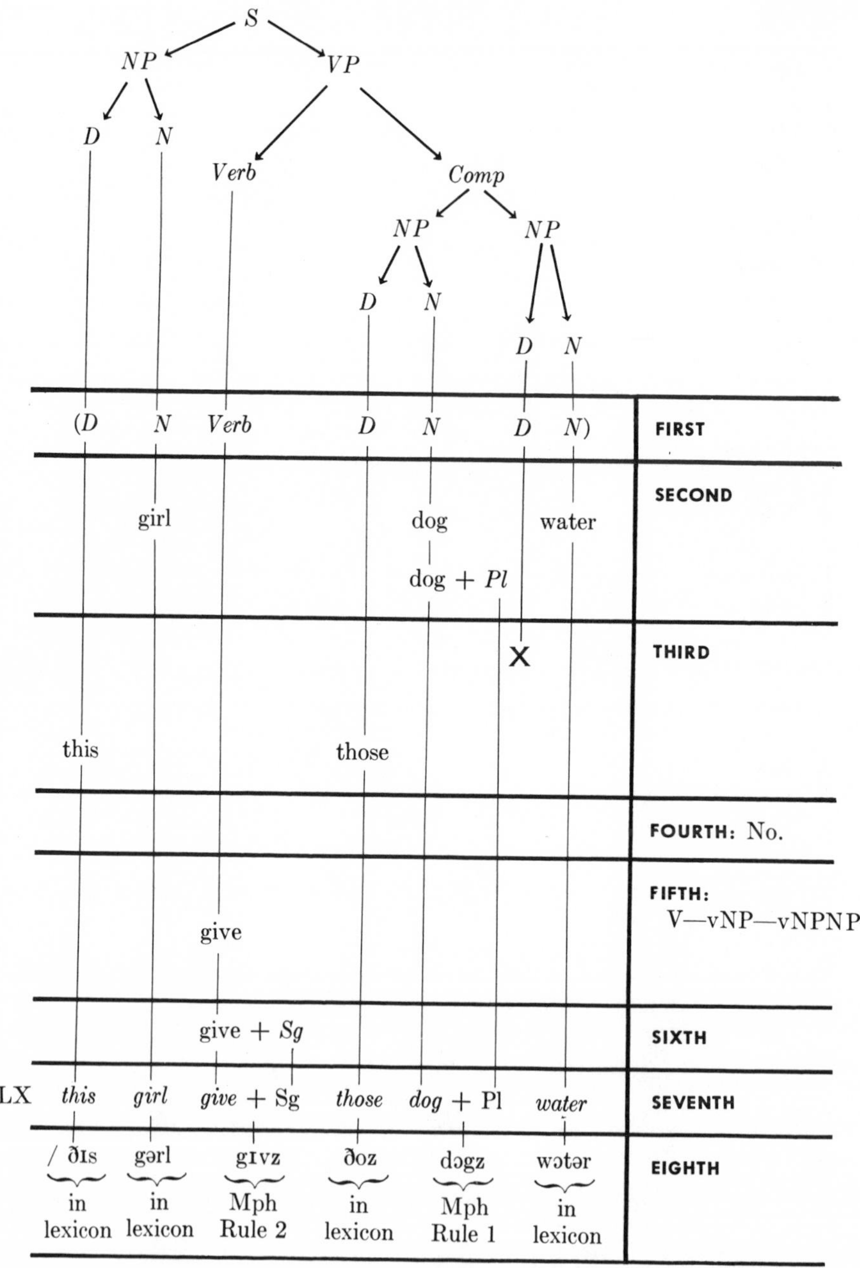

2.

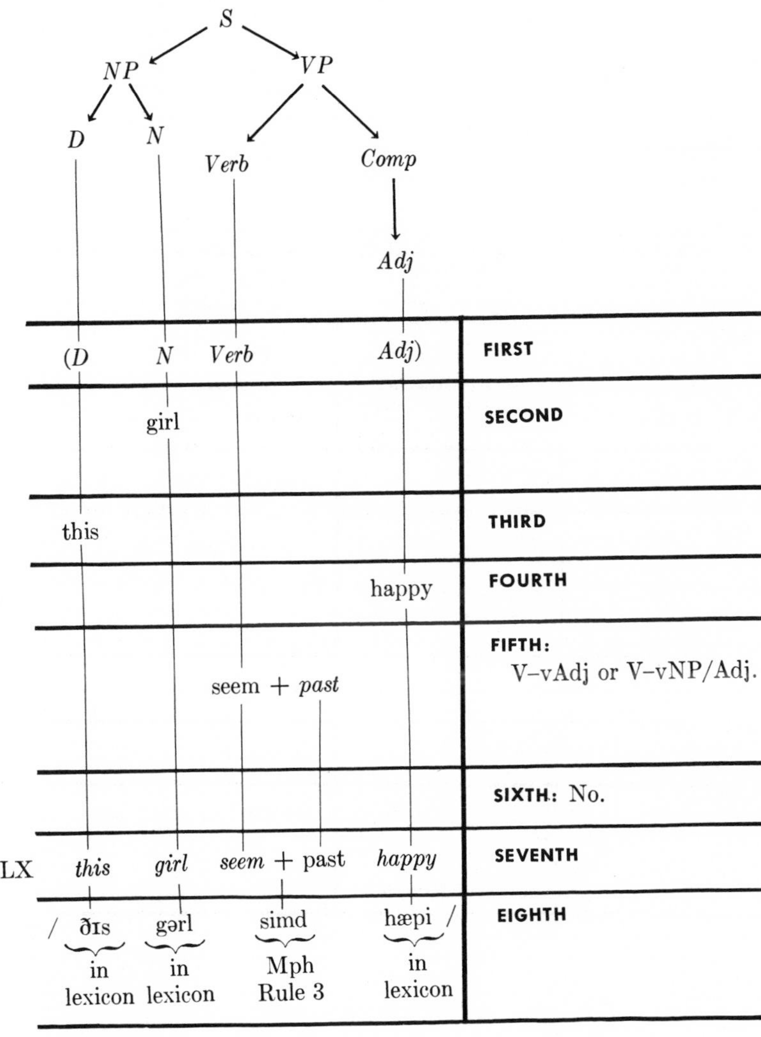
S
NP
VP
D
N
Verb
Comp
Adj
(D N Verb Adj)
FIRST
girl
SECOND
this
THIRD
happy
FOURTH
seem + past
FIFTH:
V–vAdj or V–vNP/Adj.
SIXTH: No.
LX this girl seem + past happy
SEVENTH
/ ðɪs gərl simd hæpi /
EIGHTH
in lexicon
in lexicon
Mph Rule 3
in lexicon

3.

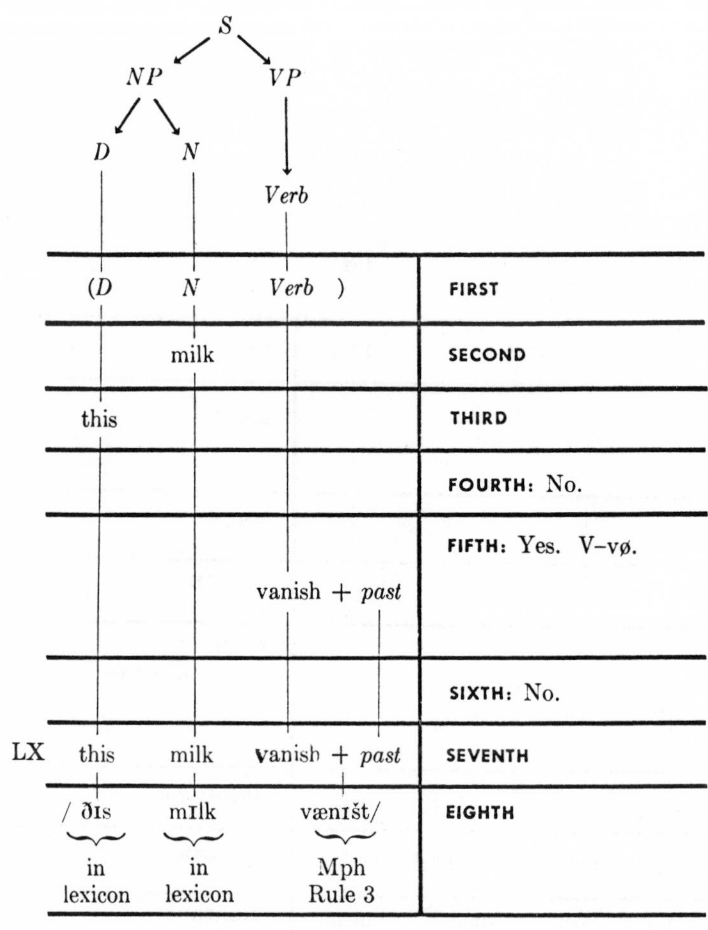
S
NP
VP
D
N
Verb
(D N Verb)
FIRST
milk
SECOND
this
THIRD
FOURTH: No.
FIFTH: Yes. V–vø.
vanish + past
SIXTH: No.
LX this milk vanish + past
SEVENTH
/ ðɪs mɪlk vænɪšt/
EIGHTH
in lexicon
in lexicon
Mph Rule 3

B. 1.

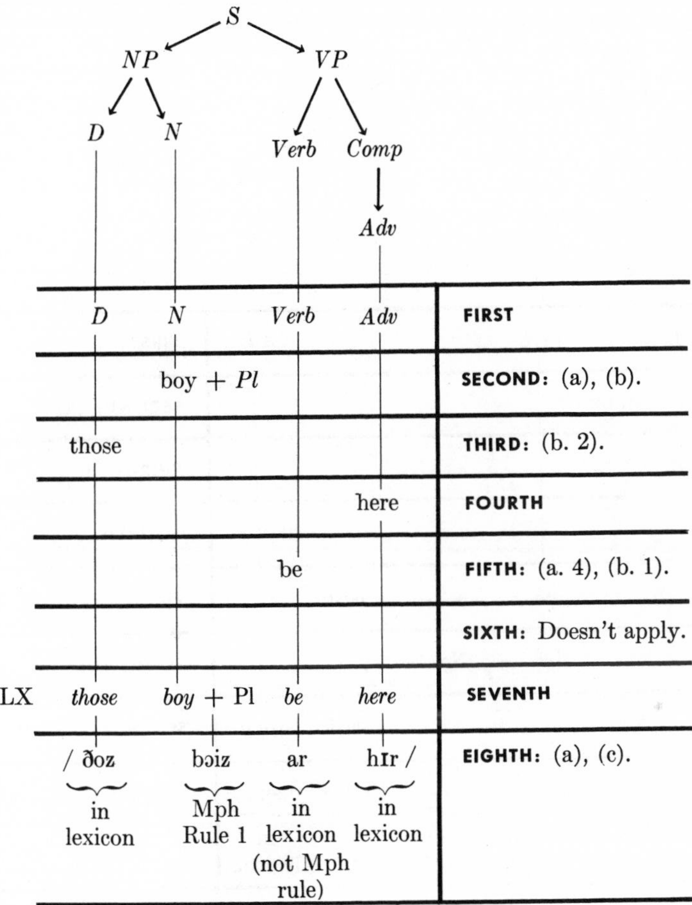
S
NP
VP
D
N
Verb
Comp
Adv
D
N
Verb
Adv
FIRST
boy + Pl
SECOND: (a), (b).
those
THIRD: (b. 2).
here
FOURTH
be
FIFTH: (a. 4), (b. 1).
SIXTH: Doesn't apply.
LX
those
boy + Pl
be
here
SEVENTH
/ ðoz
bɔiz
ar
hɪr /
EIGHTH: (a), (c).
in lexicon
Mph Rule 1
in lexicon (not Mph rule)
in lexicon

2.

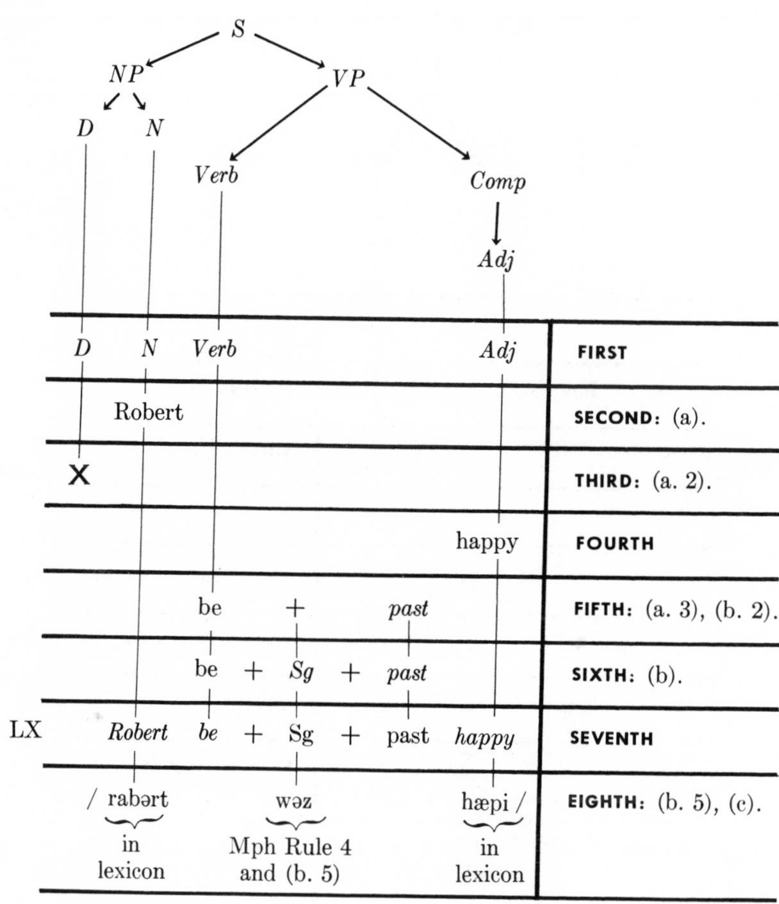
S
NP
VP
D
N
Verb
Comp
Adj
D N Verb Adj
FIRST
Robert
SECOND: (a).
X
THIRD: (a. 2).
happy
FOURTH
be + past
FIFTH: (a. 3), (b. 2).
be + Sg + past
SIXTH: (b).
LX Robert be + Sg + past happy
SEVENTH
/ rabərt wəz hæpi /
in lexicon
Mph Rule 4 and (b. 5)
in lexicon
EIGHTH: (b. 5), (c).

3.

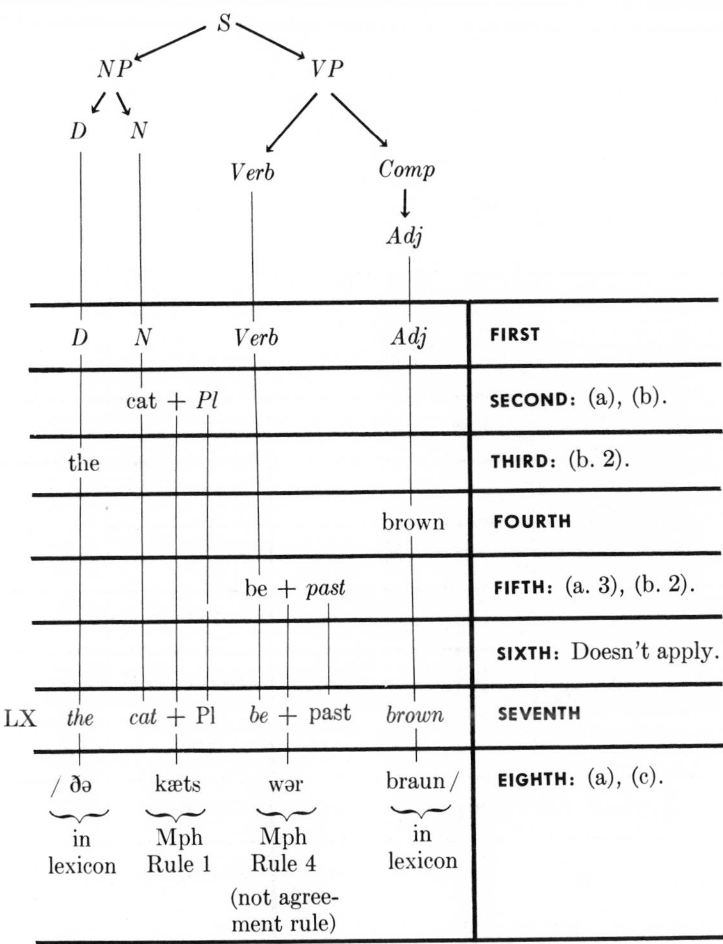
S
NP
VP
D
N
Verb
Comp
Adj
D N Verb Adj
FIRST
cat + Pl
SECOND: (a), (b).
the
THIRD: (b. 2).
brown
FOURTH
be + past
FIFTH: (a. 3), (b. 2).
SIXTH: Doesn't apply.
LX the cat + Pl be + past brown
SEVENTH
/ ðə kæts wər braun /
EIGHTH: (a), (c).
in lexicon
Mph Rule 1
Mph Rule 4 (not agreement rule)
in lexicon

4.

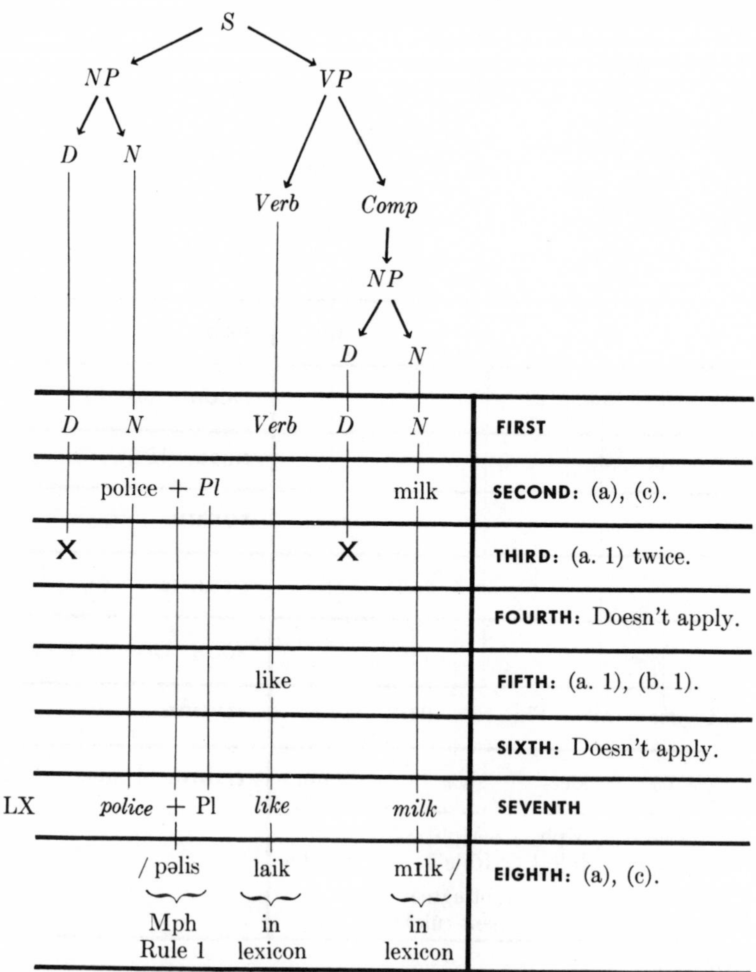
S
NP
VP
D
N
Verb
Comp
NP
D
N
D N Verb D N
FIRST
police + Pl
milk
SECOND: (a), (c).
X
X
THIRD: (a. 1) twice.
FOURTH: Doesn't apply.
like
FIFTH: (a. 1), (b. 1).
SIXTH: Doesn't apply.
LX
police + Pl
like
milk
SEVENTH
/ pəlis
laik
mɪlk /
EIGHTH: (a), (c).
Mph Rule 1
in lexicon
in lexicon

EXERCISE 309

1.

$$\text{LX}\left\{\begin{array}{c} D\text{—}\left[\begin{array}{l} \textit{Art} \\ \textit{Sg} \text{ or } \textit{Pl} \end{array}\right. \\ /\text{ðə}/ \end{array}\right\} + \left\{\begin{array}{c} N\text{—}\left[\begin{array}{l} \textit{Count} \\ \textit{Nhum} \\ \textit{Sg} \text{ or } \textit{Pl} \end{array}\right. \\ /\text{kæt}/ \end{array}\right\} + \left\{\begin{array}{c} V\text{–}vNP\text{—}\left[\begin{array}{l} v\text{ø}NP \\ \textit{Tpas} \\ \textit{Tfac} \end{array}\right. \\ /\text{no}/ \end{array}\right\} + \quad \textit{Sg}$$

$$+\left\{\begin{array}{c} D\text{—}\left[\begin{array}{l} \textit{Art} \\ \textit{Sg} \text{ or } \textit{Pl} \end{array}\right. \\ /\text{ðə}/ \end{array}\right\} + \left\{\begin{array}{c} N\text{—}\left[\begin{array}{l} \textit{Count} \\ \textit{Nhum} \\ \textit{Sg} \text{ or } \textit{Pl} \end{array}\right. \\ /\text{dɔg}/ \end{array}\right\}$$

2.

$$\text{LX}\left\{\begin{array}{c} D\text{—}\left[\begin{array}{l} \textit{Dem} \\ \textit{Pl} \end{array}\right. \\ /\text{ðoz}/ \end{array}\right\} + \left\{\begin{array}{c} N\text{—}\left[\begin{array}{l} \textit{Count} \\ \textit{Hum} \\ \textit{Sg} \text{ or } \textit{Pl} \end{array}\right. \\ /\text{gərl}/ \end{array}\right\} + \textit{Pl} + \left\{\begin{array}{c} V\text{–}v\text{ø} \\ /\text{læf}/ \end{array}\right\} + \quad \textit{past}$$

3.

$$\text{LX}\left\{\begin{array}{c} D\text{—}\left[\begin{array}{l} \textit{Art} \\ \textit{Sg} \text{ or } \textit{Pl} \end{array}\right. \\ /\text{ðə}/ \end{array}\right\} + \left\{\begin{array}{c} N\text{—}\left[\begin{array}{l} \textit{Mass} \\ \textit{Nhum} \\ \textit{Sg} \end{array}\right. \\ /\text{mɪlk}/ \end{array}\right\} + \left\{\begin{array}{c} V\text{–}vAdj \\ /\text{sim}/ \end{array}\right\} + \textit{past} + \left\{\begin{array}{c} \textit{Adj} \\ /\text{gud}/ \end{array}\right\}$$

EXERCISE 310

A. 1. a
2. a
3. a, b
4. a, b
5. b
6. b
7. d
8. a, c, d
9. a, b, c
10. b, c
11. e
12. b, e
13. b, d
14. b, d

B. 1. 1
2. 13

EXERCISE 311

1. a
2. a, b
3. b, c, d
4. a, b, c, d
5. b, d

EXERCISE 312

NP_1 + Verb-Tpas + past + NP_2^{Tpas} ⟶ NP_2 + *be* + past +
LX *the girl* + *hit* + past + *the boy*^{Tpas} LX *the boy* + *be* + past +

Verb-Tpas + pp (+ *by* + NP_1)
hit + pp (+ *by* + *the girl*)

Applying the Mph rule, we get:

LX *the boy* + *be* + past + /hɪt/ + *by* + *the girl*
or
LX *the boy* + *be* + past + /hɪt/

EXERCISE 313

1. LX *the child seem* + past *happy*
LX *the child tell* + past *her dog a tale*

2. LX *the girl run* + past
LX *the girl smile* + past

EXERCISE 314

A. 1. d
2. d
3. a
4. b
5. c
6. d
7. d
8. a
9. b
10. c

B. 1. John, who was afraid, watched the lion.
2. John knew Jack failed the test.
or John knew that Jack failed the test.

EXERCISE 315

1.

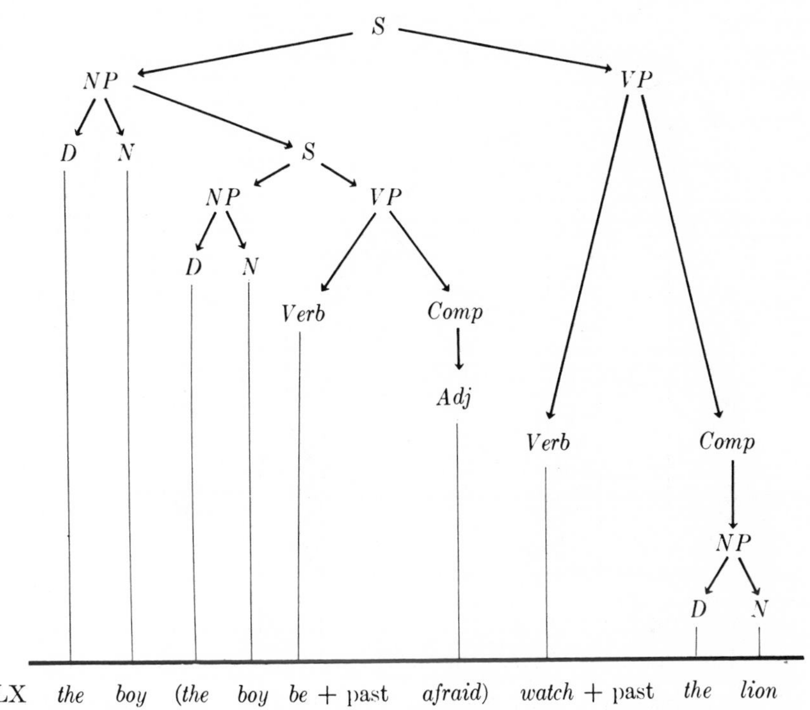

2.

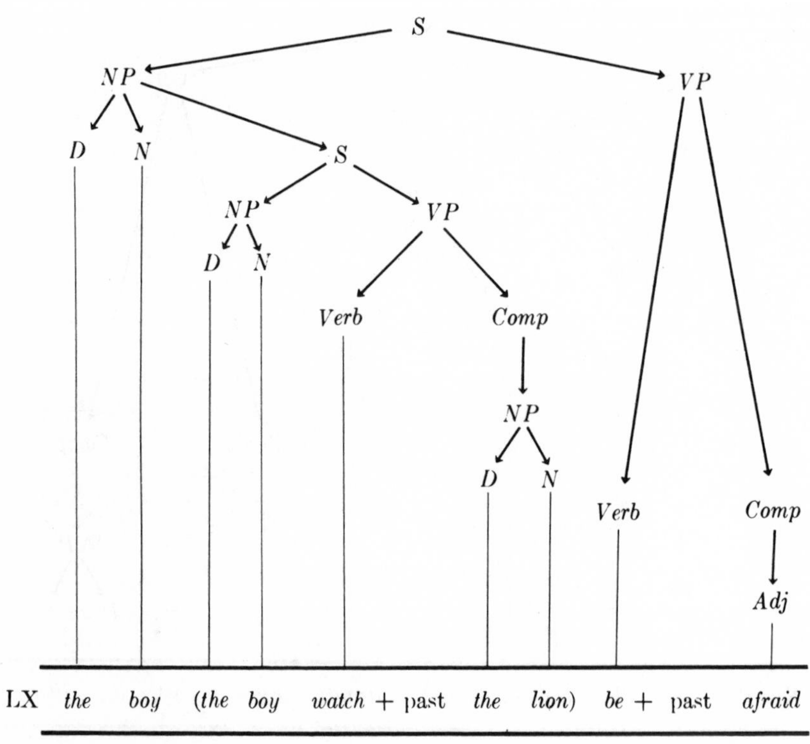
S
NP
VP
D
N
S
NP
VP
D
N
Verb
Comp
NP
D
N
Verb
Comp
Adj
LX the boy (the boy watch + past the lion) be + past afraid

3.

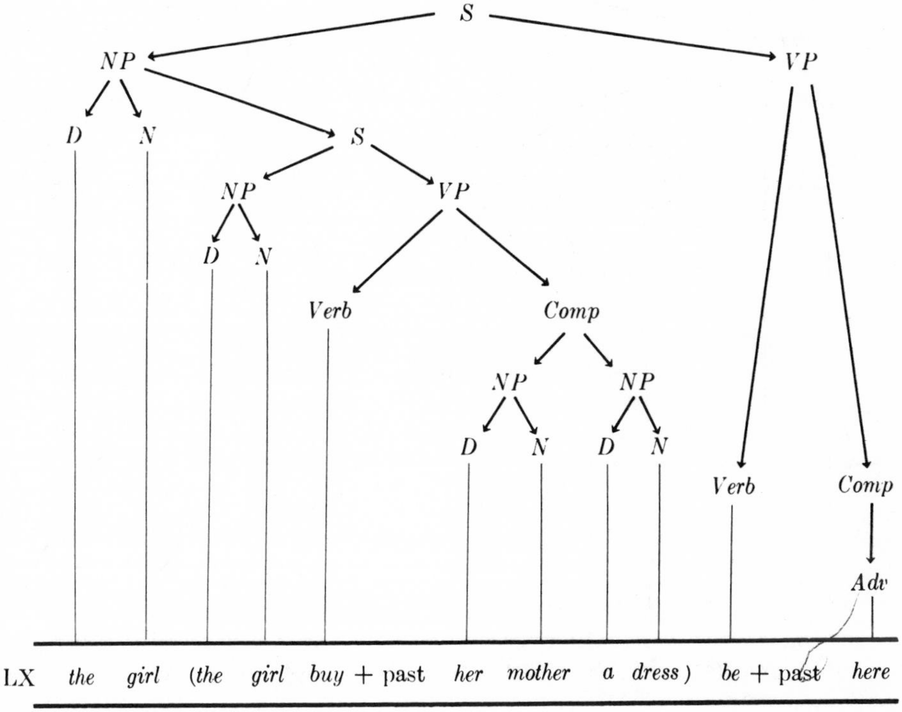

```
S
├── NP
│   ├── D ─── the
│   ├── N ─── girl
│   └── S
│       ├── NP
│       │   ├── D ─── (the
│       │   └── N ─── girl
│       └── VP
│           ├── Verb ─── buy + past
│           └── Comp
│               ├── NP
│               │   ├── D ─── her
│               │   └── N ─── mother
│               └── NP
│                   ├── D ─── a
│                   └── N ─── dress)
└── VP
    ├── Verb ─── be + past
    └── Comp
        └── Adv ─── here
```

LX *the girl (the girl buy* + past *her mother a dress)* *be* + past *here*

4.

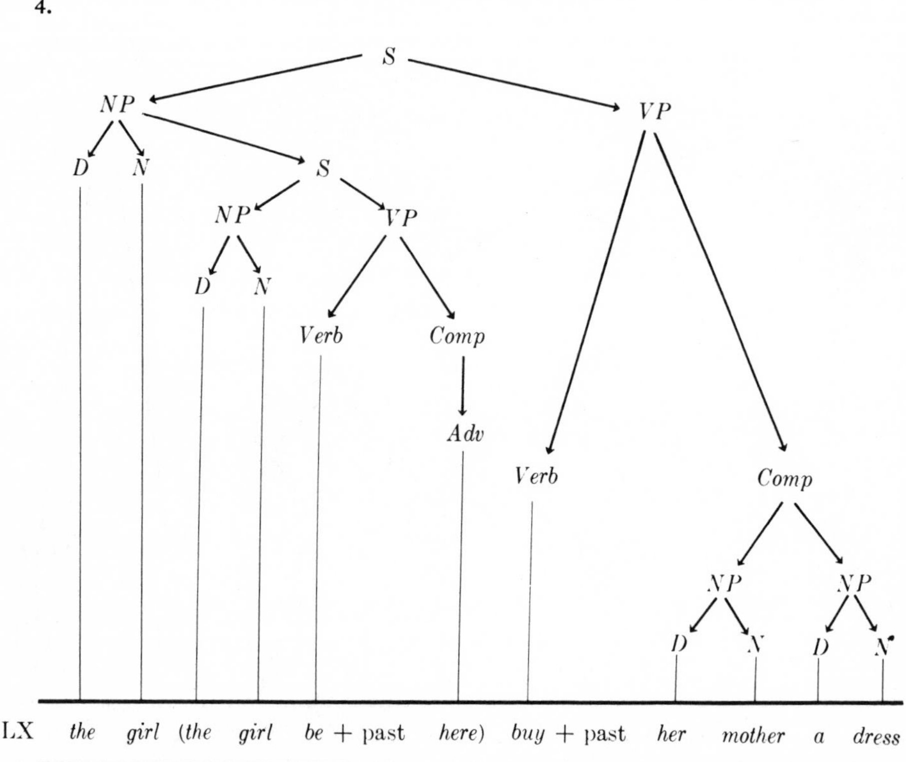
S
NP
VP
D
N
S
NP
VP
D
N
Verb
Comp
Adv
Verb
Comp
NP
NP
D
N
D
N
LX the girl (the girl be + past here) buy + past her mother a dress

EXERCISE 316

1. The boy who was afraid watched the lion (restrictive). *or* The boy, who was afraid, watched the lion (nonrestrictive).
2. The boy who watched the lion was afraid (restrictive). *or* The boy, who watched the lion, was afraid (nonrestrictive).
3. The girl who bought her mother a dress was here (restrictive). *or* The girl, who bought her mother a dress, was here (nonrestrictive).
4. The girl who was here bought her mother a dress (restrictive). *or* The girl, who was here, bought her mother a dress (nonrestrictive).

EXERCISE 317

X + D + N + (D + N +
1. LX {nothing} + *the* + *painter* + (*the* + *painter* +
Y)^{Tres} + Z
draw + past *a picture*)^{Tres} + *be* + past *happy*

X + D + N + wh$_{res}$ + D + N +
LX {nothing} + *the* + *painter* + wh$_{res}$ + *the* + *painter* +
Y + Z
draw + past *a picture* + *be* + past *happy*

X + D + N + (D + N + Y)^{Tres}
2. LX {nothing} + *the* + *cow* + (*the* + *cow* + *kick* + past *the milkmaid*)^{Tres}
\+ Z
\+ *moo* + past

X + D + N + wh$_{res}$ + D + N + Y
LX {nothing} + *the* + *cow* + wh$_{res}$ + *the* + *cow* + *kick* + past *the milkmaid*
\+ Z
\+ *moo* + past

EXERCISE 318

1. Same as number 2 of exercise 317. Applying the Mph rule for *wh*$_{res}$ + *the cow* we get:

   LX *the cow* /wɪč/ *kick* + past *the milkmaid moo* + past

2. X + D + N + (D + N + Y)^{Tres} +
   LX {nothing} + *the* + *girl* + (*the* + *girl* + *be* + past *happy*)^{Tres} +

Z
know + past *the boy*

X + D + N + wh$_{res}$ + D + N + Y
LX {nothing} + *the* + *girl* + wh$_{res}$ + *the* + *girl* + *be* + past *happy* +
Z
know + past *the boy*

Applying the Mph rule for wh$_{res}$ + *the girl*, we get:

LX *the girl* /hu/ *be* + past *happy know* + past *the boy*
or LX *the girl* /ðæt/ *be* + past *happy know* + past *the boy*

EXERCISE 319

1. X + D_1 + N_1 (wh_{res} + D + N + *be* + Y + adj)
LX {nothing} + *the* + *rock* (wh_{res} + *the* + *rock* + *be* + past + *large*)

+ Z
+ *fall* + past

X + D_1 + Adj + N_1 + Z
LX {nothing} + *the* + *large* + *rock* + *fall* + past

2. X + D_1 + N_1 (wh_{res} + D + N + *be* + Y + Adj) +
LX {nothing} + *the* + *pipe* (wh_{res} + *the* + *pipe* + *be* + past + *old*) +

Z
be + past *brown*

X + D_1 + Adj + N_1 + Z
LX {nothing} + *the* + *old* + *pipe* + *be* + past *brown*

EXERCISE 320

1.

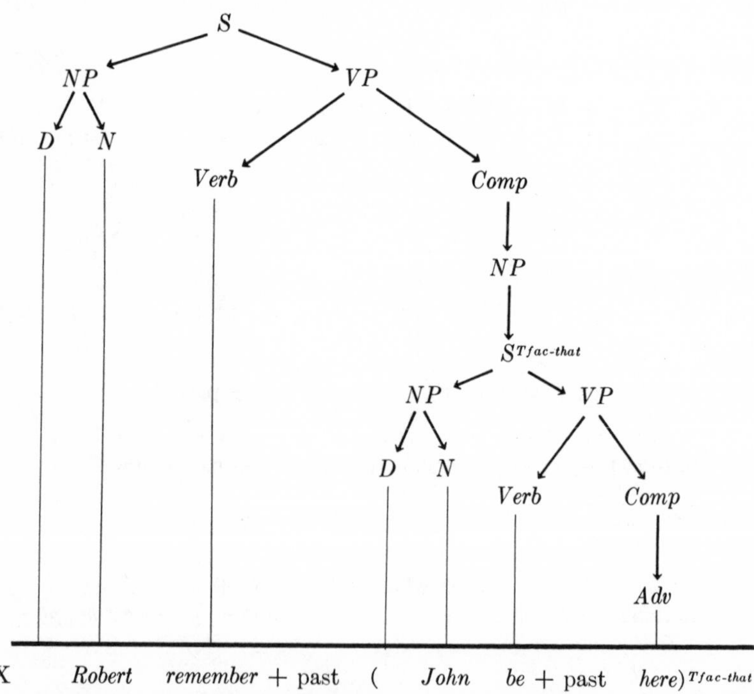

2.

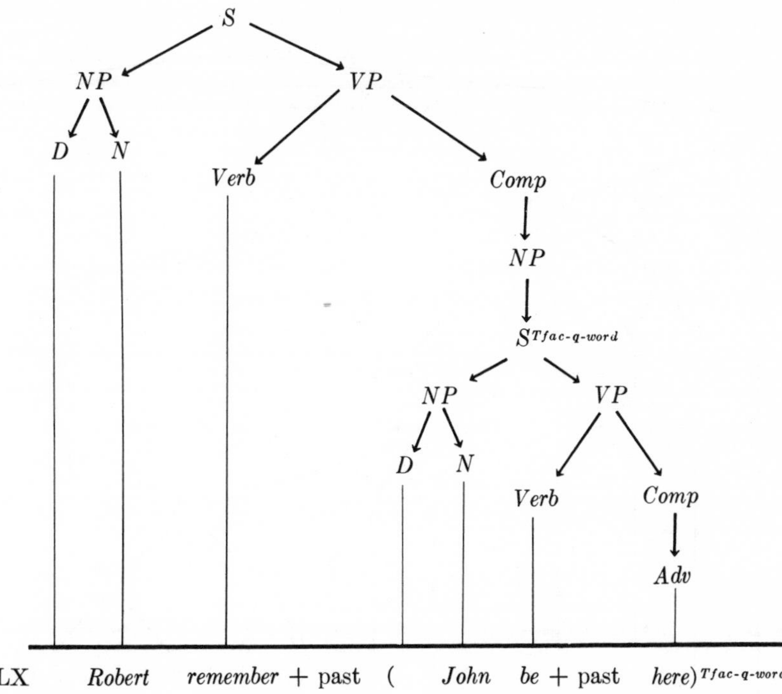

EXERCISE 321

1. LX *Robert remember* + past (*John be* + past *here*)$^{Tfac\text{-}that}$ ⟶
   LX *Robert remember* + past (/ðæt/) + *John be* + past *here*

2. LX *Robert remember* + past (*John be* + past *here*)$^{Tfac\text{-}q\text{-}word}$ ⟶
   LX *Robert remember* + past + wh + *here John be* + past

   Applying the Mph rule to *wh* + *here,* we get:

   LX *Robert remember* + past /wɛr/ *John be* + past

Notice that in the answers above we did not write the transformation formulas above the lexical strings; we just carried out the transformations on the lexical strings by following the formulas.

EXERCISE 322

A.

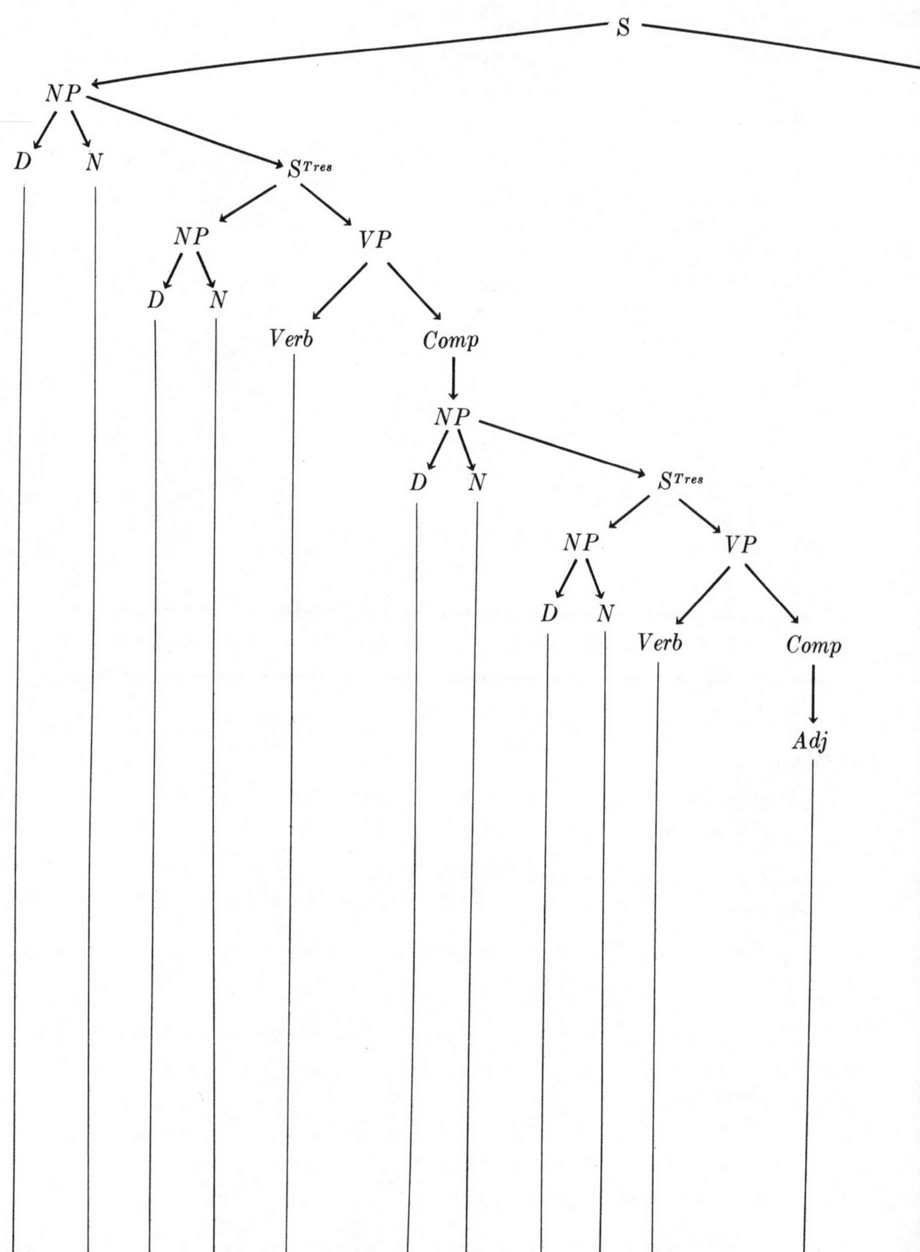
S
NP
D
N
S^Tres
NP
VP
D
N
Verb
Comp
NP
D
N
S^Tres
NP
VP
D
N
Verb
Comp
Adj
The painter [the painter draw + past the picture (the picture be + past beautiful)^Tres]^Tre

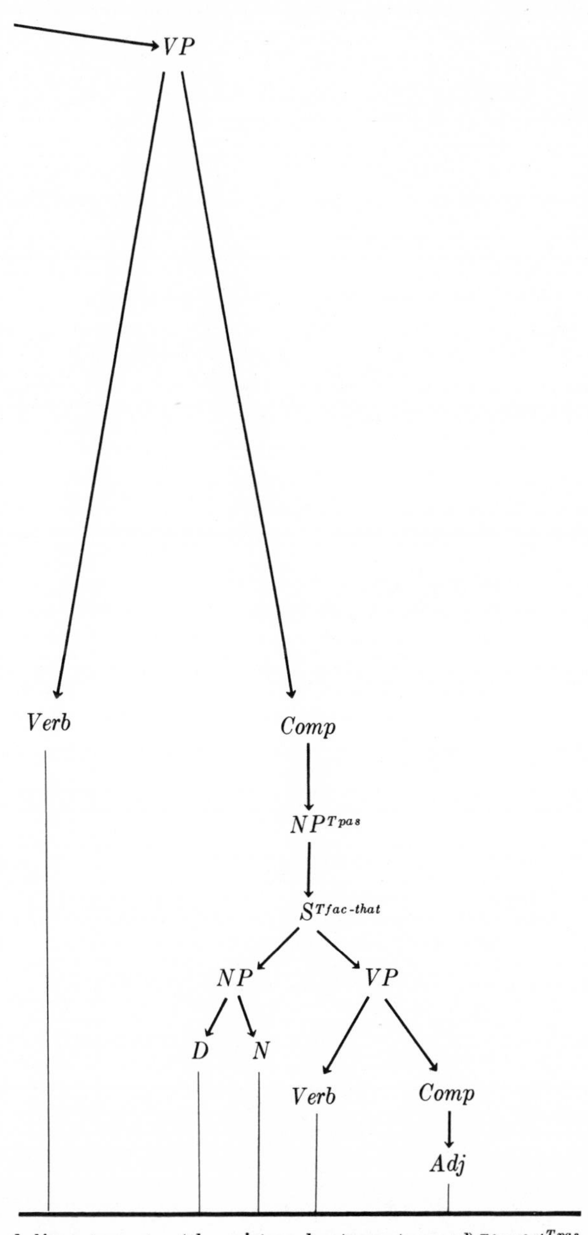

VP
Verb
Comp
NP^Tpas
S^Tfac-that
NP
VP
D
N
Verb
Comp
Adj
believe + past (the picture be + past good)^Tfac-that^Tpas

B. That the picture was good was believed by the painter who drew the picture which was beautiful.

EXERCISE 323

1.

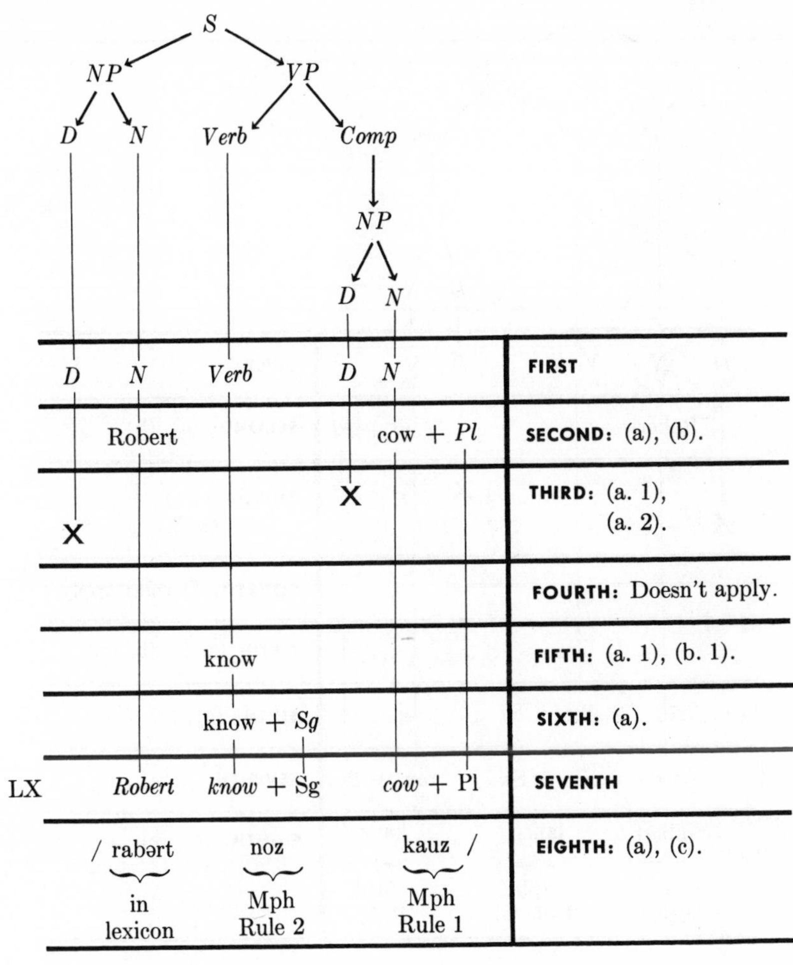
S
NP
VP
D
N
Verb
Comp
NP
D
N
D N Verb D N
FIRST
Robert
cow + Pl
SECOND: (a), (b).
X
X
THIRD: (a. 1),
(a. 2).
FOURTH: Doesn't apply.
know
FIFTH: (a. 1), (b. 1).
know + Sg
SIXTH: (a).
LX
Robert know + Sg cow + Pl
SEVENTH
/ rabərt noz kauz /
in lexicon
Mph Rule 2
Mph Rule 1
EIGHTH: (a), (c).

2.

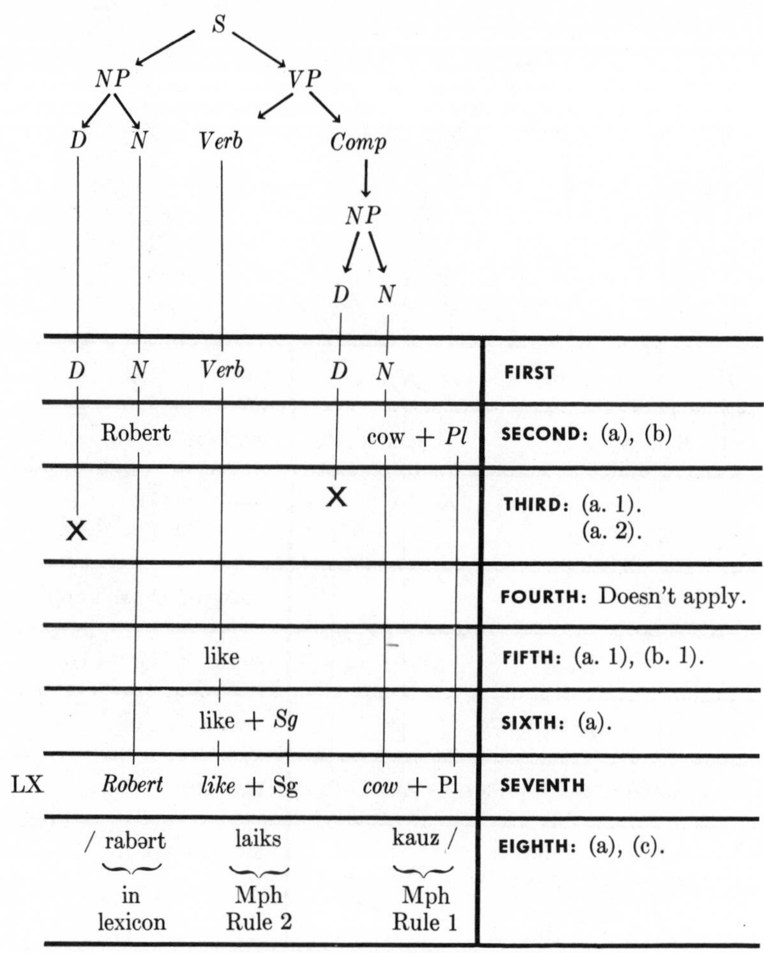
S
NP
VP
D
N
Verb
Comp
NP
D
N
D N Verb D N
FIRST
Robert
cow + Pl
SECOND: (a), (b)
X
X
THIRD: (a. 1).
(a. 2).
FOURTH: Doesn't apply.
like
FIFTH: (a. 1), (b. 1).
like + Sg
SIXTH: (a).
LX
Robert like + Sg cow + Pl
SEVENTH
/ rabərt laiks kauz /
in lexicon
Mph Rule 2
Mph Rule 1
EIGHTH: (a), (c).

3.

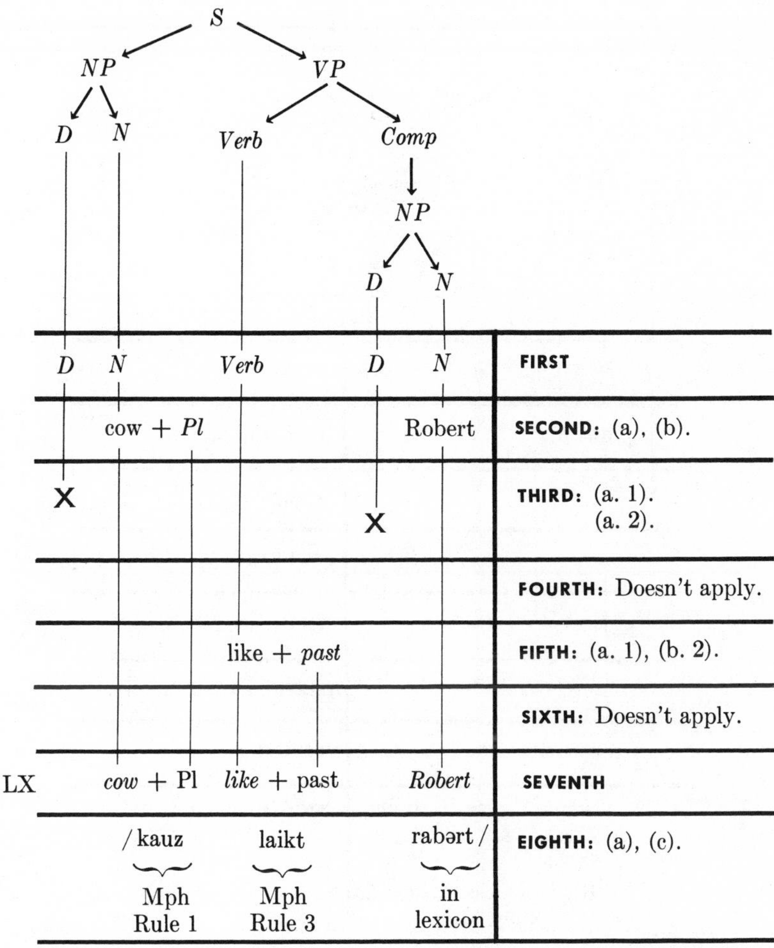
S
NP
VP
D
N
Verb
Comp
NP
D
N
D N Verb D N
FIRST
cow + Pl
Robert
SECOND: (a), (b).
X
X
THIRD: (a. 1).
(a. 2).
FOURTH: Doesn't apply.
like + past
FIFTH: (a. 1), (b. 2).
SIXTH: Doesn't apply.
LX
cow + Pl like + past Robert
SEVENTH
/kauz laikt rabərt/
Mph Rule 1
Mph Rule 3
in lexicon
EIGHTH: (a), (c).

4.

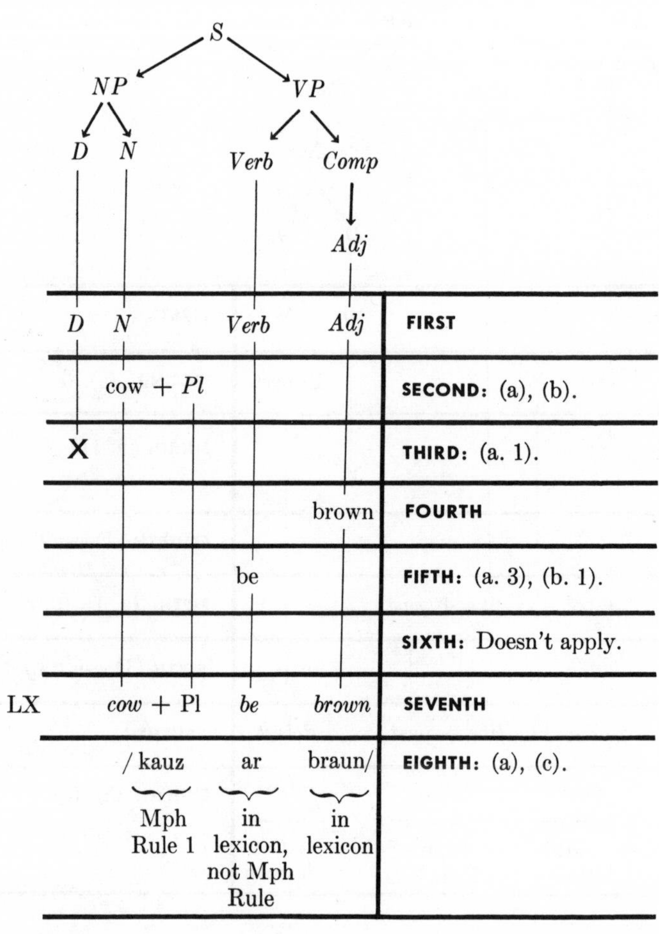
S
NP
VP
D
N
Verb
Comp
Adj
D N Verb Adj
FIRST
cow + Pl
SECOND: (a), (b).
X
THIRD: (a. 1).
brown
FOURTH
be
FIFTH: (a. 3), (b. 1).
SIXTH: Doesn't apply.
LX cow + Pl be brown
SEVENTH
/ kauz ar braun/
EIGHTH: (a), (c).
Mph Rule 1
in lexicon, not Mph Rule
in lexicon

5.

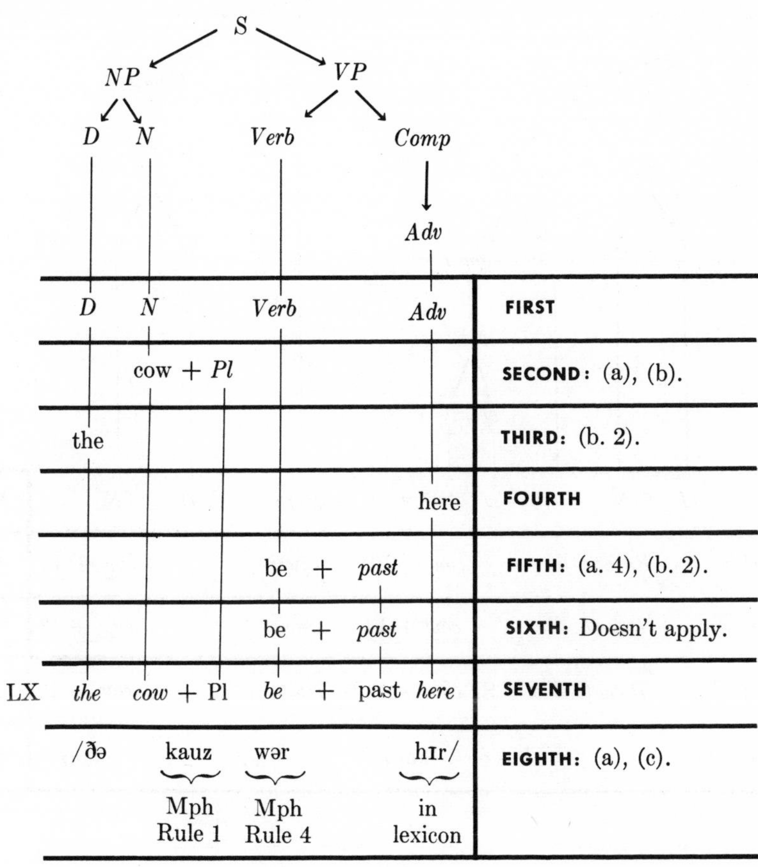
S
NP
VP
D
N
Verb
Comp
Adv
D N Verb Adv
FIRST
cow + Pl
SECOND: (a), (b).
the
THIRD: (b. 2).
here
FOURTH
be + past
FIFTH: (a. 4), (b. 2).
be + past
SIXTH: Doesn't apply.
LX the cow + Pl be + past here
SEVENTH
/ðə kauz wər hɪr/
EIGHTH: (a), (c).
Mph Rule 1
Mph Rule 4
in lexicon

EXERCISE 324

1.

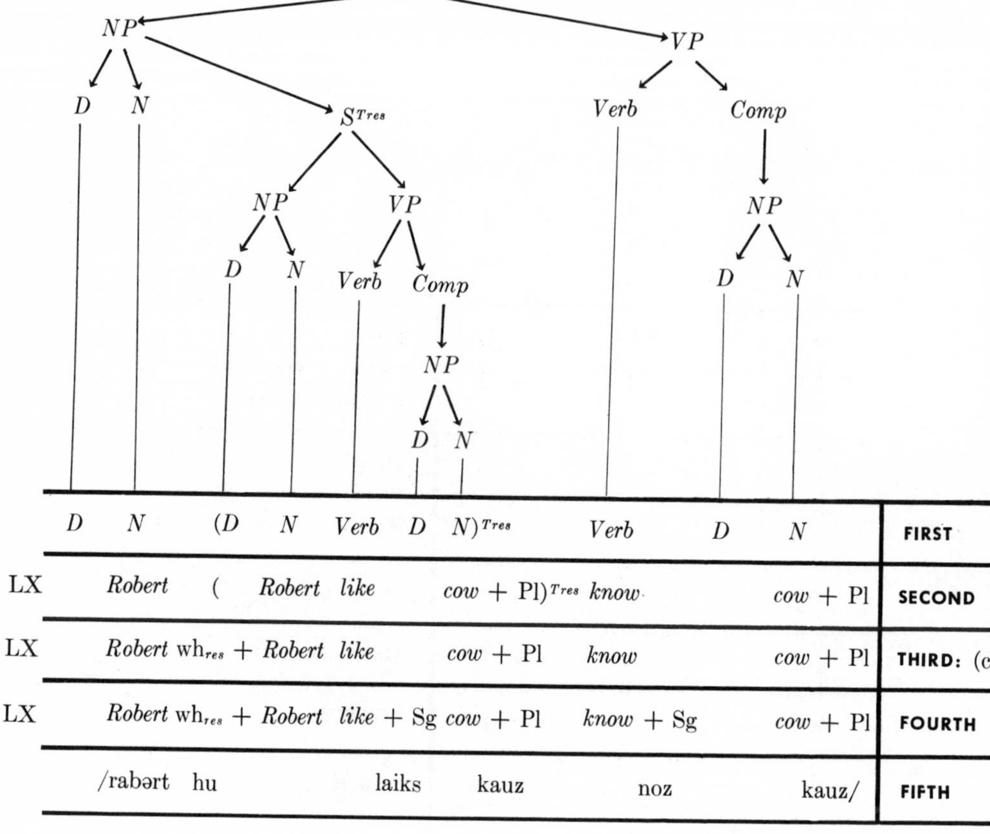
S
NP
VP
D N
S^Tres
Verb
Comp
NP
VP
NP
D N
Verb Comp
D N
NP
D N
D N (D N Verb D N)^Tres Verb D N FIRST
LX Robert (Robert like cow + Pl)^Tres know cow + Pl SECOND
LX Robert wh_res + Robert like cow + Pl know cow + Pl THIRD: (c)
LX Robert wh_res + Robert like + Sg cow + Pl know + Sg cow + Pl FOURTH
/rabərt hu laiks kauz noz kauz/ FIFTH

2.

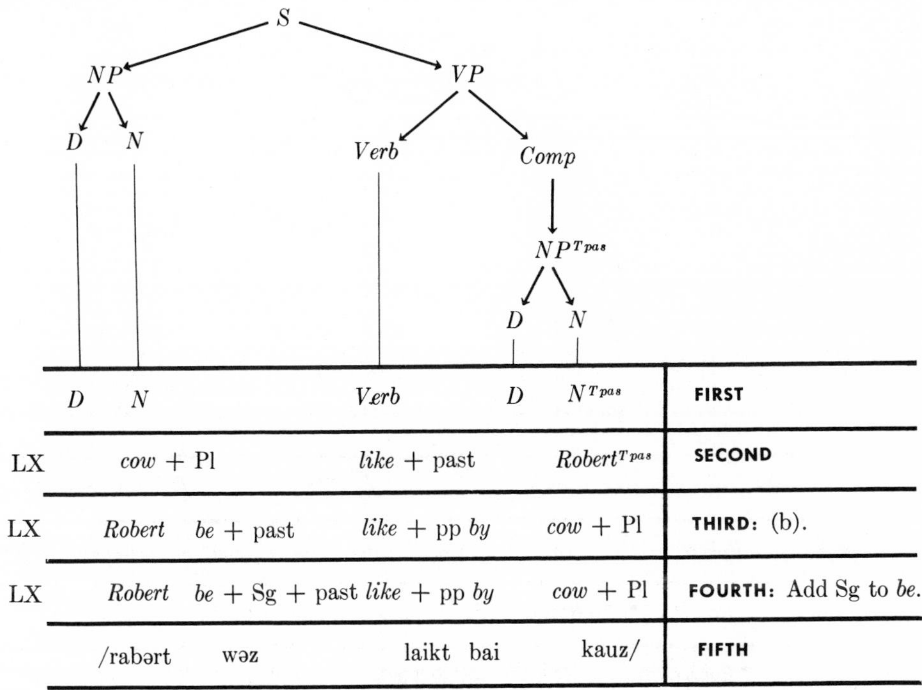
S
NP
VP
D
N
Verb
Comp
NP^Tpas
D
N
D N Verb D N^Tpas
FIRST
LX cow + Pl like + past Robert^Tpas
SECOND
LX Robert be + past like + pp by cow + Pl
THIRD: (b).
LX Robert be + Sg + past like + pp by cow + Pl
FOURTH: Add Sg to be.
/rabərt wəz laikt bai kauz/
FIFTH

3.

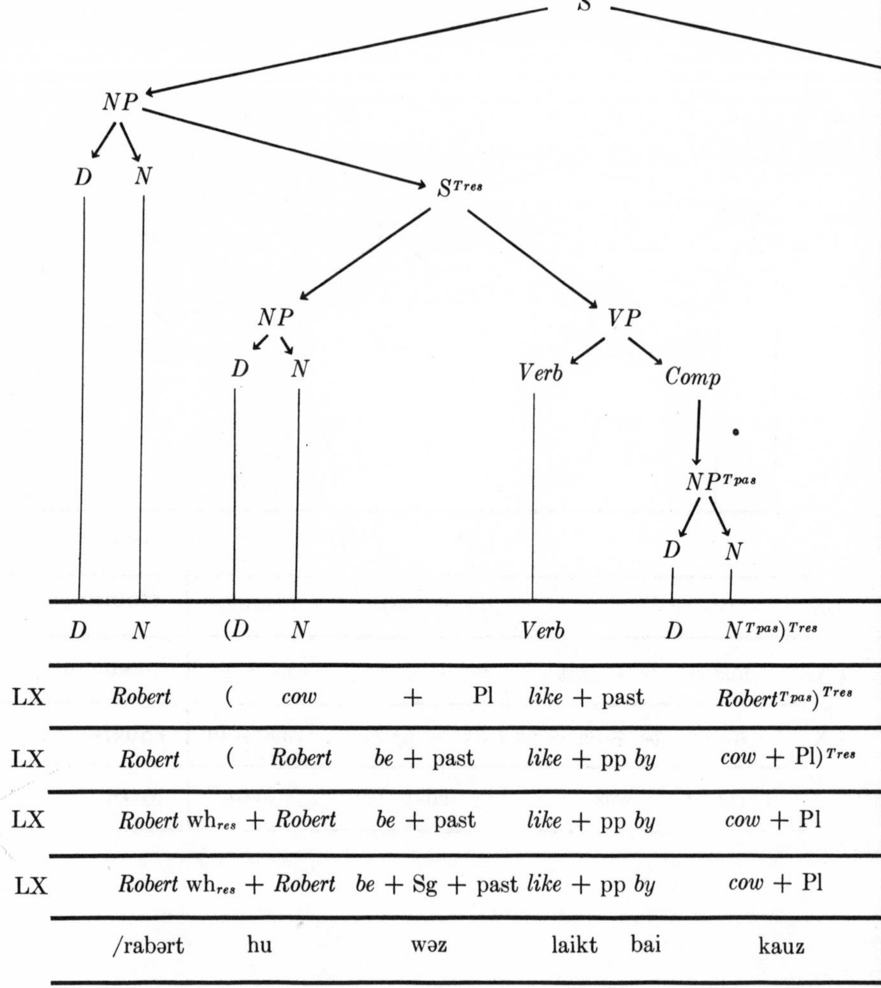
S
NP
D
N
S^{Tres}
NP
D
N
VP
Verb
Comp
NP^{Tpas}
D
N
D N (D N Verb D $N^{Tpas})^{Tres}$
LX Robert (cow + Pl like + past $Robert^{Tpas})^{Tres}$
LX Robert (Robert be + past like + pp by cow + $Pl)^{Tres}$
LX Robert wh_{res} + Robert be + past like + pp by cow + Pl
LX Robert wh_{res} + Robert be + Sg + past like + pp by cow + Pl
/rabərt hu wəz laikt bai kauz

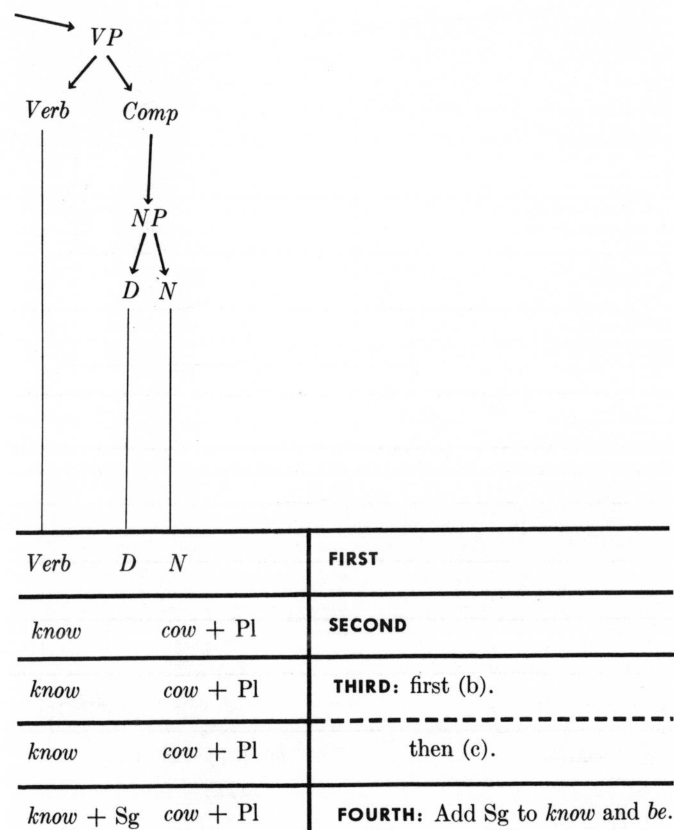

Verb *D* *N*		**FIRST**
know	*cow* + Pl	**SECOND**
know	*cow* + Pl	**THIRD:** first (b).
know	*cow* + Pl	then (c).
know + Sg	*cow* + Pl	**FOURTH:** Add Sg to *know* and *be*.
noz	kauz/	**FIFTH**

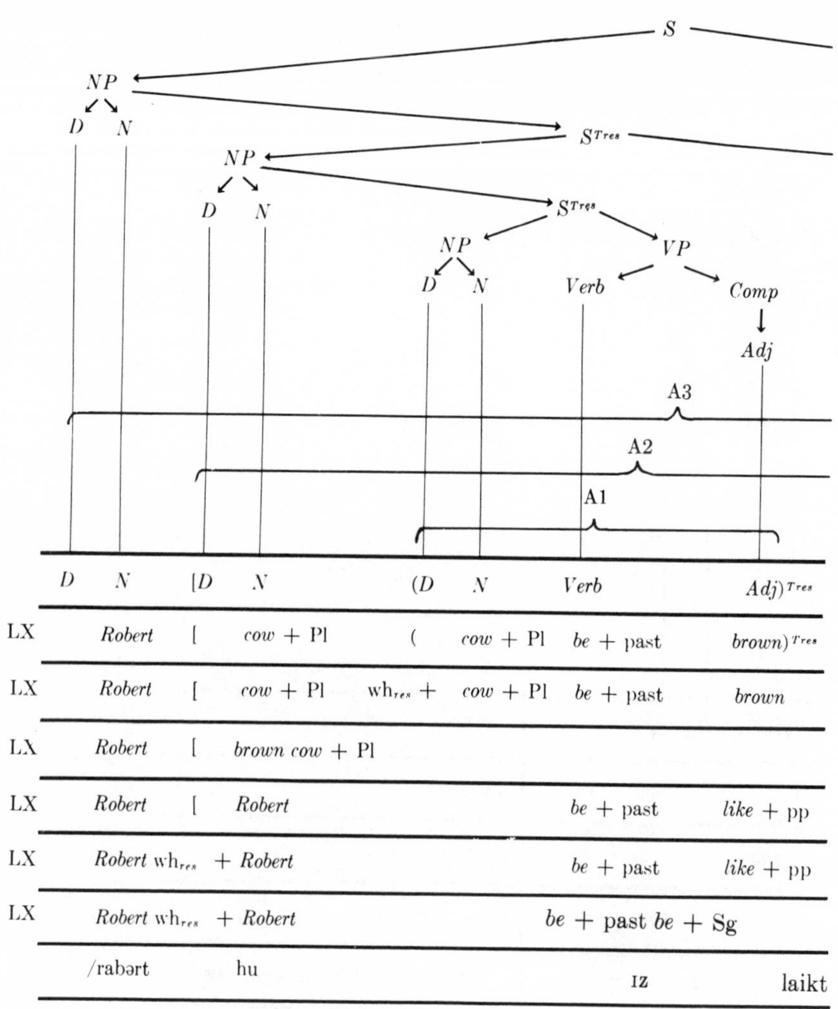
S
NP
D N
S^Tres
NP
D N
S^Tres
NP
D N
VP
Verb
Comp
Adj
A3
A2
A1
D N [D N (D N Verb Adj)^Tres
LX Robert [cow + Pl (cow + Pl be + past brown)^Tres
LX Robert [cow + Pl wh_res + cow + Pl be + past brown
LX Robert [brown cow + Pl
LX Robert [Robert be + past like + pp
LX Robert wh_res + Robert be + past like + pp
LX Robert wh_res + Robert be + past be + Sg
/rabərt hu ɪz laikt

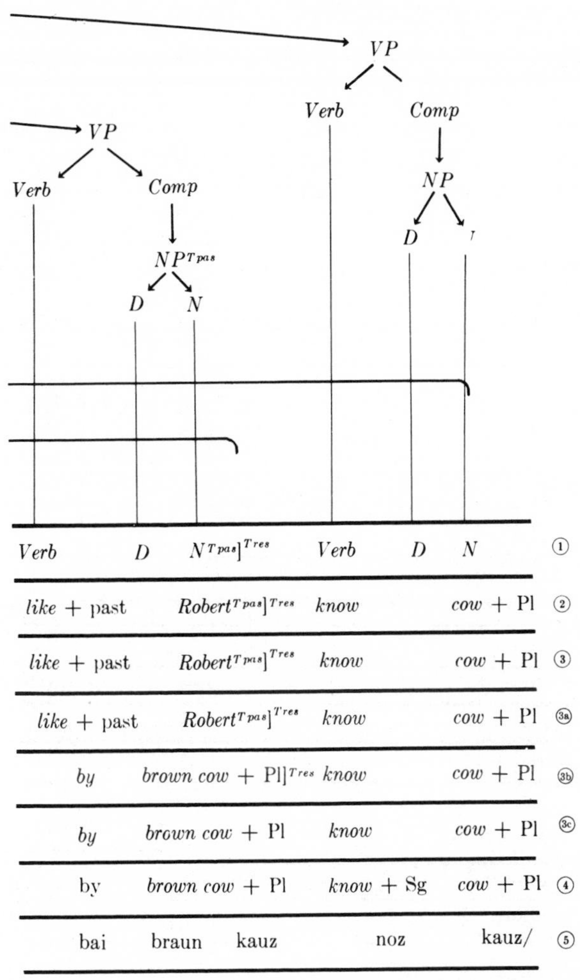

Explanation of each row:

① **FIRST:** A1 embedded in A2, A2 embedded in A3.

② **SECOND**

③ **THIRD:** first (c), string A1

③a then (d), string A1

③b ③c then (b) followed by (c) again, string A2.

④ **FOURTH:** Add Sg to *know* and *be*.

⑤ **FIFTH**

5.

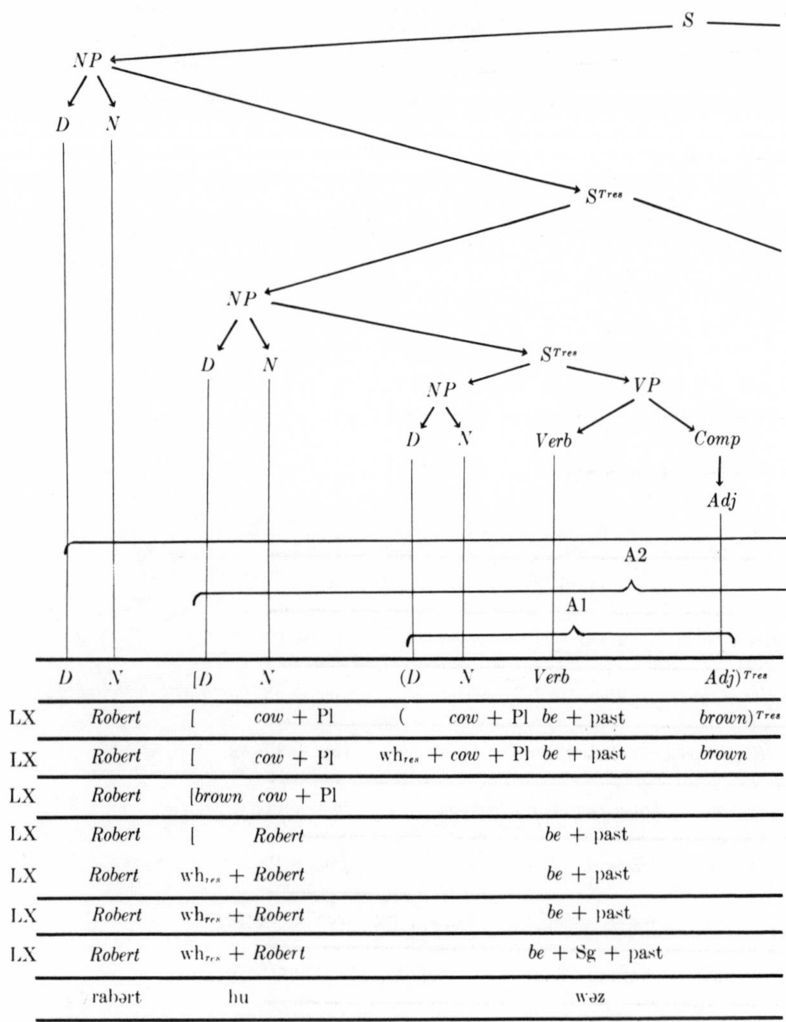
S
NP
D N
S^Tres
NP
D N
S^Tres
NP VP
D N Verb Comp
Adj
A2
A1
D N [D N (D N Verb Adj)^Tres
LX Robert [cow + Pl (cow + Pl be + past brown)^Tres
LX Robert [cow + Pl wh_res + cow + Pl be + past brown
LX Robert [brown cow + Pl
LX Robert [Robert be + past
LX Robert wh_res + Robert be + past
LX Robert wh_res + Robert be + past
LX Robert wh_res + Robert be + Sg + past
rabərt hu wəz

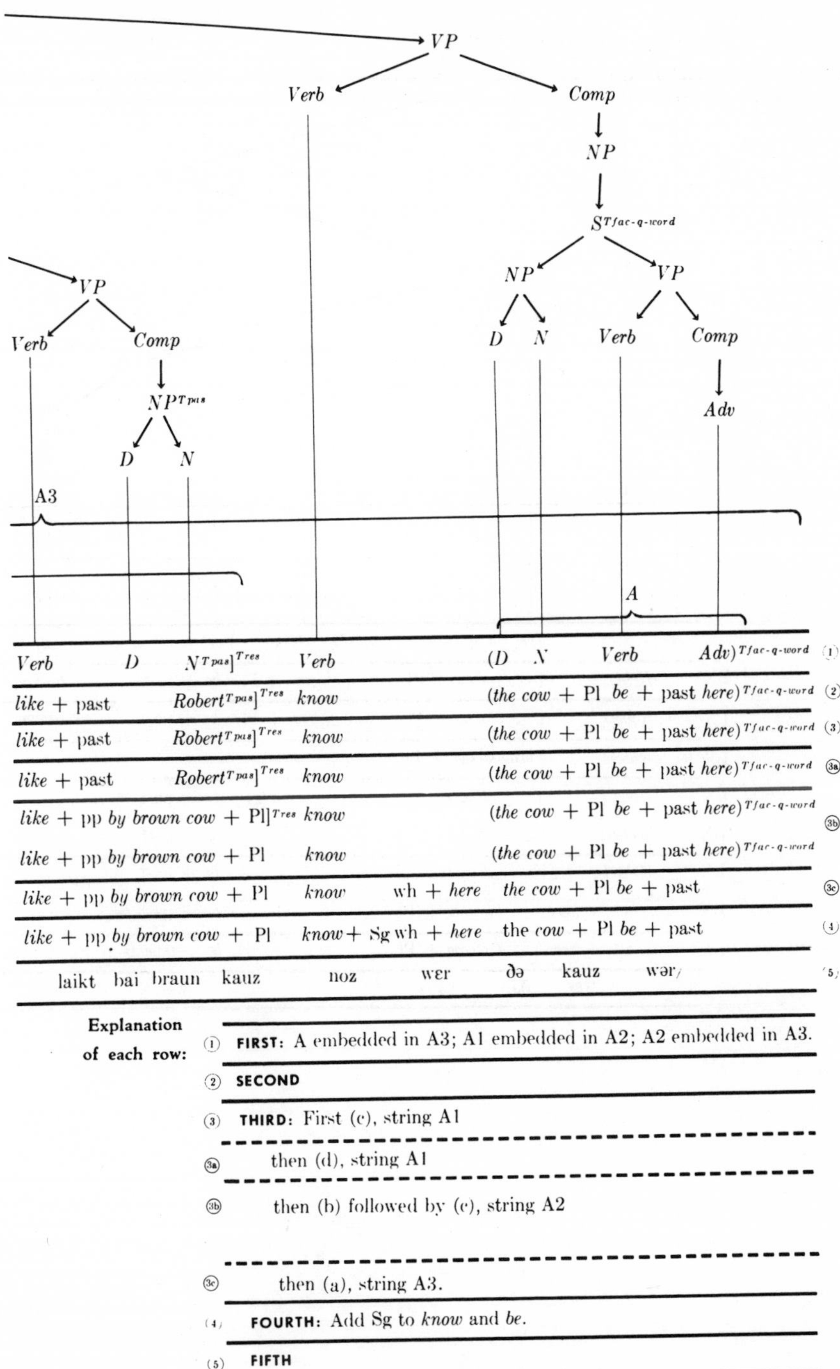
VP
Verb
Comp
NP
S^Tfac-q-word
NP
VP
D
N
Verb
Comp
Adv
VP
Verb
Comp
NP^Tpas
D
N
A3
A
Verb D N^Tpas]^Tres Verb (D N Verb Adv)^Tfac-q-word (1)
like + past Robert^Tpas]^Tres know (the cow + Pl be + past here)^Tfac-q-word (2)
like + past Robert^Tpas]^Tres know (the cow + Pl be + past here)^Tfac-q-word (3)
like + past Robert^Tpas]^Tres know (the cow + Pl be + past here)^Tfac-q-word (3a)
like + pp by brown cow + Pl]^Tres know (the cow + Pl be + past here)^Tfac-q-word (3b)
like + pp by brown cow + Pl know (the cow + Pl be + past here)^Tfac-q-word
like + pp by brown cow + Pl know wh + here the cow + Pl be + past (3c)
like + pp by brown cow + Pl know + Sg wh + here the cow + Pl be + past (4)
laikt bai braun kauz noz wɛr ðə kauz wər (5)
Explanation of each row:
(1) FIRST: A embedded in A3; A1 embedded in A2; A2 embedded in A3.
(2) SECOND
(3) THIRD: First (c), string A1
(3a) then (d), string A1
(3b) then (b) followed by (c), string A2
(3c) then (a), string A3.
(4) FOURTH: Add Sg to know and be.
(5) FIFTH

6.

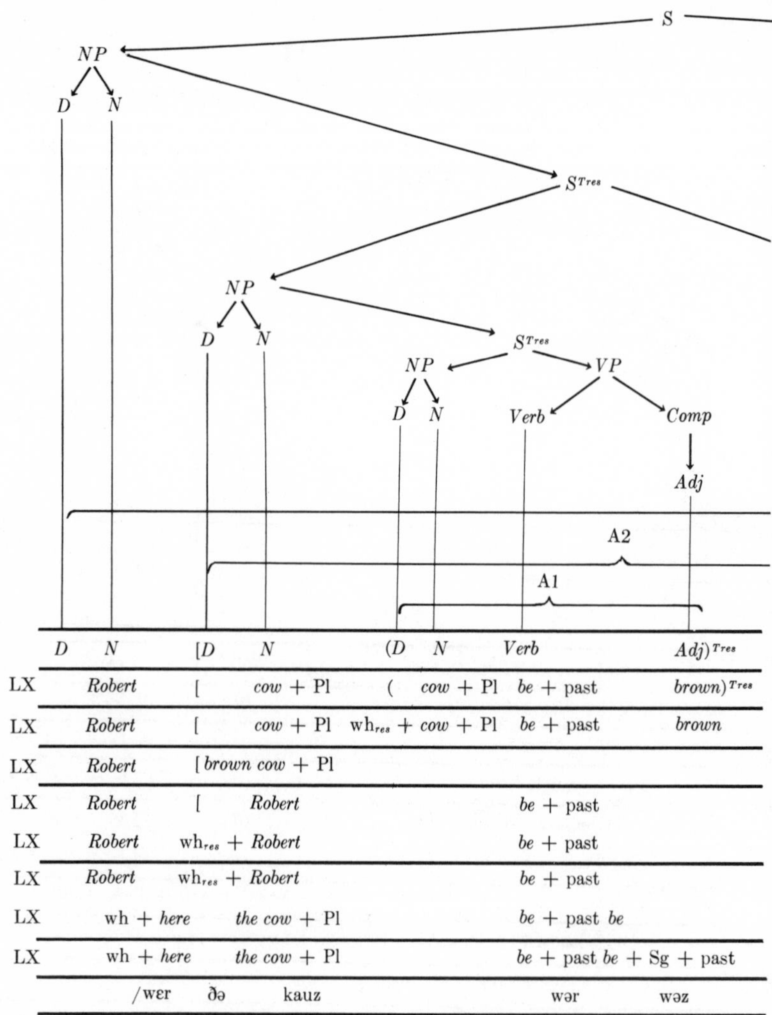
S
NP
D N
S^{Tres}
NP
D N
S^{Tres}
NP
VP
D N
Verb
Comp
Adj
A2
A1
D N [D N (D N Verb $Adj)^{Tres}$
LX Robert [cow + Pl (cow + Pl be + past $brown)^{Tres}$
LX Robert [cow + Pl wh_{res} + cow + Pl be + past brown
LX Robert [brown cow + Pl
LX Robert [Robert be + past
LX Robert wh_{res} + Robert be + past
LX Robert wh_{res} + Robert be + past
LX wh + here the cow + Pl be + past be
LX wh + here the cow + Pl be + past be + Sg + past
/wɛr ðə kauz wər wəz

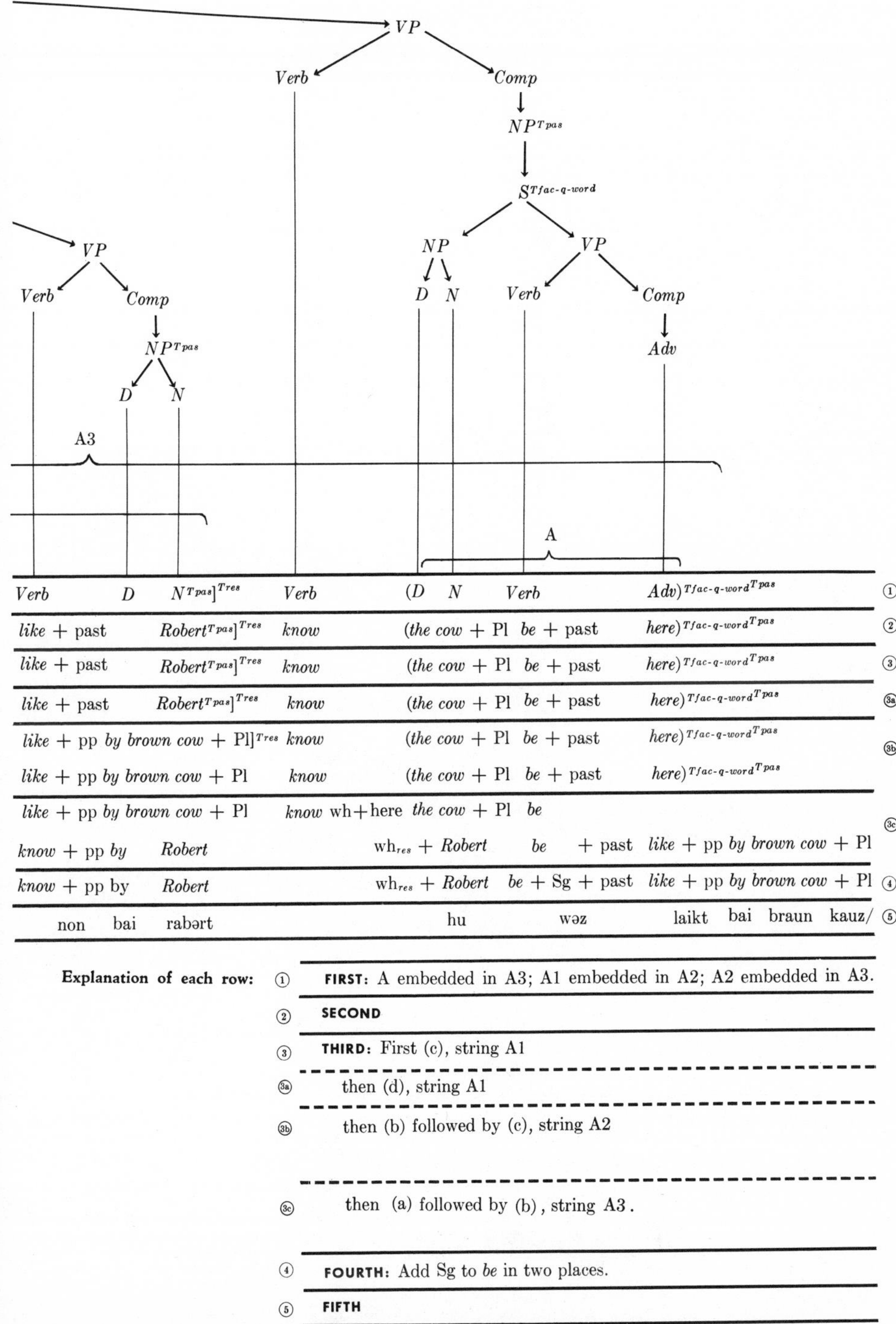
VP
Verb
Comp
NP^Tpas
S^Tfac-q-word
NP
VP
D N
Verb
Comp
Adv
VP
Verb
Comp
NP^Tpas
D N
A3
A
Verb D N^Tpas]^Tres Verb (D N Verb Adv)^Tfac-q-word^Tpas ①
like + past Robert^Tpas]^Tres know (the cow + Pl be + past here)^Tfac-q-word^Tpas ②
like + past Robert^Tpas]^Tres know (the cow + Pl be + past here)^Tfac-q-word^Tpas ③
like + past Robert^Tpas]^Tres know (the cow + Pl be + past here)^Tfac-q-word^Tpas ③a
like + pp by brown cow + Pl]^Tres know (the cow + Pl be + past here)^Tfac-q-word^Tpas
like + pp by brown cow + Pl know (the cow + Pl be + past here)^Tfac-q-word^Tpas ③b
like + pp by brown cow + Pl know wh+here the cow + Pl be
know + pp by Robert wh_res + Robert be + past like + pp by brown cow + Pl ③c
know + pp by Robert wh_res + Robert be + Sg + past like + pp by brown cow + Pl ④
non bai rabərt hu wəz laikt bai braun kauz/ ⑤
Explanation of each row:
① FIRST: A embedded in A3; A1 embedded in A2; A2 embedded in A3.
② SECOND
③ THIRD: First (c), string A1
③a then (d), string A1
③b then (b) followed by (c), string A2
③c then (a) followed by (b), string A3.
④ FOURTH: Add Sg to be in two places.
⑤ FIFTH

Index